£31·65

Kirkeley fose 22·92 .

The Way
the World Is

The Way the World Is

Cultural Processes and Social Relations among the Mombasa Swahili

Marc J. Swartz

University of California Press
Berkeley / Los Angeles / Oxford

University of California Press
Berkeley and Los Angeles, California

University of California Press
Oxford, England

Copyright © 1991 by
The Regents of the University of California

Library of Congress Cataloging-in-Publication Data

Swartz, Marc J.
    The way the world is: cultural processes and
social relations among the Mombasa Swahili/
Marc J. Swartz
        p.   cm.
    Includes bibliographical references and index.
    ISBN 0–520–07137–9
    1. Swahili-speaking peoples—Kenya—Mombasa.
2. Swahili-speaking peoples—Social life and
customs. 3. Mombasa (Kenya)—Social life and
customs. I. Title.
DT433.545.S93S93   1991
306.4′08996392—dc20   91–13198
                                              CIP

Printed in the United States of America

1   2   3   4   5   6   7   8   9

To my sons, Bill, Matt, and Bob

Contents

Preface

Dunia, Bwana: *[The way the] world [is], Sir*

This book is concerned with the world of the Mombasa Swahili. At the same time, there is an important focus on theoretical issues, especially those dealing with how culture works. But its empirical focus is on the Swahili of Mombasa, and it seeks to describe some aspects of their lives.

The saying *"Dunia, Bwana"* is used by community members to indicate that reality is as it is. In this life, it implies, one must expect that people are, at best, no better than they should be. Although things work, often they do not work just as one would like them to. In Paradise, where God rules directly, it implies, pious Muslims know that truth, justice, and virtue reign. In this world, where humans are in charge, things, real as they are, fall substantially short of that.

The Mombasa Swahili are a prepossessing people. They have lived where they are now for many centuries, and their way of life is one they, and other peoples who know them, characterize as having *utu,* a word that can only be glossed as "civilization" or "humanness." It is no accident, no artifact of the ethnographic enterprise, to find that the Swahili view themselves as truly civilized and "human" beyond many others of our species.

Their influence on the peoples they have had contact with over the centuries has been a profound and lasting one. They are the residents and probable founders of what may be East Africa's greatest entrepôt. Their trading with other groups over centuries has carried their influence beyond that of other communities far larger than theirs. Their deep allegiance to Islam has made them a very conscious part of one of the earth's most influential traditions, and their language is the lingua franca for most of eastern and some of central Africa.

The culture of this impressive group endures down the length of the East African coast and on the islands as far into the Indian Ocean as the Comoros. The Swahili of Mombasa have close ties with the other members of their ethnic group along the coast, but they are a proud and distinctive community. Despite economic and political upheavals of significant magnitude over the centuries, including, especially, the period from World War I until the present, their culture has retained its vitality and the community its coherence.

I count it a privilege to have had the opportunity to live among them and to chronicle some of the bases for their way of life. The friends I have in this community are among those I value most among all the people I have ever met. In some respects, this study was more difficult than the others I have undertaken, but the hospitality and charm of the community members, in addition to the challenging data, provided substantial compensation.

This book is based on what I have seen and heard in my eight field trips (1975–76, 1977, 1980, 1983, 1984, 1985, 1987, and 1988) totaling twenty-four months in Old Town, the Swahili section of Mombasa. The observations, discussions, and interviews that provided my data were based on an approach to culture that aims at tracing its operation in everyday life by giving particular attention to statuses and how they operate to distribute and organize culture as well as to guide interpersonal relations. The conceptual and theoretical orientation that led to this approach is adumbrated in the first chapter and presented more fully and generally in the final one. This orientation is intended to illuminate the findings and, optimally, to be useful in understanding the cultures of other social groups.

The data presented here are as they were collected, with the exception that individuals' names have been omitted or changed to protect them from possible embarrassment. Details about individuals such as their occupations, exact family size, or place of residence have also been altered for the same reason. Researchers who need to know the nature of these latter changes may consult my field notes, but actual names have been removed from them.

Despite my respect and affection for the Mombasa Swahili, I cannot characterize them as forthcoming or easy to study. This is a community in which most members value privacy a very great deal, and no amount of association with them changes this materially. Some men with whom I had spent hours over coffee on scores of occasions and with whom I felt I was on very good terms would not tell me how many children they had or what their wives' names were, much less discuss any but the most superficial aspects of their social lives.

This study exists only because everyone in the group does not share the dedication to privacy ("secrecy" is another word that comes readily to mind) that many do. A number of men and some women were willing to talk frankly about their lives but only after I had been in the community for a long period and most people knew who I was and that I was a serious student of their way of life, with proper respect for their beliefs and values.

My study might have been much easier and the results fuller if I had been able to live with a Swahili family. This, however, was impossible during my first field trip with my wife and three sons, as no one had room for all of us. Subsequently, although many were kind and hospitable, I could find no one who would house a solitary, outside man during my solitary, summer stays. Part of this is due to the difficulties in having an unrelated male in the house, but another part is probably due to my unavoidable reputation for asking questions. A woman field-worker would probably have had more access to Swahili home life, and I look forward to the results of such a researcher's work.

When I worked among the Bena of southern Tanzania and the Trukese in Micronesia, I lived in villages, and much of community life unfolded in open and public ways that made clear to everyone, even resident ethnographers, what was happening in families, neighborhoods, and among close associates generally. But the Mombasa Swahili are an urban people, and they spend a great deal of each day in their houses, as urban people do in many other societies. What goes on there is generally concealed from all those not directly involved. There is a Swahili proverb that says, *Nyumba husetiri mambo*: [The] house [regularly or usually or as an expected thing] conceals [embarrassing or shameful] events.

This emphasis on privacy often makes getting information painfully difficult and renders such things as a proper door-to-door census or a random sample survey quite impossible. If people whom one knows well are unwilling to say how many children they have and what the children's names are, it is not surprising that those who answer knocks on their doors will tell nothing whatever to an interviewer whose interests and objectives are unknown. I did manage to get a sample of more than a hundred families who responded to a questionnaire that included census information (see table 1, chap. 5) and, for a subsample of that group, information on beliefs and values concerning the nuclear family, its members, and their relationships. I also succeeded in getting survey information concerning the relations between generations and concerning illness and its treatment.

Some of these data were obtained with the help of young men and women from the community. They, as well as some of the people who allowed themselves to be interviewed, were paid. There are definite disadvantages in paying informants, but without payment, much of the information I collected would have eluded me.

Over the years, my research in Mombasa has been supported by the John Simon Guggenheim Foundation, the National Institutes of Mental Health, the National Geographic Society, the Wenner-Gren Foundation for Anthropological Research, the Research Committee of the Academic Senate of the University of California, San Diego, and the Biomedical Research Fund of that same institution. I am grateful for the generous support of these agencies without which this study could not possibly have been done.

Only a small proportion of the data in this study come from the questionnaire sort of interviews that provided the basis for the survey of beliefs and values concerning the nuclear family, generational relations, and illness.

The main source of data was intensive, completely informal "interviews" about a very wide variety of matters concerned with community life. These interviews are indistinguishable from discussions, save that I encouraged my companions to do most of the talking and followed their lead in choosing topics whenever that was possible. I did much of this interviewing myself, but my wife, Audrey M. R. Swartz, and Prof. Joshua J. Akong'a of Moi University contributed importantly during the 1975–76 visit. I am much indebted to them for their help.

My friend, Sheikh Yahya Ali Omar, has been my mentor and guide during much of this study. His endless help with the subtleties of the Swahili language provided an invaluable resource, and his brilliant insights into many aspects of his own society contributed vitally to my understanding of that community. I note his contributions throughout the book as appropriate, but it is impossible to express fully my gratitude to him.

My dear friend and mentor, the late Mohammed Suleman Mazrui (Abu Suleman), was a patient and generous guide from the first days I arrived in Old Town until his much felt passing. Similarly, the late Kamal Khan was a valued and generous friend whose knowledge of Swahili *utenzi* (epic poems) provided perspectives I would otherwise not have had. Thabit Hamisi Suleiman, his wife, Miriam, and their children were most generous in their help. Bwan Dumila and Mwenye Karama are *matabibu* (herbal doctors) who stand out among my informants on Swahili medical belief and practice and who asked that they be mentioned by their real names. The same is true of Shumi Yusef and her family who were unfailingly kind and helpful to me, as was Bi Rukia Ali and her family. My friend, Sh. Rashid Azzan, cheered and supported me when I was tired and discouraged.

I cannot thank all my friends individually, but my gratitude to them is lasting and deep.

This book is the result of a research plan that I followed for more than a decade and probably will continue to use as a guide. Some of the approaches and propositions found in the book and some of the data have been published as papers, but no chapter here is a republication of any of my earlier work in an unaltered form. Every chapter has its own contribution to make to the overall thesis of the book, and only three of the chapters, 5, 6, and 9, develop arguments that have substantial similarities to earlier publications (Swartz 1982*b*, 1984, and 1988, respectively). Each of these chapters, like all the others, also contain new data that have not appeared previously. Chapter 7 includes some of the data and argument found in Swartz 1985 but takes as its central theoretical issue a concern that is barely touched on in the earlier paper. The same is true of chapter 10, which draws on data and analysis found in Swartz 1982c and 1983 but emphasizes and develops a theoretical issue that is fundamentally different from the ones that occupy the papers.

In its early stages, this manuscript has benefited from the comments of Myron Aronoff, Michael Meeker, Michael Murphy, Fitz John Porter Poole, Melford E. Spiro, Donald F. Tuzin, and H. U. E. Thoden Van Velzen. Carol Eastman gave me the benefit of her advice and her deep understanding of Swahili language and culture. Ronald Cohen lent his wide knowledge of Africa and of the theoretical issues that are of concern here. The University of California Press copy editor, Sheila Berg, is that rarest of gems, an intelligent and forbearant editor with a sense for style and argument. As with the other kind people who helped in various aspects of this study, they are not responsible for what is said here. They are, however, to be credited for serious attempts to make it better than it is.

1

Ethnographic and Theoretical Introduction

This is a book about culture and how it actually works in guiding the behavior of those who, in the broad sense, share it. It is also a book about the Swahili of Mombasa and how their culture operates to guide their social lives and to provide them with a means for dealing with the problems and opportunities they encounter. The aim is to contribute to our understanding of the processes whereby culture works for all humanity and, specifically, to examine its constituent processes as they are seen among the Mombasa Swahili.

Ethnographically, field work focused particularly on interpersonal relationships, especially marriage and family life, generational relations, the ties among neighbors, and community structure. The social aspects of shame and the beliefs and practices concerned with health and illness are given special attention from the perspective of their cultural foundations. Taken together, they provide a reasonably broad and inclusive ethnography, despite the fact that they were chosen as much because of their theoretical interest and the availability of information in a community where information is remarkably difficult to obtain.

In examining the various aspects of Swahili life, the main goal is to identify their cultural bases and understand the processes whereby culture guides the behavior of community members to produce the social phenomena observed. The central thesis is that culture's functioning is best understood from a perspective that puts particular emphasis on the part played by a pervasively important combination of cultural elements, "status." This cultural complex will be shown to be central to the fact that culture's effects are not limited to those who share the cultural elements in question. It is through statuses, in fact, that the crucial processes of distribution, organization, and differential promotion of conformity will be shown mainly to operate.

The Ethnographic Focus

As will be seen in chapter 2, the Mombasa Swahili are part of an ancient urban community that has been in its present location on the coast of what is now Kenya for centuries. The members of this group view themselves as the heirs to cultural traditions that remain vital guides to behavior despite changes in their community and in the city their forebears founded nearly a millennium ago.

Part of the group's tradition is seen in the two-section organization of the community. As chapter 3 shows, in recent decades, this community has been strained by a weakening in the division between the sections through individuals claiming statuses that would place them outside the community and unite them with others from whom they were previously separated. This strain has been intensified by what are seen as claims for community membership from occupants of statuses that were not formerly understood as members. These strains have diminished the community's integration and stopped most joint activity. They have not, however, undermined the community's effectiveness as, in many senses, the arena for its members' lives. It still provides its members with the cultural foundation for living and the social framework within which they are born, work, marry, raise children, and die.

Chapter 4 examines the Swahili nuclear family and shows that in this largely endogamous community, it is far the most significant grouping in its members' lives. Kinship beyond the nuclear family is quite important, and ties with neighbors are lasting, but it is in relationships with parents, spouse, children, and siblings that most community members spend most of their time and much of what is vital to each person takes place.

Despite this importance, chapter 5 shows that even in this effectively functioning community, the sharing of cultural elements concerned with some of the fundamental issues in nuclear family relationships and group concerns is strictly limited. Members of long-established and stable nuclear families were interviewed concerning nuclear family issues (e.g., "Who makes decisions in your house?") and values ("Should children love their fathers more, their mothers more, or both the same?"). Informants' responses were compared with their fellow family members, with members of other families who occupied the same family statuses, and with all other informants without regard to family membership or status.

This study showed that even in the groups with the highest level of sharing, that is, among members of the same nuclear family, more than a quarter of the items were not shared and that within the community as a whole, almost a half were not shared. It was also found that individuals belonging to the same status, for example, "daughter," shared the cultural elements concerned with that status less with other occupants of that same status than they did with those who shared with them the status "member of my family."

Since the nuclear family among the Mombasa Swahili is a co-resident group whose members spend a great deal of every day together, since marriage in this group is mainly endogamous to the community, and since no questions were asked about matters beyond the scope of the nuclear family's life, it seems a reasonable working hypothesis that cultural sharing in other social settings (i.e., outside the nuclear family) concerning other issues is unlikely to be much greater save, perhaps, in the area of technical knowledge shared among those in the status devoted to its employment.

There is some basis for believing that, in fact, there is less sharing in other areas of life (as work by Fernandez [1965, 1982] on ritual, Keesing [1987a] on eschatology, and Holland [1987a] on academic matters among students suggest) than within the nuclear family. However, even if sharing is as great as within the family, the probability that it is less than complete in all relationships and concerning all issues is, unless specifically shown otherwise, taken as a basic element in discussing culture's functioning in the highly integrated Swahili community.[1]

The fact is that the social lives of the members of the community are, aside from limited relations based on schooling and occupation, almost entirely within the community. Further, membership in the community is an unquestionably important part of the identity of every one of the scores of members I have talked with over the years, and the ethnocentrism to be expected in a functioning community is decidedly present. Taking these facts together with the nearly endogamous patterns of friendship and marriage shows that the group's culture remains vital and effective.

Incomplete Sharing and Cultural "Explanations"

The fact that there are demonstrated limits on the sharing of culture in this community's most closely associated group, the nuclear family, provides a well-marked opportunity to study culture's functioning with the invocation of "shared beliefs and values" clearly an insufficient explanation of what is observed. The basis for such an invocation has been removed by a series of studies showing culture's elements to be only partially shared (see Roberts 1951; Wallace 1970; Schwartz 1978; Willis 1972; Pelto and Pelto 1975; Swartz 1982; D'Andrade n.d.; Holland 1987a; and others). How culture works despite its incomplete sharing, including incomplete sharing within statuses, is only beginning to be investigated (e.g., Gearing 1976a and 1976b and Holland 1987b, for a mainly cognitive approach).

Even if culture were fully shared by everyone or, at least, fully shared within particular status groupings, the nature of the relations among its parts and the sources of its effectiveness would still call for close study. The dynamics of culture, the processes whereby it guides the behavior of individuals and serves as a foundation for social relations, have never received much attention beyond broad characterizations such as their being controlled by evolution, diffusion, or environmental adaptation.

"Molecular" Processes and the Enduring Myth of Complete Sharing

The grand processes of cultural development have been, and continue to be, of great interest, the perspectives being the sweeping, universal ones associated with such writers as Marx, Toynbee, and Weber. But the everyday processes whereby culture actually accomplishes what anthropologists say it does, that is, provide the basis for the distinctively human mode of adaptation, have received far less attention. Cognitive anthropologists are currently in the forefront in this molecular approach where those interested in culture and personality once led and still make important contributions. These studies, however, mainly limit their focus to the psychological aspects of cultural dynamics. The study of the social aspects is still surprisingly neglected.

A main theoretical basis for that neglect is the enduring view that culture's part in individual adaptation and the regulation of social relations can be accounted for by reference to "shared beliefs and values." Although explicit support among students of society for the view that any culture is universally shared has vanished, much of the general understanding of how culture works is based on the implicit position that if a belief or value is truly part of culture, that is, if it is shared by group members, the invocation of that belief or value is sufficient to explain social phenomena.

Never mind that the invoker has usually granted that all beliefs and values are not, in fact, shared by all group members. Questions of cultural distribution, of who shares what with whom and how cultural elements find their way to the situations where they are used, are only rarely raised (Schwartz [1972, 1978] has been a leader in broaching these issues), and the questions concerning the relations among culture's elements are far more often left aside than considered. The issue of how cultural elements affect those who do not share them, clearly of central importance to culture's functioning if its elements are not uniformly shared, is almost never examined. The same is true concerning how cultural conformity is encouraged given the diversity that is part of incomplete sharing.

The tacit acceptance of completely shared culture, despite an avowed rejection of the view, makes it possible to ignore these and related issues, although the cost from the perspective of understanding the functioning of the human adaptation is substantial. Here the interest is in the dynamics of Mombasa Swahili culture at what might be called "ground level." Explicit attention is directed to cultural distribution, organization, and differential conformity from a perspective that totally forswears the invocation, tacit or otherwise, of any but demonstrable sharing. This perspective is intended to contribute to raising new and, sometimes, different questions aimed at advancing understanding of fundamental cultural processes.

Culture and "Culture"

Culture, as it is understood here, is not the only source of influence on human behavior, but it affects everything people do and is the indispensable base for social relations. There may be some merit in the vertiginous, Weberian metaphor wherein humans are suspended in a web of meaning whose substance is culture, but the trope distorts the realities of human life.

Unless "meaning" is understood so broadly as to be almost useless in analysis, Weber's web is spun of only one of the two broad contributions culture makes to human life. The other is to provide instructions for doing things such as making money, friends, and love; what I call "procedural understandings" (Swartz and Jordan 1980:49) and in some ways similar to what Goodenough calls "recipes" (1971:30–31).

"Culture" is a concept referring to the propositions or understandings that exist in the minds of individuals and that are similar to the comparable propositions in the minds of their fellow group members. That is, the understandings that make up culture are shared, so that culture's locus is both social and psychological. The basic units of culture are in people's minds, but the fact of their being shared, manifested and influenced in interaction, is a social fact. The component shared understandings have both direct and, as we will see below, vitally important indirect influence on the members of the group, some of whose members share them.

The direct influence comes from the guidance the understandings provide both for behavior and for the evaluation and assessment of whatever the actor views as relevant to that behavior. This direct influence is psychological in origin, and its primary operation is in the cognitive processes of the culture sharers. But culture's effects are not limited to those processes, crucial though they are, that occur in the human mind.

The manifest, public activity that is guided by culture is not itself culture, but it is, in considerable part, produced by it in the sense that the behavior of those involved is guided by shared understandings. This behavior, when assessed and evaluated according to understandings shared among those who express it and those who are concerned with it, is itself an influence on the subsequent behavior of those involved and, often, on the behavior of those who become aware of what was done. The behavior produced under cultural guidance thus serves as a vehicle for further, but indirect, cultural influence (see Goodenough 1971:18–20).

Some of the phenomena addressed in my approach, including the simultaneous occupancy of a number of "statuses" (in the sense explained below) and the importance of different sorts of situations to how statuses function as guides to behavior, are interestingly and differently developed in Goodenough's pioneering work (1965:12) as well as in Keesing's Chomskian-ethnoscientific "building blocks model" of social participation and cultural competence (1970, esp. 432–436).[2] I did not have the advantage of reading Keesing until the field research on which this book was based was completed, but I am struck by the thoughtfulness of his formulations and the fact that many of his suggestions work well with the data presented here.

"Status": Culture's Action Arm

The heart of the approach here is what I am calling "status," which is nearer Keesing's use of "role" than any other single concept in his or Goodenough's work (see Keesing 1970:427). The basis for my usage, as for Goodenough's and Keesing's, is Linton's unelaborated notions of "status" and "role" (1936:113–115), but my use of the concepts is much modified and has benefited from the work of the others.[3]

Clearly, an approach to culture's effect on behavior that seeks to examine the complete range of relevant phenomena must include provision for considering the ways behavior is affected by the products of culture as well as by the direct effects of culture itself. As will become clear in the course of this book, especially in chapters 9 and 10, although statuses are complexes of cultural elements and nothing but that, their operation in guiding behavior has vital effects on behavior that are independent of culture's direct influence. In other words, statuses guide behavior, and that behavior, a product of culture but not itself culture, has its own effects.

Statuses are uniquely important to cultural dynamics. They are what might be called "the action arms of culture." Not all of the understandings shared among the members of a group are parts of statuses, but most of them are. Only speech rivals status in the breadth of its influence on life; not even technology surpasses these two potent culturally based sources of influence. Sociolinguists have developed a thriving inquiry into the effects of speech on social life and culture itself, but status has not been so thoroughly studied.

To show how status comes to have so central a part in influencing behavior, it is useful first to consider what exactly "culture" refers to.

Culture and Its Distribution

"Culture" as used here refers to all the understandings that are socially learned and transmitted and that are shared by two or more actors who consider themselves to belong to some common grouping. This definition is closely related to those used by D'Andrade (1987:195), Goodenough (1971: 22), Keesing (1970:440), Frake (1962:85), and Spiro (1984:323), to name only some. By confining "culture" to understandings, the concept not only focuses on mental processes but also only on those that are cognitive. It is not that emotions and perceptions have nothing to do with culture, far from it, but rather that they are not definitionally part of it.

It is worth noting that in this definition, cultural elements need not be shared by all the members of a group. The understanding that they belong to the group will always, by definition, be shared by virtually everyone, and some other understandings may, as a matter of fact, be widely shared, but such universal sharing is not part of "culture" as defined here. So long as two people who consider themselves to be members of the same group share an understanding, it is included as part of the culture of that group. Generally, it appears that each group member shares some understandings with some group members and others with others. Complex and overlapping networks of incomplete sharing of particular cultural elements are what is characteristic of human groups.

In fact, the differential distribution of cultural elements among individuals and categories within a group is itself one of the key influences on behavior within the group as a whole. This fact needs to be emphasized by explicitly including as cultural those understandings, and they are a very large part of the total, that are shared by only a limited part of the whole group's membership. The contents of culture, the famous "beliefs and values" that group members actually share, are what students of society and behavior have most attended to. But a focus on what everyone shares slights the vital importance of the distribution of culture, which is itself, independent of the contents involved, a significant part of culture's influence.

Status: The Action Arm of Culture

To appreciate this, it is essential to understand that statuses are the instrument through which cultural distribution takes place. It is through statuses that it is established which cultural elements are associated with which individuals according to the categories they are understood to occupy in different circumstances. It is also through them that culture comes to bear on the problems and opportunities of life through particular understandings being associated with particular people according to the statuses they assume and are assigned in various situations. Statuses, then, are the core of culture's part in social life. Although statuses are at the heart of culture's ability to serve as the basis for group life and individual adaptation, they are themselves culturally constituted. All of the components of statuses are cultural elements that can be divided, for purposes of analysis, into three different kinds of understandings distinguishable according to their different functions.

The logically prior of these three kinds of elements are the "identifiers" that serve as the basis for recognizing individuals as members of different categories. Another component, "expectations," indicates how category members are expected (by themselves and others) to behave and react both in general and in particular kinds of situations and contexts. The third type of status component, "salience understandings," concerns the appropriateness and relative weight accorded different category memberships in various situations. Since everyone classifies himself and is classified by others in what is invariably a very large number of statuses, salience understandings serve an essential function in indicating which one or ones are called for and acceptable in what circumstances. Since people often serve in more than one category at a time, salience understandings serve to indicate not only which understandings apply but also what priority is given particular statuses when more than one is called for in a single situation.

Identifiers

I agree with Goodenough (1965:2) and Keesing (1970:424) that the understandings that define status category membership may be different from those concerning the behavior and responses expected from category members. This can be seen, for example, with respect to the question of who is properly categorized as a Swahili. The differences between a "Swahili" and an "Arab" living in the Swahili neighborhood have long concerned the members of this community.

Controversy and shifting social alignments focused around this status assignment have been going on since the turn of the century and before. In fact, the question of who is and who is not a Swahili is, as shown in chapter 3, a major source of the change in social life that has taken place in Old Town in the second half of the twentieth century. Despite its importance, within the group itself, the status "Swahili" or "community member" is an unmarked category without a generally used name. One never hears the words *Mswahili* or *Waswahili,* the singular and plural of the noun that would be used to refer to group members if such a term were used.

There are, as we will see in the historical and ethnographic sketch given in chapter 2, specific traits, more or less directly observable, that members of the Mombasa Swahili group all share including, notably, being Sunni

Muslims of the Shafi canon. But the fact that this and other traits are widely or, even, universally shared by community members does not necessarily make them either sufficient or necessary as the basis for the understandings that lead someone to be categorized as a Swahili. Thus, religious affiliation and belief is not enough to serve as the basis for classification by itself, since there are followers of the Shafi canon (including many whose forebears fairly recently migrated to the city from the Indian subcontinent) who are universally understood by community members as belonging to other groups.

Further, in addition to being not sufficient for membership in the unmarked "Swahili" category, there is a case that suggests that religious affiliation by itself may also not be a necessary characteristic. A Swahili poet from Lamu, Mohamed Kijumwa, went so far as to convert to Christianity—among many other behaviors viewed as bizarre and outrageous—but even this did not affect the fact that he is unquestionably viewed and evaluated as a Swahili.

In the case of Sh. Mohamed, the absence of an identifier, being a Muslim as all other Swahili are, did not block him from being categorized as a Swahili and being subject to the expectations associated with that status, so that the two types of understandings are seen to be partly separate. Sometimes, however, the understandings that provide identification are the same ones as those that serve as expectations. Thus, all those who give the prayer call (*adhan*) from mosques are *muadhini,* and no one is who does not. Nevertheless, even in these cases, more is gained in analytic ability by saying that the identifiers and the expectations are part of the same construct than by keeping them entirely separate, as Goodenough's "rights and duties" and "social identities" approach docs (1965:3–18).

There are immigrants, and the children and grandchildren of immigrants, from Oman or elsewhere in the Persian Gulf who live in Old Town. Most of those who are the children of immigrants and all of the grandchildren speak Swahili, and, of those, some have converted to Shafi from the Ibathi canon followed in parts of the Gulf region. If these men (I have no data on women immigrants of this sort, if, as is doubtful, there are any) associate with undoubted members of the Swahili category most of the time and smoke and shave their beards (Ibathi do neither), they are *mainly* evaluated and treated according to expectations that are part of the Swahili status.

But there is a difference in how they are treated and expected to act even if it is a subtle one. Now and again, one hears one of these immigrants referred to as *Muarabu* (Arab, *Warabu* pl.), and it seems likely that they are assigned to the Arab status category as well as the Swahili category and that the expectations focused on them include those associated with both. When they behave in ways that are in accord with understandings concerning proper behavior by Swahilis, they are mainly evaluated and reacted to as Swahili by many community members despite a personal history that is not entirely Swahili (because it involves fairly recent immigration). When they do not behave in accord with understandings that apply to Swahili, many community members treat them according to Arab status expectations.

Salience Understandings

There is nothing unusual about two or more of an individual's statuses being involved in interaction at once. That is, salience understandings include those that allow (or, even, require) that acting and being evaluated according to one status involves simultaneously acting and being evaluated according to another.[4]

The Swahili, to take one example of such salience understandings, differentiate among themselves on the basis of neighborhood. It is generally understood that all forms of manual labor are inappropriate for members of their group, with the partial exception of commercial fishing, which is practiced mainly by the men from the Kuze neighborhood of Old Town. These men are unquestionably classified as Swahili, but, unlike other Swahili, they are understood to be more blunt, uninterested in elaborate etiquette, and generally more direct and physical in what they can be expected to do.

This Kuze status is quite as real as the Swahili status, and both have expectations concerning their members. Since the Kuze men meet the identifying understandings for the Swahili status, they are classified that way, and since they also meet the identifiers for Kuze, they are classified that way as well. In some contexts, the Swahili status is dominant; in others, the Kuze status is. This can be seen in their own behavior and that of those interacting with them through inferring the expectations involved.

The occupancy of several statuses by each of the participants in a single event is quite common, and these multiple occupancies are often simultaneous, with the different statuses contributing differently to the expectations that guide the behavior of the statuses' occupants and of their social partners. Gender-based statuses, age-based statuses, and ethnic-based statuses often occur only or mainly in conjunction with other statuses, and, among the Swahili and others, almost all other statuses are occupied jointly with all three of these. But it is not only broad and widely inclusive statuses that are jointly operative in interaction.

The Swahili fisherman is a businessman when he sells his fish. These two statuses with their quite specific and limited expectations are occupied simultaneously, perhaps, with the broader statuses of Muslim, Swahili, Kuze resident, male, and person of whatever age. That this is so is discovered by inferring the expectations of those with whom the fisherman interacts and his expectations of them and comparing these to the expectations found in the various individual statuses at issue.

It would be possible, of course, to speak of a single status, businessman-fisherman or Kuze-Swahili, rather than a combination of the separate statuses.

However, so long as the understandings involved sometimes occur independently in association with only one of the sets of identifiers (e.g., so long as there are understandings about fishermen independent of businessmen), the analysis is better served by treating the statuses as occurring jointly.

Specific and General Expectations

Statuses differ in their importance both to the individual and to the group, and this difference is often associated with a difference in the kind of expectation they have. The differences can be seen in everyday life, of course, but they show themselves clearly in the attacks group members make on one another when angry. A particular sort of aggressive speech, "badtalk" (i.e., speech generally considered rude, coarse, and obscene), aims at questioning the targets' worth as assessed according to the expectations in the most fundamental statuses involved in group life (Swartz 1990a, 1990b).

The most pointed attacks concern statuses such as community member, the true child of particular parents, or proper male and the relationships involving them. The attacks are mainly in terms of general, rather than specific, expectations. Statuses involving more specific expectations in relationships, such as those in being a bus conductor in relations with passengers, are less broadly important to social participation and usually psychologically less vital. These are not attacked by badtalk as the statuses involved in more crucial relationships are. The most common badtalk used, mainly by women and young men, is, "Your mother's cunt!" implying an improper parent and an improper relationship with inappropriate expectations of so broad a scope they need not be mentioned. No one is assailed with "Your bus conductor's cunt!" because the conductor status, as such, involves only superficial relationships with quite specific expectations.

Specific expectations involve narrow ranges of behavior that require little interpretation. The conductor either gets the fare or the passenger is put off the bus. General expectations, such as children loving their parents or friends helping one another, are quite different and call for elaborate interpretation of behavior in assessing whether they have been met. The reference to the mother's sexual organ is an assertion that the target of the badtalk fails to meet the expectation that he or she be the proper child of particular parents, which is made doubtful by having a mother so sexually active that her most notable characteristic is her vulva.

General expectations are broad and rather vague, so that being accused of failure to meet them is always possible. One cannot successfully accuse a tall person of being short, but everyone can be accused of having a mother whose chastity is less than it ought to be. But the opposite is also true. General expectations can be taken as being met by a broad range of behavior, not just a few specific acts. Most general expectations concern behavior by the status occupant himself, rather than by his parent or other connected person, but that behavior is always in need of interpretation far beyond what is called for by specific expectations.

General Expectations, Cultural Sharing, and the Effectiveness of Statuses

Specific expectations are part of the substance of everyday life and must rather often be met if social life is to continue. Knowing that a butcher will accept money in exchange for meat, that those next to you at the mosque will follow the imam's example much as you do, and that a greeting will be returned with either no response or a benign one are all important to those who participate in Swahili social life.

Such specific expectations, however, are only a fraction of what is called for and supplied by social relationships in every enduring society. General expectations must also be met in their own ambiguous way. In Swahili society, for example, children in relationships with mothers expect to be helped and cared for, husbands in relationships with wives expect support, and wives in relationships with husbands expect to be shown love.

What behavior demonstrates help and caring, being supportive, and showing love is far more ambiguous than what is involved in the specific expectations concerning buying, greeting, and praying, but the general expectations are by no means less important because of that. The fact that meeting general expectations depends at least as much on interpretations as on behavior itself gives social life a flexibility and tolerance for differences it would otherwise not have. This flexibility and tolerance serves not only to reduce the need for detailed cultural sharing but also to make relationships effective in new circumstances and domains. The limited cultural sharing found among members of functioning nuclear families described in chapter 5 is partly to be understood as related to the latitude in relationships as a consequence of the importance of general expectations in them.

"Tokens" and "Guides"

The ambiguity of general expectations is by no means the only element in culture's ability to function as a guide for social relationships and individual behavior despite many of its elements being shared by only a limited number of those who are affected by them. Another is rooted in the fact that for some purposes, it is as important for those in a relationship to *believe* they share some understandings as it is to actually share them. Predictability is indispensable to social relations in that if people do not feel relatively confident that they know the limits within which others will respond to them, they are un-likely to participate in the relations.

Since members of even groups with the most intense and frequent relation-ships do not share many of the understandings about those relationships, the basis for predictability cannot be assumed to be the "shared beliefs and val-ues" often invoked to explain social phenomena. In fact, as chapter 6 shows, the appearance of sharing even in the presence of manifest differences can serve to facilitate the predictability essential to social life.

This "appearance" need not be a false one. For some purposes, it is useful to distinguish the functions of cultural elements according to whether they actually guide the behavior they most directly concern or are presented mainly as reassuring symbols to others whom the presenter believes use them as guides. A study of intergenerational relations shows (see chap. 6) that in for-mal interviews, younger Swahili say that the problems between parents and children and seniors and juniors are mainly due to their, the younger peo-ple's, lack of discipline and respect. In these same interviews, older Swahili say that their failure to be firm is the major cause of the intergenerational difficulties.

In more informal settings, however, quite different views appear: the younger people blame the older, who, in turn, blame the younger. In most contexts, it is these latter views, rather than the self-blaming ones, that actu-ally guide behavior. In many social situations, young people tell each other about their parents' (and, in general, elders') conservatism and failure to un-derstand the modern world, and they adopt various behavioral strategies to avoid the consequences of these understood attributes of their seniors. In a complementary way, the older people sometimes comfort each other about what they characterize as the abandoned and irresponsible behavior of their children and the hopeless nature of the younger generation. In fact, much of their behavior concerning young people can be seen to be affected by these last understandings even though that is not what would be expected on the basis of what they told the interviewers.

The understandings suggested by statements in the formal interviews of informants from both age groups are real enough; they do exist in the minds of those who state them. They do not, however, provide much actual guid-ance for behavior in the relationships with those they concern. The interview statements can be called "tokens," as distinguished from "guides." These tokens are intended, and often serve, to reinforce the belief that the individu-als using, often exchanging, them are sufficiently similar to be able to predict one another's behavior.

"Cultural Models"
and General Expectations

Another contributor to the effectiveness of nuclear families is connected with the effectiveness of the "cultural models" discussed in chapter 7. These are symbolic representations of desired or despised behavior that are frequently presented or exchanged in emotional and value-laden ways. They gain force from the fact that they are not general or abstract statements of abstract values and ideals. The terms and characterizations that constitute the models are usually quite unambiguous in either praising or condemning identified actions or sorts of behavior carried out by particular individuals in specific social relationships. The models, therefore, provide quite clear indications of what is positively evaluated behavior for particular kinds of individuals in particular settings and what is not.

The amount of sharing needed for the understandings that constitute statuses to be effective as guides for behavior, then, is reduced by lessening the ambiguity concerning what the expectations associated with the statuses actually call for. Further, the models not only make clear what behaviors are well received but do so in a way that promotes those behaviors by presenting them in an emotionally charged and value-laden way.

Goodenough and Keesing present pictures of society in which what I call statuses are occupied by individuals who are taken as sharing with their status mates the understandings that are central to those statuses. For these two theorists, many of the most crucial issues deal with how these shared understandings are related to and interact with one another. Their main concern is with developing a "grammar" of culture using statuses as a key means for discovering the rules. This, however, is contrary to the data presented in chapter 5 as well as the data in Keesing's own 1978 study. If, as these data suggest, culture is quite imperfectly shared even within statuses, their linguistics-based model is not as compelling as it otherwise would be. In language, people employ a vocabulary whose more obvious references, at least, are shared and whose use is according to universally shared rules.

If statuses are taken as central to society's operation and if those statuses actually depend on relatively complete sharing of their elements among those categorized in them, it seems reasonable to infer that in a society functioning well enough to continue, the more central statuses are to relations and group activity, the more the understandings central to those statuses' functioning will be shared. The Swahili data, however, indicate that this is by no means clearly so.

Specifically, the data in chapter 4 show the nuclear family in this community to be functioning at least adequately, but, despite this, cultural sharing within family statuses is distinctly limited. This limited sharing is most clearly characteristic of the understandings about what specific sorts of things status occupants can and should do and how they can and should do them.

These data do not contradict the importance of cultural sharing within statuses. The necessity of having some actual and dependable sharing remains, but that necessity brings us back again to the importance of general, as opposed to specific, understandings. Statuses are quite as important to culture's functioning as Goodenough and Keesing have maintained, and they do function by distributing cultural elements among group members and, mainly through their salience understandings, among situations. A key to their ability to do this is not complete sharing within statuses, however, but the distinctive quality of general expectations concerning different statuses augmented by the efficacy of readily displayed cultural models that teach and encourage behavioral conformity. What is shared in the most limited way are *specific* understandings, while those with less easily identified behavioral manifestations are more broadly held and more central to the functioning of the sorts of statuses central to nuclear families and other intimate groups.

Still another source of the efficacy of statuses is found in the apparently thorough sharing (discussed in chapter 4) of status identifiers. The agreement about the assignment of people to statuses seems higher than many other sorts of agreement. There are fairly unambiguous, explicit understandings about status assignment of the "stethoscope wearer = doctor" sort. But such explicit understandings are not necessary in many reciprocal assignments, since the process is one that works itself out in interaction. In actually relating to one another, participants in interaction each adjust to the partner until agreement is reached about the category to which the other is assigned. This is a failure-proof process in that when agreement is not reached, relationships are ended before they really begin.

Identifiers, General Expectations, and More on Models

In communities like the Swahili where a limited number of people spend their lives in the same small area, status assignment is even less fraught with difficulties. When the various status memberships of those around one are well known, the meeting of expectations is simplified. Since the statuses important to much of life in such a community have mainly general, rather than specific, expectations, only limited sharing (in a quantitative sense) is needed for the relationship to proceed fruitfully, that is, the participants meet one another's expectations sufficiently often for them to continue.

There are, in fact, culturally constituted means for encouraging the sort of limited conformity that is called for to meet general expectations. To be competent as judged by peers, a surgeon has to conform quite closely to the technical understandings concerning the work associated with his status, but for a man or a woman to have *haya* (modesty and concern for the rights of others) calls for no such close agreement between actions and shared understandings. By praising haya, conformity to a variety of distant expectations that are important to the evaluation of individuals in a considerable variety of statuses is encouraged. I will show (chap. 7) that there are a considerable variety of terms in the Swahili language that encourage conformity with the distant expectations of a range of statuses by providing emotionally potent models of the virtues of conformity and the costs of nonconformity.

It is not that status members in vital statuses such as "mother," "respected man," or "proper child" are led to conform to direct expectations in what they do and how they react but rather that they are encouraged in such general and diffuse conformity as these distant statuses call for.[5] An examination of the Mombasa Swahili terms most applied to admired and, more often, disapproved behavior shows that not only are these terms almost always general in their reference but they are also almost always concerned with social relationships.

Thus, for example, everyone is concerned with *fakhri* (which can be glossed as "honor"), and it is a main dimension of evaluation and assessment both of how a person acts and of how that person is treated. How people in different statuses, particularly men as contrasted with women, get fakhri and behave to show fakhri, however, depends on the different statuses they occupy. The ways group members use such value-laden terms exerts a pressure for behavior in conformity with expectations that are status specific and, at the same time, of the distant sort that is met by a considerable range of behavior, lessening the need for a full and detailed sharing of understandings between actors and evaluators.

"Shame" and Its Agents

In chapter 8, shame (*aibu* in Swahili) is seen to operate in some ways similarly to the terms concerning social relationships. On the one hand, there are a small number of specific understandings that are used as the basis for evaluating all group members as such, regardless of the other statuses they occupy. These universal values are closely associated with the community's most respected and prestigious men whom I call "the arbiters." The concern with being positively assessed with respect to these understandings leads to considerable homogeneity of behavior in certain public domains despite the undoubted differences that exist among those involved. The specific understandings that lie behind these instances of conformity (e.g., that public nakedness is possible only for psychotics and is deeply shameful even for them) are universally shared and almost never violated.

An important thing about this limited but public and ongoing conformity is that it implies a broader and more general agreement concerning understandings than may, in fact, exist. By following a few, limited understandings whose behavioral manifestations are obvious, group members reassure one another that they are quite similar in the things that matter most.

This reassurance is important because, in fact, group members differ both in the understandings that guide their own behavior and in those that serve as the basis for evaluating that of others. By following a few universally shared understandings, the implication is transmitted that similar agreement exists as concerns the foundations for all behavior. In fact, a far more substantial number of understandings than the few that are universally shared serves not only as a guide to one's own behavior but as the basis for judging most of what others do. Which of this larger number of understandings is used to guide behavior and assessment of others' behavior depends both on the statuses of the evaluators and the statuses of the evaluated. It is fairly obvious that how an individual acts toward another depends on both of their statuses. The same is true of how individuals evaluate one another.

Everyone in the society serves as what I call a "sanctioner," and the judgments of these sanctioners depend on the relationship between them and the individuals who are the targets of their evaluations. This leads to the same behavior being quite differently evaluated depending on who performs it and who is evaluating it. The evaluated suffer shame if they are negatively judged by either arbiters or sanctioners, so that shame serves, as the values attached to and expressed in relationship terms do, to encourage conformity both to generally held and universally applicable understandings and to those that apply quite specifically to particular statuses.

It is important to note that the understandings underlying evaluations by sanctioners are often general rather than specific. The broad and nonspecific nature of the understandings used in these judgments limits the amount of sharing required and, at the same time, encourages flexibility. Further, since these general understandings are part of statuses, they apply differentially to the same individuals as they move from one situation or relationship to another with the changes in statuses such moves often entail. This protean applicability of general understandings promotes both the maintenance of status differentiation and the distribution of culture among actors and across situations while requiring a minimum of sharing of specifics.

"Role" as a Part of Status

The usefulness of the status concept is increased when a distinction is introduced between "status" and "role."[6] A role is a subunit of the set of understandings that constitute a status including only the understandings concerning relations with others according to the status those others occupy. Thus, if one takes the "arbiter" status, an examination of the behavior of its occupants acting in that status (as indicated by their meeting its identifying understandings) will show that different understandings are involved in guiding the behavior of arbiters in "arbiter-arbiter" interactions as compared to those involved in "arbiter-junior person"[7] interactions. The "arbiter" status, then, is seen to be involved in two distinct roles and may be involved in others provided only that membership in the arbiter, rather than some other, status is what is salient for at least one participant in the relationship.

Turning to arbiters' function in promoting conformity and group operations, it is important to understand that the individuals categorized together as what I am calling "arbiters" rarely, in fact, can be seen to make judgments. As a matter of fairly explicit policy, those categorized in this status almost never say or do anything that might indicate what their assessment of acts or individuals may be. They serve, in fact, as a sort of culturally constituted Rorschach; they are the embodiment of the famous "they" who appear in the "what will *they* think" heard in many societies.

Chapter 8 makes clear that the arbiters' imagined judgments are not as frequently of concern as are the judgments of what I call the "sanctioners," but the arbiters play a central part in promoting conformity nevertheless. The sanctioners' judgments are concerned with detailed and specific aspects of what one does in quotidian statuses such as spouse, neighbor, or fellow employee, while the arbiters are mainly taken as concerned with one's standing as a group member, man, woman, or human being.

General Expectations
and the Effects of Unshared Culture

To this point, attention has been directed to the nature of Swahili culture, the extent of its sharing, and some fundamental processes that promote the differentiated conformity called for by the distribution of culture inherent in a social structure composed of articulated statuses. The issues still to be examined all concern the ways culture actually affects what community members do. These include how cultural elements affect individuals who do not share them, how cultural elements are organized, including given priorities, and how individuals use cultural elements and products to pursue goals whether they are aware of doing so or not.

Chapter 9 discusses how those who understand themselves as ill find medical treatment. Understandings identifying the signs of illness are widely shared, as are beliefs holding that a wide variety of kinds of medical care are available in Mombasa and that getting some kind of treatment can be beneficial.

In trying to understand how culture provides guidance in getting care for the sick, an obvious hypothesis, based on the customary invocation of "shared beliefs and values," is that the sick use an intrinsically organized schema of shared understandings as a guide to dealing with their illness. It begins with their recognizing themselves to be sick, proceeds through understandings about what to do when sickness of the kind they attribute to themselves is present, and leads to visiting medical practitioners whom they understand to be able to deal with the causes of their illness as they understand them.

In fact, the connection between the understanding that one is sick and the decision about what kind of physician to visit is only rarely composed of intrinsically related cultural elements of the sort mentioned in the hypothesis. Contrary to the hypothesis and quite different from the sorts of schemata used by, say, chess players, the common schema for sick Swahili is most often extrinsically organized.

Patients are found to have only the most limited understandings about body functioning and illnesses, and although most know there are many sorts of medical practitioners in town, they have few understandings about the nature of differences among them. The basis for their decision about what treatment to seek is usually the advice they receive, so that this advice is the basis for the connection between the understanding that they are ill and the decision to consult one sort of practitioner rather than another.

Given the central part played by the advice, it follows that their expectations of the adviser, since that is what makes the advice useful, are central to their treatment-seeking schema. Since the expectations involved in the relations between people are elements of the statuses they occupy, for the great majority of community members who do not share most medical understandings, it is the status system that makes that part of the group's culture effective.

Chapter 9 describes the elaborate set of understandings shared among practitioners of what some group members refer to as "traditional Swahili" medicine. These understandings are shared among professional practitioners and also among what I discovered was only a small, but articulate, group of dedicated amateurs. It is part of Swahili culture since a number of group members share it with one another, but even its main outlines are unknown to more than three-quarters of the group. Nevertheless, it is a functioning part of the culture that affects most group members at some time—often many times—in that it affects what treatment they receive when they are ill.

This is a case, then, of cultural elements affecting those who do not share them. There is nothing unusual about this; much of what happens in all groups depends on members being affected by cultural elements they do not share. The way Swahili patients get treatment, however, offers an opportunity to examine the process whereby cultural elements can influence even those who do not share them. In this case, the vehicle for the effects of unshared culture is advice that is followed, and the acceptance of that advice is the result of the expectations in the role involving the patient and the adviser.

My investigation showed that the adviser was a parent for a substantial majority of those who lived with or very close to one or more parents and a spouse, neighbor, or kinsman for the remainder. The patients said that they followed the advice they got either because the advice giver "knows about illness" or because he or she had had a similar illness and reported being helped by the practitioner recommended. On interviewing as many advisers as I could, I found that only about half themselves shared the basic understandings about body functioning and illness that would make an intrinsically organized illness-treating schema possible. The advisers, in many cases, were themselves advised in finding the practitioners they recommended; whole chains of advice expand the reach of the medical understandings to those who do not share them. This proves to be as true of understandings about and use of Western medicine as it is of traditional Swahili medicine.

For most patients, what is crucial to their getting the medical treatment they do are the expectations in the advisers' statuses and their part in their roles vis-à-vis the patients. As with Fernandez's (1965) ritual attenders who shared few understandings about the ritual they participated in with the specialists who arranged and staged the ritual, the patients' behavior is to be understood as a product of the understandings that connect statuses rather than directly as guided by the understandings concerning the immediate focus of the actual behavior.

As noted earlier, the distribution of understandings among statuses includes general expectations as well as specific ones. Patients told me, for example, that they followed their mothers' (and in a few cases, their fathers') advice about getting treatment because "my mother knows about these things," because "she is concerned about me and my health," and similar reasons. The patients "trust," "believe in," or (in a few cases) "obey" their adviser, and these views are rooted in general expectations about the adviser as part of the adviser's status as parent, spouse, kinsman, or neighbor. The adviser, in turn, has general expectations regarding whomever he or she found out about the therapist from. The intersection or connection of the general expectations in the different relationships (i.e., the adviser's direct or indirect trust in the therapist's ability and the patient's usually direct trust in the adviser) leads the patient to get treatment from a person whose relevant status is based on understandings shared with other therapists and with a few interested group members but often not with the patient.

It is the relationships among people guided by elements in their statuses, most especially general expectations, that lead the patient to seek and accept the treatment. If we think of social structure as the connections among statuses based in the mutual referring understandings that constitute those statuses, it is social structure, a product of culture,[8] rather than the cultural elements concerning illness and treatment acting directly as a guide to behavior that accounts for what is observed in at least some group members' choice of therapy and therapists. Culture's elements, concerned with who trusts whom as well as with who has understandings about the sources of illness or who is an acceptable therapist, are distributed among the statuses, and the distribution itself has a key part in the phenomenon of consulting a particular therapist.

Cultural Distribution
and Social Structure

In chapter 10, the distribution of understandings among different statuses and the general expectations connecting those statuses are seen to provide a powerful resource for wives based in the unique character of the spouse relationship. This resource is vital to the wives sometimes getting what they want from their husbands even though the husbands have the undoubted power to refuse. This social structural effect, like that involved in the seeking of medical treatment, is seen to work even though some of the key understandings involved are not shared by all—or, in this case, any—of the actors involved.

The husbands say they give in to their wives' wishes because they do not want them to be "unhappy," and the wives say the husbands do it because of their "love" for them and because the husbands are "good." The source of the husbands' concerns about their wives' unhappiness and of their goodness is shown to be related to the fact that in all other relationships, men are blocked in receiving emotional support. The general expectations concerning emotional content in the husband's whole network of relationships makes the spouse relationship unique in this respect and thus gives the wife a powerful resource whether she admits it or not and regardless of her awareness of it.

Again, then, the distribution of culture is itself an important agent in influencing behavior. The effectiveness of the distribution of culture depends, of course, on conformity to the understandings involved. The understandings that people share can only be a basis for social life if the understandings concerned are used as actual guides to behavior. Since there are some understandings that apply to all or nearly all group members and some that apply only to those classified in particular statuses under limited conditions, there must be two different types of pressures for conformity. One of these must be parallel to the differential distribution of culture in order to produce the differentiated behavior appropriate to members of different statuses in various contexts. The other sort of pressure for conformity must be fairly uniform leading people to behave in somewhat similar, rather than differentiated, ways in certain domains and contexts where such similarity sometimes promotes group cohesiveness.

The Organization
of Culture by Statuses

Chapter 11 brings together my findings and interpretations to summarize what has been found for the Mombasa Swahili and to propose a generally applicable status-based theory of culture's functioning. One of the theory's main propositions concerns how culture's parts are related to one another, that is, how they are organized, to form an effective guide to action. One source of this cultural organization is "organizing understandings" that explicitly indicate the relationship between other understandings, as in "better safe than sorry."

The relationships among elements may be ones of relative importance as in the example just cited, but they may also concern sequence, dependence or independence, or other sorts of relations. Whichever sort of relationship may be involved, organization is an indispensable part of culture's functioning. Although explicit organizing understandings can contribute to the relations among cultural elements, such understandings are by no means the only or, necessarily, the most common or effective contributors. Organization may, and often does, result from understandings that have no intrinsic relations with the issues to be acted on. Put simply, the relationship between cultural elements is mediated by, even sometimes produced by, the understandings that guide the relationships between people.

Organization is vital because it directs the unavoidable choices that must be made among the understandings that might be useful guides in particular contexts and situations. This choice is often on the basis of actors' status-guided relationships to other people concerned with the action at issue rather than on the basis of intrinsic relationships among the usually numerous alternative understandings that are more or less applicable to that action. That is, actor X follows understanding A rather than understanding B not because A is more important, urgent, or virtuous than B but because the relationships with actor Y makes A more appropriate. Status-guided organization of this sort results from at least three somewhat different sorts of processes.

One is the type involved in the previously described spouse relationship. Stated generally, participation in one relationship is affected by the involvement of the participants in other relationships. This leads some understandings available in the relationship to be given precedence over others of similar sorts, as in the husbands withholding their power to refuse their wives' requests for finery and expensive ceremonies.

A related but different social process that serves to organize cultural elements is described in chapter 9. Here it is seen that many individuals decide what medical care to seek on the basis of the general expectation in a relationship—typically with the mother—that is not primarily medical in nature but that involves wide-scope trust. The understanding that leads to action is not one concerned specifically with illness and treatment but rather with the adviser's commitment to the patient's welfare. Similarly, the adviser's recommendation is rather often based on her trust of still a third person in a relationship with her which is not primarily medical. Fairly often, such links form a chain of nonmedical relationships that influence or determine decisions about medical problems despite few of the participants sharing even basic understandings about medical issues.

In this way, the effects of cultural elements shared among a few members of a group are "passed" from relationship to relationship and affect people who may be quite ignorant of the particular understandings that directly bear on, and may be crucial to dealing with, the problem or issue concerning them.

Somewhat similarly, the expectations in one relationship are transmitted to another through their effects on the person who is involved in them both. The person with dual involvement transmits the effects of the expectations in one relationship to his partner in the other with that partner's reaction depending not on the provenance of the expectations but, rather, on the latter's commitment to the relationship itself. The partner may transmit those effects to still another relationship, thus continuing the "chain reaction." This organization of elements involving bringing understandings into some kind of sequence need not be itself based on culture since it does not depend on those involved having any understanding of the overall interlocking network of expectations that actually produces the organization. A whole series of understandings can be linked together in this way, with the vital connection between them being their involvement in relationships with participants who have relationships with others "higher" in the chain rather than any intrinsic relations among the understandings themselves.

The main hypotheses in this book were developed through work in the Mombasa Swahili community, but they are proposed as being universally applicable. It is not part of the proposal that the processes found among the Swahili are the sole means for promoting culture's effectiveness. It is, however, a contention that these processes are found in all groups. The status-based organization of culture may be only one of a variety of solutions to the problem of culture's ability to function despite limited sharing within groups and, even, within statuses. Similarly, it may be that it can be shown that the nature of general expectations is less central to social life than it appears to be in Old Town and that the use of cultural models embedded in relationship terms is only one of myriad devices that teach understandings to adults while, at the same time, giving those understandings an emotional and evaluative weight that makes them harder to flout. It may even be that the importance of evaluation and its dual dependence on status is overstated and that other processes play a greater part in differential cultural conformity and the maintenance of social structure in other communities. Still, all of these processes are being presented as universal even though the data presented here are from the Mombasa Swahili community alone.

And now it is time to turn to those data. To put flesh on the conceptual bones and to provide a basis for assessing the claimed significance of the cultural processes described here, we begin with a consideration of the rise of the Mombasa Swahili community and its evolution over time.

2

Akher Zamani

Mombasa Swahili History and
Contemporary Society

Swahili men and women say "Akher zamani" (the end of time) to express
their despair at the changes they see around them and at people's failure to
behave properly. They explain that the phrase refers to a decline in the quality
of life and that Muslims believe that this began with the death of Prophet
Mohammed in the seventh century and is accelerating now.

Whatever the world as a whole may be doing, it is true that the Swahili
community is declining economically, politically, and demographically when
compared to its stature in the first half of the last century. The group's members are still more affluent than most—but by no means all—of their fellow
Mombasans: they occupy diplomatic and civil service positions out of proportion to their small numbers; the community continues as a vital and effective force in its members' lives; and the commitment to Islam by all group
members could hardly be more complete and binding.

But the wealth of members of some recent immigrant groups far surpasses
that of the Swahili, who have lost most of their land and traditional occupations; their influence on governmental policy is quite limited, and they form
only a tiny minority in the city. Young group members do not dress as
conservatively or behave as decorously as those of their parents' generation
remember themselves as having done; respect for high-prestige individuals
is less obvious and complete than senior group members would like; some
of the most cherished symbols of group membership, such as the veil for
women, have been appropriated by members of other groups who have, in
the Swahili view, no right to them; and group rituals are far less commonly
held or universally attended than they were as recently as the 1960s.

There is nothing new in the fact that this, or any, group is changing. Unless archaeologists and historians have been deceiving us, every human society has changed throughout its existence, with differences between societies and eras being a matter of rate of change rather than its presence or absence. The Mombasa Swahili have changed quite noticeably in a number of respects during the brief period (1975 to 1988) I have been visiting them, but I will try to show that, significant as the current changes are, change has been the most constant process in this group during its long history.

The history sketched here is approached with an emphasis on culture and its parts, statuses, and their interrelations in social structure. Attention is mainly accorded social structure because the data from which other parts of long past culture can be inferred are far harder to obtain in reliable form than is information about groups and their arrangements. This is quite true of the secondary historical sources I used for early Swahili history and only somewhat less true of the informants' accounts that I combined with these published sources to produce the history of much of the current century.

After briefly examining the development of the community from its earliest period to the present, I close the chapter with a hypothesis suggesting an important influence on the overall structure of the community as found in the 1970s and 1980s.

The Swahili in Contemporary Mombasa

Mombasa is a major city, the most active seaport on the East African coast. The city proper is an island, a rectangular bit of land roughly three by five miles. It is set within the jaws of the coastline but is completely separated from the mainland by a narrow semicircular inlet of the Indian Ocean (each part of the inlet is called a "creek" locally) which surrounds the island on three sides. This is nowhere very wide, and on each side it has narrow parts that separate the island and the mainland by only a few hundred yards or less. The island's ocean-facing east side is entirely within the north-south line of the coast and thus completely sheltered from the open ocean while offering entrances to its harbors through the north and south creeks.

The island has been connected to the mainland beginning with a railroad bridge in 1896 and, since the 1930s, by a causeway on the east, a bridge on the north (a new one was built here in 1977), and a car ferry on the south (DeBlij 1968:39–40). Ships have been calling at the Old Port on the northeast side of the island for centuries. And Kilindini Harbor, the new port on the western side, now seethes with activity as cranes unload the endlessly arriving cargoes that supply imports and carry away exports not only for Kenya but also for Uganda, Burundi, Ruanda, and parts of Tanzania.

The city is, and long has been, as cosmopolitan as would be expected of a major port. The Old Port, in the Swahili section, is now used mainly by fishermen, local boats, and the coastal trade, but for centuries and as recently as the 1970s, it was the stopping place of traders from Arabia, India, Persia, and Somalia. The single masts of their dhows bristled from the port every year during the period when the monsoons blew out of the north, and their goods were being traded from Mombasa into the interior long before the Portuguese conquered the city in the sixteenth century.

The once vigorous dhow trade has declined after many centuries of great activity to a few coastal boats as of the 1980s (Martin 1978), but the streets of the city continue to be crowded with people from an impressive assortment of nations. One sees Arabs from different regions of what is now Yemen, Oman, and Kuwait as well as Iranians, Indians, Pakistanis, Europeans, Americans, and Japanese. In addition, of course, there are Africans from the coastal, Mijikena, peoples and many of the inland ethnic groups throughout Kenya, Tanzania, Uganda, and farther afield.

The occasional Swahili man is seen walking in this crush, but in his work clothes—sport shirt and slacks—he looks like every other middle-class Mombasan, and after work, when he wears his ankle-length white *kanzu* (the famous Arab-style "night shirt" or djellaba) and gleaming *kofia* (an intricately decorated skullcap), it is hard for outsiders to distinguish him from the Arabs. Swahili women are not often seen on the streets, but when they appear, their full-length, black veils (*buibui* in Swahili), leaving only their faces and hands uncovered, make them indistinguishable from Arab women but quite different from the women of other Muslim groups who wear colored veils or ankle-length gowns with face cloths.

The Swahili man's kanzu has a distinctive beige design embroidered on the yoke, and the kofia is embroidered in off-white rather than the darker colors favored by Muslim men of other ethnic groups. Both of these characteristics are apparent only on close examination and, as with many contemporary symbols of Swahili group membership, are muted and meaningful mainly to those who know to look for them.

Most students of the Swahili agree that, like the members of other communities of their group, the Mombasa Swahili, at least after the period when they can be identified as the *Theneshara Taifa* (see below), were understood by their neighbors as being of a somewhat medial ancestry. Thus, one of the leading students of the Swahili language wrote, "Regarded as 'Arabs' by many up-country Africans, they are deemed not-wholly Arabs by those Arabs of 'pure' descent who frequent the island, and occupy, so it seems to me, an anomalous position between Arab and African" (Whitely 1955:11).

Even members of other local ethnic groups sometimes fail to identify Swahili for what they are. For example, while walking down the Digo Road on the western edge of Old Town, the Swahili section of the city, with two men from the Mijikenda group, I saw two Swahili friends dressed in kanzu and kofia walking on the other side of the broad street. "What tribe are those men?" I asked my companions, both native-born Mombasans. "Arabs," they replied with confident error.

Despite the difficulty many Mombasans from other groups have identifying them, the Swahili have been part of the city longer than any other group. Old Town was the first settled area on the island and is now crowded and run-down. Its narrow streets admit only the smallest cars, and its houses virtually touch one another.

Members of the Swahili ethnic group founded what is now the city of Mombasa[1] not less than seven centuries ago, but the founders were members of a Swahili community different from the one now living there. As will be described below, the Swahili group, organized as it now is into two major sections or confederations that are jointly referred to as the Theneshara Taifa, or Twelve Tribes, has existed since the seventeenth century.[2] However, they finished settling in their present neighborhoods in what is now called Old Town as recently as the nineteenth century (Berg 1968:45–48, Cooper 1977:98).

Contemporary Old Town and Mombasa

The houses in Old Town are closely packed together. Winding footpaths between them lead to the narrow streets. Most houses are constructed of mud spread on a frame made of wooden poles plaited together with this core faced inside and out with cement. Roofs are generally of sheet metal, but a few are now tile, and, as recently as the 1970s, a few were still of the older and less desired thatch. Two-story houses are highly prestigious and are found primarily in the relatively affluent neighborhood of Kibokoni (the neighborhood traditionally occupied by the Three Tribes section) and only rarely in Mjua Kale (the Nine Tribes section's neighborhood). Even many of these large houses, like their more common single-story neighbors, are in need of paint and refacing, and the entire Old Town area has a somewhat neglected quality. Here and there, a few new apartment buildings and cement block houses with shingled roofs stand out, but the majority of these are owned by Indians or, in a few cases, Yemenis rather than by Swahili.

The old neighborhoods of Old Town including Kibokoni, Mjua Kale, and their subdivisions retain their traditional names. Most of the contemporary Swahili population are the descendants of families that have been in the same immediate area, often the same house, for many generations. But in most of these neighborhoods, a large proportion of the families, now a majority in most areas, are Indians or Yemeni Arabs whose roots go back a century or, more often, less and who have not merged into the Swahili group as immigrations of Omani Arabs more or less did a number of generations ago (see below).

Each Old Town neighborhood has its own Swahili mosque, and the adhan from the loudspeakers during the five daily calls to prayer rises above even the noise of the traffic in the narrow streets. There are Indian and Yemeni mosques in the same areas. Some of them, especially those of the Indians, are bigger and more expensive in construction and design than the older Swahili mosques.

Scattered throughout the residential areas are tiny shops, called *reshoni* (from the English word, rations), mostly run by Yeminis, where snacks, bread, rice, flour, cigarettes, kerosene, charcoal, matches, flashlight batteries, pots, pans, and sundries are sold. In most of the neighborghoods, these small shops are the only nonresidential buildings. Most of the larger businesses, banks, and commercial buildings are in the areas on the western side of the island, just beyond the Digo Road, the western boundary of Old Town.

In the last century and earlier, when Mombasa was inhabited mainly by Swahili and those closely associated with them, the western parts of the island were given over to Swahili fields and coconut plantations. This area now includes the business district and neighborhoods occupied by members of other ethnic groups. A substantial part of Mombasa's population lives on the northern or southern mainland, but few Swahili live outside Old Town. Those who do are either younger professional people living in affluent areas on the western part of the island or north mainland or relatively poor families whose forebears lost their Old Town house sites through some economic reverse and now live in the areas beyond the Digo Road now mainly occupied by others of limited means from different, mainly African, ethnic groups.

Old Mombasa

Beginning: 1000–1500

The first published reference to Mombasa is in the work of the geographer, al-Idrisi, in the twelfth century (Berg and Walter 1968:51), so the town has existed for at least eight centuries, but there is little agreement on just when it was founded or by whom (Mathew 1963:94–127; Prins 1967:40–42; Salim 1973:9–10). Horton's excavations at Shanga on Pate Island south of Mombasa show that the "Swahili were African [not Arab] in origin" and by the ninth century were becoming Muslim and establishing settlements at numerous sites along the East African coast (Horton 1986, 1987:88–89). Considering both archaeological and linguistic evidence, Nurse and Spear (1985:57–58) conclude that the city "was founded . . . ca. 1000" by Swahili whose ancestors came from the north in Lamu archipelago and the adjacent mainland where the Swahili ethnic group may have originated several centuries earlier.

According to at least one historian of the Mombasa Swahili community, the city founders were Swahili but not those who are the direct forebears of the contemporary Swahili community (Berg 1968:38–39). In this view, the latter, who are sometimes called Theneshara Taifa, the Twelve Tribes, did not come to live on Mombasa island until three or four centuries ago and were preceded there by two earlier Swahili groups (ibid.).

At first, what is now Mombasa was called Gongwa and was occupied by a Swahili group under Queen Mwana Mkisi (ibid., 42). Her dynasty was followed in about 1500 by a Shirazi dynasty founded by Shehe Mvita whose name thereafter became the Swahili name, Mvita, of the city (Nurse and Spear 1985:73). Early in the sixteenth century, during the reign of this dynasty, the Portuguese made their first visits to Mombasa. They found it to be a stone-built city with twenty to thirty thousand Muslim inhabitants trading with other parts of the East African coast and with ports on the west coast of India (Berg and Walter 1968:51–52). In this and subsequent visits, the Portuguese ships and troops devastated Mombasa three times: in 1505, 1526, and 1589 (Berg 1968:45). Despite this, during the early sixteenth century, Mombasa was de-scribed by the chronicler of Indian Ocean trade, Tomé Pircs, as "a place of great traffic" in produce of every kind (Freeman-Grenville 1963:152).

The ethnic orgins of all these active early residents of the city are not en-tirely clear, but, despite the vital and large part played by African sources in much that is Swahili (Nurse and Spear 1985; Horton 1986, 1987:87), there were doubtless cultural and biological contributions from peoples from out-side the continent. Thus, although the role of Omani Arabs in the history of the Mombasa Swahili will be seen to be a significant one, it is difficult to es-tablish clearly whether or not immigrants from Oman had already become part of the community before the arrival of the Portuguese, the first Europeans to affect the group directly.

We do know that families and rulers of Omani origin were well established on Pate Island (250 km to the north of Mombasa) and elsewhere on the coast in the fourteenth century (Salim 1973:21). And it is quite likely that there were other influential immigrants from that area present on the coast as early as the seventh century (Prins 1967:40–41).

Arabs from another area, the Hadhramaut, in what is now northern Yemen, arrived on the East African coast during the fourteenth and fifteenth centuries. They profoundly influenced the culture of the Swahili ethnic group, including that of the Mombasa community, in a number of ways, including, especially, religion (Salim 1973:141).

Currently, and for at least several centuries, all members of the Swahili ethnic group are and have been adherents of the Shafi *madhahab* (canon or sect) of Sunni Islam (Swartz 1978). This faith seems to have been brought to the area no later than the fourteenth century by a large migration of Sharifs (descendants of Prophet Mohammed) from the Hadramaut (Salim 1973:141–142). The same group of immigrants also founded the poetic verse form, utenzi, characteristic of the Swahili, as well as their method of religious teaching and the according of prestige to the families of Sharifs (ibid.; Harries 1962:86–88).

If, as seems likely, the Hadhrami brought the Shafi canon to Mombasa, they arrived not later than the early fourteenth century, or perhaps the thirteenth, as can be seen from the reports of Ibn Battuta who visited Mombasa in 1329 or 1331. He observed that the people, although living in poverty, had well-constructed wooden mosques and were pious followers of the Shafi canons of the Sunni branch of Islam (Berg and Walter 1968:51).

Whatever the exact dates of arrival of the various Arab immigrants, the active trade noted by Ibn Battuta doubtless contributed to migration into the area. By the fifteenth century, this trade was largely focused on traffic to and from the Red Sea area (Pouwells 1987:38), and Mombasa, with its northern neighbor, Malindi, and, perhaps, Mogadishu, surpassed the once dominant southern town of Kilwa as the main entrepôt to Eastern Africa (ibid.). During this same period, the people of Mombasa, both slaves and their owners, were highly productive farmers in the plantations on the island and adjacent mainland (Cooper 1977:100–102).

Probably because of this economic activity, migration to the island in the sixteenth century continued despite a disastrous military campaign against neighboring Malindi, attacks by marauding groups from the north and south, and a number of political upheavals. Even as political instability grew and rulers came and went at shorter and shorter intervals, the Mombasa Swahili continued to become cosmopolitan at a rate that increased with time (Berg 1968:45–46).

The Coming of the
Two-Section Community: 1500–1836

By the time the Portuguese arrived in the first decade of the sixteenth century, the post-Shirazi period of the Mombasa Swahili community had begun. It was an era of instability and rapid change, with the Portuguese arrival occurring at the same time the city was attacked by the cannibalistic Zimba (ibid., 45). Having survived this, the Mombasans mounted an attack on the Portuguese and their Malindi allies the year after the Europeans arrived, but this was a debacle (ibid.). The defeat ended forever the Mombasa Shirazi[3] reign and led to the formation of the two-section organization, called the Twelve Tribes, that has characterized the Mombasa community for the three and a half centuries leading up to and including the present (ibid., 42–44; Nurse and Spear 1985:4–5).

The Shirazi rulers of Malindi were allied with the Portuguese and ruled in conjunction with them from 1593 until 1632, when the acquisitive Portuguese captains took control of Mombasa into their own hands (Berg 1968:45) without, however, establishing a stable peace in the area (ibid., 50). The descendants of this Malindi dynasty became integrated into the Mombasa community and now number themselves among the *Tisa Taifa,* or Nine Tribes, confederation or section, which, largely because of its Shirazi connections and its earlier presence on Mombasa island, considers itself senior to the other Twelve Tribes section, the *Thelatha Taifa,* or Three Tribes (ibid., 45–46).

While the political situation remained unstable on the coast as a whole throughout the sixteenth century,[4] sometime around 1600, various immigrant groups joined the Mvita "tribe"[5] already living on Mombasa island. Like the other tribes that make up the Twelve Tribes, the Mvita are a collection of Swahili partrilines not claiming a common ancestor but tracing its origins to a common, earlier location. They believe their ancestral area was in the north, and they claim ties of kinship and marriage with the Malindi Sherazi rulers. The Mvita settled in the area on the eastern side of the island in a location overlapping with what Berg (1968:48) refers to as the "southern portion of the [older] Shirazi town," and it was there that they were joined by other "tribes" to form what became the Nine Tribes section of the Mombasa Swahili community.

At the beginning of the formation of the Nine Tribes confederation, the Kilindini tribe, which was to become a major part of the other Mombasa Swahili section, the Three Tribes, was still living in mainland villages some distance to the south of Mombasa (ibid., 46).[6] This collection of patrilines did not migrate to the island and join the Mvita as some other Swahili groups were doing in the late sixteenth century. In fact, the Kilindini declined an invitation from the sheikh of the Nine Tribes to join the latter confederation, which was already well established on Mombasa island (ibid.).

Instead, the Kilindini first moved north to a mainland area immediately south of the island. Only after affiliating with two other Swahili "tribes" to form what became the Three Tribes sometime between 1593 and 1632 did they move onto the island where they founded the independent city of Kilindini, in the western area now occupied by the modern seaport (ibid., 47).[7] The settlements of the two confederations were initially—and for two centuries after that—separated by about two miles of unoccupied bush and fields.

When the groups that were the nucleus of the Three Tribe section moved to Mombasa island from the mainland, according to Berg, their presence led to "a breakdown in the Mombasa state system that enabled the *Thelatha Taifa* (Three Tribes) to feel a sense of autonomy on the island" (ibid., 48). Now the Nine Tribes no longer absorbed all immigrants since the newer Three Tribes grouping not only remained separate but had its own parallel political structure.

In both confederations, newcomer families retained their identity as separate descent lines (*mbari,* sing. and pl.) and banded together into "tribes" according to common areas of origin and shared political leaders. The Three

Tribes, as we have seen, came onto the island from the mainland at the beginning of the seventeenth century with all of its three subgroupings already formed and in association with each other.

It was not until the end of the eighteenth century that the senior section, the Nine Tribes or Tisa Taifa, had acquired its full complement of constituent groups. Although further Swahili immigrants, almost all from the north and mainly single men, continued to arrive in Mombasa (ibid.)—in fact, they are still arriving—following the beginning of the eighteenth century, they were included in one or the other of the existing mbari rather than forming new ones. An immigrant man's family belonged to the mbari of his wife's family (Cooper 1977:98, but cf. Eastman 1988:5).[8]

The Nine Tribes, which counting the most recent addition, Bajun, actually number ten, are, and for centuries have been, composed of the following tribes (Taifa): Mvita, Jomvu, Kilifi, Mtwapa, Pate, Shaka, Paza, Bajun, and Katwa.

The Three Tribes are, similarly, made up of the Kilindini, Changamwe, and Tangana.

All of the tribes had the same basic political organization with a leader, or "sheikh," from a particular descent line in the tribe and each mbari (i.e., descent line) having the senior man of its senior family serve as a subordinate leader and adviser (called *mzee,* pl. *wazee*) to the tribe's sheikh. It is not entirely clear whether the two sections had established rulers for the entire section before the Busaidi took control of the city in 1837 (Berg 1968:52), but from the time each of them established their separate communities on Mombasa island until about the time of the declaration of a British protectorate in 1894, the two groupings—Nine Tribes and Three Tribes—maintained separate identities under a considerable variety of regimes that ruled the city and beyond. Each of the confederations came to have a leader, a *tamim,* who was always chosen from a particular descent line in the Tangana Tribe for the Three Tribes and a designated line in the Mvita Tribe for the Nine Tribes (Kindy 1972:47–49).

The Twelve Tribes were subordinate to outsiders from the sixteenth century onward. A partial summary of the succession of the regimes that ruled Mombasa from the sixteenth century to the eighteenth century is provided by Berg (1968:49) and shows the variety of regimes that controlled the Swahili community and its sections:

> Between the end of the Shirazi dynasty and the beginning of the Mazrui hegemony, Mombasa was ruled by an uneasy condominium administered by the Sheikhs of Malindi and the Portuguese Captains of Mombasa (1593–1631), by the Captains of Mombasa alone (1632–1698), and by various representatives of the [Yarubi] Imam of Muscat (1698–1735) with a brief reversion to Portuguese control in 1728–1729.

This summary omits the brief presence of the Turks and the three times Mombasa was sacked during the sixteenth century, including the last by the cannibalistic Zimba. In 1588, these Bantu speakers from the southern part of what is now Malawi brought "a destruction of the utmost horror" (Freeman-Grenville 1963:138–139) on Mombasa. Shortly after the Zimba, as Salim puts it, "literally ate their way northwards up to Malindi" (i.e., through and including Mombasa) the city was set upon by the Galla from the north (Salim 1973:21). By 1593, this general destruction along the coast led the Portuguese to reorganize their administration and make Mombasa a captaincy separate from that of Mozambique.

In the mid-seventeenth century when the Portuguese established themselves in East Africa, they also took Muscat in Oman (Pouwells 1987:97–98). When the Omani under the Yarubi imam, Sultan ibn Saif, overthrew the Portuguese in Muscat, the people of Mombasa sent a delegation to the Omani asking that they be relieved by their coreligionists from the "iron yoke and the injustices" of the Europeans (Lambert 1958:42). The Yarubi mounted a number of raids on the Portuguese in the following decades, and, finally, in 1696, a large Omani fleet laid siege to Fort Jesus, the Portuguese citadel (it still stands in Mombasa in Kibuokoni). Two years later, the fort fell, bringing victory to the Omani (Pouwells 1987:98). This event was a further stimulus to Omani immigration. "Many Arab soldiers and their descendants remain[ed] on the Coast, first as garrisons . . . and later as permanent settlers" (Lambert 1958:42).

During the Yarubi rule that followed their victory, the tribes of the Mombasa Swahili had not yet settled into the contiguous neighborhoods that have characterized the city for the past century and a half. Unlike this still-present arrangement, the two sections of the community continued to occupy noncontiguous areas separated by unoccupied land and were united only by their being subject to the same foreign authority (Berg 1968:50–51). Competition between the confederations for power and position within the imam's government continued to be sufficiently strong to lead, on several occasions, to armed clashes (ibid.).

In 1735, Yarubi rule on the East African coast was overthrown by the Mazrui, who had been brought to the East African coast by the imam's government as soldiers and governors. Once established as rulers in Mombasa, the Mazrui mediated between the two Swahili sections. Their efforts, including the granting of considerable autonomy to each of them, managed to bring relative peace between them. Outsiders' attacks on the city helped consolidate the Nine Tribes with the Three Tribes and draw them closer together, "but bridging the gap between them required 150 years and a foreign dynasty" (ibid., 50).

The absence of conflict between the two sections was not, and did not remain, a notable feature of the Mombasa Swahili community. Soon after the beginning of their suzerainty, the Yarubi ruler in Mombasa, Salah bin Mohammed al-Hadhrami, in alliance with the Nine Tribes, drove the Three Tribes off the island, and they took refuge with kin in mainland villages (ibid.). The Mazrui ruler who succeeded Salah, Mohammed bin Athman, invited the Three Tribes back to the island and reestablished his and the Mazrui government's ties with that section (ibid., 51).

Active conflicts and ultimate reconciliations between the two sections of the Twelve Tribes are common in that group's long history. What seems to have been the last armed clash occurred about ten years after the incident just mentioned. In this case, the Three Tribes conspired with one of the Mijikenda peoples, the Duruma, with whom they maintained a patron-client relationship, as they also did with the Digo (ibid., 47–48),[9] until the end of the last century, to restore Mazrui rule after it was disrupted by the assassination of the local Mazrui ruler. This murder was committed by agents of the new Omani dynasty on Zanzibar, the Busaidi, with the collaboration of members of the Nine Tribes confederation (ibid., 50–52).

Despite their role as mediators, the Mazrui rulers often sided with the Three Tribes. This can be seen in the fact that their *wazir,* or local subordinate ruler, was always chosen from a descent line in the Kilindini Taifa, a Three Tribes constituent (ibid., 52). Because of the ties between the Mazrui and the Three Tribes, the Nine Tribes were often at odds with their Mazrui rulers (ibid.). On one occasion, the Nine Tribes, at the prompting of members of their constituent Kilifi "tribe" who wished to assault the Three Tribes and their Mazrui allies but who did not themselves want to be involved in a civil war, called in kin and allies from the island of Pate. These raiders sailed to the Three Tribes Mombasa island settlement of Kilindini where they surprised the residents and burned their town before sailing to safety (ibid., 51).

Once again, the ensuing conflict was ended when a new Mazrui ruler succeeded to power in the city and reconciled the two parties. The end of armed fighting, however, did not mean the beginning of concord and unity between the Mombasa Swahili sections (ibid.). In fact, quarreling and intrigue can only have been said to have ended, if it has ended,[10] in the 1970s with the decline of the community as an active group and the concomitant change in affiliation of some section members (discussed below).

Mazrui rule lasted more than 150 years, continuing into the nineteenth century during which, as Berg notes, Mombasa enjoyed a period of power and influence unrivaled since the first Shirazi dynasty (ibid., 52). Under the Mazrui, the coast from Tanga to the Bajun Islands was subject to or dependent on the city, with the important islands of Pate and Pemba under its control for part of this period. The great Mombasa poet, Muyaka (now so called by community members with a taste for poetry but whose full name is Muyaka bin Mwinyi Haji), celebrated this period in his epics (Knappert 1979).

The heroic and powerful image of the city that comes from Muyaka's poems and from the oral history of this period offers a sharp contrast with the comparatively powerless and far less affluent present. This may be part of the basis for the view, to be examined below, expressed by several of those most concerned with the prestige and standing of the community, that it is now and long has been in a state of decline which has accelerated over the decades of the current century.

The Busaidi and the British: 1837–1964

The "heroic era" of Mombasa history came to an end following several rapid changes in rulers and considerable intrigue among the Mazrui. The Mazrui internecine conflict eventuated in an alienation of the Three Tribes from the Mazrui and the cooperation of this section in a conspiracy that brought Mombasa and its domains under the Omani ruler of Zanzibar and Muscat, the Busaidi sultan, Sayyid Said, in 1837 (Berg 1968:52). The final struggle between the Mazrui and the forces of Said led to the burning of Kilindini Town. Instead of rebuilding where they had been, the Three Tribes decided to establish themselves in their own area of Mvita, that is, Mombasa proper, adjacent to the Nine Tribes area, to form what is now the Old Town section of the city (ibid.). This provided the basic geographic division of the area, with the Three Tribes section called Kibokoni and the Nine Tribes section called Mjua Kale.

The move by the Three Tribes did not end the tension between the two sections of the community, but it did bring the two closer together physically than they had been during the long period when they lived in separate towns. They were also both responsible to the Busaidi official who ruled Mombasa even though he dealt with the sections through their own leaders, the *matamim,* and even though each section had its own religious courts that settled most disputes within the section (Swartz 1978).

Berg (1968:54) says that the matamim were subject to popular approval, as the Swahili saw it, and direct appointment, as the Busaidi thought of it. This last mattered little, however, since the sultan in fact allowed the Swahili internal self-government according to their own practices and with the officials they wanted. The matamim had considerable internal authority: they could imprison anyone they thought likely to benefit from it and appoint or discharge Taifa sheikhs as they saw fit (ibid.).

So long as the Busaidi *liwali* (local governors) were obeyed in their rather limited demands and some—but not most—of the port taxes and tarifs were paid to the sultan's government on Zanzibar, little was asked of the Swahili. The Three Tribes received a subsidy from the sultan every year for their help in the overthrow of the Mazrui (Salim 1973:41).

With the establishment of the Busaidi rule from Zanzibar, the status of the

Omani-descended families among the Twelve Tribes became somewhat more ambiguous than it had been. The Omani-derived families, informants report, always viewed themselves as "Arabs" and thus different from other Twelve Tribes members. This despite the fact that they were, according to universal—including their own—views, members of one or the other of the confederations. Other Swahili, however, reject the Omani-based families' view that they are "Arabs" living among the Swahili, with the others claiming that they are members of the community in all respects.

As support for this last view, it is noted that the Omani-derived families behave just as other Mombasa Swahili do, both in general and with respect to rituals (funerals, weddings, and circumcisions). The Swahili who do not claim to be Arabs point out that aside from the Mazrui, who have their own cemetery, the group members who "like to call themselves Arabs" nevertheless bury their dead in the cemetery of the confederation to which they belong. Their dead are not, in fact, buried in the cemeteries for resident, foreign Muslims, as were and are the officials and families of the Busaidi sultanate and, more recently, refugees from Zanzibar.

Informants, including members of the Omani descent lines in Mombasa, are quite vague about the dates of arrival of their Omani forebears, but it appears from all accounts that whenever they arrived, the original settlers were all men who married Swahili women rather than having brought wives with them from the Persian Gulf area (Cooper 1977:98). Historical accounts are sketchy, but it is clear that men from this area, including powerful and important individuals, have been arriving in Mombasa for many centuries. One Omani-based family, the Mandhry, are known to have arrived no later than the thirteenth century (Berg and Walter 1968:60), and the presence of other Omani-based families on the coast as early as the seventh century suggests that there were considerably earlier immigrants.

Part of the reason for the insistence on Arab identity on the part of community members with ancestral ties to Oman is the high regard in which the Omani regime on Zanzibar was held. In some respects, Zanzibar was Mombasa's Paris. As recently as the 1960s when the revolution radically changed Zanzibar, what was au courant there was to be looked up to and emulated in Old Town.

The Busaidi period when this Omani dynasty ruled from Zanzibar is looked on as a time when Swahili fortunes were still great, when people still behaved as they should, and when Islam, despite the efforts of Christian missionaries, still generally received the unquestioned respect Muslims believe God wills it to have. But with the rise of British influence and their eventual assumption of rule, all that began irrevocably to change. As F. J. Berg puts it,

> The Busaidi period in one sense represents a continuation, even a further
> consolidation, of traditional Swahili life. In another sense it was a preparation

for deep-seated changes during the twentieth century. On the one hand, the Busaidi acknowledged Swahili home rule, and indirectly reinvigorated the agricultural and commercial economy. . . . On the other hand, they deprived the city of its independence and were the opening wedge for an influx of Asians, Europeans and, eventually, up-country [from the interior] Africans. Busaidi suzerainty came to an end in fact, though not in theory, when a British protectorate was declared in 1895 (Berg 1968:54–55; see also Pouwells 1987:164–172 and Salim 1973:34–35).

The difficulties experienced by the Mombasa Swahili and their Busaidi rulers with the coming of British sovereignty were most immediately and directly concerned with slavery. The interest of the British in ending the slave trade and their general opposition to slavery was a constant source of irritation between the Swahili and Arabs (i.e., unassimilated families living in Mombasa and elsewhere) together with Mijikenda slave owners, on the one side, and the British-sponsored missionaries and officials, including the sultan, on the other (Salim 1973:41).

Under British influence, but still technically acting on his own behalf, the Busaidi sultan, Bargash, issued proclamations in 1876 aimed at ending the slave trade by land (ibid., 47). Only a British warship prevented a rebellion from beginning in Kilwa in the south when the proclamations became known. In the Mombasa area, a Swahili and Arab mob attacked the Frere Town mission station (on the north mainland immediately opposite Old Town across the north creek) established earlier by British missionaries to provide freed slaves with land, jobs, and protection (ibid.).

The direct involvement of British officials began in 1887 when the British East Africa Association was granted a concession on the coast from south of Mombasa to just south of Lamu where it was to act as agents for the sultan (ibid., 61). The Imperial British East Africa Company (IBEAC) was also active and had virtually complete authority over the entire coastal region that had been ceded to it by the sultan acting with British advice. Although its charter included the requirement that it suppress the slave trade, it sought to lessen the antagonism of slave owners toward the missionaries who harbored freed slaves by paying the former owners compensation.

In 1888, for example, IBEAC paid owners $25 each for more than 1,400 former slaves who had found sanctuary in five coastal missions (there were eleven; the other six also had large, but uncounted, numbers of newly freed men and women), but this had little long-term effect because the missionaries refused to stop harboring newly freed individuals after the payments had been made for the original group (ibid., 63–64). The IBEAC encountered many and serious difficulties in its efforts to administer the coast, deal with the slavery issue, and negotiate with Italian and German interests then active in the coastal areas adjacent to the Sudan, in the first case, and Tanganyika, in the second (ibid., 65–73). The company finally chose to withdraw entirely form the area (ibid., 72).

Instead of returning its authority to the sultan, the British government decided to govern directly, and in 1895, it proclaimed the British protectorate, which, while under the nominal authority of the sultan, explicitly put all legal governing power directly in the hands of British officials (ibid., 73). The proclamation coincided with a succession dispute among the Mazrui who had been relocated by the Busaidi in the town of Takaunga to the north of Mombasa (Berg 1968:55). The Mombasa Swahili became involved in this dispute on the side of the Mazrui group opposing the intervention of the British, and some members of the Mombasa community, including the Nine Tribes tamim and his son and the sheikh of one of the Three Tribes, joined the rebels in armed hostilities against the British (ibid., 55–56).

The rebellion gave those Swahili who were deeply suspicious of European, Christian involvement in their affairs an opportunity to stand against what they, informants say, viewed as a drift toward the hated Christian missionaries, the abolition of slavery, and anti-Islamic teachings and practices. Still, many Swahili stood aside in the conflict or collaborated with the British during the rebellion (Salim 1973:76). When the British crushed the revolt and drove its leaders into exile in Dar es Salaam, the Swahili effort to remove European, Christian influence was at an end, and changes in the community were now to proceed at a much accelerated rate (Berg 1968:55).

The British administration, under Sir Arthur Hardinge, sought to staff an administration for the coast and the interior with young Arabs and Swahili "of good family." Hardinge explained his wish to do this in a report to the British Foreign Office:

> The Arabs and upper-class Swahili are the only natives [except a few Somalis] who can read or who have any comprehension of politics, justice, or government. Community of religion, language and intermarriage gives them influence over the negro coast population which the European stranger cannot as a rule possess (quoted in Salim 1973:77).

The Mombasa Swahili, however, did not fare as well in the colonial service as their fellow ethnics from other communities, and only the lowest-level government jobs were given them (Kindy 1972:27–29). Unassimilated Arabs, many from or related to the Omani ruling families from Zanzibar, got the responsible and rewarding positions in the Mombasa city administration and in that of Mombasa's Coast Province (ibid.).

In fact, the Swahili have been in economic, political, and demographic decline for all of the twentieth century. The census taken by the district commissioner in Mombasa in 1897 was the last in which the Swahili were a majority of the city's population. The opening of the Uganda Railway at about the same time played a key role in the influx of Asian and European immigrants while also encouraging the immigration of members of other African ethnic groups from the inland areas of what was then Kenya Protectorate and, later, Kenya Colony.

At the same time, the end of slavery and the changes in the trade with the interior deprived the Swahili of their most important and substantial sources of income (Salim 1973:100–138). The Mombasa Swahili, like most of their fellow ethnics on the coast, did not work the land themselves (see Cooper 1977:98) but depended on slaves to produce the generally bountiful harvests that provided quite adequate incomes for landowning families. Informants tell me that many, probably the majority, of Twelve Tribes families not only owned the land on which their houses were built on Mombasa island but also had agricultural plots (sing. *shamba,* pl. *mashamba*) either on the island or on the adjacent mainland.

The British-prompted antislavery edicts began in the 1870s. These made the replacement of slaves impossible and the expansion of slave-worked shambas unreasonable (Salim 1973:100–101). Further restrictions on slavery were promulgated at frequent intervals until, in 1907, slavery on the mainland was abolished (as it had been on Zanzibar ten years earlier) and owners could gain compensation only by bringing court cases against the government documenting their losses (ibid., 110).

This loss to the Swahili took place at the same time that developments related to the opening of the Uganda Railway were also affecting the community. The railroad ran across the paths that the ivory-trading caravans had taken for many generations and rendered them superfluous as trade routes (ibid., 105). The British inaugurated game regulations that included the requirement that elephant hunters buy a 500 rupee license and deposit "heavy security" before undertaking a hunt (ibid., 105). Europeans and Indians, many of whom were attracted by the employment opportunities and general development associated with the beginnings of the railroad, took up ivory hunting and introduced competition into an area where Swahili and Arabs had had a monopoly, so that the profitability for the original participants was greatly reduced (ibid., 105–106).

As part of the ivory trade or in association with it, the Swahili bartered manufactured goods (especially cloth and iron tools) with the peoples of inland groups. Indian traders involved themselves in this activity and did so with a vigor and organization unknown by their Swahili and Arab predecessors, thereby virtually ending the participation of the latter in this once-remunerative trade (ibid., 106–107).

Nor were the dual blows from the railroad and the end of slavery the only ones for the Swahili in the early decades of the century. The Land Titles Ordinance passed in 1908 and allowed the government to declare as Crown Land vast acreages of Swahili land that had been under cultivation when slaves were available but which had reverted to bush with the loss of that source of labor (ibid., 114–115). This alienation of land together with the loss of labor led to a sharp decline in agricultural production and made the sale of remaining lands seem both necessary and sensible so that

> the elders of the Twelve Tribes in Mombasa, sensing the wind of change, adopted the simple argument: "wait until the government wants your land and you lose it and get nothing; sell it and you [at least] get something." By the liberal implementation of this philosophy, Indians and other speculators had acquired cheaply most of the best land in the district of Mombasa by the time the government decided to introduce the Land Ordinance in 1908 (ibid., 116).

The Three Tribes confederation tried to get the colonial government to recognize their claims to lands north of Mombasa which they held to be traditionally theirs, and, separately, the Nine Tribes made similar claims. In 1915 and 1918, these claims were disallowed by the colonial courts, and both confederations lost huge acreages of what had been communal property (ibid., 129–130). While all this was going on, individual parcels of land were being sold to Indians and Europeans by the elders of the two confederations on the basis of their interpretations of Islamic law (ibid., 125–128).

The result of the abolition of slavery and the Land Titles Ordinance was to undermine the "two main pillars of the economic structure of coastal peoples" (ibid., 133). Kenya Colony reports advert to the "unrelenting depression, stagnation, apathy, and poverty" found along the coast and refer to the people of the area, including Mombasa, as "lazy and thriftless" (ibid., 133–134). Still, the position of Mombasa as an entrepôt and the origin of the railroad gave it something of an advantage over the rest of the coast, with migrations to the city from other coastal areas giving it a net growth in the 1920s (ibid., 136).

The new migration of Arabs from the Hadhramaut in the early decades of this century brought in a supply of vigorous and entrepreneurial residents who contributed to the city's, if not particularly to the Swahilis', prosperity (ibid., 135). The Mombasa Swahili were slightly better off than their fellow residents of the coast, but in comparison to their past power and prosperity, their main progress was, in their view, toward "the end of time."

3

The Brotherhood
of Coconuts

Unity, Conflict, and Narrowing Loyalties

Undugu wa nazi hukutani chunguni: *[The] brother-
hood of coconuts comes about in [the] cooking pot*

This Swahili proverb wryly notes the difficult, even hopeless, circumstances under which coconuts unite.[1] The unity of the Swahili community's
major constituent parts came about through a conflict that shattered a long-
enduring community organization and replaced it with one that is socially less
inclusive and culturally narrower in scope. Following is a sketch of the events
whereby the old organization ceased to operate and the newer one began to
function.

Introduction

The decline of the Swahili community was particularly evident in members' beliefs about the quality of community life. My informants are unanimous in their belief that Twelve Tribes community life is not what it once
was. Older people report that in their youth, neighbors and relatives were
more dependable and the community as a whole more active. Younger people
take the same basic view but refer, surprisingly, to the impropriety of their
own behavior and the failure of their parents and respected community members to control them "better." I will return to the young people's view of their
own conduct in chapter 4 when I consider the nature of culture's contents,
but for now, the point is that informants of all ages agree that community
life has declined.

Older informants sometimes mention the number, scale, and quality of
group rituals—weddings, circumcisions, and funerals—that were held until
fairly recently and the very substantial sums of money that were spent on

them. Men are quite ambivalent about this expenditure and sometimes say that the failure of the Swahili to keep up financially with their Hadhrami and Indian Old Town neighbors is due to the extravagance of the rituals held.

At the same time, there is a definite pride in their opulence. For women, this pride is particularly strong. There were still large weddings in the late 1970s, and large funerals were still held, although with lesser expenditures, throughout the 1980s. Outright regret from men at the diminished number and quality of rituals is only rarely heard, although it is heard from women, but there is a tone of regret nevertheless. As far as comparisons heard between the present and the recent past in amity, mutual assistance, and cooperation among neighbors, there is no ambivalence and no difference between male and female informants: all compare the present unfavorably.

In fact, so far as objective evidence is available, it appears that community life has declined along the dimensions informants mention. Not that the Twelve Tribes has ever been a society characterized by boundless concord, ubiquitous amity, and widespread cooperation. As we have seen, throughout the history of the Twelve Tribes, the two sections of the community, the Nine Tribes and Three Tribes confederations, have competed vigorously across a wide scope of activities, and there have been more than a few periods of sharp conflict. Still, the sections had been mainly united in a dynamic opposition that allowed the community as a whole to exist and even prosper. Sometimes the help of outside authorities, including the notably successful Mazrui rulers in the last century, was involved in overcoming the opposition when it became disruptive, but in the last century or two, a dynamic unity was usual.

As seen earlier, the confederations were made up of migrant "tribes," many of which included within themselves a variety of immigrant descent lines that, in time, became thoroughly integrated into the community through membership in one or the other of the sections, each localized in its own part of Old Town. A partial exception to this integration into the community through section membership is found for a number of families founded by men of Omani origin. These men married Swahili women and produced, over the generations, descendants who continued to emphasize their Arab identity even though in most respects they behaved in accord with Swahili, rather than Arab, culture. A majority of these "Swahili Arab," as they can be called for easy reference, families were in the Nine Tribes section, but the Three Tribes also included some. Despite their insistence on their Arab heritage, they participated in the rituals and activities of their confederations and of the community as a whole and patterned their social lives, including marriage, just as other Twelve Tribes members did.

With the ascendancy of the Busaidi in the nineteenth century, however, the internal solidarity of each of the sections was lessened by the commitment of the Swahili Arabs to the ethnically related (as they themselves understood that relationship) group and culture on Zanzibar, that is, that of the Busaidi sultan and his retainers. I shall refer to this latter group, again for ease of reference, as "Zanzibar Arabs." It will become clear that the commitment of the Swahili Arabs of each section to the Zanzibaris has worked equally against the interests of the members of the opposite section *and* of members of their own section who do not share their claimed ethnic origin.

There was nothing new about the identification of the Swahili Arabs with the peoples of the Omani region. For many generations, there have been Swahili families that traced their founders' origins to the Persian Gulf area, but when the identification was used as a resource to gain political advantage beyond the community and to benefit from colonial racial policies, it had an influence both more profound and more lasting than it had ever had before. One of the earlier advantages that came to those who could prove they were of Arab descent appeared in 1910 when "Arabs" were exempted from the colonial Hut Tax, while others, including Swahili who did not go to court to prove they had Arab ancestors, were not (Salim 1973:187).

Asserting Arab Ethnicity
and Its Effect on the Community

Whatever their gain by asserting it, my hypothesis is that the effect of the employment of the claim to Arab, rather than Swahili, status by some Twelve Tribes members was to disrupt the long-standing organization of the community. That is, the insistence on an Arab identity by some members of each of the sections united the remaining members of the sections with each other across section lines in opposition to those in both sections who claimed the identity. This realignment, I maintain, is a major factor in the weakening of the community in that it undermined the long-standing relationships within and between sections that had served as the basis for community structure since the Three Tribes joined the Nine Tribes on Mombasa island centuries before.

The details of the conflict between those emphasizing their Omani origins and other members of the community in both sections are tangled and baroque. In part, the complexity is based in the fact that there were, and are, Omanis who live in Old Town who are not Swahili. These families follow the Ibathi canon of Islam, the men wear beards, and their patrilateral, and in some cases even matrilateral, forebears came from Oman or elsewhere in the Persian Gulf region not more, in most cases, than two or three generations ago. These families speak Arabic in their homes, and although they associate with their Twelve Tribes neighbors, they are not considered by any community members to be Swahili.

The Swahili Arabs, however, are a different group, and none of the religious, linguistic, or descent characteristics just noted for the Omanis is true of them. The fact that the neighboring Bantu-speaking peoples (the Giriama, Digo, and the others who are jointly referred to as "Nyika" by the Swahili) refer to both Swahili and Arabs (whether assimilated or not) as *Wazomba*[2] indicates that from the outside, at least, the differences between the two are not always obvious or salient.

The distinction between the groups is not always an easy one to make from any perspective; this difficulty lies, in fact, at the heart of the conflict within the community that became serious and disruptive in the 1920s. Members of the Swahili Arab group denied the validity of any distinction between themselves and less assimilated immigrants from Oman. They, the Swahili Arabs, insisted that they were members of the same group as the Zanzibar Arabs. They claimed that this membership entitled them to the considerable privileges accorded the latter group under colonial rule.

This claim was mainly accepted by the Zanzibar Arab government and the British who advised and, in the twentieth century, succeeded them, and it won for the Swahili Arabs advantages not open to other community members. This was so, informants report, under the administration of the sultan up to 1895 and it continued under the colonial administration when the Mombasa area was administered by a special arm of the Kenya Colony government, called the "Arab Administration," whose highest officials were Zanzibar Arabs.

New Community Divisions

The Swahili Arabs took considerable pains to align themselves with the Zanzibaris in ways beyond simply asserting common ethnicity. Sh. Hyder Kindy, who was personally involved, gives a lengthy account of some of the key events concerning the assertion of the alignment in the 1920s in his *Life and Politics in Mombasa* (1972:26–45). The accounts I have received from three other participants in the events substantially agree with Kindy, but they, and I, do not agree that all of those he identifies as "Arabs" are, in fact, what I am calling "Zanzibar Arabs" or Omani. Some of them were Swahili Arabs, and they and their families are Twelve Tribes members with all the social, cultural, and linguistic traits appropriate to members of that community.

Under colonial rule, the political advantages of being classified as "non-native" were substantial, and the stronger position of Arabs was clear to the Swahili as it was to everyone else. Thus, despite an initial rebuff, in 1921, many men from the Twelve Tribes, both Swahili Arabs and others, joined with resident Zanzibar Arabs in a political group called the Coast Arab Association (Salim 1973:180–187, Stroebel 1979:40) with the intention of increasing their ability to influence the colonial government (Kindy 1972:29–31). In 1927, the liwali (chief administrator) of the coast, a Zanzibar Arab named Ali Salim (later Sir Ali) who opposed and was opposed by the association, chose it as the venue for the announcement that Twelve Tribes members were not Arabs and would not be allowed to vote for the Arab representative on the Legislative Council (ibid., 30).

This led Twelve Tribes members who did not claim Arab ethnicity to form their own political group, the Afro-Asian Association (ibid.). It also led to a high level of conflict between those who emphasized their Arab ethnicity (both Swahili and Zanzibar Arabs) and those who did not (ibid., 31–45). There was even a cessation of communitywide prayer (ibid., 31). Formerly, the men of the Nine Tribes and the men of the Three Tribes alternated the Friday noon prayer between the main Three Tribes mosque and the main Nine Tribes mosque. In 1929, however, a Three Tribes man rose and denounced "the Arabs" and advised everyone to avoid going to the Nine Tribes mosque any longer since it was where "the Arabs" prayed. This despite the Muslim injunction that the whole community pray together at least at the Friday noon prayer (ibid., 31–32).

The appeal was effective, and most of the other Twelve Tribes members, including some Nine Tribes members who did not claim Omani origins, prayed every Friday in the Three Tribes mosque. Those emphasizing their Arab connections remained in the Nine Tribes mosque, with few others joining them there (ibid.).

This breach in Nine Tribes solidarity was also a blow at the unity of the sections as such in that for the most important prayer of the week, the men of the community no longer assembled according to section divisions. There was a limited unity between members of the two sections who did not claim Arab status, but the structure that had characterized the community for centuries was seriously impaired.

"Natives" and "Nonnatives"

The strain on the community resulting from the separation of segments of the sections and the reuniting of these segments according to ethnic ties rather than section allegiance was continued and reinforced by the ability of some members to achieve what was, under British rule, the politically and economically more desirable status of Arab. The interest in doing this is seen in the fact that continued appeals from Swahili to the colonial government led, in 1934, to the ruling that

> persons who could prove before a magistrate that one parent was of nonnative descent could press a claim for nonnative status, thus opening the possibility for Twelve Tribes claims. . . . Until World War II bickering continued about whether Twelve Tribes persons should be allowed to claim Arab status as nonnatives. Technically, "Swahili" were given Arab status in 1952, but relations between the two communities remained strained (Stroebel 1979:40–41).

The interest in being classified as an "Arab," that is, a nonnative, which had provided tax benefits for decades, received further impetus with the outbreak of World War II when food rationing was instituted. Those classified as natives were given coupons to buy cornmeal, while those classified as Arabs were, like Asians, allowed to buy rice (Kindy 1972:109). This was especially significant because of the meanings attached to rice and to cornmeal. For the Mombasa Swahili, eating cornmeal is inappropriate for proper group members. True Swahili of noble birth (*waungwana,* sing. *mwungwana*), that is, those without slave forebears, simply do not eat *simi,* the heavy cornmeal paste[3] eaten throughout East Africa or, at least, do not let it be known that they do. Rice is the starch suitable to waungwana, and not to have it is a degrading and shameful indication of abject poverty and/or low taste.

Informants report that even for those who received it, the rationing did not provide enough rice for it to be the dietary staple, as the Twelve Tribes members I know insist it must be. Still, being closed off from legal access to the noble grain while their fellow group members, the ones claiming Omani origin, had it was an extremely bitter experience that is remembered with rancor more than forty years later.

Crucially for the thesis being developed here, the resentment went not only to the government[4] but also, and mainly, to the group members who claimed Omani roots. Again, this united part of the Nine Tribes with most of the Three Tribes against the Swahili Arab subgroup drawn from both.

Section Competitions

The rationing and the earlier blows to section unity affected the ability of the sections to unify and compete with one another. Nevertheless, until the early 1960s, the members of the Three Tribes and the Nine Tribes did engage in such sectionally based competitions as team card games, various sports, and marching societies (*quaride*) that competed in precision of marching, elegance of uniform, and the skill of their bands. These primarily male activities were paralleled by competitions between women's dancing societies, called *vyama*.

Continuing until independence in 1963 was what several male informants have said was the most basic and fundamental expression of community life: the performance of a men's dance called *tware* and a related one called *diriji*. A large proportion of the men from each section, including the "Arabs," participated in these. In tware, the men from each side formed two lines, one for the Nine Tribes and one for the Three Tribes, facing one another. To the measured beat of the tambourine-like tware drum, each side attempted to outdo the other in the gleaming whiteness of their gowns and kofia (white skullcaps worn by Muslims) and in the elegance and grace of their movements in this very restrained dance.

No prize was awarded; in fact, no judgment was made. But each side assessed its own performance against that of the other and decided for itself who had been the most "noble." And "noble" is the word for this dance. It is performed in celebration of the marriage or circumcision of Twelve Tribes members but only for those who are understood to be descended from forebears all of whom were free men and women (i.e., waungwana). Moreover, only those with this sort of family background were allowed to participate in the dance.

A similar sort of dance, diriji, was also held and was seen, informants say, as another expression of community life. It, too, was restricted to those considered waungwana and was performed by the confederations in opposition to one another.

Many of the most important relations between women in the community were, like the men's dances, carried out in sectionally organized groups. This is so despite the existence of a group made up of all the "noble" old women, the *wamiji* (*miji* refers to city; *wa-* is the suffix for nouns referring to humans). This group acted as the ritual guardians of the community without respect to section lines, condemning improper ceremonial and ritual behavior and lending their presence to important celebrations regardless of section membership. Old men had the same title but seem not to have actively involved themselves as the women did (Stroebel 1979:80–84).

Like the wamiji, section lines were not regarded for the weddings, funerals, and circumcisions that were the center of their social life in this sexually segregated society. Women invited *all* community members of their gender to the rites. This was so even though those who cooperated most closely with one another in the laborious and elaborate preparations for these ceremonies were almost always from the same neighborhood and, therefore, section.

But this does not mean that sectional opposition had no part in female activities. In women's social lives, the competition between the sections came out most clearly in the women's dancing societies, or vyama (sing. *chama*).[5] There were a number of these societies, but the two main ones were based on section membership (ibid., 160–164). In a way somewhat similar to the men's marching societies, the women's competition involved elegance of costume, skill in dancing, and excellence of music between section-based groups whose members included the descendants of slaves as well as women whose forebears were understood to include only waungwana.

The women's competition went beyond those of the men. In addition to dancing skill, they also competed in the excellence and lavishness of the food presented at their dances, the elegance of their clothing and jewelry, and, especially, in the mordant wit of the songs reviling members of the competing group. These were sung at the dances and dealt with such embarrassments of the opposite section as one of its men having elephantiasis of the testicles, the pretensions to high social standing despite having a slave forebear of one of its families, and the sexual indiscretion of one of its women. Men, especially older and more prestigious ones, disapproved of these women's competitions, but since they were mainly carried out within the confines of the women's separate groups whose activities were not held in the men's presence, their disapproval only kept their own wives and daughters out.

Unity through Competition and Its End

The pervasiveness of conflict or, at least, of sharp competition, which was sometimes difficult to differentiate, between the two sections continued in a variety of forms for roughly three decades after the end of World War II. It was mainly in competition that the whole community came together. The important joint prayer on Friday was no more, but the men's dances, dirigi and, especially, tware, exhibited and affirmed some of the most prized values for men in the context of a competitive unity. The other competitions and oppositional joint appearances did not have the dignity and value-heavy significance for community coherence that tware had and the joint prayer had had, but they did bring community members together in actively functioning alignments that took in all parts of the group.

These sorts of activities, however, received a serious blow from a single, dramatic event in the early 1940s when the long-standing contests between sectionally based women's dancing groups escalated into street fighting involving the police (ibid., 177–181). This happened in some part because of changes in the women's understandings of what limits there were on their public behavior. Particularly at issue was the extent to which they were willing to be guided by the understandings men (i.e., their husbands, fathers, and brothers) had of how they should behave, especially how they could express themselves publicly.

The most prestigious men in the community had always looked on the women's societies as unacceptable expressions of tendencies in the community that they deplored: the public appearance of women, direct and open attacks on the private lives of community members, and the participation of waungwana and the descendants of slaves in common groups. They opposed the latter because the women's organizations did not practice the exclusion of those of other than "noble" birth as the men's dances did.

The riot shocked both men and women, but it did not surprise the senior men—or so some of them told me—who deplored the women's organizations and their activities from the outset. The most important consequence of the excesses of the women's dancing competitions for the future of the community was the unfavorable light it cast on all competitions, including the traditional ones between sections.

The women's riot led directly, informants have told me, to the abandonment by members of the Twelve Tribes community of this whole type of competition. This is an exaggeration since, in fact, the men's dances, card games, and such went on for as long as two decades after the riot, and some of the boys' soccer teams are still sectionally based.[6] Nevertheless, it is probably true that the riot gave all competition a more worrisome connotation. It is a matter of fact that the experience is cited forty-five years later as an example of the foolishness and danger of competition, especially between women, given the widely shared understanding that they are uncontrollably emotional.[7]

National Politics and
Its Indirect, Profound Influence

The lessened vitality of the sections was carried substantially further by one of the general understandings of the consequences of Kenya gaining independence in 1963. As many Swahili saw it, the officials of the new government were sensitive to the fact that community members had once owned slaves, and it was (and is) believed that any reminder of that should be avoided.

As has been noted, the sectionally organized men's dances at weddings and circumcisions were performed only on behalf of families and individuals whose ancestry is understood to contain no one of slave background. Similarly, no one could participate in the dances without his being understood to have no slave forebears. At least during the period of my visits to Mombasa beginning in 1975 and, according to some informants, since independence, no men's dances have been performed in Old Town.

It is noteworthy that the cessation of the dances strikes not only at the opposition of the sections and their association with highly prized male traits but also at a key foundation of the uniqueness of the community as a whole: the noble, that is, nonslave, status of all "true" community members. All Twelve Tribes members still speak of *uungwana,* nobility, and although the term refers to the most prized forms of behavior, manners, and character, it also applies to having an ancestry free of forebears who were *wazalia* (a polite term for slaves). This fundamental value is no longer publicly symbolized, and although it is still cherished and spoken of in private circles, its public demonstration in dances associated with key rituals has been abandoned.

Current State of the
Community and the Section System

Although the absence of men's dances is not mentioned as a particularly important part of the phenomenon, everyone heard to comment on the general state of the community notes a distinct decline. A number of sources for this have now been seen.

It is of considerable interest to note that two of the most important sources concern the boundaries of the community and the statuses of those who are at those boundaries. It would be more than bold to single out some particular aspect of community life or set of circumstances as sufficient to have brought about the state of the community as at least some members currently assess it. But this does not mean that particular elements cannot be singled out as having played identifiable parts. I will argue that the nature of the relations between the sections played one of these roles and that this, in turn, is shaped by the statuses of those who compose the sections.

Another important role will be shown to have been played by the nature of membership in the group. Here the issue is the group's boundary, as this is expressed in the status of group members. There are, as suggested above, two sets of individuals whose category membership presents difficulties. The first are those with known slave forebears. They are understood by group members as seeing themselves as belonging to the group but whose membership is denied by a majority of group members. The second problem set is composed of the Swahili Arabs. They are seen by a majority of community members as rightfully belonging, but in their own assignment they do not.

"Ethnic" Status and the Destruction of the Two-Section System

This last problem in status membership involves a category of people who are understood as rejecting the group member status in favor of being categorized in the Zanzibar Arab group, with the prestige and material advantages under British rule such membership entailed. The Zanzibar Arab status has implications for the social structure of the community as a whole in that it brought together the individuals who claimed it in a unity that crossed the lines bounding the two Swahili sections. Resistance to their being categorized in it united against them, again across the boundaries, members of both the sections. These status realignments affected the internal unity of the sections in such clearly manifested ways as the abandonment of the weekly prayers as part of the resistance to the Zanzibar Arab status for community members. This diminished unity lessened the ability of the sections to establish and affirm the community's vitality in the manner that had long been characteristic, namely, through competitive activity.

The division between the sections had been, in classical Gluckmanian dynamics (Gluckman, Mitchells, and Barnes 1963:1–2),[8] a key base of social unity for the Swahili. It was in many respects destroyed by the formation of new unities across what once had been section lines. These new "ethnic" unities produced no wide-scope solidarity because they benefited the Swahili Arabs as individuals (through better rations, jobs, and taxes), not as a group, and united their opponents from the two sections only in opposition to them. Attempts to unite the two new groupings into political action groups went on for a number of years (Kindy 1972:26–45) but disappeared after independence. They survive only as vague memories in the minds of middle-aged and elderly community members.

Another force in diminishing community vitality is the other status ambiguity mentioned above. The descendants of slaves have been closely associated with the group for generations, and not a few are widely viewed by group members as worthy embodiments of the values held by group members. However, a key identifying understanding for those with group member status is having only waungwana ("noble") forebears. To accept those whose genealogies are known to include ancestors who were not noble would be to alter the group member status radically.

An indication of how seriously this was (and is) taken is that a main reason for rejecting the proposal of marriage from a man's family, one that rated as potently as the fear that the man was a drinker of alcohol or a passive homosexual, was suspicion of his family having wazalia (nonnoble) forebears. Even if the woman's family accepted a proposal, there was the possibility that, as recently as the 1950s, the wedding ritual would be interrupted by the wamiji, the elderly women guardians of ritual and propriety who were then still active, if they believed there were genealogical irregularities.

Given the common understanding that calling attention to the fact that there were slaves in the community was at best tactless and quite possibly dangerous, holding public rituals emphasizing these differences took on a new significance. This is just the emphasis of the tware and diriji dances through their excluding all but nobles and making a central point of demonstrating the essence of "nobility" (uungwana).

According to several community members, this is why the dances stopped. Their analysis appears to be correct. The dances were an important symbol of the community's vitality based not only in the central values concerning nobility (see chap. 7) but also in the opposition of united sections competing for commonly understood and equally prized honor. These dances, in their movements and costumes as well as through the requirements for their participants, expressed and symbolized what is surely the most commonly cited (by community members) and, probably, the most crucial values in the group, those centering around nobility. Moreover, this expression occurred with the members of each section united with his fellows in competition with the other united section in expressing their shared ideal understandings and gaining prestige in terms of them. Informants say the dances were the most "beautiful" events in public life; they seem nearly pure enactments of the community's broadest social structure, including understandings about who the occupants of its component statuses were and how they should act.

The immediate basis for the end of the performances was the exclusion of the occupants of the slave descendant status and the government resentment this was understood to incur. That I have seen few indications that this resentment is actually likely and would be an active force if it were is relatively unimportant. That it was taken so is what matters.

Nor is the end of the men's dances the only change affecting community structure. If the Swahili Arab status is more salient than the status of Nine Tribes or of Three Tribes members, the oppositional basis of the community's coherence is changed and lessened. The community continues as an interconnected structure of statuses that actually guides their members' behavior. But the scope of the expectations in the relevant statuses has been decreased, their salience has been lessened in many situations, and the identifiers have been weakened. In fact, understandings about membership in the community are much as they long were, but the symbolizing of that membership is muted and privatized and this, like the change in sectional opposition, has surely affected the nature of community life, which continues but is different.

Marriage and Community in Contemporary Mombasa

Despite the general changes and the group's diminished economic and political situation during the twentieth century, the Swahili family and sense of community continue as major forces in the lives of group members. My informants and the literature (e.g., Stroebel 1979:80–94, Prins 1967:76–83) agree in indicating that for at least several decades, kinship, like community, is neither as broad in scope nor as powerful in directing activity as it was in the recent past. Still, ties based on both affect much of what most group members do most of the time. The Swahili are an urban people, and they live in an unquestionably rapidly changing environment, but they are not deracinated, their nuclear families are not isolated, and their senses of identity are still, for almost all group members, firmly rooted in being Swahili.

In later chapters, marriage and the nuclear family receive a good deal of attention, but from the perspective of community structure, it is useful to bear in mind that almost all marriages within this community are with fellow community members. Men sometimes marry Mombasa women from other ethnic groups, but when they do this—and this is true now as it has been for at least the greater part of this century—the marriage is kept secret, especially from the man's "main" wife.[9] This wife is almost invariably not only a Mombasa Swahili but, nearly as frequently, also a member of the same section as her husband and, in more than a quarter of the cases for which I have data, either a patrilateral or a matrilateral cousin.

In recent years, according to some informants, ties beyond the nuclear family have weakened, but if this is so, it is so only relative to what must have been quite powerful bonds. Households often contain kin in addition to nuclear family members, and if the sharing of houses by married brothers and their wives and families is rare, as it is, this is not a new development; a separate house for each nuclear family, especially after a number of children have been born, is generally thought desirable and was so viewed as far back as informants can remember.

It is difficult to assess whether the Swahili are virilocal or uxorilocal since crowding and the lack of availability of house sites makes it difficult for couples to live where they and their kin wish. Some informants say it is better for a newly married couple to live near the groom's family, and others (fewer) say it is better to live near the wife's family. Since an accurate census is quite impossible to carry out,[10] I can only say that if I have an impression as to where married couples live, it is that there is some tendency to locate near the wife's family. My census data (see table 1, chap. 4), as spotty and thin as they unavoidably are, indicate that couples always live in their section's neighborhood if they are from the same one (as they almost always are) and if, as the overwhelming majority still do, they live in Old Town rather than in non-Swahili parts of the city or in a distant town or nation.

Women from the group occasionally now, and in the past as well, marry men from other Swahili communities along the coast, and a few marry Arabs, either from the Persian Gulf or from the community of unassimilated Arabs in Mombasa. Even less often, they marry whites who have converted to Islam; I know of three cases, two to Europeans and one to an American. These two rare sorts of exceptions aside, however, the group's women never marry outside their own community for their first marriage.

Parents are concerned that their children may marry outsiders and, even more frightening, Christians, but this has not happened in any of the forty-six marriages since 1975 which I have data on. If there are marriages outside the community, it is in the pattern of men taking "secret" wives (all of them, so far as I can tell, Muslims) that has been part of the marriage practices followed for as many generations as informants' accounts go back.

"Clans" and Other Designations Wrongly or Rarely Used

Turning to the family and kinship, it was noted above that the community's constituent sections, or confederations, are composed of what is glossed as "tribes" (*mataifa*) and that these, in turn, are made up of patrilateral descent groups (*mbari*), called "clans" in some historians' accounts (Berg 1968:40–42, Pouwells 1987:79, 84 passim). The use of the term "clan" for any part of this society, however, is likelier to produce misunderstanding than to illuminate its social life.

The kin groupings that compose the tribes were not based on strict patrilineal descent, did not in all cases believe in a common ancestor, were not exogamous, and were only localized in the sense that all the members of a confederation or section lived in the same area without, however, any residential distinction by descent groups. The only basis for using the term "clan," in fact, is that English-speaking group members use it.

Looking at this usage, however, strongly suggests that the term is applied loosely to "kin" or "fairly close kin" rather than to any sort of unilineal descent group. For example, an informant said "the clan" was coming to a gathering at his house, and the people who came included not only his patrilateral kin but also some related through his mother and some through his wife (who was not his cousin). When I asked him if he considered them all to be "his clan," he said that he did. This is quite consistent for the use of "clan" as described by Prins (1967:80–81), whose reservations are in accord with those noted here.

The two words for groupings of kin that were used in the fairly recent past but seem not to be currently in use are *nyumba* and *mlango*. "Nyumba" is most readily glossed as "house" and is used for the nuclear family members and their siblings and parents. "Mlango" means door in Swahili and, in this usage, refers to the broadly conceived category of kin and, sometimes, affines related through either parent. It was never used to refer to a social group of any kind. It was, rather, a category used to place an individual or nuclear family in a context of kin and affines. Prins notes that the term "mlango" is an alternative to "clan" or mbari. Kindy gives a historically useful list of the names of all the mbari making up each of the tribes (1972:49–51; see also Berg 1968:40–41).

There are hints in my informants' discussions that mbari were once the basis for joint activities including warfare and dances, but if this did occur in the past, it has not done so for most of this century. Many informants, including some of those who know their "tribe," do not know which mbari they belong to. Even in the earlier period when mbari was widely known, it appears that it was not the primary framework for close relationships beyond the household. This framework, especially for women and children, was and still is provided by the *mtaa* (pl. *mitaa*), or neighborhood.

Residence

Residence was more nearly uxorilocal than virilocal, and although patrilateral cousin (both cross and parallel) marriage was fairly common, so was matrilateral cousin marriage. Marriage to unrelated individuals, mainly of the same tribe and almost always of the same confederation, accounted for more than half of all marriages. In fact, informants say, marriage with people from the same mtaa was more common than any other sort, and such marriages could be with cousins on either side or with neighbors who had no traceable kin relationship. As a thoughtful and intelligent informant put it, "The mtaa was like a group of relatives. The neighbors could be related on either side or maybe they weren't obviously related, but they had been marrying each other for generations, so they were all related."

The mtaa is still socially important as the main basis for the young people's groups of friends (still completely separated according to sex), the visiting and mutual assistance groups of women, and the men's *barazas*.[11] There are signs of the weakening of the neighborhoods of some Swahili families living outside Old Town and an ever-increasing number of houses in the old neighborhoods being taken over by members of other ethnic groups (see Swartz 1983:36–37), but as of the mid-1980s, they remain the most vital element in community life beyond that based in close ties of kinship.

Like the mbari, the tribe has not been an active group since the 1960s. Few people, and none I have met who are under 35 or so, know to what "tribe" they belong. The confederations of tribes remain symbolically important, however, and although they carry out no social activity, I have not talked to a single community member who is unaware of what confederation he or she belongs to. There is no general Swahili term that can be translated as "confederation" or "section," but it is the most frequently heard wide-scope identifier for community members, so that one hears that someone is "a Three Tribes member" or "a Nine Tribes member" on the rare occasions when broad social placement is at issue.

Outside Contacts
and Community Importance

Despite the continuation of virtual community endogamy, there is more rather close contact with non-Swahili Mombasans than there was in the past. The secularization of the community increased under the British as the Swahili became a smaller and smaller proportion of the city's population and were increasingly integrated into an economic system where most of the employed men (very few women worked for wages outside the home until the last few years when a small number got paying jobs) spent their days working with mainly Christian members of other ethnic groups.

This has not led to any movement away from Islam. Almost any conversation, even a brief one, leads to at least one reference to the Koran, or to God, or to the holy laws. Religious courts with Swahili judges (*kadhi*) learned in Koranic law are invariably used by community members for difficult domestic problems and civil disputes among themselves. Civil courts are involved only when there are serious crimes. The boundaries of the community, in fact, can be traced by examining the court—religious or secular—that disputants use (Swartz 1978).

The Swahili have always insisted on Islamic education for their children of both sexes, and I know of no one in the community who did not learn to read the Koran and to pray in the *chuo* (religious school for children). Secular schools in the area were initially, in the nineteenth century, mission operated, Christian oriented, and designed to produce converts, so it is little wonder that the Swahili (and other Muslims) avoided them. Eventually, however, by the 1930s, the economic importance of a secular education together with concessions to Muslim interests (including teaching the Koran and Arabic to students in the schools the Swahili attended) led to a substantial proportion of the community sending their sons and, later, even some of their daughters to government-run schools including secondary schools (Salim 1973:146–156) despite the high cost of tuition.

Diminished Prosperity

In the period following World War I, the Mombasa Swahili began to be acutely concerned about their economic situation and prospects and about the future of their group and their religion. As Salim (ibid., 179) says,

The aim to raise their status . . . was widespread. . . . It was the product of the economic plight which the new generation found itself heir to after their fathers' rickety system of trade and cultivation . . . had finally crumbled under the impact of the abolition of slavery and the advent of the railway, and after a good deal of land had been lost to government . . . or sold to foreign speculators [i.e., Indians and Europeans] in order to maintain a semblance of the old standard of living.

The Swahili community does continue to "maintain a semblance of the old standard of living." It appears that almost half the households have a servant, and color television sets and videocassette recorders are common (even though each one costs half a year's salary for a junior civil servant). Community members are well dressed, and informants say that as many as one extended family in three has a member who has made the expensive hajj to Mecca.

Compared to the Indians and Hadhrami Arabs who live among them in Old Town, however, the Swahili are not well off. Only one major business in Mombasa is owned by a community member, and most men are employed as civil servants, teachers, small shop owners, clerks, managers, and middle executives. A number of younger men have been employed in Saudi Arabia and the Persian Gulf area, and their remittances were important sources of income for a substantial number of families through the mid-1980s when this diminished. Mombasa Swahili have never done manual work save as fishermen, and this continues to be true, but wealth on a par with their non-Swahili neighbors has eluded them since the early part of the century and continues to do so.

The Swahili are well-to-do in comparison to many other ethnic groups in Mombasa, but compared to their past—and their memory of their past—as well as to their more affluent Indian and Arab neighbors, their situation is a difficult one. Nor is this only psychological. There are genuinely poor families in the community, and serious concerns about money and debts are more often characteristic of families than are feelings of financial security.

Less Expensive Life-Crises Rituals

Partly as a result of their limited economic resources, some of the opulent life-crises rituals that once characterized the community (Prins 1967:104–105, Stroebel 1979:8–13) have paled and others have vanished. Group members still talk about these rituals with a mixture of nostalgia (for the glory) and sorrow (for the great expense).

Funerals, especially those for prominent persons, are still attended by hundreds upon hundreds, but the spendthrift days of feeding this multitude for days and weeks have come to an end. Birth is now the occasion for only a relatively modest celebration by a few score women relatives and neighbors. Circumcision, once an occasion for a major feast, is no longer publicly celebrated. Weddings were lavish occasions to which the entire community was invited as recently as the late 1970s, but now they are less opulent and much smaller, and attendance by more than one hundred is rather unusual.[12]

As of the 1980s, some weddings and other life crises are marked only by a *maulidi* (reading of the life of the Prophet followed by light refreshments) to which only kin and neighbors are invited. The expenses involved in the grand rituals were enormous: as much as five years' earnings were spent on a wedding or a funeral. As one walks through Old Town, one is shown houses that families mortgaged and lost to pay for these rituals. But expense is not the only reason these rituals have declined in frequency and opulence.

One is that Mombasa, including the Old Town section, has gone the way of cities everywhere: crime has increased, while generally acceptable behavior has decreased. Robberies and murders, although still rare by the standards of Nairobi and most American cities, have increased sharply since the latter years of the 1970s as rural migrants streamed into the city. Now many community members have well-founded uneasiness about walking through the streets of Old Town at night. Because of this, attendance at prayer in the mosques at the predawn, *alfaqiri,* prayer and the nighttime, *isha,* prayers has declined, with more men (women do not enter Swahili mosques) praying at home. The celebration of rituals was and is held in the streets adjacent to the house of the family involved, and as crime increases, community members are less and less enthusiastic about being out of their homes after dark.

Further difficulty comes from that fact that *wahuni,* rowdy boys and young men, some of them Swahili, are far more plentiful than they were and, many say, more unrestrained in their behavior. Uneasiness about celebrations being ruined by fighting and vandalism has a substantial basis in experience. It was traditional for the groom to be escorted to his bride's house for the wedding night and for his entrance to be opposed by neighborhood boys and young men. After disarranging his clothes and making some noise, they let him in— sometimes after being given a token gift of money. Lately, however, these boys and young men have sometimes become rowdy and even dangerous, seriously beating the groom and his escorts and breaking windows and furniture in the house of the bride's family.

Even more important, perhaps, is the decline in the community discussed earlier. Men are heard to say that money spent on lavish entertainment is wasted and that people are only impressed with the foolishness of someone who provides an elaborate wedding or other ritual for the community at large. Men have long taken this view but have yielded to their wives' wishes to stage impressive rituals (Swartz 1982*b,* 1983).

It may be that women are no longer as motivated as they were just a decade ago to spend an important part of their family's wealth on one or two rituals as well as slightly less able to influence their husbands. The reasons for this are complex and will be addressed in chapter 10. For the moment, it is enough to say that the social relations that played the central role in the women wanting to hold expensive rituals and, at the same time, provided them a source of freedom in dealing with their husbands have decreased in importance for them as the community's overall integration has declined.

This is not to say that the rituals have stopped. They continue, if on a reduced scale, and give every evidence of accomplishing the ends of life-crises rites as set out long ago by Van Gennep. Like the community, they are still effective but reduced in social scale and toned down in their opulence.

The culture of the Mombasa Swahili is still effective and still guides the activity of most community members, most of the time. The center of their lives has always focused around kinship and the household group, and whatever changes have taken place and are occurring have not and do not alter that fact.

4

He Who Eats with You

Kinship, Family, and Neighborhood

Mla nawe hafi nawe ila mzaliwa nawe: *He¹ [who] eats with you [will] not die with you unless he was born with you.*

This proverb suggests the central place of kinship in Swahili life and a fundamental reason for that centrality. First, there is allusion to the widely shared concern that associates will accept your hospitality (and with it, your friendship) but, in the end, desert you. This is in contrast to kin, who are, the proverb asserts, the only ones you can count on. It is not that kinsmen are understood as always trustworthy and loyal but only that in a difficult world, they are the ones who are most likely to stay with you.

Ndugu muwi afadhali naye: *[A] bad kinsman [it is] better [to be] with him [than to be without him].*

No matter what you may think about a kinsman, he or she will always be your kinsman, and, even if he is bad, as the proverb says, it is better to have him than to be without him. On emotional, material, and social grounds, kin should not be denied.

Damu isipowasha hunyeza: *[If] blood does not burn, [it] itches.*

This proverb emphasizes the undeniability of kin ties. The proverb is heard about people who have reservations concerning a kinsman or do not seem to others to be very close to him or her. Sometimes the proverb is used to warn someone who is thought likely to say something unfavorable about a person in front of another who is that person's kin. Even agreeing with someone's criticism of his own relative can prompt this warning, because it is generally

59

believed that whatever reservations one may have about a kinsman, the tie with him or her will always remain in force. This applies to all kin but is heard most often concerning one's own and one's parents' siblings.

In this community the emotional attachment to kin is very rarely severed completely, but even if it were, there remains an unavoidable social attachment. This is based in the fact that closely related people, especially nuclear family members, are categorized into a common status as "members of a family" (*ndugu* or *ukoo mmjoa*) and, as the next proverb indicates, have a common social and material fate.

> Mchuma janga hula na wakwao: *He [who] earns calamity, eats [it] with the people of their house [i.e., his family].*

Kin are by no means viewed as always good to one another, but the closeness of their interests is understood, as the following proverb shows rather trenchantly, to lead them to work together and to avoid doing anything really harmful to one another.

> Meno ya mbwa hayaumani: *[The] teeth of [the] dog do not bite [harm] each other.*

This proverb makes a particularly important point, since, as several informants who discussed it with me agree, the strong emotional and social bonds and the commonality of interests that unite kin also puts them in a position to harm one another as no outsider can. The proverb does not mean that kin never harm one another but rather that although people may turn their hostility, acquisitiveness, or indifference on others, even the worst of them (i.e., dogs, which most Swahili, in common with many other Muslims, find revolting as well as sources of ritual pollution, *najisi*) find it difficult to direct at their kin. Like a set of teeth, kin work as a unit and do not usually harm one another, whatever they may do to others. Because of their general and pervasive importance to one another, however, kin can be more bothersome than anyone else can be.

> Chawa akuumao mbwa nguni mwako: *[The] louse that bites you is inside your clothing.*

Taken together, these proverbs suggest the broad and pervasive social, material, and emotional ties among kin and their enduring quality. It is important to note that the proverbs are all general indications of the importance of kin relations and the unity of interests among kin. They do little to indicate what kin can be expected to do or not do. In fact, insofar as they provide any guidelines for behavior at all, they are very broad guidelines that counsel remembering kinship and the permanence of its ties without reference to what is actually to be done by whom for whom in specific circumstances. This is not only true for the proverbs I have quoted here but for all the others concerning kin that I have encountered (e.g., Scheven 1981:325, 328, 329).

As the discussion of Swahili social life proceeds in subsequent chapters, it will become clear that the participants in wide-scope and long-enduring relationships such as those involving kin and neighbors share broad and general expectations regarding each others' behavior more than they do specific ones. The most generally shared specific cultural elements in these relationships are the "identifiers" (see chap. 1), but my main concern here is less with specific understandings than with the general ones that are the main contents of the relationships between those identified as belonging to family statuses.

Kin, Household, and Nuclear Family

The importance individuals give to kin relationships generally is intensified as the kin ties are closer. It is notable that a number of the proverbs affirming the importance of kinship invoke eating and commensality in ways informants with whom I discussed the proverbs agree show closeness of relationship.

It is the household group, rather than some more inclusive collection of kin, that regularly eats together (although in many homes, the commonly prepared food is eaten in two seatings: first the men and then the women). And it is the household group that contains the kin who are the most broadly important members of the generally important category, kin. Kin relations are said by everyone with whom I talked to be more important in most activities than any others. Of these, the ones involving fellow members of the same household are more important yet.

As we will see below, the household is the material, social, and emotional base for much of what its members do, and more than three-quarters of Swahili households include or are solely composed of the nuclear family (see table 2, below). In examining cultural sharing among household members (chap. 5), I limited the survey to households where the person "in charge" (*mwenye amri*) was a member of a nuclear family including both spouses and at least one child considered by them (and by the child) as their biological offspring. This was an attempt to increase comparability.

This focus on the nuclear family is justified by the prevalence of this group among the Swahili as well as by the interest in examining in a natural setting a grouping in which the sharing of understandings about the group, its members, and their relationships would be expected to be in the upper part of the range of sharing.

Narrowly defined groups focused on technical tasks (e.g., a surgical team) might be expected to have members who share more completely the understandings about their work and each member's role in that work. Monasteries or other religious communities and other highly specialized groups may have an extremely high level of sharing among members in some respects, but in dealing with others concerning the broad array of matters that make up ordinary everyday life, the nuclear family would seem to call for at least as high a level of sharing as would be found in any other social group and to provide an ideal situation for mutual socialization as a basis for that sharing.

In chapter 5, we will see that the elements of family culture, those understandings having to do with the nuclear family and how its members do and should treat one another and with what the group should and does do, are only partially shared, even by members of the same nuclear family. One reason for this could be that the nuclear family is of limited scope and importance in Swahili life, but, as we will see, this explanation is not characteristic of the nuclear family in this society.

If group interests and the relations among members were restricted in scope and intensity as those, say, of the residents of a boarding house are, even members of families that continue functioning for long periods of time (and only such families were included in the survey work that formed the basis of the study of sharing) might share only a limited range of understandings about the group and its constituent relationships. Since, however, the interests of the Swahili nuclear family are broad and of intense concern to members and since family relationships are seen as vitally important, limits in the sharing of understandings about these interests and relationships cannot be explained as based in substantially restricted joint concerns and involvements.

What is said about the importance of the nuclear family—and we will consider this more specifically in a moment—should not be taken to suggest that all households are composed of, or even contain, a nuclear family. Fourteen of the 111 households surveyed for the census I made did not include both spouses. Most of these fourteen households are headed by divorced or widowed women, but, despite the emphasis given male authority by the Swahili and the support this has in Islam, these households function in many ways much as do those with a complete nuclear family. They are evaluated by outside community members, according to the evidence I have, on the basis of the same broad understandings that apply to households whose core includes both spouses.

Similarly, roughly half of all households—whether the households include a full nuclear family or not—include one, rarely two, adult, nonnuclear family kin. These "extended" households, too, give every appearance of operating according to the same broad understandings that apply to the other half of the population of households whose only adults are the spouse-parents.

It is not surprising that there is variation in household composition and that a substantial minority lives in a household without a full nuclear family present. Death and divorce sunder nuclear families in Old Town as they do elsewhere. But this does not diminish the importance of the nuclear family even for those whose household does not contain one. None of the many individuals I talked to who lived in nonnuclear family households thought that the composition of their household was an ideal one. Most viewed their situation as more difficult economically and socially than it would be if there were a full nuclear family in their household, but the truncated (usually because of divorce or husband/father's death) household was their main source of emotional support, material assistance, and social relations. In this they were no different from the majority who live with their spouse and children or parents and siblings.

Whether a nuclear family or not and whether including "outside" kin or not, the household members are much involved in each others' activities and interests. The mother often is, as in many societies (e.g., Bott 1971:69 ff., Young and Willmott 1973:101–102), the hub of activity, and everything her children do is of immediate and central concern to her. At the same time, her views and assistance are usually crucial to the children, at least until they have established their own nuclear families and, most often, even after that.

The mother/wife is also often much involved in her husband's activities. As we will see in chapter 10, men depend on their wives as they do no one else, and if wives have a considerable set of interests (many of them shared with the children) separate from the husband, he is still the most important adult male in the vast majority of households. In many families, men have rather distant relations with their children, especially with the sons, and deal with them mainly through their wives. However, the emotional and material ties between fathers and children are deeply felt and highly influential. As we will see, there is a substantial and sharp division of labor and leisure in the Swahili nuclear family, but that group is of the first importance to all its members despite the differences according to their statuses in how much and in what ways they participate.

In spite of this, the data examined in chapter 5 show that there is only limited sharing of the cultural items directly concerning life in the nuclear family household among the members of that very same group. Among community members belonging to different, but equally stable, families, the sharing of cultural elements concerning the nuclear family is even more limited. These findings are taken as the basis for the view, quite fundamental to this whole study, that extent of cultural sharing is only one, and often not the most prominent, of the contributors to the effectiveness of the groups in dealing with their members' needs and interests.

In fact, other studies of cultural sharing among Swahili not belonging to the same nuclear family (to be seen in chaps. 7 and 9) confirm the limited nature of cultural sharing in this society. Work by others suggests that the same is true in social groups in other societies (e.g., Pelto and Pelto 1975; Holland 1987a; Kessing 1982).

To see the nuclear family's place in Swahili society and to understand more of the nature of that society, it will be useful to consider the nuclear family in the context of kin relations in general.

Swahili Kinship

As table 1 shows, Swahili kin terms do not distinguish cross from parallel cousins, but they do have different terms for matrilateral as opposed to patrilateral parents' siblings. As noted earlier, the Mombasa Swahili have no unilineal descent groups despite the use of the term "clan" by English-speaking group members. In fact, the only groups of this sort with members living in Old Town are those made up of Arab immigrants who are either fairly recent arrivals from the Persian Gulf or members of the Mazrui group, which has been in East Africa for a very long time but retains its clan, *sensu stricto*, organization.

The patrilineal mbari is often referred to as a "clan" in the literature (e.g., Pouwells 1987:79). Mbari are not localized (and may never have been), do not and never did own property, are not exogamous, and, in short, have none of the attributes of a clan other than a belief in relationship through fathers (not always excluding fathers' sisters' offspring). For the Mombasa Swahili, in fact, there are no corporate unilineal descent groups.

As far as contemporary relevance of the mbari is concerned, there is no activity of any kind attributed to them in the last four decades or more prior to which they are said to have played a minor role in wedding rituals.[2] I could find only a few elderly people who knew which of the mbari they belonged to, and a number of younger informants said they were not even familiar with the word "mbari."

The extended family is commonly referred to as mlango (lit., door), but *ukoo* is also used even though it refers to the nuclear family in some contexts. The mlango is basically an ego-centered category of bilaterally related kin whose members do little or nothing requiring organization or general participation. Ad hoc groupings, usually made up of women kin and neighbors, form for particular, limited purposes (mainly to prepare for and participate in weddings, funerals, the now very rarely publicly celebrated circumcisions [*tohara*], and maulidi, or public readings of the life of the Prophet followed by refreshments). These activities aside, group activities limited to or arranged by kin drawn from beyond the nuclear family are nonexistent. Participation in such jointly arranged activity as is carried out depends as much on the affectional ties and current interests of members as it does on their kin statuses, and unrelated neighbors are often as prominent in them as kin are.

Save for living parents and their dependent children, who share the proceeds from wealth inherited by one of the parents, property ownership is virtually never shared among kin, even siblings. When a father or mother leaves land, a house, or an apartment building to his or her children, it is either sold and the money divided according to Islamic inheritance laws or the building or land is physically partitioned so that each heir has his or her share as separate, personal property.

People of means sometimes create trusts (*wakf*) supervised according to Islamic law to benefit their children and grandchildren. Several informants said that this was done to conserve the property (only its income is available to the heirs) and, also, to lessen the chances that an adult brother (or, rarely, some other surviving kin) of the deceased would misappropriate the inheritance while serving as the children's guardian until they reached their majority.

Disputes about inheritance are settled by local kadhis (judges of Islamic courts) according to Koranic principles. A Swahili language book presenting the principles of the Islamic laws (*sheria*) of inheritance is taken as the final arbiter of disputes and is consulted both by kadhis and by lay persons concerned with questions of inheritance (Kasim el Mazrui 1952).

Parents and Children

There are some generalities regarding relations among kin[3] that can be inferred from informants' statements and observed behavior. These include respect and deference for parental generation kin which diminishes somewhat as the ego generation kin reach adulthood but does not disappear until and unless the parental generation kin becomes senile (*pishwa*), and even then some indications of respect and deference are retained. Outside the nuclear family, there is general similarity in behavior toward parental generation kin regardless of sex, although, given the pervasive division of the sexes and the isolation of women (*tawa*), there is generally more interaction within one's own sex.

Relations between mothers and children are usually closer, freer of conflict, and less restricted than relations between fathers and children. Fathers are said—including, sometimes, by themselves—more often to get along well with daughters than with sons. In fact, boys and young men rather often make use of their sisters' good relations with their father to get the father to do things the sons want him to do. A daughter asking her father to do something is likelier than a son, several informants say, to succeed even if what she wants is for her brother.

Some young men report excellent relations with their fathers, and observation in these cases is in accord with their reports. Others, however, say that although the father-son relationship is warm and close when the boy

Table 1. Kin Terms

A. Mostly Consanguines

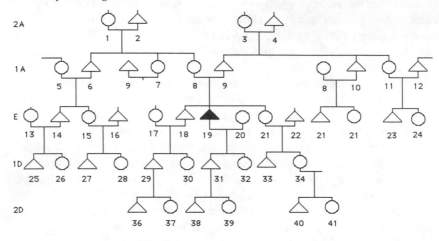

Generation	Number	Term	Generation	Number	Term
2A	1, 3	Nanya	E	14, 15	Mtoto wa Mjombe or Ndugu
	2, 4	Babu			
1A	5	Mkaza Mjomba		13, 16	Shemeji*
	6	Mjomba		17, 22	Shemeji*
	7	Mama ya Pili		18, 21	Ndugu
	8	Mama		20	Mke
	9	Baba		21	Ndugu or Ndugu bin Ami
	10	Baba ya Pili or Ami			
	11	Shangazi		23, 24	Mtoto wa Shagazi or Ndugu
	12	Baba			
1D	25–34	Mwana			
	26, 28, 30, 32, 34	Mwana or Binti			
2D	36–41	Mjuku			

*This is also pronounced and spelled "shemegi."

Table 1. (continued)

B. Mostly Affines, Male Ego

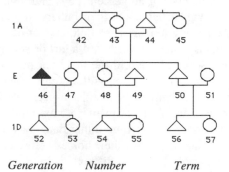

Generation	Number	Term
1A	42–45	Mkwe
E	47	Mke
	48–51	Shemeji
1D	52, 57	Mwana
	53, 55, 57	Mwana or Binti

C. Mostly Affines, Female Ego

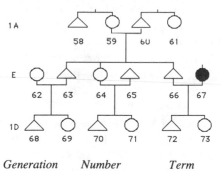

Generation	Number	Term
1A	58–61	Mavya
E	62, 64	Witi
	63, 65	Shemeji
1D	68–73	Mwana
	69, 71, 73	Mwana or Binti

is small, as adolescence approaches, the relationship becomes more distant and/or characterized by conflict.

I have talked to a number of adolescent boys and young men who have critical, even bitter, things to say about their fathers. A number of sons criticized their fathers for being too strict, too old-fashioned, and too unwilling to provide needed funds. I have never heard a girl or young woman criticize her father. However, several have told me that their parents (*wazee*) are too strict or old-fashioned but without being willing (or able?) to differentiate between their fathers and their mothers in this respect. Aside from whatever share they have of the general criticism of parents, mothers are not, in my experience, subject to open criticism by either daughters or sons.

A few boys and young men leave their homes before they marry, and the reasons given are uniformly based on difficulties in getting along with their father or, somewhat more commonly, their mother's husband whom she married either following divorce or the biological father's death. In all seven of the cases of this sort that I was able to record, the son visited his mother even though, as in two instances, the husband/father told her not to see him.

As will be seen below, mothers almost always have greater involvement than fathers in their children's lives. In some families, the fathers are mainly peripheral to the children's activities except for providing (or refusing) money for these activities, including schooling.

Relations between parents and children are by no means free of conflict. Mothers' day-to-day relations with their daughters are fraught with conflict, and much of the most colorful obscenity in the Swahili language (and it is a language rich in abusive resources) is directed by mothers at their daughters (Swartz 1990*a*, 1990*b*). I have no evidence to indicate that fathers and sons or fathers and daughters exchange insults, but tensions in these relations—often related to differences regarding the use of money—frequently are expressed in silences and withdrawal.

Some conflict is taken as natural. A proverb says *Pesa zikiwa mfukoni haziwati kugongana* (Money that is in [a] pocket does not stop knocking together). This emphasizes the inevitable and constant minor conflict among those who are close to one another (in the same pocket) and the harmlessness of that conflict. Another proverb asserts that the familiarity that allows minor conflict is strengthened by that conflict: "*Nyoko, nyoko—ni faida ya kuonana*" (Mother, mother [this is an archaic form that appears only as part of fairly mild obscene insults and refers to that insult here]—is [to the] advantage of [a] relationship).

But the recognition that some strife is natural and harmless in parent-child (and other household) relationships does not obviate the fact that serious ruptures can and do occur. As noted, there are sons who leave the parental home before marriage and not in order to work at a distant job. I know of no Swahili woman who has left her parents' home as dissatisfied sons sometimes do, but the restrictions on women are such that departures are extremely difficult unless the woman marries or goes to the house of a kinswoman, in which case I would not be likely to hear that family trouble was at the root of the move.

As understood among the Swahili, it is a tenet of Islam that a child cannot go to heaven if the parent does not have *radhi* for the child when the parent dies. "Radhi" means a blessing and comes, informants report, from the parents' satisfaction with the child's behavior. A parent cannot control radhi; it is a natural consequence of the child's behavior, and a child who has behaved intolerably toward a parent will not get radhi regardless of how great the parent's love for him or her may be. Radhi need not be given explicitly, and at death a parent may give or withhold it without necessarily knowing that it has been given or withheld.

Since the Swahili, including the members of the younger generation, are almost all deeply religious Muslims, the importance of radhi would seem a significant resource for parents in their relations with their children. To some extent this is true, and an element of children's general wish to please their parents is, they say explicitly, based in concern about this blessing.[4] Much more active in shaping relations with parents, however, are the very strong bonds that unite parents and children. A mother is said to feel deep sympathy and love for her children because of *kitei* (Johnson 1959 [1939] renders this as *kite*), the pain she suffers at the birth of her child. Sometimes a person who refuses a child's request or withholds sympathy from a child is told, "*Hukuzaa*" (You have not given birth). Even fathers are said to have given birth and to have sympathy and love for a child because of this.[5]

Although fathers are said genuinely to love their children, some part of this is understood—at least by some male informants—as a consequence of their love for the child's mother, their wife. A proverb used mainly with respect to stepchildren but explicitly said to apply to own children as well maintains that a man who loves a woman must also love her children: *Mtu akipenda koa, hupenda na kilicho ndani* ([A] person [who], if [he] loves [the] oyster shell [customarily or usually] loves that which is inside [it]).

Mother's Siblings and Father's Siblings

The mother's brother, *mjomba,* occupies a fairly distinctive position in the parental generation, and informants agree that this man is more likely to be sympathetic and helpful than a father's brother, *Baba ya pili* [lit., second father] or *Baba mdogo* [lit., little father]. Several informants say that if one's father dies while one is young, it is better to be in the charge of a mother's brother than a father's brother because, given the partrilateral emphasis in Islamic inheritance laws, the former is not in a position to try to appropriate your share of your dead father's estate as the latter is. Further, and at least as important, there is more likely to be "love" (*upendo*) on the mother's side of the family. The mother's brother's wife is referred to by a distinctive term, *mkaza mjombe*.

Like mother's brother, father's sister is referred to by a term, *shangazi*, that distinguishes her from other kin of the parental generation, although there is no distinctive term for her husband. However, no particular distinctive qualities in the relations between people of either sex and their father's sisters were observed or reported by informants. If anything, it is my impression that mother's sisters play an active role in people's lives more often than father's sisters do. When I mentioned this impression to informants, they uniformly agreed and said that it was due to the fact that when children are small, they go with their mothers when the latter go visiting. Since mothers visit their sisters more often than their husbands' sisters, the children become more accustomed (*zoea*) to them and, therefore, have closer relations with them.

Siblings and Cousins

Own generation kin are treated quite differently according to sex. There is often a good deal of interaction among same sex, same generation kin, although it is my impression that sisters, sisters' daughters, and similarly related women are more likely to spend a great deal of time together than comparably related men.

Still, in many families, brothers are together a good deal before they marry. The elder serves as a mentor for the younger, and the younger helps the elder in whatever tasks the latter may be involved in. With marriage and the beginning of their own families, relations become more formal and distant, and sometimes competitiveness, even mutual hostility, emerges.

Relations between sisters are frequently close and warm in childhood when they are almost constantly together as a consequence of the isolation of women, which led—and, to a slightly lesser extent, still leads—to girls and young women spending much of their time in their own house and those of female relatives and neighbors whom they visit with their mother. After marriage, relations between sisters generally remain quite positive and lack the competitiveness that sometimes is seen between brothers.

Brothers and sisters are together less as children than are same sex siblings, since while the girls stay in the home when they are not in school, the boys, after the age of seven or eight, are either in school or wandering the neighborhood and playing games with other boys. There is some conflict between brothers and sisters deriving from brothers attempting to control their sisters, especially with regard to the sisters being allowed to go out of the house. Sisters often depend on their brothers to do errands for them which involve going outside, and brothers depend on their sisters for part of the cooking, cleaning, and mending they require. As might be expected, this work for brothers by sisters sometimes leads to resentment, but it also serves as a check on brothers' attempts to control their sisters' activities.

Matrilateral Association and Affection

Several informants have said that both men and women are closer to their mother's kin than to their father's as a consequence of closer emotional ties to the mother and of going with her to visit her kin when they were young. My observations (as well as the data in the survey reported in chap. 5) tend to bear this out. Nevertheless, beyond the confines of the nuclear family, common interests and personal affections are the most powerful determinants of which kin associate often and closely with one another and which have more distant relations.

In accord with this, group members consistently affirm that there is no general difference in one's relations with father's brother's children, mother's brother's children, father's sister's children, and mother's sister's children. All own generation kin can be referred to as ndugu (the same term, in fact, is used for all kin regardless of generation or nature of relationship), but there are terms that distinguish between brothers (*kaka* and *mdogo* are fairly common) and sisters (*dada* or the more Arabized *ukhti*).

There are limited terminological differences found in alternate terms which distinguish the children of one sort of parents' sibling from another and from own siblings, but there is little basis for believing that these differences have much sociological or psychological significance. They seem mostly to be used to clarify a relationship for the benefit of visitors or anthropologists. The alternate terms are used only in reference and clarification and mean, literally, "child of mother's brother," "child of father's brother," and so on.

Cousin marriage is quite common, and more than a third of all the marriages about which I could collect genealogical information were between kin.[6] I have been told that it does not matter if the cousin you marry is related to you through your father or through your mother (although a number of informants are quite emphatic about how important the difference is to "Arabs"), but that it is slightly better to marry someone who is not the child of an actual sibling of either parent. In fact, two marriages about which I have relatively full data involved the child of a parent's true sibling, and neither of these caused any observable comment.

Generational Kin Term Uses

The terms for members of the child generation are basically the same for all kin on both sides. The females are referred to as *binti* and the males as *mwana*, with the latter term sometimes used for children of both sexes. I found no use of terms differentiating among child generation kin on any basis other than sex, but explanations are added ("the child of my sister" or "the child of my mother's brother's son") when needed.

The terms for parents are extended in an interesting way to members of the child generation. A crying child is comforted by, among other ways, being addressed as *baba* (father) or *mama* (mother) by his or her parents or older siblings. Informants say this is done to give the child respect or prestige (*heshima*) and, thereby, cheer him or her. The fact that little boys of ten or less are sometimes addressed as *Bwana Mkubwa* (or the diminutive of that, *Chubwa,* meaning Great Sir or Great Lord) seems to serve the same function, since this same term is used not only for rich men, political officials, and important employers but also for the father's father, the mother's father, and, sometimes, for others called *Babu* (grandfather).

Child terms are extended outside the family to children, particularly members of other ethnic groups, from whom favors are being asked. Swahili women, especially older ones, have a particular, ingratiating inflection they use in addressing an unrelated child as *Mwanangu* (my son) when they are trying to get the child to run errands for them.

Grandchildren are spoken to in a quite familiar way, and relations between grandparents and grandchildren are ideally and actually warm, friendly, and as nearly egalitarian as they can easily be given the differences in resources and physical abilities.[7] A grandparent who is present when a grandchild is scolded or punished will, especially if the punishing parent is the grandparent's child, take the child's side and urge the parent to forgive him or her. I heard a grandmother tell her daughter in what appeared a serious way that it would be better if she, the grandmother, were punished rather than the grandchild for what the latter had done to annoy the mother.

Kin and Expectations

Within the substantial range of variation in relationships involving kin, one thing is universally true: the main expectations in these relationships are general rather than specific. These general expectations are the heart of relationships not only within the household and nuclear family but also with fairly distant kin such as grandparents and grandchildren, parents' siblings and their children, and, to a considerable extent, neighbors who have lived near the family for long periods.

There are also specific expectations in these relationships, of course. For example, wives and mothers and, to a slightly lesser extent, sisters are expected to prepare meals for the household and to see to such domestic tasks as laundry and cleaning.

Husbands and fathers are expected to provide money to the rest of the household and, together with sons and brothers, to do most shopping and errands involving any substantial traveling around the town. These last expectations involve highly specific activities such as producing cooked food at a particular time or paying a particular bill. There is usually little or no difficulty for the participants in a relationship in determining whether or not specific expectations have or have not been met, although there may be difficulty in agreeing on the significance of meeting or not meeting them.

The Importance
of General Expectations

The main expectations in these relationships, the ones that participants most often use as the basis for evaluating performance, are general rather than specific. Establishing whether general expectations have been met or not is much more difficult than doing the same for specific expectations and, at the same time, is often more important. A person who is judged to meet the general expectations in his or her kin status will be positively evaluated in the status by those in relationships with him or her even if that person is not particularly adept at meeting some of the specific expectations in the status. The reverse is less often true.

Since the difference between general and specific expectations is one of degree rather than kind, it is not surprising that the two shade into one another. Specific expectations such as the wife's housekeeping or the husband's provision of money become most important when they are seen as affecting general expectations. A key difference is that general expectations can be met in a variety of ways, which is not so true of specific expectations. A husband who loses his job may fail to meet the money-providing expectations but still be evaluated positively in the spouse role if the wife recognizes other bases for viewing him as loving, conscientious, and having good intentions (*nia*, see below). The same is true for a wife who cooks badly or fails to keep the house as the husband might want it to be.

General expectations may include telling a child or, sometimes, a spouse about mistakes they have made and how to correct them, but they are characteristically positive in nature. As will become clear below, "upendo," which can be glossed as "love," is one of the main aspects of relations among nuclear family members and, beyond that, with kin and neighbors generally. Some of the more obvious manifestations of upendo are displaying concern, trust, affection, and a regard for the interests of the object of the love. "Accustomedness" and, less, "one character" function much as "love" does, but for the present discussion, love alone will be considered and the others left for later examination.

It is not always obvious whether particular acts meet general expectations, and even those directly involved can sometimes make a judgment only by considering a whole pattern of behavior rather than specific acts. In part, this is so because the connection between acts and the meeting of general expectations is so dependent on interpretation that a given behavior and its opposite can be taken to have the same significance. Thus, as we will see in chapter 10, a man shows his love for his wife by giving her money for clothing and such even if he thinks buying the clothing is wasteful and unnecessary. Showing love for a son, however, sometimes involves not giving him money when the same man, now in the status father, thinks the use of the money would be wasteful and unnecessary.[8]

Nor are opposite behaviors given the same interpretation only when they occur in different relationships involving different statuses. A woman shows her love for her sister (i.e., meets general expectations in the relationship with her) by criticizing her even to the extent that the sister weeps, but love can also be shown by denying to the sister the truth of criticism, perhaps leveled by others, of her. In short, general expectations are illusive as concerns their behavioral reference, and this is not just an observer's problem. Participants in relationships often find it difficult to assess whether or not general expectations are being met, but the assessments are nevertheless made and remade with the future of the relationship, as well as the judgment of the individual, depending on them.

Community members are explicit about the difficulty in assessing behavior in relationships where general expectations are the crucial ones. A number of people have told me that in dealings with those who are close, that is, with spouses, children, close kin, and neighbors, nia can be more important than what the person does. "Nia" can be glossed as intentions, purposes, or general orientation. A person whose nia is "good" (*nia nzuri*) can do things that may seem bad but that are recognized, perhaps on reflection, as at least well intended. Understanding whether a person in a close relationship has met the general expectations in that relationship, then, depends not only on his or her behavior but also on the view the other participant(s) in the relationship have of his or her nia.

Just what is called for by general expectations is not always clear until a situation arises involving them. Thus, for example, several young Swahili men were arrested for loitering one evening. It was difficult to tell why they had been arrested since they appeared to be doing nothing unusual but only sitting on a low retaining wall near their houses chatting as they generally did in the evening. Because of the vague reason for the arrest and because they were handled rather roughly by the police without any obvious reason (I saw the arrest), the event caused severe anxiety in the young men's households. On hearing what had happened, one of the fathers rushed from his house to that of a neighbor who was friendly with a number of the city's more important officials. In a remarkably short time, the neighbor left his house, although he had been about to go to bed, and went to the police station where, after long discussions with police officials, he was able to win the young men's release.

No serious question seemed to occur to the fathers of the young men about the willingness of their neighbor to help them. Nor did the neighbor, then or later, indicate that he thought he had done anything particularly surprising or unusual even though he said he had not actually intervened with the police before on behalf of neighbors or, for that matter, anyone. "We help each other," he explained to me in discussing the incident and his role in it.

The neighbor's intervention is in accord with the general expectation of mutual help and support that is characteristic of relations between kin and neighbors. Thus, when the child of a household is being married, the mother's women kin and neighbors speak of "our wedding" and work impressively long hours helping to prepare for it. When the son of a household is ready for a job, not just his father and older brothers but many of his parents' brothers and parents' sisters' husbands, older cousins, and neighors will all make efforts—some more vigorous than others, of course—to find him a suitable position.

Precisely what neighbors and kin do for one another is mostly not specified, but the expectations in their relationships are, nevertheless, powerful. Just as a politician is supported because he is understood to provide vague but vital goals and states such as "prosperity" or "peace," so kin and neighbors are positively evaluated when they provide "help" and "support." The Arab owner of a "ration shop" is expected to return goods and change to a customer who says what is wanted and gives him money, but expectations of such a clear and specific kind are not the main characteristic of relationships between kin and neighbors. In those relationships, more accurately, in the statuses of the individuals involved in them, the key expectations are broad and general, giving those relationships a flexibility and an ambiguity that relationships based on statuses involving mainly specific expectations cannot have.

Mutual Choice in
Forming a Social "Pool"

In general, my observations and discussions with group members support the conclusion that each Swahili is part of a pool of individuals whose members choose one another for relationships of varying intensity, frequency of association, and duration. Some of these relationships are rather distant, and others involve regular mutual assistance, exchanges of some kinds of confidential information, and strong emotional bonds. Ties of kinship make up a substantial part of the basis for forming this ego-centered pool, but neighbors from adjoining houses are another important element, especially for women.

For men, membership in the pool is also affected by the mosque they regularly attend with a man's closer relations—both with kin and nonkin—often mainly with others who attend the same mosque. Since which mosque a man regularly attends is commonly more influenced by proximity than anything else, neighborhood (in the sense of the general area, about which see below) is important for men but is generally a wider area than it is for women.

Individuals choose and are chosen from their pool according to personal preference, leaving the other pool members as more or less available sources of material help, social support, and, for women, emotional warmth when limited or exceptional circumstances make these desirable. This availability is maintained through relationships kept active in occasional visits to one another's homes and joint participation in weddings, funerals, and maulidi.

Particular kinsmen may or may not be active in preparing for one another's life crises or religious rituals, but they will make some contribution and will almost always be present. Men who attend them use their pools as the basis for choosing a baraza. Some men do not attend a baraza regularly, but there is an explicit value on men associating with one another rather than being isolated in their homes, and a main venue for such association, second only to the mosque before and after prayers, is the baraza.

In my limited experience with them, women are more often in close contact with more of their kin than men are. Women seem to draw on the "pool" of their husbands' kin, however, rather more selectively depending on their and their affines' preferences, on the women's relations with their husbands, and on their husbands' relations with the members of his extended family.

Men are generally more distant and more selective in all their relationships save, often, with their wives (more of this in chap. 10). There are men who see a great deal of several of their father's brothers' sons and little of their mother's brothers' sons even though informants report that warmer and more satisfactory relations are likelier on the mother's side. There are mature men, including some with children of their own, who associate closely with their fathers and are involved with them in a range of financial, religious, and social matters. But there are others who see their fathers only rarely and have little to do with them. The same can be said of relations between brothers.

Neighbors

For both men and women, the pool of possible close and/or especially significant associates is not limited to kin. Neighbors, including those who are unrelated, are often among those with whom there are the closest relationships, often involving mutual assistance and strong emotional ties. There is a proverb that, if it lacks the trenchancy of many others, nevertheless characterizes the nature of relations with neighbors as compared to kin: *Hallah, hallah jirani kuliko ndugu mli kule* (God, God [much used to give emphasis] the neighbor [is more] than [a] kin [who] is over there [i.e., at a distance]).

As with kinship, ties based on proximity are a likely basis for close relationships without there being any necessity for such relationships to develop. To be *jirani* (neighbors; *wamtaa* is a less common alternate term) is to have the basis for a close relationship, but normatively, informants agree it need only be a cordial one. Some neighbors are likely also to be kin, and the dual tie increases the likelihood of frequent and close association. Other neighbors, however, may not even be Swahili, and close relations even with such outsiders are, within limits to be described, fairly common.

Old Town is no longer a purely Swahili area and has not been since the railroad to Nairobi and Uganda was completed before World War I. The steady increase in the presence of non-Swahili in the area has resulted in greater and greater population density, with much of the additional housing, as well as some formerly Swahili housing, being occupied by outsiders. The limited census I was able to make indicates that outsiders, mainly Indians and Arabs of various sorts (but most commonly those from the Hadhramot area of Yemen), now occupy more than half of the houses in the area. The eastern part of Mombasa island, which was almost purely Swahili prior to World War I (when the rest of the island was used for agriculture), is now a cosmopolitan area only slightly less polyglot than the area adjacent to Old Town that has become the business district and, to the west of that, a mainly non-Swahili residential and industrial area leading to the modern port.[9]

Despite its greatly increased non-Swahili population, Old Town is not completely heterogeneous. There are almost no resident Christians there, and almost all of the minority of non-Muslims are Hindus. Among the Muslim majority in Old Town, the Swahilis' fellow Sunni are the largest group, although there are some Shia (all or almost all from India), a small number of unassimilated Omanis of the Ibathi canon, and, again mainly Indian Muslims from other non-Sunni groups. Ethnic heterogeneity is, as this suggests, rather greater than religious.

Relations with Non-Swahili Neighbors

Many Swahili women and some men have close relations with unrelated neighbors, some of whom are from other ethnic groups. This close association with outsiders, however, is almost exclusively with those who are Sunni Muslims. Close relations with Indian neighbors, even if the Indians are Sunni, are not very common unless they are Baluchis (see chap. 2), whom the Swahili view as far more like themselves than members of any other outside group. Close relations with Hadhrami Arab neighbors (and the Mombasa Hadhrami are all Sunni) are, however, by no means unusual.

Close relationships between whole Swahili households and unrelated neighboring households are quite common, and people often speak of their neighbors as being "ndugu" even when, on inquiry, it appears there is no known blood relationship. Such relations are very positively evaluated by everyone I talked to, and the issue of whether "real" kin might be unhappy about close relations between their relatives and unconnected neighbors was dismissed as farfetched. A number of informants pointed out to me that Islam enjoins neighbors to care for and love one another and quoted Prophet Mohammed as saying that the only thing that remained to be done to make neighbors the same as kin was to find a way for neighbors to inherit from one another.

Warm and mutually supporting relationships are extremely common between Swahili families that have lived in the same nearby houses for generations, but even neighbors who have lived near one another for only a matter of years often have wide-scope and intensive relations. Such relations sometimes develop even when the neighbors are Sunni from some non-Swahili group.

In many cases, of course, the members of neighboring households differ in the closeness of their ties with one another. Most frequently, it is the wife-mother in the Swahili household who is close to her counterpart in the neighboring household, and other relations between members of the two households vary from cordial or polite to truly friendly. Occasionally, the relationship between households focuses on the husbands-fathers, but this is far less common and these relations, like most men's relations, are usually restrained and polite rather than close, even if the men sometimes do important practical favors for one another.

"One Character," "Accustomedness," and "Love": The Emotional States Understood as Usual in Close Relationships

Long presence in the same nearby houses is important, but more important yet is whether someone in one household sees someone in the other (always of the same sex and almost always women) as having *tabia moja* (lit., one character or disposition, i.e., being sympathetic to one another and/or similar in personality). This mutual attraction or similarity is said by several informants to be the surest source of close relations between individuals who are not kin and neighbors. The relatively few men and women who have lasting friendships with people who are neither kin nor neighbors also attribute the relationship to tabia moja.

Tabia moja is far less important for kin. The proverbs at the beginning of this chapter make clear the same thing that one observes and hears from infor-

mants: kin relations benefit from personal compatibility, but if the relationships are within the nuclear family, such personal preferences matter far less.
Mazoezi (accustomedness) comes from long, close association, and I have
been told repeatedly that with mazoezi, being mutually sympathic (i.e., tabia
moja) is not an issue. Tabia moja refers to mutual affection and similarity
of interests, while accustomedness makes this unnecessary since becoming
"accustomed" to someone renders whatever lack of affection or incompatibility of interests there may be manageable and, eventually, unimportant.[10]

As discussed earlier, one has love (*upenzi*) for the parents and siblings
and spouse with whom one lives, or, failing that, especially if they are step-
parents or children, one is "accustomed" to them. Selections from the pool
of possible associates made up of more distant kin and neighbors, however,
is on the basis of personal compatibility, tabia moja. Accustomedness and/or
love seems the basis of the household group where constant and close association takes place. Compatibility and mutual affection are enough for the less
constantly demanding relations between more distant kin, neighbors, and
friends. Fellow household members are rarely characterized as having tabia
moja with the speaker, but close associates from outside the household frequently are.

Inclusive Neighborhoods:
Old Town Sections

As has been true for centuries, the area of the town in which a family lives
(mtaa, pl. mitaa) provides a basis for organizing social relationships. The importance of these now is less than it was twenty years ago, but everyone
is actively aware of what his neighborhood is, and it still affects social relationships. Each of these areas (see maps 1 and 2) occupies a fairly substantial territory, far more than the few adjoining houses whose occupancy offers
the possibility of people having a close relationship as "neighbors" in the
sense just discussed.

The residents of each of these areas are likelier to associate substantially
more with those from the same area than with people from other areas, and
close ties are likelier within than across area boundaries. Each of the areas
is understood as having economic, social, and personality traits that distinguish it from each of the others, with the understandings about each area
differing, mainly in emphasis and valence, according to whether they are
expressed by the residents of the areas in question or by the residents of the
other areas.

As noted in chapter 3, each of these areas was a part of one or the other
of the two sections that were the basis of community organization until a few
decades ago. This organization has lost its effectiveness as a basis for joint

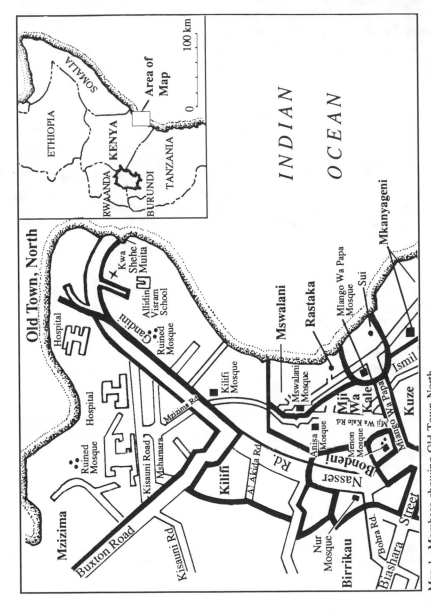

Map 1. Mombasa showing Old Town North.

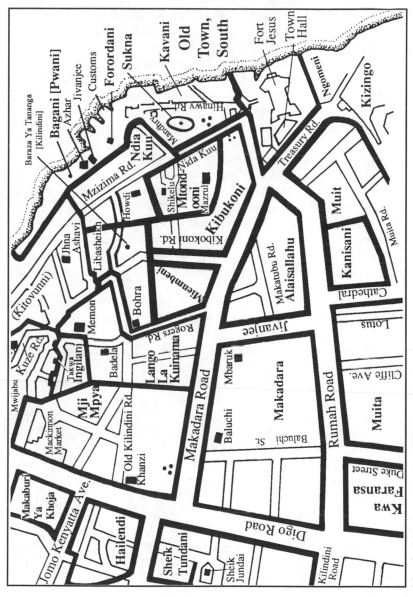

Map 2. Mombasa showing Old Town South.

or cooperative activity, but to a considerable extent, the people of a given area are still likelier to be in each others' social "pools" than people from other areas are, and marriages seem more common within areas than between them. The areas also serve as a means for categorizing community members according to what are seen as important qualities held in common.

Beginning at Fort Jesus and going northward through the areas (see map 2), the residents of Kavani (including Kibukoni, Mtondoni, and Barani) are spoken of as the richest in Old Town and as having the finest houses. This area includes the largest number of families who view themselves as being of relatively recent Arab descent. They are generally, informants say, seen as educated, refined, and physically unimpressive as concerns fighting for men and hard work for women.

Among non-Swahili Mombasans, a Swahili man is sometimes referred to as *Bwana Badi,* where "Bwana" (the title meaning "lord" or "sir") is used to mock what is taken to be the Swahili claim to nobility (remember this quality, uungwana, refers to slave-free descent and is a central quality for full membership in the community) and "Badi," the short and familiar form of "Mohammed," a very common name for men in the community. The men of Kibukoni are the ones who are most commonly referred to as "Bwana Badi," including, at least once in my presence, by Swahili from other Old Town areas.

The people of Mkanyageni (including Kuze) are considered the bravest, strongest, friendliest, and most loyal members of the community. They are also considered the poorest, the roughest, the least cultivated, and the most insultingly outspoken and quarrelsome. The people of this area include the newest immigrants (although they have been there for generations) coming from Bajun, the Lamu archipelago, and other Swahili communities along the coast.

The famous fighters of Old Town are all Kuze men, and men from other areas have been heard more than once to say of them (collectively or about individuals), "Walizaliwa na bakora na kisu," i.e., that they are born with a walking stick and a knife. A great fighter from this area who died in the 1940s was said to be able to hit an enemy twelve times with his walking stick and leave a single mark. The most recent murder committed by a Swahili which I am aware of was the stabbing of an outsider by a Kuze man who had been insulted by his victim.

The residents of Mjua wa Kale are characterized as being in between the other two in wealth, refinement, and fighting ability. There are some Omani-derived families in this area, called "the Mjua wa Kale Arabs," who are—or were—associated with the Nine Tribes rather than the Three Tribes as most "Swahili Arabs" (as that term was used in chap. 3) are. The main trait of the residents of this area is thought of as pride expressed as interest in precedence, so, for example, it is said a man from here always refused to follow the prevailing practice of standing when the Prophet's name is mentioned in Maulidi because "nobles don't stand for one another." In a story I heard several times, an Mjua wa Kalc man came into a mosque before prayers and was greeted by a neighbor resting on the floor without his hat or *gizbau* (the traditional men's vest—now rarely seen—worn over the ankle-length kanzu). The new-comer took off his hat and gizbau, lay down on the floor, and, only then, returned the greeting.

Residence Choice and Household Location

My inability to get a complete door-to-door census makes it difficult to say with any certainty whether there is a pattern in newly married couples' actual place of residence and, if there is, what pattern is present. A majority of informants say that in their view, residence for a newly married couple is ideally in or near the groom's father's house. Further, a majority also say that if the choice is between living near the wife's parents or living equally far from both, it is better to live equally far from both.

Despite these fairly generally held ideals, my limited direct observation reveals no clear pattern of residence. Some couples live near the groom's family, some live near the bride's family, and many (seemingly the largest group) live about as far from one as from the other. The situation is complicated by the fact that Old Town is very crowded, and couples often have to live wherever they can find space. It may be that the majority's reported preference for virilocal residence is followed less than it is because people simply cannot find housing where they would like to find it. Whether this is so or not, the best assessment of the facts available to me is that there is no clear pattern of residential choice.

Table 2C shows who lives with whom rather than what household is near what other. It shows that the nuclear family is, generally, the most important domestic unit. Seventy-six percent of our sample involves people living in a household with their nuclear family kin. Almost half the households contain no relatives other than nuclear family kin, that is, no adults other than spouses and unmarried offspring. Since nonrelatives only rarely are part of households,[11] this means that a large majority of community members live with a spouse and their children or, before they marry, with their parents and siblings.

Still, many households contain kin other than the spouses and their children. About half of the 111 households for which I have census data include at least one adult kin of the person who is said by the members of the household to be *mwenye amri* ("having authority," i.e., the household head). Widows and widowers, if they do not remarry, usually live in the house of one

Table 2.   1976 Census Figures from 111 Swahili Households (Gathered in 1976)

Male-headed households: 94
Female-headed households: 17

A. *Adults in Household with Head*

Number of households with these adults present:

	Household head's			*Head's Spouse's*		
	Spouse	*Parent*	*Sibling*	*Parents' sibling*	*Parent*	*Sibling*
With male head	87	22	17	17	5	20
With female head	3	3	4	0	0	0

B. *Children in Household by Sex, Age, and Sex of Head*

	Male head		*Female head*		*Subtotal*		*Total*
Age	M	F	M	F	M	F	
Less than							
7	37	34	3	2	39	36	75
8–10	42	29	3	4	45	33	78
11–17	54	63	12	8	64	71	135
18–25	39	24	11	10	50	34	84
26–35	13	7	4	7	17	14	31
Totals	185	158	30	31	215	188	404

C. *Household Composition*

	No.	*%*
Spouses living together	90	81
Spouses without other adults	54	49
Resident children		
Male head	74	78
Female head	15	88
Both spouses and children		
Male head	71	76
Female head	1	6

of their children (or have one or more of them live in their house). Those without children or without those who can or will take them live where they can, most often in their siblings' or siblings' children's houses.

Married children living with one or both parents together with childless widows and widowers living with collateral relatives account for the roughly one-third of the surveyed households that include either the househead's parent or a parent's sibling.

The average number of children per household was 3.65 for male-headed households and 3.59 for female-headed households. This includes both biological children and children who are *lelewa* (roughly "adopted"; see below).

"Adoption"

Although reliable census data, including information on number of families with adopted children, are very difficult to obtain, more than half my informants (the men and women I worked closely with over extended periods, perhaps a total of 35) were either themselves adopted ("lelewa" is the passive form, "be adopted," and *lea*, "adopt," is the active form), have adopted one or more children since becoming adults, or both. Some informants say the practice is "not rare, but not even a quarter of all families do it." Others say as many as a quarter of all families contain one or more children who have been "adopted." The general reticence about private matters is the main factor inhibiting the collection of data about adoption. There is no suggestion that there is anything disfavored about being an adopted child. On the contrary, men and women report that adopted children, if treated differently from biological children, are treated better and loved more.

This is especially so for those children, and this seems to be the larger category, who are adopted as acts of friendship. Many informants report that if two women like one another and one gives birth, the other will request (*omba,* which can also be used as "beg" is) that she be given the child to raise. If the birth mother accepts the request, and it appears that it often is, the child will be turned over to its *mama mlezi* (adoptive mother) at forty days, after which it will be brought to its birth mother (*mama mzazi*) for breast feeding several times a day for a year or so, when it will be switched to a bottle to supplement solid food.

It is by no means true that all such relationships begin so early in the child's life. Many are "adopted"[12] much later, and the relationship can be terminated, with the child returning to the biological parents usually because the birth parents are displeased with the way he or she is treated or because the adoptive parents can no longer keep him or her. Such terminations are rare and are taken very seriously by all involved.

The women involved in these relations are, more often than not, kin. Sisters often adopt one another's children, and the same is true for women of the same generation closely related through either their fathers or their mothers. Neighbors also adopt each other's children despite the absence of any kin ties, and cross-generational adoption with a grandmother adopting her own daughter's child, while not common, is not unknown. Men sometimes adopt the children of relatives or even friends, but these adoptions are far more often because of "need" (*ya lazima*) than friendship.

Informants all differentiate between two types of adoption: because of need and because of friendship. Men generally instigate adoption when the child of someone to whom they are closely tied is in pressing need of a home because of parental illness or death or other such circumstances. Women are occasionally the main movers in an adoption on such dire grounds, but they are mainly the central figures when adoptions are based on the wish to strengthen relations.

The Lives of Adopted
Children and of "Natural" Children

When a child is adopted, he or she continues to see the birth parents on a regular basis and continues to call them *baba* and *mama* while using the same terms for the adoptive parents. The visits with the birth parents are just that, visits. The child's home is with the adoptive parents. So far as I could determine, all of the adopted school age boys and girls I know of regularly *shinda* (spend the whole day as opposed to stopping in for a shorter time) with their biological parents. This type of visit is made by all children, adopted or not, to various relatives. But it is an occasional thing as regards visits to other relatives, while it is often a never missed weekly visit, often on Friday, for those who are adopted.

An adopted child is treated much as a biological child is. In paying the bride-price, for example, the adoptive parents provide the whole amount if they are well-to-do or, at least, a substantial part of it if they are less prosperous. Even as concerns radhi (the parental blessing), many biological parents say that they give theirs if the adoptive parents do and withhold it on the same grounds. I know of adoptive children who provide the funds to support their adoptive parents when the latter are old and unable to provide for themselves.

In general, children leave their parents' home to establish their own household in their early or middle twenties and, as table 2B shows, very few children remain in the parental home beyond their mid-twenties. A few sons, but almost no daughters, leave their parental home before they marry. The sons may leave to take employment in another part of Kenya or abroad, but few sons leave—generally because of quarrels with their fathers—to live with other kin (generally married siblings) or, in unusual cases, in a rented room in the house of a distant kin or unrelated community member.

Marriage for Women, Jobs for Men

The nuclear family, with or without one or two additional relatives, is the household unit for most Swahili. The beginning of these families, marriage, is considered the key event in the individual's entrance into adulthood. There are virtually no women who fail to marry at least once, and only very few men remain single. Such unmarried men are viewed as, at best, impotent and, quite likely, the passive partner in homosexuality (*mshoga* or *hanithi*).[13]

Women who have never married are considered extremely unfortunate and, until the last few decades, denied the company of married women other than their mothers and sisters lest they hear talk of marital sex and be stimulated to improper behavior. In fact, the young women I have been able to interview are unanimous in saying they want to marry. Without exception, the single girls and young woman I talked to[14] told me that the most important thing that would happen to her, and the thing she looked forward to most, is getting married. The reason given for this was invariably that in getting married, she would begin her own life, have her own home, and become independent.

Every boy and young man I asked told me that the most important thing that would happen to him in the foreseeable future was to get a job. Just as marriage is said by women to bring them independence, employment is cited by men as the source of their independence. The men say this comes through escape from the father's financial control and with this, as many note, the ability to marry and found a family.

Arranged First Marriages

Informants of both sexes say that their first marriage was or will be in large part determined by the wishes of their families. Repeatedly, this was characterized as a community "custom" (*mila* or *desturi*), or, sometimes, a Muslim custom, that has been followed by many previous generations. The mother and father are identified as the main actors in marriage arrangements, but older siblings, especially brothers, were sometimes said to be extremely influential. I know of two cases in which wedding plans agreed to by parents were affected by objections to the groom by the prospective bride's older brother.

There is no disagreement among informants about the desirability of arranged marriages, and many of them talk as though all marriages, at least first marriages, are, in fact, arranged. This, however, proves to be one of those statements (a "token" in the sense explained in chap. 6) that reflect something other than observable reality. When specifically asked, informants all agree that there are, in fact, children who want to marry someone not chosen by their parents. When the child is very insistent, informants say, it is better to accept his or her choice than to be shamed by the child running off and marrying without parental approval.

Some informants say that marriage on the basis of the choice of those being married is much more common now than it was even as recently as the 1960s and 1970s, and this may well be so. However, having encountered a few middle-aged and even elderly men and women long married to non-Swahili, I discovered that although a few external marriages are, in fact, arranged, these are mainly with outside men who are either rich or prestigious. Such cases involved Arabs or European men converted to Islam and local women whose parents accepted the proposal of the outsider man.

Such marriages to prestigious outsiders, although not common by any means, seem to have been occurring for several generations at least. Obviously, the families that claim Omani forebears and who claim ties with well-established Swahili mbari (the now mainly forgotten collections of families) through their mothers must have involved extracommunity marriages that took place many generations ago. It seems very likely that these are of the same sort as those now involving rich Arabs and European Muslims.

Occasionally, a marriage is arranged between Muslims of ordinary prestige from outside the community and community women. In all the instances of such marriages involving a woman from a family of waungwana (i.e., a family without known slave forebears) I could find (a total of 11), the woman's family was poor and the man was from another Muslim Mombasa group. In most of these cases (7), the man was ethnically a Hadhrami Arab, but there were cases where the groom was Indian (3) or from another African group (1).

These marriages seem to be *faut de mieux*. If both families are poor and neither partner has prospects of a marriage that will provide much in the way of wealth or prestige, informants agree that any marriage, so long as it is to a Muslim, is better than no marriage, especially if the union does not involve someone believed to have one or more slave forebears.

All the first marriages involving more prosperous families that I could get information about were arranged and were either within the community or between a woman from the community and a man who was a Persian Gulf Arab, an Islamicized European or American, or from another Swahili group elsewhere on the East African coast or offshore islands.

When the proposed marriage is between kin, the negotiations described below are truncated and more informal than when the proposal and its acceptance involves a nonrelative. If the parents of the couple are close kin (and occasionally they are siblings or the children of siblings), much formality and consultation can be dispensed with since everyone involved knows all the others quite well and since the interests of both parties are much more nearly identical. As the kin relationship between the parents is more and more distant, the marriage decision is more and more like that concerning a nonrelative.

The initiative in arranging a marriage is with the prospective groom's relatives. The decision about which woman should be proposed to (*posa* [v.] is "propose") is made jointly by the groom's family, with all adult members having a say. The decision is sometimes said to be that of the father and the groom's adult brothers, but all agree that the mother and adult sisters play a key role in providing information about the prospective bride and her family and that their views, especially the mother's, are extremely influential. There are, I have been told, marriages in which the father extended a proposal even though his wife, the groom's mother, disagreed, but such events are said to be rare. Hardly less rare are mothers who convince their husbands, the fathers, to extend proposals the latter strongly resists.

The prospective groom himself often plays an active role in the decisions concerning his prospective marriage even though he usually hardly knows the prospective bride before the wedding. Until the last decade or two, the groom had not normally seen his bride until the wedding night, but now he has often seen her at school and may, in these days of greater mobility and less supervision for young women, know her rather well from meetings at school and in the neighborhood.

Sometimes the young man instigates his family's discussions of his marriage proposal by telling his father and mother that he would like to marry and is particularly interested in the young woman he names who, normally, he has met at school or seen in the neighborhood. The young man's preference is taken very seriously and overridden only if there are compelling reasons for doing so (of the sort indicated below). It is widely understood that young people "these days" (*siku hizi,* a phrase one hears a good deal when discussing marriage and young people in general) cannot be made to do things they do not want to do, and if the attempt is made, painful consequences (even elopement, a very rare occurrence) may eventuate.

In addition to the prospective groom and his resident nuclear family, other household members (including nonnuclear family kin) are ideally and usually consulted in a serious way, and, in some families, so are senior kin (especially grandparents on both sides and parents' siblings) and parents' siblings who do not live in the household. When kin other than those in the groom's nuclear family are involved, unless one of his parents is missing (through death or divorce), their participation is generally more a matter of form than of substance, although sometimes they will be asked to accompany the father and brothers to the young woman's house when the proposal is actually made. As a friend told me about notifying his son's mother's (my friend's wife) parents of the decision to propose marriage to a particular young woman's family, "We ask them, but really it is only notifying them."

Even though it is almost entirely a matter of form, consulting kin about a marriage proposal is very important to continued peaceful relations between those involved. When people who consider themselves descended from a common forebear on either side are not notified about a prospective proposal concerning someone they view as a kinsman (or kinswoman after the proposal has been made and is being considered), they may view themselves as having been offended. In one instance I know of, a man—who was generally viewed as rather quarrelsome—was enraged at not being told of a proposal involving someone whom he said was his kinsman until he heard the wedding was about to take place. "They throw me away," he said. "They don't want me because I am poor." He was, in fact, not particularly poor, and one suspects he made that statement to impute the basest motive he could to people whom he considered kin but did not, in his view, treat him accordingly.

Once a choice has been made, one or more men from the groom's family (sometimes including kin from beyond the nuclear family) call on the men of the bride's nuclear family to make the marriage proposal. When the proposal is made by several men from the groom's family, ideally and typically led by his father or, if he is dead or incapacitated, by the young man's adult oldest brother, it is viewed as more prestigious for the bride's family and more difficult for them to reject.

The proposal is made to the prospective bride's father or, again, if he is dead, to the young woman's oldest brother. The prospective bride, as well as the other women of the household, are never present when the proposal is made. The man with authority over the prospective bride has formal authority to accept or reject the proposal, but, in fact, he should and, informants say, always does consult other family members before making a decision. The consultation follows the same lines and concerns the same kin as are involved in the decision by the groom's family to extend the proposal.

Similarly, the young woman's own views are considered by her family much as the young man's are by his. I heard of no marriage initiated by the bride, but her wishes are taken seriously. She cannot get her family to initiate a proposal, but her preference in accepting or rejecting one is never lightly dismissed. At a first marriage, the Swahili believe that, in accord with Koranic law, the bride need not actively assent to the match proposed to her. However, should she explicitly refuse by telling her parents she will not accept the marriage, it will not take place. Although some men and women say that young women only rarely reject the decision of their parents, siblings, and other kin, I know of at least two cases (and suspect there are an unknown number I did not find out about) in which marriages did not take place because the prospective bride did not want to marry the man for whom the proposal was made.[15]

Selecting the Families
of Those Who Are to Marry

A central factor in the extending or accepting of a marriage proposal is the view that the two families have of each other's standing as waungwana (nobles). The suspicion of the existence of a slave forebear, which, as noted previously, bars the object of suspicion from the muungwana status, will almost invariably put the suspected family beyond consideration save by families who are themselves suspect.

The Swahili follow the Shafi canon of Sunni Islam, and that canon, informants tell me, requires that those to be married be *kufu*. This means that they must be of the same "tribe," the term used for this by English-speaking informants but probably referring in some part to prestige and economic standing. An informant told me that the founder of Shafi said that the child of a religious judge (kadhi) should not marry the child of a blacksmith.

Just all of what is involved in kufu is not entirely clear, since, as seen, Swahili do marry people from other ethnic groups, but community members agree that a proposed marriage can be rejected if the proposed partners are not kufu. At the same time it is also agreed that a rejection on such grounds is the most insulting possible. This suggests that objections based in kufu are at least sometimes used as a way of saying the proposer is not a muungwana, a person of undoubted free birth, or, at least, is of such low station as to be unworthy.

The economic situation of the two families is important to those involved, and although each generally prefers, *pari pasu,* the other to be equal or somewhat more financially secure, only extreme poverty is a likely source of serious objection to the marriage. The prestige of the occupations has significance in itself, with highly remunerative but low-prestige positions less desirable than less remunerative but more admired ones.

The significance of kufu, equality, is seen in some uses of kin terms for nonkin. Women, usually of different generations, who are fond of one another sometimes address one another as *mavya,* a reciprocal term for husband's mother and son's wife, even if the actual relationship does not exist. The term, it was explained to me, is a friendly one asserting the equality of the women and the propriety of a marriage that would unite them in the relationship it indicates. Similarly, women fondly call boys of their daughter's age *Bamkwe* (a contraction of "Bwana Mkwe," where "mkwe" is a reciprocal term for spouse's parents and child's spouse), even if the boys are young children.

Birth and economic status are by no means the only basis for evaluating marriage proposals. The suspicion of serious, unacceptable behavior or character traits on the part of either of the young people will bring the other family to oppose the marriage. If the young woman is thought to have a quarrelsome or difficult character or if her association with the other sex is thought to have been too free, the proposal is unlikely to be made by the groom's family.

Rejecting or Not Extending Proposals

The most common objections leading the woman's family to reject the proposal from an otherwise acceptable family are that the young man drinks

alcohol or smokes *bhang* (marijuana), has engaged in passive homosexual behavior, is a brawler and troublemaker (*mhuni*), or has no economic prospects
because of a poor school record or poor work history. Respectful behavior
toward others, especially seniors, is considered important for both the bride
and the groom, but it is mainly young men who are found deficient in this
quality. Informants say that "these days" this proper respect from the young
is so rare that even quite disrespectful young men must be accepted if one's
daughter is to marry at all.

In one case I am familiar with, the prospective bride's older brother, although absent from Old Town (he had a job in Europe) and not the one seen
as having authority over her, nearly succeeded in blocking the acceptance of
a proposal because he suspected that the young man (who had an unusual
manner) was a passive homosexual. The wedding only took place after the
bride's grandmother (her father and mother were both dead), with the help
of other relatives including the grandmother's brother, convinced the brother
to withdraw his threat to stay away from the wedding and not to contribute
to its very substantial cost.

Suspicions that young women have any association with unrelated males,
other than the most transitory ones at school, or have excessive interest in
sex are taken very seriously. An *mkware* (a woman with strong and active
interest in sex) is considered a splendid mistress but a risky wife. Young
women suspected of this quality are by no means favored by families as prospective wives for their sons or brothers. Laziness, however, seems to be the
character trait that most often leads members of the groom's family to oppose
extending a proposal.

I have been told that a bad reputation for any of the members of the family
of the groom can lead to hesitance on the part of the bride's family in accepting a proposal and that, similarly, a groom's family may be reluctant to propose to the family of a prospective bride if there are suspicions about her
sisters, brothers, or parents. This is, in part, I am told, because of the difficulties anticipated with the in-laws and, in part, because the prospective bride
or groom may not be as desirable as she or he seems but, rather, to resemble
the family member of doubtful reputation. I do not know of any cases of
such considerations actually preventing a proposal or an acceptance, but such
may exist.

The Basis for Successful Marriages

Young men tell me that some brides (I suspect that the number is still quite
small) are not actually virgins, but the ideal that they be is very strongly held
by the community in general and by both her family and that of the groom.[16]
These same young men say that the groom would mind less if his bride were
not a virgin than would his father and the woman's father.

Until recently, the failure of the wedding night to result in evidence of the bride's virginity (in the form of blood on the cloth that had been beneath her hips on the marital bed) could lead to serious difficulties. From the mid-1970s to the end of the 1980s, no quarreling of this sort came to my attention, as I am sure it would have had it been public. Nevertheless, informants say the groom's family would accuse the bride of promiscuity and the bride's family would insist she was a virgin but that the groom was impotent. In such cases, the marriage would be ended without delay. A few marriages, in fact, do end very quickly, and it may be that some of these are due to difficulties related to understandings about the bride's virginity and/or the groom's potency.

The successful marriage, a number of men and women have separately told me, is based on love (upendo). This despite the fact that marriages are often arranged and that, even in the later 1980s, marriages contracted because the prospective spouses are attracted to one another before the wedding are considered less likely to flourish than those based on family choices. The expressed understanding is that parents and adult family members have sounder and more mature judgment than the young prospective spouses do and that family judgment is likelier to bring together a couple who is truly suited.

When such a couple is brought together, the ideal view holds, they will develop a lasting love for one another. Even initial incompatibility will, informants say, be overcome as the couple gets to know one another. A proverb, sometimes used with regard to people getting used to things quite outside of marriage, holds, *Walioana, wataambana* (They were married, they will [learn to] speak to one another, i.e., as they stay together, they will learn to get along).

Bride Wealth

The bride wealth (*mahari*) has been rising fairly steeply in recent years. In 1980, I recorded a bride wealth payment of KSh 15,000, or around $1,000 at the rate of exchange as it was then, and in 1985, I recorded another one, this time of KSh 32,000, or $2,000 at the exchange rate at that time. The mahari is used by the bride's family to buy furniture and household goods for the newly married couple. The bride's parents ideally keep none of it (I heard of no cases when they did keep even part) and are expected to (in the cases I could follow, actually did) add money of their own to it in order to buy more and better things for the couple's new household. I have been told that the groom can provide furniture rather than money, but I have not recorded an actual case of this happening.

Divorce

The return of the bride wealth when divorce occurs did not occasion serious conflict in any of the cases I have information about. If the furniture is sold, the groom's parents expect to get the money paid for it, but if it is not, they will accept the chairs, tables, and pans and, even, not necessarily pursue every item bought.

Divorce is fairly common, especially for first marriages. I estimate that somewhat more than a third of first marriages are dissolved by divorce. It is substantially less common for subsequent marriages, and it is not common to find men or women who have been divorced more than twice. Divorce is generally viewed as an extremely unfortunate event that is, however, sometimes a necessity. One commonly hears people say, "Of the things God allows, He hates none more than divorce."

Nuclear Family Life

Nuclear family ties are close ties in all respects. The division of labor is clear and sharp. The mother/wife with the assistance of the family daughters (and, in most even moderately prosperous families, the family servant) cares for all household needs, and the father/husband, generally the only family member with paid employment, is the source of the family exchequer. In some families, there is rent-producing property belonging to either or both spouses adding to family income, and if there are children with paid jobs, they contribute most of their earnings until they marry. Even married children are expected to make some contribution toward the living expenses of their parents and dependent siblings and to help with the costs of educating the latter.

Socially, family members spend a good part of every day together. However, the women and younger children are in the house a good deal more than the men and older boys. The family takes its meals from the common kitchen, though in many families the male and female members do not actually eat together. The wife/mother or a daughter/sister brings food to the husband/father and sons/brothers who eat and leave the table (or, more traditionally, mat) in the living room, at which time the servers eat the remaining food, usually in the kitchen. In some families now, I was told, the whole group eats together, but I have never actually seen this and am told it is not common.

The separation of the sexes, an explicit value, leads to the nuclear family itself being separated for a good part of every day, and this is furthered by the sharp division of labor. Men are never to set foot in a kitchen. Swahili lore has it, a boy who goes into the kitchen after puberty will pay for it by having rain on his wedding day.

Family Activity

The most common joint family activity is talking together (44% of the families surveyed chose this as the main nuclear family activity; see chap. 5).

There is some constraint on fathers talking with daughters, and several informants have told me that until two or three decades ago, it was common for daughters to avoid any face-to-face contact with their fathers. Thus, daughters did not remain in the same room as their fathers and a daughter would only converse with her father by addressing him through the door from outside the room he was in.

Such avoidance is not common now, but there is still constraint so that, for example, when the family television is on, the daughters of the household usually sit together, often with the mother, on one side of the room while sons sit with their father on the other side. The separation of women from men affects not only the daughter but also the mother/wife. A grown, married woman typically and usually has a rich social life with her female kin and neighbors, but her movements are restricted and much of her time is spent at home or visiting in the homes of nearby kin and friends. Women venture out to buy their own clothing and make small purchases from the tiny food and sundries shops (called *reshun*) scattered throughout Old Town. The main shopping for groceries, meat, fish, and other household supplies is done by the men of the house.

The sons spend more time away from the family home than anyone else, playing with their male kin and neighbors when they are young and going off to school and work as they mature. The daughters spend a fair amount of time with their same sex kin and neighbors, but they are more restricted in what they do than their brothers are and one rarely sees girls and young women outside their houses.

Both boys and girls attend religious school (chuo, pl. *vyuo*) beginning at the age of 5 or so and generally attend for at least a year or two as they learn to read the Koran and to write, usually with limited ability, in Arabic. These schools are timed so that the older children can attend secular school, but many religious schools have long sessions on the days when the secular schools are closed.

Children all shinda (spend the day) with kin in other households, but this is of limited importance for boys who, although they continue to visit, mainly stop spending a whole day at the house of a kinsman when they are old enough to spend their time playing soccer and wandering around the neighborhood with other boys of their age. For girls, the days at the houses of kin are their main opportunity to leave the family home, and they generally continue this more-or-less supervised, daylong kin visiting until marriage.

The Division of Activity by Gender in the Family and Generally

The supervision of girls has become less strict in the 1980s than it was even in the 1970s. Many now go to the same secular schools that their brothers do, and some young women now get jobs in offices and shops after finishing school and before marriage. A few women continue working after marriage, but almost all stop paid employment when the first child is born. There is still, however, a good deal of concern about girls' activities on the part of their parents and grown siblings. The explicit reason for this is fear that the girl may indulge her sexual appetites before marriage. "Having a daughter," a middle-aged Swahili father told me, "is like having an egg in your hand. You cannot be careless for a minute without it being ruined forever."

Men and boys are free to roam the city as they wish but ideally should avoid bad company and late hours. Men and boys attend the mosque, go to work, chat with friends, and some—now a minority but formerly a much larger percentage—regularly attend small-scale men's gatherings (baraza) that generally take place at the same time and in the same location. The Swahili men understand themselves to be very sociable, and whether in a baraza or not, they stop to chat with kin, neighbors, and acquaintances whenever they see them. There was a very strong value on men "being known" among other men which still exists if, perhaps, somewhat less explicitly than I was told was the case some decades ago.

Men, like their wives, sisters, and daughters, however, are almost always at home at mealtimes. Houses are generally locked up at the completion of the evening prayer (isha, rarely later than 8:30), and the entire family retires early. It is quite rare to see middle-aged Swahili men on the streets after the last prayer, but small groups of Swahili young men can be seen on street corners chatting until 11:00 or, sometimes, a little later.

Other than chatting on the streets, the main activity outside the home is attending cinemas. There are two in Old Town which show mainly American and European films (preferred by many community members who attend films) and another showing exclusively Indian films which some Swahili attend. It is now fairly generally accepted for men and boys to go to cinemas, and some men even go with their wives. Conservatives view this attendance with something between caution and alarm, but that view seems less prevalent in the community at the end of the 1980s than it was at the beginning of the decade and earlier.

During the holy month of Ramadhan, the Old Town area is transformed. The streets, usually deserted in the early evening, teem with men and boys, and the usually darkened, quiet houses are full of music, talk, and life. Following the afternoon prayer (*magharibi*) when the sun goes down, everyone eats the first food of the day (*futari,* traditionally a date) and goes home to prepare for the main meal (*daku*), which is eaten sometime after the final prayer (isha) but generally at 10:30 or 11:00. Following the meal, people amuse themselves with games, music, or visiting with neighbors. The streets are full of men and boys chatting or playing checkers or cards (but not for money since gambling is forbidden in Islam), and women's voices ring from the houses. Some families spend this festive time together, but mainly the

men and women celebrate separately. After the brief sleep characteristic of
Ramadhan, some families eat a heavy breakfast to sustain them through the
day of fasting to come, but others sleep a bit longer and have only tea and
whatever snacks are available just before dawn and the reinstitution of the
fast.

It will be clear from this brief sketch of leisure activities that men and
women, boys and girls have quite different activities: the women's center in
the home and the men's outside. Nor is this only a matter of the separation
of the sexes. Proper men should go around visiting and be known to the community. Women should stay near their houses and those of their close kin.
Women do not veil their faces any longer, although it is only in the 1980s
that they have ceased doing so, but they should not be seen in public.

Employment

Save for the more conservative members of the community, it is not understood as wrong for women to have jobs outside the home. But, in fact, few
have. In part, this is because of the scarcity of employment combined with
a general disinclination to hire women, and, in part, it is due to the restrictions
of the job market where few occupations save nursing, teaching, and office
work are open to women. Except for baby nurses (aya), even house servants
are generally men, and although Swahili would not consider accepting such
jobs, this restriction suggests how limited women's employment opportunities
are.

With virtually no exceptions, Swahili men have a job, are looking for one,
or are retired from one. This means that while women's lives tend to focus
around the home and immediate neighborhood, men's are centered outside
the home and, often, include employment that is beyond not only the home
and neighborhood but also the community.

The Central Place
of the Nuclear Family

For women and their children, the nuclear family is obviously the vital
center of their lives. They are together much of the time, cooperate in much
of what is most important to each of them, and are united by strong emotional
bonds. For men, the situation is less of a piece. Men have few close ties, but
the closest of all are with their wives (see chap. 10). Their relations with their
children, especially their sons, can be rather distant, and their relations with
both sons and daughters are not close in comparison with those between the
mother and children. Still, these are the closest relations the men have from

an emotional perspective and the most responsible from a material and social perspective.

We have seen that neighbors and nonnuclear family kin play crucial parts in people's lives, but this does not diminish the role the nuclear family plays. Much of what all group members do is either with other nuclear family members or, as regards men's work, viewed as largely in the interests of those members. Members are in constant contact with one another and are interested in almost everything done or happening to any of the others.

In nuclear families that do not break up through divorce, one would assume that members' activities are guided by similar understandings about the way the family life is and how it ought to be. If the members did not share these beliefs and values initially—as when a couple first marries and as children grow up—there is ample opportunity for mutual socialization, so that the importance of cultural sharing is accompanied by what may be a unique opportunity to achieve that sharing.

Thus, the cultural elements concerning this group, it would seem, are at least as likely to be shared among its members as most others. In the following chapter, the extent of this sharing will be examined and it will be shown that it is, in fact, substantially less than complete.

5

Understanding Is Like Hair

Limited Cultural Sharing and the
Inappropriateness of "All by All" and
"Some by Some" Models for Swahili Culture

Akili ni nywele, kila mmoja ana zake: Understanding is [like] hair, each one has his [own] (i.e., people's views of everything differ).

There can be no question that nuclear family life works among the Swahili. Some families are broken by divorce or death. Some are hindered by endemic conflict. But most members of this community spend their lives within the framework of the nuclear family, beginning with the one founded by their parents and continuing with the one they found themselves. The nuclear family is not all there is in the lives of the members of this group, but it plays a central role for almost all of them.

Introduction

Given this importance, the cultural elements concerned with nuclear family relationships and operation would seem at least as likely to be shared among its members as most other sets of understandings would in this or other sorts of groupings. If culture serves as the basis for group life—and if it does not, it is more than difficult to think what does—it unquestionably serves as the basis for the Swahili nuclear family. To the extent that culture's role in social life depends on sharing, it seems justifiable to expect that as much sharing would be found in the Swahili nuclear family as would be found in most other groups.

In this chapter, I examine the extent of sharing in Swahili nuclear families. This examination assesses the extent of sharing of cultural elements concerned with nuclear family life and relations among all Swahili ("all by all" sharing) and the extent of sharing among individuals belonging to the same nuclear families and among members of the same statuses. The theoretical foundation for this has been adumbrated in chapter 1 and will become clearer as the data are presented.

It will be shown that three-eights of the beliefs, values, and procedures concerning nuclear family members, their relationships, and the group as a whole are not shared among members of the same nuclear family and that almost half of these cultural elements are not shared among community members who belong to different families. To simplify a bit, the operative (if often disavowed) view of culture and its operation used by social scientists is that people get along with one another and take advantage of the traditional understandings and values that make life possible through sharing these cultural elements with those around them. This sharing was once viewed as greater in "traditional" and "small-scale" societies than in urban and industrial societies, but everywhere it was sufficient to allow explanation to be based on the undoubted similiarity in belief and values group members hold. In "complex" societies, the similarity was obscured by variation having limited effect on such groups as families, but in "simple" societies, the similarity is held to be manifest and easily seen. Durkheim's (1961:18) view regarding religion was not different from many others views of culture in general:

> . . . the variations of ritual, the multiplicity of groups and the diversity of individuals [makes] the fundamental states characteristic of religious mentality . . . [difficult to find]. . . . Things are quite different in the lower societies. The slighter development of individuality, the small extension of the group, the homogeneity of external circumstances, all contributes to reducing the differences and variations to a minimum. The group has an intellectual and moral conformity of which we find but rare examples in the more advanced societies. Everything is common to all.

The classical and still powerfully influential view is that social life must be understood in the light of all, or at least all *relevant,* beliefs and values being uniformly shared among all group members. As was noted in chapter 1, a number of students of culture have shown that culture is *not,* in fact, universally shared. These findings have not, however, displaced the general explanation of culture's effectiveness as due to "shared beliefs and values."

As Holland (1987a:234) points out, some of what appears to be lack of sharing may not really be that but rather contextual differences, differences in expression, or simply errors. But the existence of these false appearances of variation does not gainsay the results of the growing number of studies that show real differences in the beliefs and values held by members of the same group. As seen in the proverb that opens this chapter, the Swahili themselves clearly recognize differences in the understandings held by individuals even if not all social scientists do.

The fact that sharing is limited is true not only of the Swahili but also of other groups, including four directly compared with the Swahili as concerns the culture of nuclear family life (Swartz 1982*a*). These limitations, more-over, are not limited to the complete inventory of a group's culture but also occur as concerns sharing among members of the same status categories. This fact presents difficulties to the position, first advanced by Ralph Linton (1936) in his formulation of "status" and "role," that regardless of limits in general sharing, sharing within social categories was sufficient to account for culture's effectiveness.

Individuals may not, according to this view, share everything with every-one else, but those with the same rights and responsibilities (i.e., the members of the same status) share the cultural elements concerning those rights and responsibilities. Put otherwise, this position holds that the members of the same status do share the cultural elements concerned with that status with one another even if these elements are not completely shared with those in differ-ent statuses. To be concrete, this view holds that mothers may not share all the beliefs and values concerning being a father, but the mothers do share with one another the cultural elements concerning being a mother.

Rather startlingly, the data presented here and elsewhere (Swartz 1982*a*) suggest that even this modified view of sharing is inaccurate and, therefore, cannot be used as the basis for understanding the ways culture works. It would not be startling to find that mothers share the cultural elements concerned with the father status less than fathers do, but it is contrary to the Linton view of status to find that sharing among mothers is a good deal less than complete even as concerns the understandings directly involving and concerning the mother status itself. In fact, in many cases, sharing among individuals *not* belonging to a status about issues concerning the status is greater than sharing by status members.

This suggests that a sound view of culture's operation needs to proceed not only from an understanding of the limits in cultural sharing generally but also with attention to the incomplete sharing even among members of the same statuses.

"Status"

"Status" is a key concept in the understanding of culture's operation. As noted earlier, a status is taken to be a collection of three distinguishable sorts of shared understandings (i.e., cultural elements). The sort concerning the distinguishing characteristics of category members is called "identifying un-derstandings." The understandings about how category members are expected to act and how they expect others to act toward them in their capacity as cat-egory members are called "expectations," and it is important to note that these may concern quite specific behaviors (e.g., mothers cook food at mealtimes) as well as very broad ones (e.g., mothers are concerned with the welfare of their sons and daughters and act accordingly).

A final sort of status component can be called "salience understandings." These concern which status or statuses (vis-à-vis others) properly serve as a guide for behavior in particular situations and, when more than one status is involved, which ones are appropriate with what relative importance in guiding behavior.

It is important that "status" refers to nothing but a complex of cultural elements. As will be seen, it is through statuses that culture's constituent parts come to bear on the problems and opportunities of life (personal as well as social) of those who share the parts. Later, it will be shown that despite their purely cultural contents, statuses have an effect on behavior separate from that of the culture that constitutes them.

Measuring Cultural Sharing

There are two serious problems involved in the assessment of the extent of cultural sharing. They are doubtlessly part of the reason for the fact that only limited attempts to make this assessment have been carried out since Roberts's (1951) pioneering effort.

First, what it is, exactly, that actors do or do not share needs to be specified. If this difficulty is overcome, there remains the problem of determining whether this sharing is present. Put otherwise, how can we isolate the units that make up culture, and how can we determine whether these units are shared or not? Cognitive anthropologists have made progress in dealing with these two related problems (e.g., Berlin and Kay 1969). I follow one of their leads by keeping the immediate scope of investigation narrow and mainly limited to data that are readily quantified.

In the study focused on this issue (Swartz 1982a), I took, of necessity, a provisional and partial approach to the two problems just noted. In this approach, the units of culture are identified with responses to items on a questionnaire (see Appendix and ibid., 335–338). Without doubt there are serious problems in taking responses to questionnaire items as equivalent to cultural elements. In my 1982 study, I used the same multiple-choice questionnaire (appropriately translated) for the Swahili and the other four European and American communities where the interviewing was done.

To take an obvious problem, it is quite possible that what I intended as different items are, in fact, reflections of a single cultural element and that what was a separate element of culture in one of the groups where we worked was not in another. The questionnaire was devoted entirely to questions concerned with nuclear family life. It asked informants to choose among alternatives concerned with issues—61 in all—such as who the family peacemaker was, how children should treat their aged parents, and where most children live after they marry. The status of these questions as cultural elements has to remain in doubt, and the only basis for treating them as elements is pragmatic: if the problem of cultural sharing and cultural dynamics is to be studied directly, the effort must begin even if all the problems in making the study have not been solved.

A similar rationale was used to justify the approach to cultural sharing that was used. This approach is to take cultural sharing as present when two informants chose the same response to a question. A sharing coefficient was calculated based on the number of questionnaire items on which two informants made the same response as compared to the total number of responses from the two minus the number of identical responses according to the following formula:

$$\frac{\text{Same answers}}{(\text{Number of questions asked}) - (\text{Same answers})}$$

So, for example, if two informants answering sixty-one questions each chose the same responses on all of them (61/122–61), they would have a sharing coefficient of 1.00.

It is true, of course, that people can have some—even a good deal—of cultural sharing concerning the subject of a question without choosing the same response and that they can choose the same response without much cultural sharing. Nevertheless, the sharing coefficient as defined for the study gives some approximation of what two actors share on the issues they are asked about, and there is no reason to believe that the responses are systematically biased toward either error.

For the Swahili (and the other four groups studied), we interviewed only people who belonged to families that met the following conditions: (1) they contained a wife and a husband who lived together at the time of the interview; (2) the spouses considered themselves and were considered by their child or children as the natural parents of the child or children included in the study; (3) the spouses had at least one child twelve years of age or older who lived with them and who had never been married. We inteviewed three members of each family meeting the above conditions in each society. We chose this number because it was the largest number of interviews we found it practical to get from a particular family while at the same time being large enough to allow us some measure of intrafamilial sharing across generational and sex, as well as status, divisions. The five-society study aimed at dividing each community's families equally between families represented by two children (siblings) and a parent and families represented by two parents (spouses) and a child (see table 3).[1]

The coefficient of sharing for the total sample was obtained by comparing the responses of each member of the sample from that society to those of every other and taking the mean of all those comparisons. This latter coefficient is not really representative of the whole Mombasa Swahili community,

Table 3.   Some Characteristics of the Sample

Number of		Families with	
Males	*Females*	*2 parents,* *1 child*	*2 children,* *1 parent*
25	26	9	8

even allowing for the nonrandom sample (see below), because only individuals belonging to the sorts of families meeting our criteria are included. Thus there is not representation of adults who live alone or with others who are neither parents nor spouses or married people having no children or whose children are all either below twelve or married.

Because of these exclusions, the total sample as constituted is probably more similar to the selected family groups than to a more fully representative sample of the society as a whole. Therefore, the differences in sharing found in the sample as a whole and sharing found within families are probably understatements of the true differences in sharing within families and sharing among community members from different families (i.e., community as a whole). Since the objective is to examine the hypothesis that the level of sharing of all cultural elements is high enough to serve as a (perhaps *the*) main source of culture's ability to function as the basis for social life in functioning groups, an overstatement of sharing is more acceptable than an understatement that might wrongly falsify the hypothesis.

As indicated above, the families studied were not randomly selected. A sample based on such selection was not possible because of the demands interviewing made on the families and because of the widespread reluctance to discuss even the most distant family matters with nonmembers. We compensated for this as much as possible by choosing families so that there were representatives of the various mitaa (neighborhoods) and the range of socioeconomic and educational standings.

It should be noted that there was a difficulty in identifying families that considered themselves and were considered Swahili which was not properly resolved until the data had been collected. Because of complexities concerning the affiliations of the occupants of statuses of members of families whose rather recent forebears came from the Persian Gulf area as well as of members of families who are suspected of having slave ancestors, the initial decision (made before I had discovered the extent and profundity of the status problems as concerns group membership) to include members of families whom Swahili interviewers decided belonged to the Swahili community proved unacceptable. Among the families included by interviewers were some, I discovered, that undoubted community members did not accept as "true" or "full" members.

To try to deal with this problem, I assembled a panel of four middle-aged Swahili informants well acquainted with all sections of the group. Each of these men (mature women are difficult to employ for private sessions with other male informants and a male researcher) was, without doubt, viewed by others as a member of the community and of one of its long-established constituent families. These informants examined the names and other demographic data (but nothing else) collected from families interviewed and eliminated families they considered noncommunity members (i.e., considered members of other ethnic groups) with the result that the Mombasa Swahili are represented by only seventeen families despite data having been originally collected from thirty. All results of interviews here draw only on the seventeen undoubted member families.

It may also be that community members descended from fairly recent Arab immigrants are underrepresented if they told interviewers they were not Swahili. This is unlikely, however, since the interviewing was done by four young Swahili (three men, one woman) who consistently erred on the side of including doubtful community members. Moreover, some of those included are known by me to claim descent from Omani and Yemeni forebears who emigrated relatively recently.

The four societies compared with the Swahili in the original study need not be examined or discussed at length here. The characteristics of these families and the data collected from them are reported in the original paper, which presents the findings regarding cultural sharing from all five societies, including the Swahili, and compares the results along the dimensions to be examined here (see Swartz 1982a).

The Limits in the Amount of Family Culture Shared by Family Members and Community Members from Different Families

Despite the difficulties in this approach to studying cultural sharing, it produces findings that can provide a starting point for further investigation in a largely neglected area of empirical research. It is not that the results of this study are beyond doubt but, rather, that they give indications of having some validity.

Some of the findings are what would be expected: members of the same family share more of the understandings concerned with family life and relations than those belonging to different families (table 4A below). Rather less expected is the size of the difference between sharing among same family

Table 4.   Sharing Coefficients for Questions on "Family Culture"

A. *Mean Sharing within Families and in the Sample as a Whole*

| | For sample as a whole |
Within families	(i.e., different families)
.473	.317

B. *Mean Sharing within Status Categories (Different Families)*

Categories			
Mothers	Fathers	Sons	Daughters
.327	.342	.312	.287

C. *Mean Sharing in Pairs within Families*

Fa-Mo	Fa-Son	Fa-Da	Mo-So	Mo-Da	Ch-Ch
.606	.484	.728	.414	.569	.463

members and sharing in the community generally. Table 4 shows that within the family about five-eighths of the items (0.454 would be 5/8, 0.600 would be 3/4) are shared, while among members of different families in this long-enduring, well-integrated, and traditional community, less than half of all the items (0.333 would be 1/2) are shared.

The fact that cultural sharing is a good deal less than complete among members of the same families and also among community members is probably in accord with the assumption, now widely held, that "all by all" sharing does not occur. It may be, however, that its absence in so small and highly integrated a group as the nuclear family may carry this a bit farther than is generally envisaged.

The nuclear family was chosen as the venue for studying the role of cultural sharing in Swahili social life because it is a crucial element in this society and an undoubtedly effective group as concerns retaining its members and meeting an acceptable (to members) proportion of their social, emotional, and material needs. Given the stability and endurance of the families studied and the broad array and significance for members of the tasks taken care of within it, it is clearly warranted to view the culture of this group (i.e., the beliefs, values, and procedural understandings concerned with its tasks and relationships) as effective. If the effectiveness of culture is taken to depend on the extent to which its constituent elements are shared, there would be every reason to expect a level of sharing here about as high as would be found among the members of any group whose activities cover a broad scope of life.

It is striking, therefore, that three-eighths of the cultural elements directly concerned with family life and relationships (as represented by our questionnaire) are nevertheless unshared among members of functioning, continuing families. This limited sharing may be less than surprising, but the fact that the sample includes only members of active, continuing families, all of whom are concerned with family life and relationships on a daily basis, makes it somewhat more interesting.

The idea that there is *a* Swahili family culture is not supported by the findings in table 4, if what is meant by "family culture" is a single set of generally shared cultural elements concerned with family life and relations. The ability to explain culture's effectiveness as the basis for Swahili family life (and the results from the other four societies are quite similar in this; see Swartz 1982*a*) as a consequence of "shared beliefs and values" is put into question by these findings and made more doubtful yet by findings reported elsewhere here, especially in chapter 9.

Are the Swahili a "Homogeneous Society"?

Before turning to more detailed examinations of who shares at higher and lower levels with whom, it is useful to consider an issue of broad importance both theoretically and ethnographically: do the Swahili comprise a "homogeneous group" with its culture evenly shared among group members regardless of membership in such subgroups as families? If this were so, it could be argued that a distinction between "homogeneous" and "heterogeneous" (or at least less homogeneous) societies is an important consideration in how culture operates. Whatever may be found about culture's operation for the Swahili would quite possibly be different from what would be found in nonhomogeneous societies.

The question, then, is whether or not the Swahili give evidence of being more homogeneous in cultural sharing than other societies that differ in composition from the Swahili. Some indication of the answer to this can be found by comparing Swahili cultural sharing to that of two other groups examined as part of my earlier study (Swartz 1982*a*). Unlike the Swahili, these two groups are made up of ethnically diverse families, at least some of whose members had migrated to their current homes from other areas. Also unlike the Swahili, most family members in these other two groups associated with nonnuclear family kin only occasionally or rarely. Compared to the other two groups that experience the isolation of families common to the urban life in the Euro-American setting, the Swahili community is much more nearly a "traditional society" whose culture might be expected to be more "homogeneous."[2]

Despite having the traits of a "traditional society," table 5A shows that as concerns cultural sharing, the Swahili are not as "homogeneous" as might be expected. Although the Swahili family members do share with one another more than same family members do in the other two groups, La Jolla, one of the "heterogeneous" groups, shows more sharing among people from different families ("Total Sample"). This hints that viewing the Swahili as distinctly more homogeneous culturally than the other two groups is not fully warranted. The evidence becomes stronger with examination of table 5B.

Here we see the difference between family and group-wide sharing is substantially greater for the Mombasa Swahili than for either La Jolla or Kahl. This is just the reverse of what would be expected if Mombasa's homogeneity were reflected in a unformity of cultural sharing greater than that found in the other, more heterogeneous groups.

Extent of Sharing within the Family versus Extent of Total Group Sharing

Table 5C and 5D shows that the level of cultural sharing within the family is more distinctive of the Swahili than the level of cultural sharing within the community at large. That is, the differences between the Swahili and the other two groups are larger with respect to internal family sharing than with respect to total group sharing. Further, if these two sets of differences are compared to the differences between internal family and total group sharing in table 5B, it can be seen that the level of sharing for the Swahili community is more similar to the levels of sharing in the two other societies than Swahili communitywide sharing is to Swahili famiiy sharing.

This finding may be counterintuitive in that interaction, both within families and in the wider community, seemingly would act to increase levels of sharing. Yet the data here show that groups with no interaction among their members (i.e., groups in three widely separated parts of the globe) are more similar in levels of sharing than either coresident families or whole communities whose members interact. A hypothesis that might explain this is that the range of sharing associated with working societies (i.e., those still in existence and whose members are not all leaving in the immediate future) is narrower than the range associated with working families.

Some families, this hypothesis suggests, get along with quite limited sharing while others have substantially more, and this wide range is present in all the societies included in this study. Direct experience with Swahili families

Table 5. *Mean Coefficients of Cultural Sharing within Families and in Total Samples for Swahili and Two Other Groups and Comparisons within and between Groups*

A. Levels of Sharing Within Families and for Total Samples

Mean Sharing within	Swahili	Kahl	La Jolla
Nuclear family	.473	.377	.405
Total sample	.317	.305	.325

B. Differences for Each Group between Sharing within Families and in Total Samples

	Swahili	Kahl	La Jolla
	.156	.072	.080

C. Differences between Swahili Internal Family Sharing and Internal Family Sharing in the Two Other Groups

	Swahili	Kahl	La Jolla
Swahili	–	.060	.068
Kahl	.060	–	.052
La Jolla	.068	.052	–

D. Differences between Swahili Total Sample Sharing and Total Sample Sharing in the Two Other Groups

	Swahili	Kahl	La Jolla
Swahili	–	.012	.008
Kahl	.012	–	.020
La Jolla	.008	.020	–

suggests that some families get along quite well (carry out household activities, distribute money and goods, have members who seem reasonably satisfied with one another, etc.) on the basis of rather limited—both in scope and intensity—interaction. The members of these families talk to one another less, stay around one another less, and restrict interaction when it occurs. Other Swahili families are less restrained: they interact more and do so more unrestrictedly. But the latter families "work" quite as well as the former do in keeping together and accomplishing their members' ends.

At the community level, however, there is a narrower variation brought about by the relatively low limit on the level of sharing that *can* be attained in so large and diverse a group and the relatively high "floor" on what must be present if a group is to continue operating. The minimum needed for social continuation is, I suspect, largely made up of "tokens," which will be discussed in chapter 6, and status identifiers, which will discussed in chapter 7.

Members of different families have little need, or for that matter, opportunity, to deal with one another in nuclear family statuses. There is some pressure to be seen in conversations and to use relationship terms to praise or condemn (see chap. 7) people belonging to different families, and this may represent the basis for some part of the rather consistent, and low, level of sharing of family culture found among people from different Swahili families (and the comparison groups as well). Another part of societywide sharing is found in the agreement about who is what in the family, that is, what categories of people are found in households and who fits in them.

Less Sharing among Members of the Same Named Statuses than among Fellow Family Members with Different Family Statuses

As noted earlier, one of the first—and still one of the few—alternatives to the view that everyone in a society shares all culture with everyone else is the view that culture is distributed according to status membership. Linton (1936:113–115) holds that members of the same status category share more with one another—especially as concerns matters directly affecting the status—than they do with members of their society who do not belong to the status category in question. This view is probably more nearly in accord with observations of behavior than is the one that holds that all culture is shared by everyone. Nevertheless, there are a number of questions about sharing within statuses that can usefully be examined even if only with the limited data obtaining with questionnaires. Table 6 gives the sharing coefficients for the sample as a whole, within the families, and for the four basic family status categories.

Table 6.   Mean Sharing Coefficients within Status Categories

A. Mean Sharing	Swahili	Kahl	La Jolla
Within total sample	.317	.305	.325
Within families	.473	.377	.405

B. Mean Sharing in Status Categories	Swahili	Kahl	La Jolla
Mother's category	.327	.319	.335
Father's category	.342	.332	.333
Sons' category	.312	.288	.326
Daughters' category	.287	.276	.328

By making comparisons among these, it is possible to consider a question of basic importance to the place of statuses as foci of cultural distribution: whether members of a given status share more with one another than with fellow community members in different statuses. For the family, the question is, do, for example, mothers share more of the understandings concerning family life with other members than they do with members of their own families given that the latter are not mothers?

Table 6 shows that for the Swahili and the comparison groups, the coefficients for sharing within the designated status categories (i.e., mother, father, etc.) are uniformly lower than those for sharing within families without regard to internal status differences. That is, members of the same family share more of the total family culture despite belonging to different statuses than do members of the same statuses who belong to different families. According to the sign test, this lesser sharing among members of the same status category as compared to sharing within the family is significant for the Swahili, and the other two groups, at the 0.01 level.

"Family Member" as a Status

This lesser sharing among members of the same named status is not obviously consistent with views of culture's operation that depend, as Linton's does, on the assumption that statuses are always and uniformly the centers of sharing of the cultural elements that concern the activities involving status category members as such. The findings here suggest that for family affairs, sharing is greatest among family group members without regard to status differences within the group. This suggests that for the family, at least the part played by internal, differentiated statuses has been overemphasized and the part played by the status "family member" underestimated. This point is an important one because the data in table 6 indicate that the statuses that both group members and anthropologists think of as making up the family (i.e., mother, father, daughter, son) are less influential as concerns sharing family culture than the less obviously marked status, "family member."[3]

The fact that family members share more of family culture with one another than they do with members of their particular statuses within the family does not mean that these latter statuses play no part in the distribution of culture. What it means is that the nature of the part played by statuses in bringing particular cultural elements into different situations cannot be assumed and may be different in uniformity for different statuses. Named statuses are surely involved in cultural distribution through greater sharing of certain understandings within the status than in other statuses, but this is not necessarily so for all understandings with all statuses.

Even with respect to total family culture, there are some differences in sharing associated with statuses other than family member. Table 6 indicates that for the Swahili, sharing among mothers and also among fathers is significantly greater (at the 0.01 level according to the sign test) than sharing among unrelated members of the same society but that other statuses do not exhibit this same distinctive level of sharing. The fact that this is true for mothers but not fathers in the two comparison societies is suggestive of the variation in the part particular statuses play as foci of sharing in different groups. Mothers and fathers from different families do not share as much with one another as members of the same family do, but they do share more within their statuses than unrelated people from different families ("Total Sample") do.

This may indicate that these statuses play a distinctive part in Swahili family and community life in that they are particularly important in making family life more similar in different families than it would otherwise be. In simply understanding things more as their counterparts in other families do, the parents exert a homogenizing influence quite apart from whatever their specific behaviors guided by those understandings may be.

This implies that the basis for Swahili society is better understood if, in addition to the distinctive expectations and saliences of statuses, there is also information about the extent of sharing within those statuses. Currently used views of cultural distribution seem to assume that statuses are highly similar in the uniformity of their members' sharing of the elements associated with them, but evidence here suggests that some statuses involve more uniformity (i.e., sharing) in members' understandings and others involve much less.

It may be that statuses have levels of sharing quite as characteristic of them as are the particular elements of culture they share. Mothers may be the main or only actors in a society who have the understandings needed, for example, to deal with distraught children in ways that will be generally approved, but it may be equally important to the way the society's family culture works that it is mothers who share more of it across family lines rather than do daughters or fathers. Similarly, if there were a society in which no internally differentiated status had members who shared more with their counterparts in other families (and none of the three here are like this), that would probably be associated with a family culture working quite differently from one in which there was at least one status with greater cross-family sharing regardless of what that status was.

The clearest way in which sharing beyond the family's boundaries can influence the culture of the broader group is through the sharers exerting similar influences in their different families and thereby bringing about some pressure toward general uniformity. Sharing culture with fellow status category members in other families need not lead to pressures for homogeneity, but it does provide a necessary base for such pressures.

It also provides a possible base for conflict. This would be found in a family where the father and mother share more with fathers and mothers in other families than they do with group members generally, while sons and daughters do not have the same higher sharing with their counterparts in other families. In many Swahili families, the children, especially sons, label their parents as "old-fashioned" and "too strict." In some part, this may be because the parents are likeliest to share what is identified with tradition and, given the substantial sharing between spouses, bring the children to feel subject to old-fashioned treatment. The children, often characterized by parents as "difficult," need share little with one another or the parents to gain that characterization and to oppose the parents' views.

Status Membership and the Sharing of Status Culture

Members of the various named statuses in the family have been seen to share less of total family culture as represented by all the items on the questionnaire than do those in what might be called the "same family member" status. It would seem, however, that if what is measured is sharing of the cultural elements directly concerned with their own status and its relationships, the members of any status category could hardly fail to share more than others share those same elements.

Since fathers and mothers from different families share more across family boundaries than members of other family statuses do, an examination of their sharing provides a useful test of the hypothesis that understandings concerning statuses are shared more fully by those who are classified in those statuses than by those who are not.

Tables 7 and 8 present the results of comparing informants' responses on questionnaire items (all available in Swartz 1982a:335–338) concerned with the mother/wife and the father/husband statuses, respectively. Table 7 concerns the elements that make up what can be called "the mother/wife scale." This scale is simply a list of questions concerning beliefs and values bearing on the mother/wife's behavior. It has five component questions, and the comparable scale for father/husbands has the same number.

The items in the two scales differ only in their subject, with each focusing on the status concerned. Thus, one question in each scale asks whether or not wives advise husbands (for the mother/wife scale) or husbands advise wives (for the father/husband scale) about the work the husband or wife (respectively) does; another asks who wives (or husbands) consult when something is worrying them; another asks whether or not most wives (or husbands) are happy in their marriages; and the final one asks how much fathers (or mothers) take into account the interests and wants of other family members in what the fathers (or mothers) do.

Obviously, the questions in these scales are removed from behavioral reality, but taking the scales as wholes, it seems reasonable to argue that if members of a status do share more of the cultural elements concerning their status with one another than they do with members of other statuses, this will be seen in the results of tabulating responses to these questions. In fact, such status-centered sharing is not what is found for either the father or the mother status.

In Part A of tables 7 and 8 are the coefficients of sharing for the mother/wife and father/husband scales among pairs outside the family (i.e., "Total Sample"). If it is true that sharing of cultural elements concerned with a status is at a higher level within that status, table 7 would be expected to show that the pairs of mothers (Mo-Mo) have the highest coefficients and table 8 would show that the pairs of fathers (Fa-Fa) have the highest coefficient.

In Part A of table 7, it can be seen that neither for the Swahili nor for the comparison groups do mothers have the highest sharing coefficient for the mother/wife scale. Part A of table 8 shows that fathers have the highest sharing coefficients for the father/husband scale in one of the comparison groups but the lowest coefficient in the other and somewhere in the middle for the Swahili. In neither case does the data strongly support the Linton-derived hypothesis that those classified in a status category share items directly concerned with their own status at a substantially higher level than do those in other categories.

Thus, for both mothers and fathers, our data drawn from comparisons among members of the same societies but different families fail to show a higher level of sharing among those actors classified in the same status category even when the elements in question are all directly concerned with that status.

Table 7. *Sharing Coefficients for the Mother/Wife Scale Pairs Inside the Family and Outside the Family*

A. *Outside Family Sharing*

Total sample pairs	Swahili	Kahl	La Jolla
Fa-Fa	.361	.325	.266
Fa-Mo	.348	.307	.307
Fa-So	.361	.281	.286
Fa-Da	.335	.262	.311
Mo-Mo	.337	.291	.341
Mo-So	.370	.249	.334
Mo-Da	.347	.235	.353
So-So	.368	.225	.316
So-Da	.365	.231	.337
Da-Da	.299	.250	.337

Pairs with highest and lowest sharing coefficients

Highest	Mo-So	Fa-Fa	Mo-Da
Lowest	Da-Da	So-Da	Fa-Fa

B. *Inside Family Sharing*

Family Pairs	Swahili	Kahl	La Jolla
Fa-Mo	.606	.462	.381
Fa-So	.484	.323	.294
Fa-Da	.728	.270	.296
Mo-So	.414	.329	.397
Mo-Da	.569	.290	.449
Ch-Ch	.463	*	.445

Pairs with highest and lowest sharing coefficients

Highest	Mo-Da	Mo-Da	Fa-Da
Lowest	Fa-Da	Mo-So	Mo-So

* See note, table 8 below.

Table 8. *Sharing Coefficients for the Father-Husband Scale by Pairs Inside the Family and Outside the Family*

A. Outside Family Sharing

Total sample pairs	Swahili	Kahl	La Jolla
Fa-Fa	.380	.328	.310
Fa-Mo	.405	.314	.350
Fa-So	.330	.302	.311
Fa-Da	.369	.245	.329
Mo-Mo	.427	.296	.367
Mo-So	.361	.288	.333
Mo-Da	.383	.230	.345
So-So	.315	.276	.321
So-Da	.353	.245	.324
Da-Da	.370	.207	.321

Pairs with highest and lowest sharing coefficients

Highest	Mo-Mo	Fa-Fa	Mo-Mo
Lowest	So-So	Da-Da	Fa-Fa

B. Inside Family Sharing

Family Pairs	Swahili	Kahl	La Jolla
Fa-Mo	.606	.462	.381
Fa-So	.484	.323	.294
Fa-Da	.728	.270	.296
Mo-So	.414	.329	.397
Mo-Da	.569	.290	.449
Ch-Ch	.483	*	.445

Pairs with highest and lowest sharing coefficients

Highest	Fa-Da	Fa-Mo	Mo-Da
Lowest	Mo-So	Fa-Da	Fa-So

*The number of two child, one parent families in the Kahl sample was too small to allow this coefficient to be calculated.

Family statuses may well be quite different from such technically focused statuses as surgeon, potter, or navigator, among whose members we would expect far more sharing of the cultural elements directly concerned with the status than among nonmembers. The fact that there are *any* statuses whose members do not clearly share cultural elements concerning the statuses at a higher level than nonmembers is striking and the additional fact that these statuses are part of so broadly important a group as the nuclear family makes the finding even more challenging.

However distinctive the mother and father statuses may (or may not) be as concerns sharing, the data collected for this study do seem to raise serious doubts about the fruitfulness of continuing to assume that all statuses are equally uniform foci for cultural sharing with all that entails for the way culture operates as a guide to social life. The role of statuses in cultural distribution has long been taken as a central one and as the main alternative to an all by all model of cultural sharing. This alternative model, some by some, has received little empirical attention since Linton introduced it, although work by Holland (1985, 1987a) provides a notable contribution. The indications from this study, and they are in accord with Holland's findings, are that, useful as it is, it requires a good deal of elaboration and modification if it is to serve as an adequate basis for understanding culture's operation.

It is not that statuses have no role in the distribution of culture but rather what role they have and how they can function with only limited sharing among those who occupy them requires examination. Even granting that all cultural items shared among some members of a group are not necessarily shared among all group members, we still are called on to account for the finding that classification together in a status does not ensure a high level of sharing of even the cultural elements concerned with that status.

As noted in chapter 1, the all by all model of cultural sharing is no longer respectable, and Holland's work together with the findings here suggest that even the some by some model (i.e., the portion of the group's total cultural inventory which concerns the operation of a status is shared by those who occupy the status) cannot be used with confidence.

The fact that the understandings concerning statuses are by no means uniformly shared among the occupants of the statuses in question throws into doubt some aspects of the view formulated by Goodenough (1965) and elaborated by Keesing (1970) that if we fully grasp the schemata in the minds of status occupants, we will have most or all of the basis for understanding how culture operates as the basis for social life.

Important as the distribution of culture by statuses is, recognizing its existence by no means provides all—or even most—of the answers to the question, how does culture work as the basis for social life if it is only partially shared? The data just considered suggest that not only is there substantial variation in the general sharing of culture but there are also important differences in sharing among the occupants of the same status even as concerns those statuses directly.

Relationships: Do Participants Share Their Culture More?

One area of culture that has not yet been considered and that might provide the expected support for the idea that status members share more among themselves than with others remains to be examined: relationships between members of different statuses. The scales for mothers and for fathers concern elements dealing with what the status category member says he or she does, values, or believes, but examining elements concerned with joint or reciprocal activities involving relationships between members of different status categories might produce results more in accord with conventional theoretical assumptions concerning status membership and cultural sharing.

Table 9 reports the sharing of answers to questions concerning the relations between parents and children. There are ten such questions, and together they form the parent-child relationship scale. The questions in the scale ask about such things as informants' beliefs about how jointly owning property affects parent-child relations; how best to avoid parent-child conflict and deal with difficult problems; whether parents and children love one another; and what sorts of things parents and children do together (Swartz 1982a:336–338).

Part A reports sharing on the parent-child scale among informants from different families. This sharing outside of the family shows that for the Swahili, same generation pairs are about as high in sharing as cross-generation pairs are so that the relationships seemingly subject to understandings concerning parent-child relations fail to show consistently higher sharing than other relationships do.

These findings are particularly noteworthy since, as our earlier examinations showed, those assigned to status categories failed to share at distinctively high levels either general family culture or the cultural elements concerning their own statuses. The absence of particularly high-level sharing in statuses and relationships where it would be expected given the Linton view of how statuses operate will be discussed below. For now, the point is simply that unrelated members of the participant statuses in the parent-child relationship do not share our scale for that relationship at a notably high level.

Part B of table 9 presents data on sharing within the family, and it, too, offers little support for the idea that the participants in a relationship share culture concerned with that relationship at a uniquely high level. For the Swahili, and the comparison groups, a parent-child pair is the one that shares the relationship scale at the highest level, but for one of the comparison groups, it is a parent-child pair that shares at the lowest level.

Table 9. *Sharing Coefficients for the Parent-Child Relationship Scale Inside the Family and Outside the Family*

A. Outside Family Sharing Coefficients

Total sample pairs	Swahili	Kahl	La Jolla
Fa-Fa	.651	.618	.585
Fa-Mo	.630	.645	.598
Fa-So	.648	.628	.606
Fa-Da	.602	.610	.617
Mo-Mo	.602	.675	.628
Mo-So	.625	.655	.648
Mo-Da	.596	.634	.650
So-So	.654	.634	.666
So-Da	.632	.616	.658
Da-Da	.586	.586	.674

Pairs with highest and lowest sharing coefficients

Highest	Fa-Fa	Mo-Mo	Da-Da
Lowest	Da-Da	Da-Da	Fa-Fa

B. Inside Family Sharing Coefficients

Family Pairs	Swahili	Kahl	La Jolla
Fa-Mo	.749	.738	.681
Fa-So	.710	.677	.685
Mo-Da	.788	.590	.566
Mo-So	.762	.692	.689
Ch-Ch	.698	*	.690

Pairs with highest and lowest sharing coefficients

Highest	Mo-Da	Fa-Mo	Ch-Ch
Lowest	Ch-Ch	Mo-Da	Mo-Da

* See note, table 8.

This can hardly be taken as strong support for the assumption that members of the two statuses participating in a relationship share more of the culture concerning that relationship than do any others. Once again, then, the evidence indicates that for the nuclear family, the relationship between status membership and cultural sharing appears to be a good deal less clear than would be expected according to the Linton view.

Table 10 offers a somewhat different perspective on the relationship between being party to a relationship and sharing the cultural elements concerned with that relationship. This table reports sharing of the items in the spouse relationship scale. There are six items in this scale concerning such jointly or reciprocally relevant issues as who wins arguments between spouses, whether spouses share friends or not, and which could get along best without the other (see Swartz 1982a:337–338).

Part A reports sharing among actors belonging to different families. Only among the Swahili is the mother/wife and father/husband pair the one that shares at the highest level for members of different families. Part B, which reports sharing among members of the same family, gives different results, however. Here we see the statistically nonsignificant result that the mother/wife and father/husband pair is first not only for the Swahili but for both comparison groups as well.

This last offers some support for the intuitively appealing notion that parties to a relationship share cultural elements concerned with that relationship more than others do. More broadly, however, the results are quite mixed. We saw that for both of the relationships examined, members of the directly involved status categories in the society at large (i.e., informants from different families) did not share at a consistently higher level than did members of other status categories. For the parent-child relationship, the same lack of higher-level sharing among members of the directly involved statuses was also seen for members of the same family. These findings also fail to support a close association between status occupancy and high levels of cultural sharing.

However, the findings regarding sharing of the spouse relationship scale by members of the same family (table 10B) support the traditional view of statuses despite the fact that they are just short of statistical significance. It appears that spouses who are actually married to each other may have more sharing of the spouse scale than do spouses who are not married to each other (i.e., husbands and wives from different families) and also more than do other members of their families. If this is so, it suggests that spouses in the same family do not bring the cultural elements concerned with their relationship into that relationship—spouses in different families would show more sharing than they do if that were so—but, rather, that they *developed* shared elements in the course of their marriage. This would be what Wallace's "equivalence structure" (1970:27–36) view of cultural distribution would predict. That is,

Table 10. *Sharing Coefficients for the Spouse Relationship Scale by Pairs Inside the Family and Outside the Family*

A. Outside Family Sharing Coefficients

Total sample pairs	Swahili	Kahl	La Jolla
Fa-Fa	.411	.565	.367
Fa-Mo	.437	.549	.354
Fa-So	.383	.508	.390
Fa-Da	.343	.464	.369
Mo-Mo	.427	.520	.342
Mo-So	.394	.487	.360
Mo-Da	.340	.446	.345
So-So	.383	.449	.385
So-Da	.298	.417	.388
Da-Da	.243	.377	.360

Pairs with highest and lowest sharing coefficients

Highest	Fa-Mo	Fa-Fa	Fa-So
Lowest	Da-Da	Da-Da	Mo-Mo

B. Inside Family Sharing Coefficients

Family Pairs	Swahili	Kahl	La Jolla
Fa-Mo	.738	.647	.612
Fa-So	.640	.594	.504
Fa-Da	.326	.546	.476
Mo-So	.590	.537	.576
Mo-Da	.468	.597	.480
Ch-Ch	.432	*	.552

Pairs with highest and lowest sharing coefficients

Highest	Fa-Mo	Fa-Mo	Fa-Mo
Lowest	Mo-So	Mo-So	Fa-Da

* See note, table 8.

through associating with one another, people work out understandings of what is happening (including what the partners in interaction will do) that are equivalent but not necessarily even similar in different families.[4]

It seems very likely that in some family relationships, the participants do develop the sort of "structures" (i.e., collections of distinctively shared cultural elements) that Wallace alerted us to. It is my distinct impression that this takes place in developing relationships in the Swahili community and that, for example, the men in the same baraza (see chap. 4) over time come to share understandings about, at least, what topics will be discussed, when to say prayers, and what refreshments will be served. Men join the group with some understandings brought from earlier experience with other groups (including those involving members of their households which took place when the men were quite young) and develop new ones specific to the group they now participate in through their experience with it.

It is important to note that the understandings vital to groups and relationships are not always just those that adult participants bring to them when they begin their participation but also may well include understandings developed through experience. It is less than startling that such development of cultural elements is important in some relations and groups, with the processes of becoming accustomed (zoea) to people and groups a recognized occurrence among the Swahili and in many other societies. That it should occur for children and the relationships involving them in the nuclear family is what would be expected given the family's role in enculturation. That it should be so central in the spouse relationship in an ancient and relatively stable group like the Swahili is, perhaps, less obviously in accord with how culture is often thought to operate in a "traditional society." More generally, the statistical data support the general proposition that culture, the set of understandings shared among those in interaction, is fluid even in such well-established groups as the nuclear family and even in societies as traditional as the Swahili.

Neither "All by All" Nor, without Modification, "Some by Some"

The findings of this comparison of survey interviewing data indicate that substantial revisions in traditional views of cultural distribution (i.e., who shares what with whom) are called for. The data here show that the once-prevalent view that all culture is shared by all members of a society is, as expected, without factual foundation even in a small and long-established group like the Swahili. This is worth noting because the all by all view of sharing, despite its universal disavowal, has by no means lost its place as the basis for formulations explaining how culture, either that of particular societies or generally, actually operates. What is called for is a useful alternative to an approach to cultural dynamics that does nothing more than invoke "shared beliefs and values." The processes whereby beliefs and values affect those who do not share them have received less attention than they require, and giving this attention begins by demonstrating the inadequacy of formulations based, explicitly or implicitly, on all by all sharing.

This is made more challenging by the findings that show the main alternative to "homogeneous" cultural sharing, Linton's status-centered approach (the "some by some" view), is also far from well supported by the facts. The limited sharing within statuses does not gainsay the part statuses play in cultural dynamics, but it does raise new questions about how they operate.

In chapter 6, where attention moves beyond the family into the general community, we will see that as concerns quite different sorts of understandings and quite different statuses, the sharing by (and about) members of mainly age- and gender-based statuses is extensive despite the fact that these statuses do not have the linguistic marking internal family statuses do. In that discussion, it will be suggested that "specific expectations" regarding statuses play a quite different part in social life than "general expectations" do and that "identifying understandings" (the cultural elements that serve as the basis for assignment to cultural categories) have a unique role in cultural operation.

These results indicate that it is as important to refine and develop the "some by some" model of cultural sharing (that is, Linton's basic view as he formulated it) as it is to reject the all by all model. Statuses are crucial to the distribution of understandings, but among the Swahili (and elsewhere), sharing within statuses is quite incomplete so that members of a given status cannot be assumed to share with one another all understandings seemingly relevant to that status in the various contexts and situations in which the status is involved.

If this last is so, as the data in this chapter suggest, an approach to culture's operation that is based wholly on finding the schemata in the minds of status occupants cannot explain culture's ability to serve as the foundation for social life. This is a consequence of the finding that some of the components of these schemata, including those directly concerned with the statuses, are different for different status occupants; that is, they are not shared.

This limited sharing of culture does not prevent statuses from operating, as will be seen in the following chapters. This is vital in a number of ways that go beyond the functioning of social relationships. As this discussion develops (and especially in chap. 10), it will become clear that a crucial aspect of culture's operation can be understood as a result of the "organization of culture" (a concept to be introduced later but concerned with how the various understandings group members share are related to one another). This organization is not entirely the result of shared understandings that put different cultural elements in relationships with others as some understandings (e.g., "it is better to be liked than wise") do. A vital part of cultural organization comes from the ways statuses operate to make available the results of the guidance of understandings to those who may not themselves share those elements.

Dealing with the Fact of Diversity

But before addressing the problems of cultural organization, it is useful to consider how people deal with the fact that many of the understandings that are basic to life are not shared by all those around them. The recognition that each person is different from every other in what he believes, in what he values, and in what he wants is probably universal. A Swahili proverb reminds those who are pleased with achieving a desired end, *Kizuri kwako, kibaya kwa mwenzako*: Your good thing [can be] a bad thing for your companion.

This proverb and the recognition of differences it affirms is like the one that gives this chapter its name: Intelligence is [like] hair, each one has his [own]. Another that makes the same point says, *Penye wengi pana mengi*: [Where] there are many people, there are many views.

The diversity seen in the data on cultural sharing is not only a finding of research but it is explicitly familiar to the community members themselves. Yet group members have to be able to predict, and to believe they can predict, within broad limits what those around them will do if social life is to continue (e.g., Parsons 1964 [1951]:10, 27–29, 36–37). This suggests that people, like anthropologists, do not allow their knowledge of diversity to interfere with their belief in uniformity as concerns important values and beliefs. The next chapter examines a main device Swahili use to obscure the absence of general sharing.

6

Close One of Your Eyes

Concealing Differences between
the Generations and the Uses of "Tokens"

Ukenda kwa wenye chongo, fumba lako jicho: *[If]
you go to the land of the blind, close [one of] your
eye[s]*.

Introduction

We have seen that the Swahili have far less than universal cultural sharing. This is the same result found in studies of sharing in other groups (e.g., Holland 1987a; Fernandez 1965; Pelto and Pelto 1975; Pollnac 1975; Sanday 1968; Sankoff 1971; Schwartz 1972). In all cases, there was no evidence of less than adequate group functioning or individual adjustment.

Since culture is the basis for social life and individual adaptation, there can be a question as to whether or not culture "works" despite the absence of uniform sharing. If culture's operation is to be understood, it is clearly necessary to examine the processes involved rather than sweeping them aside with allusions to "shared beliefs and values." This would be useful even if there were all by all sharing of culture's elements. In the absence of such sharing, it is surely not less useful.

The last chapter suggests that some of culture is shared by some group members but not others, while other elements are shared with the latter and not the former. Although there is no evidence to support the notion, there may be some grand, unifying understandings shared by all. Even if there are, the means by which these presumably broad tenets (e.g., "Avoid shame" or "Maintain privacy" are two that might be shared among Swahili) are used to guide particular actions cannot confidently be attributed to uniform sharing of further beliefs and values of greater specificity. Sometimes there is such sharing, but sometimes not.

Culture often affects behavior when the relevant elements are shared by those concerned with the subject(s) of the elements. It also often affects behavior, however, when there is little of this sharing, as will be seen in chapters 9 and 10. The basic question is, what are the processes whereby culture has similar effects that, at least sometimes, fall, like the rain, equally on sharers and nonsharers?

The remainder of this study is addressed to this question as it applies to the Swahili community. In this chapter, the process of interest draws its effectiveness from the importance of appearance as contrasted with what is, in important senses, reality. *Seeming* to share understandings will be shown to have socially cohesive consequences essential to culture's operation even when the understandings that actually guide the behavior in question are by no means shared.

Specifically, data are presented concerning an important class of cultural elements that, although shared, are not connected to behavior in the same ways many other sorts of elements are. The existence of this sort of cultural element is partly recognized in Western folk wisdom by such statements as, "They say it, but they don't do it." The strength of these elements in influencing social relations will be shown to involve actions that suggest people believe that being thought similar to others is worthwhile whether you are truly like them or not. "When in Rome . . ." is surely among the more quoted proverbs in English. It will be suggested that it is less important in some circumstances to do as the Romans do than to *seem* to.

The creation of the appearance of sharing will be seen to occur through exchanges, indirect as well as direct, involving the passing back and forth of statements and other sorts of symbols that suggest similarity in the beliefs and values of those concerned. The appearances so created may involve actual sharing as established independently from the symbol exchange, but they also may not.

Symbols exchanged in this way will be called "tokens," and it will be shown that it is useful to distinguish their functions from those of another category of cultural elements that will be called "guides." Guides are understandings that affect behavior in ways directly traceable to their content, while tokens—and the same element of culture can serve the same actors as either or both—serve to indicate similarity of understandings. In the generational relations currently of interest, the difference between tokens and guides is strongly marked since they are represented by opposite understandings concerning the same evaluations and action, but this is not always—or, perhaps, even usually—so.

Differences between
Younger and Older Men and Women

In Old Town, men in their thirties or older dress in neat slacks and carefully buttoned sport shirts during working hours. During weekends and after hours, they wear the ankle-length white gown, kanzu, and embroidered cap, kofia, that are the traditional outer garments. Although few of these mature men follow the practice, common until the 1950s, of shaving the head completely, most still keep their hair very short.[1] In bearing and gait, many mature men remain much as men were said to have been in the last century and, quite possibly, earlier. They walk with measured stride and carry themselves erectly. Sometimes their hands are clasped behind their backs as they go, or, occasionally and more commonly for elderly men, they carry a *bakora,* the traditional walking stick.

Younger men and boys present quite a different picture. They are rarely to be seen in kanzu, and, if they are not wearing T-shirts bearing the usual assortment of advertisements, slogans, or university names, their shirts are open to the middle of their chests. Many have long hair worn in Afros. Instead of the deliberate step of their fathers and older brothers, some glide along with loose-shouldered lubricity. Instead of the invariably quiet conversations of their elders, the younger men often raise their voices and occasionally make the buildings ring with their shouts and laughter.

Nor are these obvious and immediately striking differences between the young and the old found only among males. The younger women, although still rarely to be seen save when in school or on their way there or back, are very different from their mothers and, even, elder sisters in ways that go beyond manner and dress.

As recently as the middle 1970s, mothers worried that a daughter might have *mato ya nde* ("eyes of the outside"), meaning that she often looked out the windows of her home with the intention of catching a glimpse of passing young men. There was no question but that she would remain confined inside the house according to the strict segregation of the sexes and the seclusion of women, but the worry was that she might be so willful as to try to see passing males and somehow arrange meetings.

In fact, this is still a source of concern, but now there is much in addition to worry about with some adolescent and slightly older women going to discos and out-of-the-way "cold houses" (small cafés that serve cold drinks, snacks, and tea) disporting themselves until long after dark. The horrified mothers and fathers forbid such practices, but a minority of young women, usually by subterfuge, do it anyway.

One rarely sees young Swahili women abroad on the streets after dark, but some probably do actually go out in the early evenings, as young men and a few young women say they do. The belief that they do is very common. The older people deplore such behavior, often passionately, but, they say, there is little that can be done to stop it because that is "the way the young people are these days."

Still, daughters and their mothers and fathers usually get along quite well despite the language mothers use on their daughters (see chap. 8 and Swartz 1990*a*). However, informants say that it was never really rare for there to be families where the fathers and sons were at odds, and the fairly recent change has been for conflict to be more serious and to focus on such things as mode of dress, spending too much money, associating with young men of bad reputation, and acting like a *mahuni* (a gadabout, a disrespectful and willful person). There have always been some young men in the community who were considered mahuni, but now, many older men and women say, all of the young men are.

All of this suggests the existence of a "generation gap" between parents and children and between younger and older people more generally. The actions and statements of those involved show quite clearly that there are real differences in some of the understandings shared among those in the two age groupings. These differences concern such things as dress style, deportment, and restrictions on seeking the sort of entertainment available in contemporary Mombasa, and they extend to differences concerning the assessment of the younger people's behavior and the older people's authority.

Many long conversations with members of the two generational groups and years of associating with them strongly indicates that the members of each cohort guide important parts of their behavior with understandings that are shared among age-mates much more than across generational lines. Puzzlingly, however, interviewing does not seem to confirm this cross-generational cultural difference. Interviews using a standard set of questions (see below) produced data suggesting that as regards some aspects of culture, including some of those concerned with the very areas of life where differences between the generations are most obvious, there is as much sharing across generational lines as within generations.

Differences between Age Groupings, Uniformity within Them

In addition to the contrasts in dress and public behavior, many of the explicit views and beliefs heard from members of the different generations suggest substantial cultural differences. This can be seen in the sort of people the young men admire. They can fairly often be heard praising the behavior of the American blacks they see in movies, and although the ability, size, and strength of American black athletes are mentioned with great admiration, it is the "superfly" sort of character (a "sharp"-dressing, smooth-talking person who attends little to conventional constraints) or irreverent rock musician seen in American films (and occasionally on Voice of Kenya TV) that is most prominently and admiringly mentioned.

Most or all of the fathers do not share this approval. They view movies in general as suspect and only acceptable when, on an individual basis, they are found not to be possible sources of corruption and avenues for undermining proper behavior and the Muslim faith. Television is more broadly accepted, but it too causes unease. Many of the particular traits some of the youth admire in actors, musicians, and athletes—"wise-guy" talk, "sharp" clothes and grooming, swaggering, attendance at discos, contempt for authority—are ones the older men understand as most objectionable and dangerous.

The older men give their admiration to those displaying unusual piety and, especially, religious learning. The young men believe in and practice Islam, and there is no question that they are quite serious about it, but it does not completely dominate their view of the world and of what is admirable as it does for their fathers.

The young admire pious and learned men but not to the extent their fathers do. The term "sheikh," a title of respect used for older men which especially refers to their religious learning and piety, is a mildly derisive sobriquet used by the youths for any of their peers who are particularly zealous in their religious commitment.

More directly concerned with the obvious differences in behavior, each group is quite explicit in its disapproval of the activities and style of the other group and, sometimes only implicitly, in its approval of its own. The older men condemn the behavior of many or most of the young and characterize them, as we have seen, as irresponsible, disrespectful, wastrels. The elders suggest that the sorry state of the contemporary youth is mainly a result of outside influences such as secular schools and association with non-Muslims.

The young men and boys, for their part, say that although their activities are different from those of their parents when they were of the same age, there is nothing wrong with going to discos, behaving informally, and expressing themselves (in clothes and speech) more freely than their parents did. Parental condemnation of their behavior is less due, according to the young people, to reasonably based objections to that behavior than it is to their parents' failure to understand modern ways.

There are, then, substantial differences between the understandings held by the members of the two generations as these understandings apply to guiding and judging the behavior of the young. Both groups have understandings about the same general thing (i.e., the desirability/acceptability of the behavior of own and other groups), but the understandings held by each are at odds with those held by the other.

In addition to holding what amounts to opposed understandings of this sort, members of one generation have understandings that are simply absent among members of the other. In 1978, for example, boys and young men had elaborate understandings about platform shoes: how to walk in them, how to judge them as regards price and beauty, and what sorts of people did and did not have them. Older men simply did not possess such understandings. All platform shoes were understood identically by them as both expensive and as a sign of the decadence and intrusion of Western culture they deplored.

There is, then, substantial evidence indicating material differences between young and old in the understandings held regarding general deportment, acceptance of parental restriction versus personal freedom, and, for boys and men, such things as clothing, the sort of man to be admired, and personal demeanor. There is also evidence showing that despite the differences between the age groups, there is substantial sharing within each of them.

Attempting to Measure
Generation Gap Differences

Having found differences between the generations in behavior and in those aspects of culture that seemed quite closely connected to that behavior, I decided to try to determine how broad in scope and general the differences between the bodies of understandings shared by the generations were.

The members of both generations almost always mentioned family relations in their discussions of differences between the younger and older people. As has been shown, the nuclear family is uniquely important for the vast majority of community members and plays an undeniably central role in the social life of the group. Although extended family kin are fairly important, children are primarily responsible to their parents and parents are far more concerned about the actions of their own sons and daughters than about others' actions.[2]

When discussing generational differences, statements always focused on parent-child relations rather than those between younger and older people generally. Remembering the Swahili emphasis on privacy, it is not surprising to find that parents did not all refer specifically to their own children, but some did, and all focused their attention on relations within the family more than on general community relations. Similarly, younger people phrased their comments about generational differences almost entirely in terms of parent-child relations, with rather more discussion of personal relations within their own families than was heard from the more restrained, older informants. Older men quite often made statements such as, "There is no controlling children these days; they will not listen to their parents." Young men said things such as, "No matter how much I explain, my father pays no attention."

Because of this focus on family relationships and because of the importance of the nuclear family in Swahili social life, I designed a survey interview form concerned with the nature and quality of family life and family relationships. I asked about ideal and actual qualities associated with the statuses father, mother, son, and daughter. The questions produced a wealth of material that was quite parallel to but, as will be seen, remarkably different from what I gathered in being present during general discussions of generational differences and in my informal conversations with both older and younger men.

The Survey Study of Generational
Differences in Sharing Understandings
Concerning the Generation Gap

Given the uniformity of findings from observation and informal discussion, my hypothesis was that more formal techniques would produce similar results. A main objective of the use of formal techniques was to discover the extent to which sharing within generations was similar to or different from the sharing among members of the other social groupings reported in chapter 5.

My expectation (which, as will become clear, has been proved incorrect) was that the members of each generation would share far more with one another than they would with members of the other generation, so that intragenerational sharing indexes would be significantly higher than cross-generational indexes. It seemed so obvious that this would be so that the survey-based study of generational sharing was undertaken more to provide a measure of the extent and nature of the differences between the generations than a test of whether or not such differences were present. The latter would be tested, of course, but I viewed it as pro forma more than anything else.

There was another aim in doing this study. The findings regarding the sharing of family culture were based on results obtained with a multiple choice answer format, and it seemed possible that this distorted the results. In the study of sharing in generational groupings, the interview form (see Appendix) used in the survey did not ask informants to answer questions by choosing a single, prepared response from among a few alternate responses. It proposed fairly broad questions and the informants answered them in their own words and as they chose. The first question on the form can serve as one example of the sorts of questions asked: "In your experience and for the families in your immediate neighborhood, how do the family members get on these days? Would you say they get along as well as they did in the past, less well, or better?"

Two further examples may help give the flavor of the interviews. The examples are chosen to give some idea of the scope of the questionnaire.

"Thinking about your own family and others you know well, how is it with the father? What are the contributions he makes in your family and in others?"

"Tell me about relations between mothers and daughters. In what ways are those relations similar to those between mothers and sons and between fathers and daughters?"

The interview forms were administered by four Swahili assistants, two males and two females, all in their late teens and early twenties. The questions were translated into Swahili by me and then checked by both the assistants and by my friend and colleague, Yahya Ali Omar, who is credited in the community as being the leading scholar of the language. It is quite possible, of course, that the fact that the formal interviews were all carried out by young Swahili influenced the results, but since it is impossible to get older Swahili to serve as interviewers and since any outsider administering the interview, including me, would be unable to get many individuals to participate, there was no choice but to proceed as I did. In the analysis of results given below, the effect of the questions being asked only by younger community members known to be working for me (as they were) is considered at length.

The difficulties in getting Swahili to participate in these interviews were predictably substantial, and it was quite impossible to get anything approximating a random sample. The interviewers got their informants where they could find them, which doubtless led to an overrepresentation of their kin and friends. Since the four were from three different neighborhoods and unrelated, however, this was not too serious. The interviewers drew their informants from all of Old Town's neighborhoods and from the different educational and socioeconomic strata, so there is a fair representation of the whole community in the study.

The results of the interviews were coded by a research assistant whose code-recode reliability was above 0.80.[3] Informants were taken to agree in their answers to a question when the coding for their answers was the same, and this agreement (what is called "sharing" here) was used as the basis for computing sharing scores.

These were calculated in exactly the same way the scores discussed in chapter 5 were. That is, overall scores were obtained by comparing the scoring of responses of each individual in the sample with every other (i.e., the members of all possible pairs were compared to each other) and using the results of the comparison in the same formula used for calculating the sharing coefficient in chapter 5. Using this formula, if two informants agreed on every one of the twenty questions they were asked, they would have a sharing coefficient of 1.00 (i.e., $20/40 - 20 = 1.00$).

By averaging the resulting scores for pairs, it was possible to get scores for the groups of which the pairs were members. Thus, averaging the scores for pair agreement when all the pairs were members of the same families gave "same family" scores, and averaging the scores for pairs whose members belong to different generations gave "different generation" scores.

The sample was made up of forty-eight individuals chosen so that every person has either a same sex parent or a same sex child from his or her own family in the sample, with none of the "children" being married. Thus, everyone in the sample is unambiguously in one or the other of the two generations studied and has a parent or child of the same sex in the sample. That is, the sample is made up of twenty-four parents and twenty-four children with no cross-sex parent-child pairs from the same family.

Before going into the generation gap results, it is worth noting that the open interviewing with scores derived from an evaluation of the informants' own answers are not radically different from the results of the multiple choice questionnaire study of family and community sharing of nuclear family understandings as reported in chapter 4. Sharing on the "open response questions" is higher, as would be expected from the lessened need to take a clear position on the open interviews (what might be called the "waffle factor"), but in both cases, the sharing within the family (and family membership was not known to the scorer in the generational study) is substantially higher than in the community at large. The level of sharing in both is substantially higher for the members of the same nuclear family than for those from different families (see table 11).

Interpreting this roughly in percentages, the open questions show a sharing of about 70 percent within the family, while the multiple choice questions yield an estimate of sharing at around 65 percent, and, for those from different families, open questions indicate 62 percent sharing, while multiple choice gives 48 percent. Since the questions, not just the kind of reply informants are asked to give, are different in the two assessments of sharing, the differences between the two sets of findings are less striking than their similarities.

As table 12 shows, contrary to my hypothesis, there is substantial cross-generational uniformity with respect to the questions in general (table 12A) and with respect to the questions divided into groups according to their subject matter (table 12B). This is true both within families and across family lines.

It appears that there may be differences between gender categories such that males agree with males more than males with females and females with females more than females with males, but this holds across generational lines as well as in the same generation. Similarly, members of the same family share more with one another than nonrelatives. However, it is important to note that the internal family sharing reported here is between members of different generations since every family interviewed is represented, but only by a parent and a child, never by siblings or both parents.

In short, despite the evidence for a generation gap that can hardly be avoided in observing public behavior as well as with respect to the understandings concerned with public behavior expressed in informal settings, the survey data suggest that there is no such gap concerning such things as the nature of family life, the nature of family relationships, and the sources of responsibility for the tension in family life.

Since parents deplore their children's public behavior in conversations with one another and in casual discussions with me and since, in the same sorts of contexts, children make it clear that they believe that their parents' views of proper public behavior are outmoded and inappropriate, the absence of differences between the two groups in the results of the survey interviews is striking. It is true that the topics of the two sorts of data—those resulting from

Table 11.   *Sharing on All "Open Questions" versus Multiple Choice*
           Questions on Different Samples

Means sharing	On multiple choice	On open questions
Within nuclear family	.473	.537
Within total sample	.317	.439

the scheduled interview and those resulting from conversations among informants and between them and me—are slightly different, but they are unquestionably closely related. The scheduled interviews focused on the nature of
family relationships and the sources of the quality of these relationships, while
the informally obtained data focused on overall behavior with an emphasis
on public behavior. Still, the two foci are closely associated in informants'
views as well as according to connections outsiders can readily appreciate.

An examination of the contents of the survey interviews summarized numerically in table 12 illuminates the "sharing" between generations and makes
the issue of the culture gap—or its absence—sharper. These interviews show
that without regard to generation, informants agree that family relationships
are characterized by tension and conflict and that this is particularly, but not
uniquely, true of the father-son relationship.

Without respect to the generation they belong to, informants agree that
there are two main causes for the tension found in family relationships. One
of these is the undesirable, undisciplined, and unconventional behavior of
children, especially, but not uniquely, of sons. Another cause for family dis-
cord agreed to by both parents and children is the weakness of parents and
their refusal or failure to exercise the authority that is theirs as a consequence
of their occupancy of the parental statuses. Fathers, members of both generations agree, are more culpable than mothers, but mothers are also said to be
at fault. It is agreed that in the rather rare families where children behave
more nearly as they should and (not or) where parents are forceful, family
life is "better" (again the characterization is that of the informants) and its
constituent relationships more nearly free of conflict and tension.

What the survey interviews indicate, then, is that parents agree with their
children that their, the parents', weakness plays a key part—many in both
generations say it is the most important one—in producing the troubled state
of family life and the tension characteristic of most or all family relationships.
Children, in turn, agree with parents that the children's behavior is deplorable
and that although parents are at fault for not controlling it, the children must
accept responsibility for their own actions. This acceptance is particularly
striking in that members of both generations characterize these actions in
the survey interviews with such terms as "undesirable," "bad," "wild," and
"hopeless."

Table 12. Sharing of Responses Concerning Family Statuses and Relationships between Members of Same Family and Members of Different Families (n = 48)

A. Sharing Coefficients for All Questions Calculated Together as Found between Statuses as Indicated

| | Same family | | | | | | Different families | | | |
	Fa-So	Mo-Da	All	Par-Par	Ch-Ch	Par-Ch	Male-Male	Female-Female	Male-Female	All-All
	.529	.544	.537	.431	.439	.442	.441	.453	.431	.439

B. Sharing Coefficients for Questions Concerning the Family as a Group, Family Statuses, and Family Relationships

Family	Fa-So	Mo-Da	All	Par-Par	Ch-Ch	Par-Ch	Male-Male	Female-Female	Male-Female	All-All
Group	.546	.566	.556	.386	.462	.426	.446	.408	.423	.425
Father	.591	.566	.577	.489	.526	.478	.455	.509	.478	.480
Mother	.433	.637	.540	.501	.423	.473	.388	.486	.450	.468
Spouse	.463	.525	.494	.424	.397	.416	.400	.420	.417	.413
Son	.556	.479	.517	.361	.428	.393	.405	.412	.380	.394
Daughter	.538	.437	.517	.410	.380	.410	.446	.421	.374	.402

Apparent Differences
between Culture and Behavior

It is initially quite puzzling to see that in the survey interviews parents and children agree that the members of their own, as well as the other, generation are failing to act as they should according to their own standards. It is not unusual for individuals to see themselves as wrong in particular instances and as personally responsible for specific, undesirable events or states. Still, to characterize themselves as behaving badly over a length of time and across the spectrum of training children or growing up is surely remarkable.

Karen Horney (1937) held that neurosis was characterized by continuing behavior contrary to the values of those who displayed the behavior. Since the Swahili survey interviews show that those interviewed do condemn what they say is their own behavior, the possibility must be considered that they are neurotics in Horney's terms.

Another possibility, of course, is that although informants *say* that a crucial factor in producing the family life and child behavior they themselves condemn is their own behavior, they do not "really" mean what they say. It is less than startling to observe that people in a wide variety of societies say things for reasons other than that they believe them to be true.

If we must choose between characterizing the Mombasa Swahili informants as neurotics who cannot restrain themselves from acting in ways they themselves find objectionable or as characterizing their statements as reflecting something other than a straightforward expression of the understandings they hold, it would seem that there is more support for doubting the full and complete accuracy of their statements than for doubting their mental health.

Taking the members of the Swahili group in general, I have no evidence indicating that neurotic tendencies among them are beyond what is found in other groups. They make their livings, raise their children to become functioning adults, carry on many reasonably gratifying social relationships, and give no signs of suffering more than the rest of humanity. However, members of this group have shown themselves to be no less willing to bend the truth, exaggerate, omit, and plain fabricate when it serves their purposes than do members of other groups I am familiar with.

This is not to say that informants were not telling the truth in their responses to the survey. A statement made independently by a substantial proportion of a group's members surely takes on a special status even if it is ultimately judged to be one that those who make it know to be other than an accurate representation of reality. What can be said about the survey interview data is that they are at odds with the informally gathered information about the same issues and that they do not seem to be in accord with observed behavior.

The statements in the survey must have some significance for those who make them; otherwise, why would so many different people independently say the same things? They cannot, however, be taken as straightforward statements of "real" beliefs and evaluations. If the elders blame themselves as much as they blame the younger generation, as their statements in the survey indicate they do, why do their informal statements and observed behavior only manifest disapproval of the young and no effort to change their own actions?

Similarly, if the younger people recognize their own behavior as "bad" and accept at least part of the responsibility for it being that, why is there no evidence that they attempt to abandon their current patterns of behavior? The responses in the survey are shared, as the statistics in table 12 show, but they do not seem related to the behavior they address in any straightforward and observable way.

What people say concerning the behavior of the younger generation in the informal discussions of that behavior is consistent with what they are observed to do, in that each group deplores the activity of the other and implies or states a view of itself as blameless. Unlike the implications of the responses given in the survey interviews, the understandings inferred from the informal discussions are entirely consistent with the behavior that the members of each generation manifests. What explains this seeming contradiction between what is said in the interviews and what actually guides behavior?

"Phatic Communion," Interpersonal Relations, and Questionnaires

Decades ago, Malinowski (1960) formulated a description that can serve as the basis for understanding such things as the Swahili assertion of responsibility at the same time that there is no behavioral evidence to support this assertion. He wrote of a kind of use of speech he called "phatic communion," which he characterized as fulfilling "a social function and that is [its] principal aim. . . . Each utterance is an act serving the direct aim of binding hearer and speaker to speaker by a tie of some social sentiment or other" (ibid., 315).

His idea was that phatic communion bound people together through the uses of statements whose external or empirical accuracy was mainly irrelevant. He believed, as many did in the 1920s, that "primitives" were different from other sorts of humans and that they used phatic communion more than "civilized" people did but that, nevertheless,

> the binding tissue of words which unites the crew of a ship in bad weather, the verbal concomitants of a company of soldiers in action, the technical language running parallel to some practical work or sporting pursuit . . . serves to establish bonds of personal union between people brought together by the mere need of companionship and does not serve any purpose of communicating ideas. (ibid., 315–316)

Although Malinowski did not limit phatic communion to greetings, he thought it particularly noteworthy and common in them. Reisman (1977) reports the meaning of greetings among the Fulani group with which he worked as follows:

> When two people greet each other, each reveals to the other two important facts, namely, that he knows the formulas and that he is ready to participate in the ritual of saying them. . . . They express for the speakers, then, the sharing of group life (*gondal*) and the desire to maintain it. (ibid., 171–172)

What I am suggesting is that the Swahili response to the survey questionnaires can usefully be viewed as a phatic communion that is similar to the greetings Reisman reports for the Fulani in Jelgoji. The members of the two generations express responsibility for the situation they deplore not (or not mainly) because they actually see themselves as responsible but because they wish to assert a social bond with other members of their group. This bond may well include the interviewers, who were, it will be remembered, young Swahili, or it may be that the bond was with the members of the other generation who might become aware of the contents of the interview.

The basic idea here is that members of a social group assert solidarity with one another by averring or implying similarity, especially in public contexts, when relatively low-cost opportunities present themselves to do that. One such kind of opportunity is the utterance of greetings, but assertions of solidarity are not limited to the kind of greetings Reisman discusses.

The sort of thing I am suggesting as occurring when the Swahili are interviewed about generational differences also takes place in ritual performances, as becomes clear when the absence of sharing among participants regarding the significance of these performances is revealed. This can be seen in Fernandez's important work among the Fang of northern Gabon. In examining the principal subcult of the Bwiti cult, Fernandez found that the ordinary participants in the ritual all carried out the activities appropriate to them as performers but that they had extremely limited agreement about such things as the meaning of the cult's symbolism and what it was intended to accomplish.

> . . . it appears that the cult in the eyes of the members queried had a number of manifest functions and that these members differ in assigning priorities to, or even recognizing, these various functions. Of the 20 cult members, seven said that the main purpose of the ritual was to find and establish proper relationship with the Christian God, who lies beyond death and of whom the Fang had no traditional knowledge. Eight said that the main purpose of the cult was to establish contact with the abandoned ancestors and regain their tutelary blessing. The remaining three declared the purpose of the cult ritual to be various. (Fernandez 1965:906)

Fernandez's important paper (see also his recent book, 1982) makes the point that people can carry out activities without sharing the meaning of those activities. They share only the understandings of what is to be done, when, and how but not what the meanings are. He interprets this as a "solidarity in the forms of cultural interaction . . . so that they need no longer seek it in cultural forms" (ibid., 912). He goes on to say that the participants in the ritual hold in abeyance their differing understandings of what they are doing in the ritual. He writes, "They do so for the sake of a social-satisfaction—the satisfaction of orienting their activity towards each other with the resulting psychobiological benefits whatever they may be—the security of acceptance, exaltation, *esprit de corps,* morale, we-feeling, enthusiasm, exstasis" (ibid., 913).

Fernandez's main concern in examining the Bwiti cult ritual is very similar to the one that is the focus here: to understand how people can act as though they share understandings when, in fact, their sharing is much less than it might seem to be. The cult members know how to act in the ritual, but they do not share the meanings attached to those actions; the Swahili informants know what responses to give in a survey interview, but they give every evidence of holding quite different views that are masked by those answers.

The survey interviews were public situations in that the interviewers were not only all young people but also known employees of an outsider (i.e., the anthropologist) whom everyone knew to be concerned with gaining an understanding of the community. In that situation, as in the Bwiti rituals and Reisman's Fang greetings, the actors took unified action (i.e., common answers) as the proper way to behave. None knew how the others had responded, but that presented no difficulty since the regnant understanding here—as in many other contacts with outsiders—was to present a face of unity to affirm solidarity. The answers the informants gave the survey interviewers were tokens just as ritual actions and greetings are in the two instances just discussed. It is generally true of tokens that their exact content matters less than that they be of a nature that asserts unity or similarity.

The informants gave these tokens with, I hypothesize, the aim (not necessarily fully or consciously articulated) of giving a good impression of their group and themselves to the young interviewers and "the professor" for whom the latter worked. The responses also showed the informants to be truly integrated members of the community who shared the views of the other group members as they imagined those would be. They did not have to know what views others expressed to know that putting all the blame on "the others" (i.e., the young blaming the old and vice versa) would set them apart from the others and would suggest that they did not share important understandings with them.

"Tokens" and "Guides"

This would explain the disparity between the presence of important differences between the members of different generations as seen in various behaviors such as dress and demeanor and the absence of evidence of these differences in formal interviews. It suggests that shared understandings need not be related to behavior only or mainly as guides for that behavior. The responses in formal interviews can serve as symbols whose exact reference is relatively unimportant but whose proper production (i.e., when to produce them and who to give them to) is crucial. This is a point that the ethno-methodologists in sociology have examined in many important studies (e.g., Cicourel 1987).

It is not that these—or most—symbolic expressions of understandings, that is, tokens, have no relation to behavior. Rather, it is that the relationship is not necessarily what it might appear to be. Saying that one is responsible for generational tensions is not the statement of an understanding that guides be-havior in intergenerational relations. Instead, it is the production of a symbol seen as important in their relationship with the interviewers, the anthropolo-gist who employs the interviewers, and their community as a whole. In effect, they are asserting that they share with their fellow group members vital un-derstandings about aspects of group life, and this assertion is by means of tokens—in this case, statements about behavior—given to those with whom they are speaking.

In fact, the use of tokens is by no means limited to responses to interview questions. One of the consequences of successfully passing tokens is the af-firmation of various memberships and commitments. Swahili of all ages, for example, exclaim *Hamdulila* (God be praised) when things go well and *Alla-huakbar* (God is great) when surprised, and begin most undertakings by as-serting *Besmilla* (In God's name). This asserts their unity with other Muslims and separates them from Christians and others, just as their dialect of the Swahili language differentiates them from Swahili speakers belonging to other groups. Carol Eastman has argued that language is "culture loaded" (1979) and that it serves to establish social identity (1984, 1985). This applies to the Swahili, with whom she has worked, as well as to speakers of other languages.

More than asserting identities and commitments, however, exchanging to-kens also provides confidence that those exchanging them share important understandings. The parents who say they are responsible for their children's behavior are asserting the existence of common ground with those children and anyone who sides with them, and, mutatis mutandis, the children's asser-tion of responsibility for themselves does the same with their parents and their allies.

The distinction between cultural elements serving as tokens and as guides is useful in understanding how culture works despite the quite incomplete sharing of many of its constituent parts. Malinowski, Fernandez, and, prob-ably, many others saw the importance of this distinction in accounting for some aspects of culture's functioning. Surely, although Reisman is an unusu-ally accomplished and sensitive field-worker, he is not the only one who has noted the importance of tokens and their frequency of use in particular areas of life.

Swahili men, to take another example, wear kanzu and kofia as other Muslims do. But Swahili men, and no others, wear white kanzu embroidered with small beige designs on the placket and kofia that are white with white embroidery. These are tokens presented to all who see them which will be understood by those who matter most as what they are: assertions of group membership and acceptance of group understandings.

Some tokens, then, are purely communicative symbols as well as statements of understandings that do not actually reflect guides for behavior but, rather, serve to assert the existence of sharing. It is doubtlessly also true that some guides are also tokens. Among the Swahili, for example, proper performance of the daily prayers is a crucial token that community members give one another every time they pray publicly.[4] The understandings that lie behind this token are, so far as I can tell, nearly completely shared.

Every Swahili more or less fully shares the Sunni view of how to pray and the meaning of the movements in prayer taught him or her as a child. Using informal evidence, the understandings about the meanings, unlike the understandings about the Bwiti cult ritual, are nearly universally shared. These shared understandings about prayer actually guide people in the way they pray. Nevertheless, the way praying is done serves as a token of group membership, joint and shared belief, and a raft of common values and beliefs about the supernatural, humanity, and the world. It is not sufficient to pray properly to be recognized as a Swahili—various Muslims of Indian origin and from other African groups also do it—but it is a necessary token.

Understandings need not be divorced from the activities they concern in order to serve as the basis for tokens. They may, in other words, be both guides and the basis for tokens. The willingness of group members to use and to accept tokens, in fact, probably rests in considerable part on the fact that some tokens are also guides. Since they sometimes are, it is not groundless to take symbolic expressions of agreement, unity, and solidarity as at least possibly reflecting the true (i.e., active and effective) condition. The understandings that are not, in fact, guides for the behavior they address *might* be; others are. The fact that Swahili prayer behavior actually symbolizes understandings that are guides for other behaviors and beliefs, together with other behaviors that both assert sharing and actually guide activity, contributes to the appeal of making such statements as those about intergenerational relations.

Tokens may be consciously intended as such or not, but they always serve to indicate the presence of particular understandings. Sometimes tokens can be recognized because, as with the responses to the survey interviews, they are clearly not guides, but they can also be recognized by finding out what significance others attach to what people say, do, and otherwise communicate.

The basic distinction between "guides" and "tokens" is a functional one.

Guides are understandings applied as determinants of behavior in the areas indicated by the statements. The Swahili understanding that the left hand is not properly used in eating is readily expressed and often heard being directed to small children and anthropologists. Observing the Swahili eat, one sees the left hand kept out of action even for rather difficult one-handed tasks such as breaking a piece off the flat, pancake-shaped breads the Swahili often eat. Seeing the eating, one concludes that the expressed understandings about using the right hand and avoiding the left hand are guides. They also serve as tokens, of course, but they are quite redundant ones in most contexts where group membership and the sharing of understandings about eating are symbolized by the way the people sit, the food they prepare and eat, and so on.

Regarding the behavior that was the focus of much of the discussion of intergenerational relations in the interviews, young people report in informal conversations that there is nothing wrong with how they act in public. Difficulty, they say, arises from the fact that older people use inappropriate standards for judging them. Taking their statements as representing understandings concerning their evaluation of their own behavior, these understandings are clearly guides. This view of the understandings is confirmed by the fact that they continue to behave in the ways they say are unobjectionable without changing what they do to take account of the objections of the older people.

Guides, to put this generally, are understandings whose effects can always be seen in behavior beyond (in addition to) statements about what is or should be. Tokens may or may not be linked to observable activity beyond communication. The existence and use of tokens is an important support for social life and for those cultural processes, to be examined in subsequent chapters, that depend on social life.

Recognizing the possibility that understandings can be shared but connected to behavior only as tokens rather than as guides, or guides that are also tokens, appears to have analytic usefulness. It suggests an explanation for phenomena such as the two sets of data concerning the Swahili generation gap. As will be seen below, it also seems to make easier the recognition of a process that plays an important role in culture's ability, despite its quite incomplete sharing, to serve as effectively as it does as the basis for social life.

Sharing, Nonsharing, and Social Life: Predictability

A key social function of sharing understandings is that they provide a basis for interaction. As noted in chapters 1 and 5 and as Parsons (1964 [1951]:27–28) and others have observed, group members must have at least some ability to predict one anothers' behavior if they are to continue in interaction with one another. However, the group members need not share every understanding about everything to have this predictability. The existence of different understandings as concerns music, food, or sports need not interfere with social relations and usually will not, if the differences are not brought to the fore. The same is true of differences in views about the evaluation of and responsibility for the behavior of young people.

The absence of sharing of understandings can disrupt social life, of course, but the disruption is not automatic. One of the ways disruption can result is from those involved recognizing what they take to be serious differences between them. Such recognition hardly promotes confidence in one's ability to believe one can accept or even predict what they are likely to do. When differences are not displayed, this source of social disruption (but, of course, not all sources) deriving from this is diminished in its effects.

Concealing differences by avoiding the issues involving them is a way of promoting confidence, and denying the existence of these differences by asserting common understandings is another that is at least as effective. It is noteworthy that intergenerational relations came up in a public sort of way because of the interviews. I have not heard Swahili discuss these relations with fellow group members of different generations in public settings. Parents and children do this in private, of course, and the results are rarely to make relations between them easier. Since the interviews made it difficult to conceal differences, another route was taken by most participants in the study: the use of tokens implying a sharing of views when, from the point of view of guides for some kinds of action, they do not exist.

But tokens can accomplish something further. They actively indicate sharing. Predictability is essential to continued interaction, but it is not sufficient by itself. It is easy enough to predict the behavior of a hungry lion, but nevertheless one does not willingly interact with him. The anticipation of acceptable behavior in the areas of mutual involvement is also needed if interaction is to proceed. Tokens can, and in this case do, indicate the existence of the sort of sharing that supports this type of anticipation.

It is worthwhile to note that tokens can do this given either of two interpretations of them by those using them. On the one hand, they can be taken to indicate the actual sharing of the understandings they concern. Tokens, after all, are in many cases also guides. In the area of intergenerational relations, however, it seems likely that many members of both generations are aware that at least some of those who express the understandings in the interviews do not employ them as guides. In this case, the tokens can be taken to indicate a willingness to avoid the *expression* of behavior that is unacceptable even if understandings that would lead to such behavior are known to be present. In the land of the blind, as the proverb quoted at the beginning of this chapter advises, one does not really become blind. By closing a single eye, one partly feigns blindness, thereby signaling a willingness to make concessions and be agreeable with limited cost.

Despite the importance of tokens,[5] it is not my view that their existence is enough to explain how culture is able to serve as the foundation of social life, despite the absence of universal sharing or, even, complete sharing within statuses. Tokens *are* vital elements in social life, but so are some kinds of fairly extensive sharing of actual guides among members of the same status. The next chapter concerns some of the issues in this sharing among members of the same status.

7

Liking Only Those in Your Eye

Relationship Terms, Statuses,
and Cultural Models

Apenda mtu matoni: *He [only] likes [a] person [when
the person is] in [his] eye (i.e., when the person is
in sight).*

For people to take care of themselves and for social relations to proceed,
there must be some common basis for action, some available repository of
the procedures and approaches evolved in the group over the generations.
Earlier chapters have shown that such a basis and repository do not result from
all by all sharing or, even, complete sharing within statuses. Since, however,
social life and its products must depend on some group members sharing some
understandings, the question is, what is shared by whom and, more important,
how does this limited sharing provide the basis for individual and group life?

Status, Culture's Action Arm

Statuses are the action arm of culture. They bring culture's elements to
bear on actual situations and problems through categorizing the actor and his
associates in the actor's mind and indicating not only who does (and does
not) belong to the categories relevant at a given time or situation[1] but also
what is expected of category members and those who associate with them.
The three different functions of the understandings that constitute any status
need not be carried out by different understandings; a single understanding
may serve two or even all three functions.

Those in interaction categorize each other and themselves as belonging to
various categories that are taken as salient in the applicability of their particular expectations. The agreement of their categorizations and the saliences understood to apply are probably never complete, but, as will be seen, there
are powerful processes that make a necessary minimum likely.

When I attended barazas, my fellow participants, judging by what they said and did, accorded me the statuses of visitor (rather than regular member), married man and father, European (i.e., white), university professor,[2] non-Muslim, and probably others. I did not categorize myself in just the same ways, I suspect, but double contingency saved me—as it usually does most people most of the time—from inappropriate behavior. Similarly, I categorized the other baraza attenders as friends, senior community members, Muslims, my hosts, senior men, and family heads.

All persons categorize themselves in a substantial number of statuses at any given period of life according to the situation currently relevant. The actor, in turn, is categorized in a substantial number of statuses by the others involved. The agreement between the various classifications is neither complete nor uniform from instance to instance. Still, social life often proceeds relatively smoothly within the community, indicating a substantial agreement in expectations and in the identifying and salience understandings that "deliver" them.

The complex and simultaneous assignment of similar categories with equivalent salience and expectations by a number of different individuals is daunting to consider in the abstract. Since, however, all members of the Swahili community including two-year-olds have a fairly well developed ability to use statuses in shaping their own behavior and assessing that of others, the complexity can be seen as manageable for participants and, in principle, for observers as well.

Role, a Subunit of Status

Part of the effectiveness of statuses comes from the fact that only a portion of their constituent understandings need to be shared for them to function. Occupants of any one, and those dealing with them as such, need share only those directly concerned with their relationship rather than the status's total inventory of understandings. A student in a chuo (religious school for children) need only share, and that only roughly, the expectations the occupant of the teacher status (mwalimu) has of him and he has of the teacher. The other roles in the teacher status, including that involving the teacher and the student's parents, need not be shared in any detail as far as his own relations with the teacher are concerned. The parent-teacher role may well affect the student, of course, but the student need not, and probably usually does not, have the understandings required for actually participating in that role.

This is not to say one role relationship may not vitally affect another, as the parent/child relationship sometimes affects the teacher-student relationship. Rather it is to say that a status can play a part in guiding the behavior of those in a relationship involving one of its occupants without either the occupant or those in relations with him sharing all the elements in the status.

The part of a status that contains expectations concerning members' relations with members of the same or another status is called a "role" here. This concept is useful in directing attention to the fact that limited sharing between two individuals in a relationship need not lessen the effectiveness of culture's guidance in that relationship. The fact that a status's roles can connect the status to a variety of others in quite different relationships is, of course, vital in understanding the processes whereby social structure operates. Several of these latter processes are examined in chapters 9 and 10, but for the present, the point is that these depend on quite limited sharing, even of the components of shared statuses, for their operation.

In order for statuses and their subdivisions, roles, to operate, it is essential that people be fairly confident about which statuses they occupy, which are occupied by those with whom they are in interaction, and what expectations are associated with that occupancy. As will now be seen, this is not entirely a matter of shared understandings leading to inevitable social consequences. Rather, a dialectic between social relations and the cultural elements concerning them proves central to the effectiveness of culture in this, as in many other, processes central to community and individual functioning.

Cultural Models,
Language, and Statuses

The expectations and salience understandings vital to statuses' functioning are by no means completely shared, but there are "cultural models" of these embedded in the terms that are used to characterize individuals and relationships. These models play a role in promoting social life and individual satisfaction. As Roy D'Andrade (1985:321) notes, the use of what he calls "character terms," which are included among the relationship terms dealt with below, is an important element in learning the complexes of cultural elements involved in social life.

Keesing argues persuasively for the view that knowledge of a language is contingent on knowledge of "a culturally defined model of the universe" (1979:15) and that cultural assumptions are at the very heart of language use (ibid., 25). His focus is on the usefulness of a knowledge of the group's culture in describing language, while the approach here employs the same nexus but focuses on language use as a means group members use to present each other with cultural models and to promote conformity with them. The Swahili are by no means unusual in this usage, as indicated by Holland and Skinner (1987:79) who found a similar one among American college students, but its universality remains to be established.

The existence of these models does not, naturally, assure conformity with their constituent understandings, but they do provide a basis for sharing, a sort of ongoing socialization in what is acceptable and desirable behavior in interpersonal relations. By characterizing the behavior of particular individuals in strongly evaluative ways, they offer the prospect of encouraging conformity. Such encouragement extends not only to the individuals characterized, if they learn of or anticipate the characterization, but to others who are reminded of the constant evaluation of their behavior according to the understandings that are contained in the models.

D'Andrade has examined another aspect of this same phenomenon. He says that "[a] cultural model is a cognitive schema which is intersubjectively shared by a social group" (n.d.:18). This sharing itself, he argues, imparts a force that would otherwise not be present. As he puts it, "Because cultural models are intersubjectively shared, interpretations made about the world on the basis of a cultural model are experienced as obvious facts of the world" (ibid., 18–19).

What is encouraged by the models implicit in Swahili relationship terms is mainly behavior differentiated according to status differences. The ways young men are encouraged to act by the terms concerning their participation in relationships is quite different from the ways senior men are encouraged to act by the terms applying to them, for example. The main force of the models is to promote conformity, but this is less a conformity to a general culture that applies equally to everyone than it is a conformity to the expectations and salience understandings distinctive of particular statuses. Statuses are the basis for distributing culture among group members and across situations (see Schwartz 1972, 1978, 1989), and the models provided by the relationship terms encourage conformity to the different understandings applicable to different actors in the varying situations they are involved in.

The existence of substantial cultural conformity in the Swahili community is obvious. The sources for this conformity, however, can usefully be examined. The Swahili community works because its members act in ways they find more often and more nearly mutually acceptable than not. Men, for example, who have spent time working in Saudi Arabia recount at length their dissatisfaction with almost every aspect of life there save their pay and their association with the fellow Swahili with whom they share quarters. Their reports always involve accounts of the unacceptable behavior of the Saudis and the Saudis' failure to respond properly to the Swahilis' behavior. These accounts imply, and sometimes explicitly involve, comparisons with their home community, which is, at least relatively, pictured as the desirable standard.

Other examples could be adduced of the Swahili view that proper behavior and desirable relationships are characteristic, even uniquely so, of their community. Such evidence of ethnocentrism, however, is hardly problematic in any functioning group and needs only to be brought out to emphasize the general acceptability to community members of much of what their fellow members do.

There is only one possible basis for the community's effective operation and for its members' satisfaction with it, and that is, of course, a shared culture. Chapters 5 and 6 show that an appeal to a general sharing of beliefs and values is factually unacceptable and theoretically blinding. Even occupants of a common status are shown to share only partially understandings concerned with that status.

Here the aim is to take statuses as the foundations of social life and, recognizing the absence of complete sharing even in these, to try to contribute to an understanding of how statuses actually operate in Swahili society. Specifically, attention will be directed to two issues: first, the difficult question of how people identify one another as members of particular statuses in various circumstances, and second, and at greater length, how terms characterizing behavior in social relationships provide representations (or models) of the expectations and saliences of a variety of statuses, thereby encouraging their sharing and promoting conformity to them.

Four Kinds of Statuses

Before going further, two distinctions are useful in understanding how statuses operate in Swahili culture. The first of these concerns two different sorts of relationships and the differences in the statuses, especially in their expectations, associated with them. The second distinction concerns the uses of statuses.

Simplex and Multiplex
Relationships and the Statuses Involved

The statuses that figure in the kinds of relationships Max Gluckman (1955:19) called "simplex" and those in the relationships he called "multiplex" differ in ways important to culture's operation. A simplex relationship contains expectations that are quite specific in reference and limited in scope. "Bus driver," "passenger," and "sales clerk" are the typical sort of statuses here. The expectations in multiplex relationships cross a number of cultural domains and are usually broad and general rather than specific and concrete. "Mother," "neighbor," and "friend" are typical of the statuses in multiplex relationships.

A status in a multiplex relationship can also be involved in a simplex relationship. A Swahili mother's relationship with her child is undoubtedly multiplex, but her relationship with a physician who is treating her child may well be simplex even though she is acting and being responded to as a mother in both relationships. The statuses that form the main base of simplex relationships cannot serve as a basis for carrying on a multiplex relationship.

Two Functions of Statuses

The multiplex-simplex distinction, then, concerns the scope and specificity of expectations in statuses. Another important distinction is between statuses as guides for the behavior of those categorized in them and statuses as ways of placing or identifying people.

The guidance function can be seen in, but is by no means limited to, using status categories as a basis for calling for specific sorts of behavior from those categorized. For example, in a pamphlet written in the 1950s by one of the community's most outspoken leaders, he commanded, *Rere jamani* (Be prideful, family members). This was, I have been told, a demand that his fellow community members, whom he addresses as family members to emphasize their ties to one another and to him, behave themselves according to his somewhat heroic view of how Swahili should act. Similarly, but from the negative side, women sometimes berate one another by saying *Si mwanamke, we!* (Not a woman, you!) meaning that the object of the phrase is not acting as a woman should. In both cases, the guidance offered is, it appears, salient across a wide range of situations and relationships.

Statuses guide behavior through indicating when they are salient and what expectations they involve. They are not always, of course, presented as explicitly as they are in the above examples. In addition to guiding behavior, statuses also serve to characterize people and to indicate how they are connected to others and to social groups as wholes. Thus, in response to asking friends who someone is, I have often been told things such as, "That is Sheikh Mohammed. He is my neighbor and works for the government."

The two dimensions of statuses—one being the nature of their expectations and salience understandings and the other their use in social placement—each have two varieties that come together to make four combinations. That is, both types of statuses, multiplex and simplex, are used as guides to behavior and both are used in placing and characterizing people. More important for our present purposes, the identifying-characterizing function and the guiding function, though distinguishable, are not independent of one another. Thus, if Sh. Mohammed and my informant had stopped being neighbors (either because one of them moved or my informant felt Sh. Mohammed was not acting as a neighbor should), it is possible he would only have mentioned his name, as sometimes happened when others identified people I asked about.

As concerns both simplex and multiplex statuses,[3] part of the result of placing and characterizing someone can be to provide guidance for behavior toward him or her. This guide may be directly useful to the one for whom identification is made by suggesting expectations and salience understandings appropriate in dealings with the identified, or it may indicate the identifier's relationship to the one identified, or both. In short, multiplex statuses can usefully be distinguished from simplex, but both types are used both in placement-characterization and in behavior guidance. These latter functions, though separable, often involve one another.

Statuses, Expectations, and Evaluations

As the complexes of cultural elements that bring shared understandings to bear on the actualities of life, the effectiveness of statuses is as much due to their serving as a foundation for evaluation as their serving as a guide for behavior. The latter function, obviously, depends on status occupants having understandings that individuals not in the status may or may not share. The evaluative aspect, however, depends on elements shared by many who are not status members. Indeed, they may be shared by nonmembers more than members.

Since at least some expectations are associated with identifying status occupants, some bases for evaluation are available not only to the status occupants and those in roles involving them but to many others in the group. Thus, although statuses distribute culture in the sense that only those occupying a status may share all the understandings necessary to meeting the expectations of that status, others may well have understandings that form the basis for evaluating the behavior involved.

Soccer players are by no means the only ones who evaluate performance in the games that go on constantly in Old Town. A young man who is an outstanding player will, in fact, be admired by some community members outside contexts in which soccer is the focus. More generally, evaluations of performance in a status can affect an individual's social relations and prestige beyond the situation in which the performance occurs, and these evaluations may be made by people substantially removed from involvement in the performance. More than that, since statuses are connected to one another in a variety of roles whose expectations interlock, the meeting, or failure to meet, of expectations in one status can affect performance and evaluation in others.

Taking a simple example of the interconnection of expectations, it is not altogether unknown for Swahili men to have trouble meeting the expectations in their work statuses. A small proportion of men, especially young men, cannot get and keep jobs that provide them with the pay they need fully to meet their financial expectations as husbands, fathers, sons, and, sometimes, siblings and neighbors. Failures to meet status expectations in the simplex work relationships which lead a man to be discharged can make it impossible for him to meet some broad and general expectations in multiplex family relationships that call for his having money.

Similarly, behavior called for to meet expectations in multiplex relations can affect performance in simplex relations. This is obviously so when the practical necessities in meeting expectations in a multiplex relationship, such as a mother's need to take time to care for a child, clash with meeting expectations in a simplex relationship, such as the expectation that the same woman be on time for her job as a sales clerk.

Clashes in expectations in the two kinds of relationships are not limited to practical matters. Thus, *haya* is a complex virtue involving definite but modest assertion of one's own rights combined with active consideration for the rights of others. It is valued in many Swahili multiplex relationships, but it can be quite harmful to meeting expectations in simplex relationships in business and commerce where being forward and demanding can be advantageous.

Who Is a What?

For statuses to work as they do, participants in social relationships must share with their partners in interaction understandings of what categories each is assigned. As far as simplex relationships are concerned, recognition of own status and that of the other seems to depend on little beyond an understanding of what the interaction is about. If one had never been on a bus,[4] it might be difficult to understand what being a passenger involves as well as what a "bus driver" is, what he expects, what can be expected of him, and the range of circumstances in which the driver-passenger role is salient. Even in this unlikely case, however, one would quickly learn or stop trying to ride buses. The same is true, mutatis mutandis, for many other simplex statuses.

Even for multiplex statuses, there is so much agreement about categorizing those in broad-scale statuses that it is difficult to get people to discuss the issue. An extract from my field notes on a discussion concerning how one knows who is assigned to a category indicates something of what is encountered when such inquiry is approached directly. The informant, "BR," is a woman in her late fifties whose husband is dead and who lives with her two sons, one seventeen and one twenty-three.

> MS: (BR has just given me an example of what a friend is by discussing a friend of her oldest son. The son's friend is Hamid.) How do you recognize that Hamid is your son's friend?
> BR: I know he is my son's friend because my son has known him for a long time and they go around together.

MS: But how is he different from other young men whom your son has also known for a long time?

BR: They like each other. They are friends.

MS: So a friend is anyone you like and you go around with?

BR: Yes, that is a friend. (If he goes away?) Yes, if he goes away [as to another city or country], he can still be a friend if they continue to get along and remember each other.

MS: But, so I can be sure I understand, when does someone become a friend?

BR: Don't you have friends in America? It's like how you know your neighbor or anybody. You know them.

However limited cultural sharing may be, the idea that one may be in doubt as to who is a friend, an enemy, a brother, or a neighbor is seen as ridiculous. It may be that a person identifies another as a friend or a neighbor but is not similarly identified by the other who, instead, classifies the first as an enemy or vague acquaintance. As far as their direct interaction is concerned, this need make no difference so long as each behaves according to the expectations held by the other as concerns whatever interaction is taking place.

It may be that one acts toward the other as friend and the other acts toward the first as "person who thinks he is a friend." The overlap of the expectations in the two categories may well be sufficient to allow direct interaction of some kinds to proceed. Difficulties would emerge only when one of those involved followed an expectation (e.g., getting help) that is not consistent with the other's classification. Even when direct interaction is proceeding smoothly, the disagreement in classification may affect other relationships (where participants may know of the unshared classification) in ways that shared mutual classification would not.

I have been told by an older man that a younger was an *mshenzi* (uncultivated, uncouth person; see below), but when I saw the two interacting in the limited ways they did, as when entering a mosque at the same time, they acted toward one another as others do who share the community member status. It is clear, however, that the older man's "true" (or, at least, unfavorable) identification of the other affects his behavior in some situations since he did tell me the young man was an mshenzi. In fact, neither identification excludes the other, and it is a matter decided by his salience understandings as to which status, or combination of statuses, guides the older man's behavior toward the younger.

So long as the older man treated the younger as "community member," the young man responded to the expectations in that status and treated his elder, in turn, as "community member." The identifying understandings each used resulted from the mutually contingent status assignment each made of the other so that the interaction proceeded. It is likely it would not have continued as it was when the two met at the mosque had the young man wanted to marry the daughter of the elder, since that would involve expectations beyond the "community member" status, and these would probably touch on the elder's expectations associated with the "mshenzi" status.

From the point of view of how culture works, it appears that agreement on mutual classification is not difficult to achieve in face-to-face relations and depends as much on mutual adjustment of expectations as it does on a pre-existing set of shared understandings. Multiple identifications and assignment to more than one status at a time provide flexibility in different settings according to their different expectations without necessarily obstructing interaction in any of them. There is an effective limitation on conflict arising from unshared mutual classification. This is that those who cannot agree on mutually acceptable categories for one another most commonly cease interaction.

In simplex relationships, the basic identifications involved are nearly unavoidable and leave little room for error. Bus drivers and passengers either place one another in those statuses or interaction concerned with bus riding is impossible.[5] In multiplex relationships, mutual identification is also vital, but, as with the example above in which one person classified the other as friend while being classified himself as enemy, the identifications may be only partially shared. A number of Swahili men, mainly former administrative officers,[6] have told me that in the colonial days, the British officials who came to the coast from Nairobi did not "know how to act." These outsiders, unsocialized by the Swahili and Arabs of the coast, treated all "Africans" the same—to the Swahili, an obvious failure to make important distinctions and one that made the upcountry colonials undesirable partners in interaction.

As Holland (1987a) discovered in her important study of American college students, the ability to differentiate among statuses depends in part on the interest and involvement of the actors in interaction with one another. In what she calls "the romantic sphere" (i.e., the relations of male and female students in dating and such) she found substantial agreement among the students concerning the elaborate classifications of their associates, but in the "academic sphere," where classification was according to subjects studied and similar matters, there is much less agreement (ibid., 240–242).

This finding is important here. It may be that identifying understandings even for the statuses active in multiplex relationships are not completely shared. That they should be fully and generally shared seems unlikely given the generally limited nature of cultural sharing. Since, however, these statuses always involve crucial areas of the lives of those involved, it is likely that the sharing of mutual identification is very substantial. This is made more so by the operation of the mutual adjustment that is the heart of double contingency (see below) in the frequent interaction characteristic of such relations. This is probably the reason Holland's results show that those in high-frequency interaction, common to multiplex relations, come to agree on mutual assignment.

It is important to note that the behavioral importance of mutual assignment in large part resides in the expectations that are part of that assignment. Some expectations are quite specific, and behavior is easily assessed as having met them or not. Other expectations are broader and more diffuse, and establishing whether these have been met involves substantial interpretation. In multiplex relationships, specific expectations and salience understandings of the "passenger gives money/driver issues ticket" sort are usually distinctly secondary. The general tone and significance each participant assigns the behavior of the other matters more in these relationships, and there is a great deal of room for variation in what is acceptable.

Expectations and Double Contingency

Given the flexibility this suggests in multiplex relationships, it might appear that such relationships are being taken as less useful in accomplishing the particular tasks that make up life than simplex relationships are. In fact, this is not so. Simplex relationships are based very substantially on specific expectations, but they are easily ruptured and are not very flexible. Multiplex relationships are more lasting and more flexible, but the very flexibility, based on the less specific nature of the expectations involved, makes them seemingly less useful in getting specific things done. This, however, is countered by the process Parsons calls "double contingency" (1964 [1951]:37 passim). This has been referred to here with respect to identifiers, but it also operates to achieve at least some sharing of expectations.

Thus, for example, in a Swahili family I know, an unmarried daughter got a job, partly prompted by her understanding of what her mother expected her to do given the family need for money. The mother responded in part to the daughter's having done this by taking the major part of the daughter's earnings in accord with what the mother views (she says) as her right. She also leaves part of her daughter's earnings for the daughter's own use (as well as supplying the daughter with a place to live and food) in part in line with her understanding of what she says her daughter expects her to do. When the mother forbade the daughter to use the household telephone because she thought the bill was too high, the daughter objected and said her earnings entitled her to use the telephone when she needed to. The mother acceded to the daughter's wish but increased slightly the proportion of the daughter's wages she took.

The mother-daughter interaction proceeds in this way with each behaving in a way that is partly contingent on what the other does and partly on what the other is thought to expect. So long as both mother and daughter continue to adjust their behavior to the other's response as well as to their view of the other's expectations, interaction can continue without necessary disruption.

In the case cited, the daughter confided that her mother took too much of her pay, but she continued to supply it since, as she said, her mother wanted it and "what else could I do?" Similarly, the mother said that her daughter wasted money foolishly but was, mainly, a "good [girl], not like some 'others.'"

There may be minimal sharing regarding each other's specific expectations, but if each finds the other's actual behavior broadly acceptable (as in Wallace's [1970:27–36] "equivalence structures"), the relationship can continue despite the initially limited agreement on expectations and salience even if the low level of agreement continues. The mother and daughter are by no means fully satisfied with each other's meeting of expectations, but both agree the other continues as a central figure in her life and continues to satisfy the broad expectations that go with being a mother and a daughter.

At a minimum, however, despite double contingency and the existence of some sharing, people do not, indeed cannot, meet all the expectations in their multiplex relationships with one another. That this is so would hardly seem surprising. It does not surprise the Swahili. Every Swahili I talked to about this agreed that no one, "not even a saint," does everything that is expected of him or her. No one, it was often noted, is perfect; only God is.

The proverbs quoted at the beginning of chapter 4 are quite explicit in saying that a bad relative is better than no relative at all. In the terms being used here, an acceptable partner in a multiplex relationship is preferable to having no such relationship. In multiplex relationships, so long as behavior can reasonably be interpreted as meeting their broad expectations,[7] the relationships usually proceed despite imperfect sharing of some of their expectations and salience understandings.

"Relationship Terms" and Shared Understandings

An examination of the terms used to characterize people and their participation in various sorts of social relationships reveals that the meaning of the terms depends on the existence of a number of general values and beliefs. These cultural elements are found to be part of the expectations in an array of the statuses involved in many of the multiplex relationships found in Swahili society. These general understandings are expressed quite explicitly and, often, as parts of the evaluations of particular individuals and their specific behavior. Sometimes the evaluations are general, but more often, they focus specifically on particular statuses of variable inclusiveness ranging from the broad "community member" to the narrow "member of the nuclear family involved."

These expressed evaluations involve using the qualities referred to by particular terms as bases for assessment of the categories of individuals and, sometimes, relationships to which they are applied. The terms are emotionally as well as evaluatively charged, so that their application carries intrinsic support for conformity to the standards they entail. Since the terms are used differently according to the statuses of those to whom they apply, they militate for the differentiated conformity called for by distributed culture rather than for a uniform conformity that would blur functional distinctions among statuses.

Investigating Terms Concerning Expectations and Relationships

To study the terms characterizing individuals and relationships, I began by compiling a list of seventy words and phrases referring to character and behavior. These were originally taken from conversations with various community members. Each term was discussed with three different male informants of high prestige who were native to the community. Each was asked to comment and provide any additional terms he could think of. After analyzing the results of this (Swartz 1985), I discussed these same terms with three older women (one in her fifties, two in their sixties) in the same way on a later field trip (1988). The results of the discussions with the women confirmed my hypothesis that there was little gender-based difference in the models for behavior which can be seen in the uses of the terms.

After eliminating alternate terms and phrases for the same traits and behavior, I have twenty-nine remaining. Each of these is considered below.

The Swahili are very private people, one of whose main values is *sitara*. This can be glossed as "secrecy" or "privacy" with an implication that honor can be maintained only if the specifics of life are kept secret. The basic unit for the sharing of secrets is the household group (usually including a nuclear family and often no one else), and this is expressed in a fairly commonly heard proverb, *Nyumba yasitara mambo*: lit. The house hides the things that happen, with "things that happen" referring to unfavorable and undesirable events.

This pervasive concern with concealing even the most ordinary aspects of life applies to family members and forms an active force in much of what everyone does. The values suggested by this term not only apply in relations with neighbors and fellow community members but with anthropologists as well. These understandings affect the way community members treat one another and limited my ability to observe and discuss community life.

The next terms to be considered are unusual in two respects. First, they concern the broadest sorts of expectations applying in all public relationships involving adults. Second, they are positive in that getting or having what they refer to is unquestionably desirable and positively evaluated by everyone I talked to. A proverb notes, with respect to positive attributes, *Jina jema hung' aa gizani*: [A] good name (always or as a regular thing) shines in [the] dark.

No term is more laden with emotion and value than *uungwana,* referring to the quality of being a noble as opposed to being a slave. It is most often heard as *mwungwana,* meaning a noble person. To say someone is not a mwungwana is a profound insult, which, if accepted, bars the individual and his or her family members from marriage with those who are considered waungwana (pl. of mwungwana). Being a mwungwana always involves the belief that the person so characterized has no slave forebears. This is both a necessary and a sufficient condition in that if one is believed to have slave-free ancestry, one is a mwungwana even if, because of bad behavior, one is a wretched example of the category. This does not, however, mean that category membership is not evaluated according to the performance of certain kinds of behavior and the avoidance of others.

Thus, a mwungwana always shows *utu* (civilization or refined behavior) and avoids brash, noisy, demanding behavior if he wishes to be evaluated positively. Waungwana do not eat cornmeal (or, if they do, let no one know they do), gossip, raise their voices, or squabble with those beneath them. Silence is said to be the anger of a mwungwana, and the general understanding is that a mwungwana, something all community members must be if they are fully part of the community, behaves with restraint, a concern for high standards, and an abiding concern with the rights of others.

Fakhri refers to an attribute informants say is indispensable for honored standing in the community, and, in strict usage, only waungwana can be characterized in this way. My senior male informants, all of whom speak excellent English, as a substantial majority of the community does, say that the English words most fully approximating its meaning are honor, prestige, and dignity. The utu required for being a mwungwana is essential for fakhri, but being a mwungwana is not sufficient for having fakhri. The absence of both slave ancestry and grossly unacceptable behavior makes one a mwungwana, but more positive qualities are needed for fakhri. The most important and obvious of these is the active respect of senior community members.

Fakhri mainly comes from notable accomplishments in religion, education, politics, or the professions. It can, however, be based in personal character and demeanor. A man or woman who is admired for his or her consistently impressive behavior over a period of years may win fakhri despite not having university degrees, great religious learning, wealth, or power.

A person who has fakhri has what really matters even if he is poor to the point of having no regular place to live and only an indefinite source of food, as some learned, holy men (*sheikh* is the term used for such a person) might. Further, if you are without fakhri, not even a shiny Mercedes and a new two-story house will redeem you. A person whose money comes from sin—a bar

owner, a person profiting from selling fermented coconut toddy, a pimp—
may be rich, but he will not have fakhri if people know the source of his
wealth. Even building a mosque may not win him the esteem and respect
referred to by the term "fakhri."

Fakhri has few synonyms or modifiers. There is little elaboration of the
idea as far as vocabulary is concerned. It is a highly desirable condition, and
everyone knows that it is. There are, as we will see, a variety of ways to get
it, but there is little embellishment of the basic idea. It may be that the
Eskimos have many names for the snow that is the base for much of what
they do, but the Swahili have only one name for what observation shows to
be one of the most significant—publicly, the most significant—parts of life
for them.

Women are most concerned with their fakhri with their female neighbors
(the women of their mtaa), while men's fakhri is affected far more by their
relations throughout the Old Town community. Women gain fakhri according
to their relationships with and evaluation by their neighbors. Men's fakhri
has a broader base, depending, as it does, on all their relations throughout
the community.

Women in their relations with one another are benefited in meeting expectations if their husbands provide them with sufficient funds to dress and
ornament themselves well. A woman who succeeds in getting her husband
to provide her with the needed funds for proper dress, ornament, and the
staging of reasonably impressive weddings and funerals is well along to having at least a minimum of fakhri. Unless a man is viewed as a great sheikh,
he must find employment, almost always outside the immediate community,
that will pay him enough to allow him to dress properly and to entertain his
fellows on great occasions.

Men's fakhri, however, appears independent of providing funds for wives
in that a man receives no honor for a wife who has high prestige among
women and loses none if she has a low standing with her peers. The division
of the sexes, in fact, makes it almost impossible for men to know what women
are doing save through the reports of their wives, and, similarly, women depend on hearsay for their knowledge of the doings of men.

All men are expected to be pious and, preferably, learned in the holy works.
When small, everyone goes to religious school to learn sufficient Arabic to
be able to read the Koran and pray, but ever-increasing knowledge of religious
matters is an important source of male fakhri that is less open to women who
may, however, contribute to their fakhri by their general piety. The idea that
there could be a female sheikh was viewed as risible by the women I asked
about it.

Children who do well in secular school and who demonstrate general competence in life's affairs—especially boys but also, in the women's domain,
girls—are much admired and are a source of fakhri for their mothers and,

less, their fathers. However, children's attainments should never be mentioned since this is understood to incite *hasadi* (jealousy) and the evil eye (*mato*), which can lead to the admired child losing his admirable ways or, even, his life.

Women are viewed—and view themselves, as best I can tell—as emotionally freer, less logical, and less tied to the practical concerns of life (especially money) than men are. According to both male and female informants, this is women's proper state,[8] and although women who are careful planners and successful in business (there are currently several who are) are admired, they may also be feared by members of both sexes (but evidence about this from women is conflicting). I have heard of a number of these businesswomen that they dominate their husbands, which is said by members of both sexes to be a bad thing and contrary to Islam.

Men derive much of their fakhri from their dignity, which entails not suffering others to act as though they are being deferred to. So, for example, if two men take tea together in a teahouse, there is sometimes a spirited discussion of who should pay, especially if one feels that the other's paying would indicate his acceptance of the other's largess. Men are reluctant to accept anything that appears to be charity, and even children will not accept clothing that has been used by another unless the first user was a same-sex sibling.

Part of the tension between men and women stems from women's inclination to push their husbands to spend freely on rituals, clothing, and jewelry and the men's fear that lack of money may put them in a position where they cannot always defend their prestige. Similarly, men fear that knowledge of their poverty (which may or may not be real) may be spread through the gossiping of women. A man does not lose fakhri for being poor but only for being known to engage in the behavior associated with poverty such as eating cornmeal. Although women also prize being "nobles," men fear that the women's garrulousness together with their weak, as men see it, commitment to fakhri many undermine both their own honor and that of the men associated with them. There is a proverb that men sometimes repeat which brings together their fear of women's talkative natures and their scorn for women's commitment to the standards of fakhri: *Hakuna mwanamke mwungwana*: (There is no woman [who is a] noble).

Adabu is the only other term concerning general standing in the community. This one, more than fakhri, has to do with relations between people according to their respective statuses and, also, their prestige.

Adabu can be glossed as "proper relations and behavior between superiors and inferiors." In standard Swahili, adabu is often glossed as "manners," and a book entitled *Adabu Njema* was used as a sort of manners guide in Tanzanian schools in the latter part of the colonial period and the early years of independence. For the native speakers in Mombasa, however, the meaning is much narrower.[9] Broadly, the term refers to being properly deferential to superiors and, at the other side of asymmetrical relationships, not being un-warrantedly overbearing with inferiors. In fact, the term is mostly used for a young person who deals with his elders with unfailing respect. Adabu implies a hierarchy in social relations, and experience with the group shows that this hierarchy involves both age and fakhri. A young person with adabu treats all older people with a certain deference but is far more circumspect and respect-ful in behavior toward an older person with firmly established fakhri than with one who has little.

Honor and Deference:
How Terms Encourage Conformity

The understandings involved in adabu and fakhri provide an important illustration of how interconnected complexes of understandings are mani-fested in speech and how, in turn, they affect manifest social behavior. A junior who meets the general expectations in behavior toward his seniors is characterized in a positive way by those seniors and is likely to gain prefer-ence when there are limited goods at the senior's disposal (e.g., marriage with the senior's daughter).

At the same time, a fairly senior man or woman who has met the ex-pectations in his or her status as adult community member gains fakhri, which leads younger people to behave toward him or her with adabu, thus provid-ing manifest (i.e., behavioral) confirmation of the older person's fakhri. Such demonstration, in turn, wins respect and esteem for the younger person and confirms that he or she has utu (civilization).

To generalize this, and similar processes are involved in terms to be con-sidered below, meeting expectations for positively evaluated behavior by members of one status (adult community member in the example) imposes expectations on relations with occupants of another status (young community member) which, if met, bring rewards to both parties to the relationship. By so doing, the sorts of status expectations central to valued relations are dis-played and the merit of conforming to them is demonstrated in observable behavior.

The interconnections of the expectations inherent in fakhri and adabu entail sequences of behavior from different individuals which demonstrate the vir-tues of both sets of expectations by manifestly (i.e., socially) rewarding them. The expectations involved provide a script, as it were, for converting broad understandings about honor and "good" behavior between individuals of dif-ferent ages into directly observable action that affects the individual's com-munity standing and, at least in some cases, self-esteem.

Interestingly, for men, I recorded no words for negative aspects of standing in the community. To be without fakhri is less a negative condition than it is lacking a prestigious but nonessential positive one. Such a person may well be seen as a mwungwana if his genealogy is acceptable (or, at least, not known to be otherwise), and, unless he is known for egregiously violating the standard expectations of the community member status, he will be characterized as such without further qualification. He is just not a prestigious and honored community member.

For women, the situation is rather different. If they do not stage the impressive weddings and funerals that bring fakhri but do attend those of others (and all women do attend), they are said by informants to risk bringing shame (aibu) on themselves. It is only a "risk" of shame because so long as they have an unmarried child or a living parent, the opportunity to meet the honor-bringing expectations still exists. When all chance of meeting expectations has passed, however, the woman who has not held the rituals is likely to be negatively evaluated as a man who has failed to meet equivalent expectations is not.

Adabu, as concerns young people, does not have the optional quality fakhri has for men. *Huna adabu* (You have no adabu) is a strong reproach when delivered from a senior to a junior. A young man or boy (girls and young women are rarely in situations where such issues arise since they are generally secluded in their houses) who consistently fails to manifest adabu is called a *muhuni,* a pejorative term concerning failure to meet a range of expectations to be considered below.

A middle-aged man cannot be a muhuni no matter how he acts. Although both fakhri and adabu apply to behavior in general, they refer to different sorts of behavior for members of different statuses and their presence or absence is evaluated according to the status of the person involved. Just as mature men cannot be judged as muhuni, without adabu, children cannot have fakhri. They can only contribute to or detract from that of their parents. Further, women's fakhri comes from different behavior as evaluated by a different audience than men's does.

Unfavorable Terms and Understandings Mainly about the Young

Somewhat more broadly applicable but related to muhuni and closely connected to adabu, there is the characterization *mshenzi,* uncivilized and uncouth person, mentioned in the general discussion of status in chapter 5. Like the epithet, "Huna adabu" (You have no manners), "mshenzi" is an insult sometimes hurled at an offensive person rather than being only a characterization used in discussion or in describing someone. An mshenzi is a person who lacks the attributes of civilization, utu. It is someone who fails to meet the most immediate expectations in interaction (e.g., by failing to dress properly or speak acceptably). Most often, this trait is attributed to noncommunity members, but some community members who are understood to violate seriously the standards of decent behavior are included. It is generally a young person who is characterized as an mshenzi. Still, an older person is occasionally also referred to in this way if he (I have only rarely heard it used for female community members) is viewed as an egregious violator of direct expectations concerning dress, speech, and interpersonal relations.

An even more serious pejorative used almost exclusively for young people is based on a term, *fadhla*, used in Old Town but not listed in any of the standard Swahili dictionaries (Krapf 1882; Johnson 1959; Akida et al. 1981). It refers to gratitude and reciprocity between those in junior statuses and those in senior statuses. Although the term is positive, it occurs mainly as an accusation or denunciation by an older person (often a parent or other relative) of a younger and concerns the younger's failure to reciprocate for what the older has done for the younger.

The general importance of fadhla in relations among peers was readily agreed to by informants, but in conversation, I rarely heard people mention or talk about it save in relations between juniors and seniors. Moreover, all of my recorded instances of its occurrence are references to a junior's failure to do what a senior thinks the junior should have done. These failures sometimes refer to specific instances of help not given (e.g., not taking a sick person to the hospital) or consideration not shown (e.g., failure to visit a parent) but can also be quite general, as in failure to live in a way that reflects credit on the parent.

The word is used as a serious denunciation of a junior by a senior: *"Huna fadhla!"* I am told that a young man can be moved to tears by his father or some other highly respected senior telling him he has no fadhla and that the same is true for young women and their mothers, although the term may be in less frequent use among women. So far as I can establish, the term is not used as an epithet across gender lines.

The general expectation involved in fadhla is a broad and vital one in relations between individuals in statuses with quite different prestige. Unlike adabu, fadhla is not an expectation in all relationships between juniors and seniors. Fadhla refers to expectations of juniors as held by seniors in very close relationships, especially between parents and children but possible in any relationship where the interests of the two are closely identified.

Expectations in Specific Relationships

Turning to the expectations in specific relationships, a meager vocabulary appears on my list, but the terms used refer to some that are quite central where they apply.

The first of these, *shibana*, refers to a role where the statuses (and there are rarely or never kinsmen in this relationship) of the participants include expectations that are unique among those in the community. The male participants (women seem never to have this relationship) can ask each other for anything without haya ("shyness," see below) and can take each other's food or money without asking permission. Such freedom with other's possessions cannot, informants tell me, cause a quarrel in a role characterized in this way. The relationship is one that grows up slowly over a long period between men who get on with and trust one another.

This relationship is a rare one. It was only after much inquiry that I was able to get a single example of it, and subsequent searching has revealed only one other. The fact that the shibana relationship rarely occurs, however, should not obscure the important ideals and expectations it entails. The rarity of the Western honest man, disinterested party, or unbiased judge does not lessen the broader implications of the understandings forming those statuses, and the same is true of the shibana relationship. It serves, I suspect, to underline the nature of expectations in ordinary men's relationships by its contrast with them. Every man I talked to about this relationship knew what it was and what its expectations are even if they could think of no participants.

The fact that shibana, with its broad expectations and mutual accessibility, is so rare and difficult of attainment emphasizes the markedly different and much narrower expectations in more common relations between unrelated men. Knowing the expectations in the shibana relationship and its rarity does not ensure conformity to comparable and opposite expectations in other men's relationships, but it certainly calls attention to them. This is especially so as concerns the potential shame arising from being free with another man's confidence and possessions.

Women, whose possessions are closely controlled (ideally, at least) by their male kin, could not easily be in a relationship whose central expectations specifically concern the use of possessions. Perhaps important, however, is the fact that shibana-like freedom is more characteristic of relations between women in areas not concerning the free use of possessions. The expectations in women's relations with one another allow, sometimes require, that they embrace each other, shout together in joy and anger, hurl insults, dance together, and gossip. Shibana-like lack of restriction is not unusual in the expectations in many women's relations, and it would not offer a sharp contrast as it does to what is common in relations involving men.

Effects of Relationship Terms through Contrast

The general point suggested by the shibana relationships is that the expectations in particular relationships can be made socially visible and psychologically effective in ways other than those we saw for "honor" (fakhri) and "manners" (adabu) where the meeting of expectations receives manifest social rewards.

As will be seen, Swahili shared understandings are often displayed by focusing attention on the badness of not meeting them. Shibana calls attention to the expectations in ordinary men's relationships by focusing on the rarity, rather than the badness, of their absence. Shibana may call attention to expectations such as generosity, openness, and selflessness, but since these are appropriate for men, if at all, in relations with children and wives, it would seem likely that the main cultural effect is that of emphasis by contrast.

The Virtues of Reserving Special Treatment for Those in Special Relationships

Liking Only Those in Your Eye   The more usual sort of contrast, that between commendable meeting of expectations and condemnable failure to meet them, is seen in the clearly disapproving characterization of a particular sort of participation in relationships: *Apenda mtu matoni* (lit. He or she likes a person [while he or she is] in [his or her] eyes [i.e., sight]).

This, informants told me, refers to a person who likes people and pays attention to them only when they are with her (it is used most for women) and forgets about them when they are not present. Some informants say the characterization means the person has no real commitment to anyone and treats everyone basically the same. The implication, I was told, is that people should differentiate between those who are closely related (by kinship or, less, neighborhood) to them and those only distantly connected and that the salience of a relationship should not depend wholly on the presence or absence of those involved in it.

Informants are unanimous in saying that liking those who are in sight is a negative trait and that people would be quite angry if they knew someone was using the phrase to characterize them. An important quality of this phrase is that, unlike shibana, it focuses on a person rather than a relationship. This, in fact, is characteristic of most of the terms concerning meeting or failing to meet expectations. By focusing on individuals, the implied evaluation becomes forceful to the extent that people wish to avoid being unfavorably characterized. Thus, the implied model not only formulates and displays valued expectations and saliences but does so in a way that can promote conformity to them.

A related and highly similar cultural model to the one found in the "liking those in sight" phrase occurs in two proverbs, one that states the understandings abstractly and one that makes an accusation against a particular person.

The abstract statement is made in a proverb quoted at the beginning of chapter 4: *Mla nawe hafi nawe ela mazawa nawe* (lit. He [who] eats with you will not die with you unless he was born with you).

The understanding here is people who are "born with you," mainly your nuclear family kin, will stand by you, unlike those who share your largess but who have no strong tie of kinship. Informants say that the message is that it is a mistake to treat everyone the same, especially to waste your resources on "strangers," since only close kin are committed to you. The proverb, like the accusation that someone has no lasting affection, emphasizes the virtue of differentiating between those with whom one has lasting ties (i.e., of close kinship) and all others.

The same message is contained in an unusual proverb used as criticism of whomever the user wishes to name for neglecting their close kin while being generous with "outsiders": [Someone's name] *ni uvuli wa mvumo hufunika walo mbali* (lit. [The named person] is [like] the shade of the Mvumo, it covers those who are far away).

The mvumo is a tree with a long, branchless trunk and a crown of branches and leaves at the top so that it gives no shade near its base but only at a distance. This proverb says that the person it names gives his good things only to those who are distant from him while neglecting those near him. This message is the same as that seen in the previous two statements, but here it is a culturally constituted trope for use against a named person.

Informants agree that this proverb would not be used in the presence of the person named and that that individual would probably not find out the comparison had been made. Community members agree, however, that those who hear the comparison involving another would be likely to consider who else, including themselves, it might apply to.

Being Accustomed   Broadly, the preceding three proverbs all emphasize the importance of distinguishing between those with whom there are close ties, mainly kin based, and all others. They specifically enjoin the reservation of affection and other scarce goods to relationships with kin or, at least, people whom one has associated with for very long periods. A related but different message mainly concerned with neighbors and friends is found in the personal trait, *hanamazoea*.

The verb *zoea* can be glossed as "become accustomed to" or "being used to." *Mazoea,* the nominal form, is used to refer to the state of habituation or being accustomed. "Hanamazoea" can be glossed as having no habituation or not becoming accustomed to people or things. It is an unfavorable characterization applying to one who does not develop closer relationships over time. It is applied to a person who fails to be friendly and return hospitality through failing to manifest signs of friendship such as invitations despite having often accepted such signs from others.

The positive state, mazoea, can be seen in the keening of a woman at her stepfather's funeral: "Habituation," she wept, "is worse [i.e., more deeply felt] than love" (*Mazoea mabaya kuliko mapenzi*). Lasting relations are most valued, and kin relations are the prototype of these, but failure to treat long-standing associations with due regard is disapproved even if they involve those without kin ties.

Broad Personal Traits, Broad Expectations, and Hierarchy

The absence of valuable traits, such as "habituation," is understood as unfortunate, even deplorable, but not usually remediable. It is the general Swahili view that character traits are fixed and, although controllable, cannot be changed. Thus, the proverb, *Tabia ni chanda cha mwili*: lit. Character is [a] finger [i.e., part] of [the] body.

Character plays a vital part in Swahili understandings in how people behave, and, although character is mainly fixed, it is worthwhile, as an informant put it, "to praise what is good so there can be teaching." Some of the most praised traits are those involved in meeting expectations in roles, especially in those involving seniors. Similarly, some of the most generally condemned traits are those manifest in failing to meet such expectations in these relations. Description of the traits, then, provides explicit statements of the understandings that are central expectations in important roles and offer a basis for "teaching" through praising, or condemning, them.

One of the admired traits, particularly important for younger people but praiseworthy in everyone, is *haya*. This word describes the main characteristics of a person who is modest rather than boastful or brazen and who is considerate of the rights and sensibilities of others. A child who is offered an attractive toy and, instead of enthusiastically accepting, remains quiet and averts his eyes is said to have haya. A man or a woman who behaves with modesty and restraint when successful and who is reluctant to impose on others is showing haya, as is a person who is generous in assessing the behavior of others. A person with haya knows his or her rights and entitlements and does not forego them without strong reasons, but is readier to view others as having met expectations than to view them as having failed to do so.

As noted above, the participants in the extremely rare shibana relationship use each other's possessions without haya. This means that they need not be concerned, as good people in most relationships are, about accepting things from others beyond what is called for by closely calculated reciprocity. Save in the shibana relationship, those with haya are concerned to see that the rights of their partners in relationships will receive primary attention while being ready to interpret what has been done by the partner as satisfying their own rights. Haya is, generally, a reluctance to view one's self as slighted or neglected while manifesting concern about the other.

Because of its haya, the lion, an animal admired by the Swahili for its bravery and lack of guile, is said not to attack those who look straight into his eyes. A brave soldier has the same characteristic, which is seen in his knowing his duty and doing it, while, at the same time, being respectful of others, even opponents, who know their rights and stand up for them.

While haya is a highly valued trait that strongly affirms the general significance of others' rights, its emphasis on consideration for others brings it closer to leading those having it to be easily victimized by those without it. Informants say that those with haya know their rights as well as those of others, just as the lion does, and that being victimized is *upumbafu,* foolishness or idiocy. In fact, however, assessments of people sometimes lead the same person to be characterized by haya or by upumbafu depending on the assessor's own character and his overall view of the person involved and of the acts in question.

Respect and Reciprocity

Closely related to haya, *heshima* refers to the trait of respecting others and not being arrogant or proud in dealing with them, while, at the same time, behaving with dignity so as to be worthy of respect. There is a proverb that says, *Heshima apewa mjuwaye heshima*: "Heshima" is given to he who knows [recognizes] heshima.

A person with haya accords heshima to others and is, therefore, a likely object of heshima. The understandings basically involved in heshima are more reciprocal than those in haya. A young person with haya is sure to accord heshima to those with whom he or she deals, but he or she may receive little heshima personally because of his or her junior position. In a similar way, adabu, "manners," always inclines a young person to accord heshima to seniors but will win the junior only limited heshima. Both haya and heshima concern the expectations involving rendering unto others, but heshima involves more of also expecting to be treated with the respect one's dignity and accomplishment deserve.

Hierarchy as a General Understanding Supported by the Use of a Variety of Terms

It will be clear by now that Swahili talk about a series of praiseworthy and desirable character traits having to do with hierarchical relationships and the expectations, especially but not exclusively, of the junior in those relationships. All of the terms—fakhri, adabu, haya, heshima—involve a distribution of the understandings that call for a modest and respectful manner, mainly from those in junior statuses directed especially but not exclusively toward those in senior statuses. These terms all express a positive evaluation of generally being concerned with the rights of others and with meeting broad expectations in a range of relationships.

Not only do the terms provide a recurring reminder of the different expectations in the various statuses involved in important relationships but they can also serve to support conformity by providing desired, or to be avoided, characterizations of the participants in those relationships. Thus, haya and heshima are held up as characterizing valued behaviors in particular statuses, and, at the same time, they are represented as essential traits in those whom others admire. It is a cutting reprimand for a senior to say to a junior "Huna adabu" (You have no manners) or, on the positive side, approvingly to characterize a young person as *mwenye haya,* (having respect for the rights of others and also his own). The terms, in other words, not only provide a model of culturally approved ways of meeting expectations distributed among different statuses but they also can serve as forces for conformity by applying directly to specific individuals.

None of this would come as a surprise to an observer of Swahili interaction. Two-year-olds walking gravely up to friends of their fathers and lightly kissing their hands are demonstrating adabu (manners), acknowledging fakhri (honor), and showing heshima (respect). It may be going too far to say that their behavior is connected with some kind of permanence in their relationship with the owner of the kissed hand and with the permanence of their fathers' relations with that person, but the fact is that they are not urged to do this kissing (not publicly anyway) and seem to do it only with senior kin and regular, respected visitors to their houses.

The negative aspect of the complex just seen appears in the words *kibri* and *jeuri.* "Jeuri" refers to behavior of people who can best be characterized by English phrases such as "disrespectful youth," "street hoodlum," "boor," and the British "cheeky." My best informant tipped his kofia over one eye and slumped in his chair so that he was half lying down (in sharp contrast to the erect sitting posture and carefully centered hat of the individual with adabu) when explaining this word's meaning to me.

A jeuri person, more often a young person than an old one and usually a male rather than a female, is said to use people's things without permission, speak rudely to everyone, and take things from people's hands abruptly when accepting food or other objects. Young men who are rough in their ways, who spend their time with undesirable companions, and who are suspected of drinking and smoking bhang (marijuana) are called muhuni, and the characteristic behavior of muhuni is to be jeuri. It is the opposite of the behavior, conduct in relations, and character implied by fakhri, adabu, and heshima. Informants say that formerly people would not allow their daughters to be betrothed to young men who were muhuni and whose behavior was jeuri, but these days, they say, that is no longer possible since all the young men are muhuni and are at least sometimes jeuri. This view is generally delivered with despair and sometimes comes with bleak comments about *akher zamani,* the end of time, a lament discussed in chapter 2.

Whether all young men are muhuni or not, I have never met one who wanted to be characterized in that way. The most abandoned and hopeless young men, older informants say, are those who spend their days—and sometimes nights—in the clubhouses (*gahdens*) that are erected in small, unused open spaces in Old Town. These young men include many of those who wear their hair long, contrary to the traditional style of cutting it short or shaving it altogether, and who most obviously reject the restrained behaviors practiced by older men. They are numbered prominently among the youths who bring despair to their elders and who, in turn, say the elders do not understand modern times. Even these young men bridle at the suggestion they might be jeuri and are muhuni.

The understandings put forward in their positive form by the terms "adabu," "haya," and "heshima" are also involved in the pejorative terms "jeuri" and "muhuni." The fact that the young men reject these characterizations suggests their potency. It may be that the young men of the gahdens—and their less-dissatisfied fellow youths who do not spend their time in these disfavored hangouts but who dress and act in a similar way—do not meet the expectations invoked by adabu and the other positive terms as their elders see it. But the youths believe they do meet them. They say they are as respectful as their elders deserve, that they always show concern for the rights of others, and that their behavior is modern (*ya sasa*) rather than rude.

Terms and Conformity

It is not that the descriptive terms ensure conformity to everyone's expectations but rather that they make these expectations known and do so in a way that emphasizes the value of meeting them. Occasionally, terms are used in openly expressed denunciations such as "Huna fadhla" (You have no gratitude) where they serve as coercive instruments, but most consistently they display the valued expectations attached to particular statuses and indicate the virtue of meeting them. The terms exert pressure for conformity according to the wishes of those who are aware of them to avoid condemnation or win approval, but this may be distant and contingent on the characters and, especially, relationships between the terms' subjects and their users.

As we will see in chapter 8, the effectiveness of the evaluations of behavior depend on the statuses both of the evaluator and of the evaluated. The young men who are characterized as muhuni often reject evaluations from members of the older generation. Even so, the youths are reminded of what the expectations are which form the basis of these evaluations and they concede some force to them by insisting that in their own view, and that of their peers, they meet them.

Some General Understandings of the World and Relationships

The Swahili share what they say is the general Muslim belief that the world has been disintegrating steadily since the days of the Prophet in the seventh century. Several have told me that they believe that their group may be among the leaders in this disintegration because of what they understand as their poverty and the pervasive, destructive influence of the outside, Christian and Indian, worlds. It is not without significance that I collected more words referring to personality traits and general behavioral characteristics that are disapproved than words referring to approved traits and characteristics. It is notable that it is in relationships involving seniors and juniors, the fakhri-adabu relationships, that decline is thought by at least some group members to have been most serious.

Not all aspects of interpersonal relationships are taken to have changed equally. Interpersonal conflict is understood as having altered rather less than meeting expectations in hierarchical relationships has. Fighting and open quarreling are not at all common among men, although men who have acquitted themselves well in a fight are at least covertly admired. Overtly, they are in danger of being characterized as muhuni unless the fight is with an outsider, was clearly started by the other or, preferably, was started by both.[10]

In relations within the community, amity is the general expectation. There are no descriptive words for those who promote amity unless the already considered complex words concerning manners, respect, deference, and honor can be looked on as doing that. There are, however, a number of terms concerned with failures to meet expectations that, if met, would contribute to amity.

Characterizations of Conflict Bringers

Gossip and tale-mongering among women is common, the men say, and the negative words regarding bringing conflict into interpersonal relations focus around gossiping. *Fidhuli,* a person skilled in insulting others, is feared, and the unwary are warned against associating with such people, but there is also a bit of admiration for the hurler of especially pointed insults. The underlying understandings, of course, involve the expectation that insults will be avoided, and a person who does not meet this general expectation is negatively evaluated to the point of being considered dangerous. If, however, the fidhuli does it well, there is admiration—and one cannot avoid seeing the admiration in people's comments about a skilled fidhuli—for the aptness of the insults rather as there is admiration for a skillful thief.

Kufye means easily insulted and offended. It is a trait, most commonly found in women but present in some men, that is little admired. It exists in a nearly dialectical relation with fidhuli in that your skill as an insulter is related to my perception of insult, while my reluctance to be affronted limits your ability to insult. The implication that there is a value on interpreting what others do as meeting expectations rather than the reverse when there is a doubt is supported by informants who say that a reluctance to view others as having failed to behave properly is part of the valued haya.

Insults come not only from things said but also from failures to meet expectations. If a woman fails to notice another's new dress (and women do quite openly comment on one another's clothing at weddings), the wearer might be insulted because her expectation that her dress would be admired was not met. Such an insult, however, would often be viewed as an indication of kufye unless the neglect were pointed. A person with kufye is one who holds unshared expectations of a particular kind. It is interesting and instructive to contrast this with the sensitivity of the person having the valued trait, haya.

The person with haya is sensitive to indications that expectations are not being met because his or her haya would result in a loss of self-esteem should that happen. Such suffering due to haya is admirable, while that of the person with kufye is not. The person with kufye makes everyone a fidhuli, a skilled insulter, and puts in question everyone's ability to meet expectations, while a person with haya shows how proper regard for real expectations and their fulfillment can operate to bring credit to the individual and to make his or her social relationships more satisfying.

Insults, Conflict, and Secrecy/Privacy

Insults and being offended by them are connected to a central value in all close Swahili relationships, sitara. This highly desired condition involving concealing a substantial proportion of all information concerning self and family was mentioned above. This condition, sitara, is based on *siri*, secret[s], and is connected to insults and offense by the fact that others' ability to shame or insult depends on their knowing about the life and activities of the insulted and his or her family. Being accused of being kufye, too easily insulted, or any other undesirable trait, depends, as informants explicitly formulate it, on people knowing about what you do. If you conceal what you do by maintaining sitara, you are protected so that, quite literally, one cannot have too many secrets. To have siri is not so much an admirable trait, the way having haya is. Rather, it is a prudent and sensible one whose absence is "idiocy" (upumbafu).

With "privacy" or "secrecy" there can be little basis for insults or, to carry this further, for "shame" (aibu), a singularly important process to be considered at length in the next chapter. It is worth noting that the only Swahili dictionary written in the Swahili language (Akida et al. 1981) defines "sitara" as "hali ya kuficha jambo la aibu" ([the] condition of hiding [a] thing [i.e., matter, source of] shame). The state of having sitara is obviously a desirable one from the perspective taken by the Swahili I know. Openness is not valued, as far as I could determine, by any community member, although there was substantial variation in how much people wanted hidden and how vigorous they were in doing that.

The importance of privacy and concealment is seen further in the disapproving term, *mwazirifu* (lit. exposer), referring to someone who talks quite openly about shameful things in the family. Children and elderly widows are said to be the usual "exposers," both because they talk too freely with anyone who will listen to them and because they go to people's houses at mealtimes and accept food. This last is viewed with horror by the family of the one who does it, because it is understood to imply that there is not enough food at their own houses. Worse yet, an exposer may go to people's houses and actually ask for food.

Such people spoil the privacy/secrecy, sitara, of their families and provide the material the insulters can use and the thin-skinned can be offended by. The *mdaku* is an outsider who seeks the facts the "exposer" is quite ready to give away. This last creature, like the first, provides the ammunition for insult.

Insults, Honor, and Expectations

It will be apparent that the insulting, the revelation of shortcomings in the family of the target of the insults, is closely related to the whole complex of understandings focusing around honor (fakhri) examined above. Insults are not easily attached to those with fakhri. When this honor is based on piety or excellence of character, what insults can reach the honored one? When it is based on style of dress, elegance of manner, or success in worldly things, the insults can only be effective if they attempt to attack character. In short, a person with fakhri is, by virtue of having it, less open to harm by insult because he or she meets rather demanding expectations of at least one important kind. Insults and fakhri are opposed sets of understanding and both depend on how expectations are met.

Insults reduce fakhri through implying or saying explicitly that the expectations bringing honor have not been met. In fact, most of the qualities that confer honor (fakhri) are qualities that meet broad expectations in social relationships, and failure to meet them makes such relationships difficult. There are people who are understood to impede others' social relationships by making these others believe that their expectations of partners in social relationships are not being met. Such people are called *sabasi,* and their specialty is trouble making.

A sabasi causes quarrels between people by telling each of them that the other is saying bad things about him or her. The closest English counterparts to this are "troublemaker," "tale bearer," or the almost archaic and only vaguely appropriate "buttinsky." The sabasi functions in a community where there are a variety of understandings alerting those who share them to the possibility that others are maligning them. The term itself seems to stir negative feelings in those who told me about it.

An aspect of interpersonal relations that is not clearly suggested in any of the above but which is a vital concern in relationships is found in the trait called *hasadi,* jealousy. Any positive quality a person seems to have may induce this jealousy, and this is very much the same as regards honor. The trait is much invoked in Swahili ethnopsychology and points to some of the central expectations in several multiplex relationships.

One such understanding is that everyone has hasadi and that it is normal to be jealous to a certain extent but that some people carry this to pathological extremes. Such people have a constant predisposition to it, *husudu,* (to) covet. This trait is often attributed to a less rewarded brother by a brother who feels more rewarded (by parents or by life), but the suspicion of coveting is widespread and by no means limited to siblings or other close kin.

Covetous people are much feared in that they are understood to feel that anything the object of their jealousy gets is rightfully theirs. These people are dangerous in that they are understood to retaliate by telling bad stories about the objects of their jealousy and, less openly mentioned but vital, in other ways.

The "other ways" include a quite involuntary evil eye called, simply, *jito,* or "eye." This jito operates to harm any object of open admiration. The cautionary tale is told, for example, of a *mwadhin* (the one who calls others to prayer) with a beautiful voice.

A person with jito was visiting Old Town and heard a mwadhin issuing the call to prayer. As the call was being issued, someone remarked to the visitor that the mwadhin's voice was beautiful. In midcall, the voice was stilled as the visitor's "eye," acting without conscious intention on his part, silenced it forever by making the mwadhin mute.

The part of coveting in Swahili social relationships and its relationship to the expectation that group members keep group, usually family, affairs to themselves is now clearer. We have seen that it is considered important to keep knowledge of the shortcomings of one's family from reaching the attention of "insulters" and that this is connected to sitara, with disapproval being accorded those who give away the secrets from the inside and those who try to dig them out from the outside with inquisitiveness. We now see it is also important—sometimes a matter of survival—to keep the family strengths and successes private as well. Failing to do so can arouse jealousy and the revenge of the jealous (hasadi) in the form of bad stories circulated and, even, the dire effects of the evil eye, jito.

The Part of Relationship Terms in Cultural Dynamics: Cultural Models

In the multiplex relationships that are the heart of Swahili social life, the identifying understandings that allow community members to know who is what under what circumstances are quite generally shared. So much so, in fact, that people take them as self-evident. Even when sharing of identifying understandings is less than complete at the beginning of an interaction, double contingency operates to create sufficient sharing for interaction to proceed. Further, less than complete sharing of identifying understandings is seen neither to halt interaction in many situations and contexts nor to prevent the differences in status assignments from having consequences in the relationship at issue and/or in others.

Thus, people disagree about placing one another with one set of identifiers, such as those for the statuses of friend and enemy, but may well be able to interact with one another in a variety of settings using statuses on whose identifiers they do agree, such as community member. At the level of interaction, identifying understandings are, by their nature, either shared or unimportant for immediate relations. Failures to share broader identifiers may well have consequences for broader relationships, if such exist, but they need not hamper day-to-day contacts.

The general effectiveness of status identification, however, is not sufficient by itself for social life to proceed. There must also be some sharing of expectations and of the salience understandings that make statuses effective guides to action. One of the sources of this necessary sharing is the same double contingency that is involved in identification. Another, seen to be particularly important for spouses, is the mutual socialization of those in close relationships with one another.

Another source, which has occupied most of this chapter, comes from cultural models that indicate how people are to act and interact. The terms that characterize people's behavior and relationships have been seen to provide statements of many of the broad and general expectations and salience understandings that constitute vital aspects of the multiplex relationships in the Swahili community. More than that, these models differentially associate expectations with specific statuses promoting conformity not only to the few broad understandings that ideally govern the behavior of all community members but also to the particular understandings concerned with how specific categories of people behave, or should behave, in their relations with other community members.

These term-based associations of statuses and desired behaviors provide potent reminders of the understandings central to the different statuses involved in relationships central to the community operation. More than that, through focusing on specific individuals the value-laden and often emotionally charged characterizations of relations and behavior have the potential, at least, for encouraging the meeting of the expectations contained in those understandings. The effectiveness of the terms in doing this depends on the extent to which people see the terms as applying to them and their concern with approbation and disapprobation. Relationship terms are not the only source of cultural models, but they are a potent one that is frequently and pointedly brought to the attention of all those who hear their own or anyone else's participation being characterized.

The next chapter examines a related but different basis for harnessing the emotional energies of the individual to cultural conformity through the operation of shame, aibu.

8

Tongues Are Spears

Shame and Differentiated
Conformity

Ulimi arobaini, fimbo arobaini: *Forty tongues [are]
forty spears.*

The term "aibu,"[1] shame, refers to the painful emotional state resulting
from the belief that others have or will evaluate one's behavior in an unfavorable way. Aibu rests on those experiencing it having two understandings: that
others know, or will learn, of what one has done or may do and that they
hold beliefs and values in which the behavior is held to be improper or
undesirable.

There is, in fact, no single term heard more than aibu in discussing behavior of questionable acceptability. I asked a room full of prestigious, middle-aged men at a baraza what they thought the main source of concern in
the community was. Several suggested that it was the young people, others
mentioned the changing world, and still others said poverty, but when one
of the men said "aibu," there was a general murmur of agreement.

This chapter will show that aibu is not only a nearly constant concern for
virtually every member of the community but that it is also a powerful social
and emotional force promoting conformity to the expectations and salience
understandings that are at the core of the community's most important statuses. As is true for terms such as *kibri* (pride, a sin in Islam), aibu refers to
understandings that indicate what is valued and appropriate behavior by pointing out the opposite. Unlike other terms, however, aibu refers to a painful
emotion everyone is understood to experience.

Shame, Status, and Limited Sharing

The importance of shame in producing conforming behavior has been reported for a number of societies (e.g., Epstein 1984; Obeyesekere 1981; Spiro

1958), and it works in the same general way for the Swahili. An issue that occupies an important place here, however, is how shame based in the sharing of understandings about what is not desirable behavior can function given the limitations in such sharing that have been demonstrated in this community. Further, there is the question of how shame can encourage conformity to the expectations in statuses when those expectations differ, sometimes markedly, from one role to another.

In fact, the hypothesis here is that shame is produced both by the relatively few cultural elements that are shared by virtually everyone and by the values and beliefs shared mainly within limited categories of people (i.e., those resulting from statuses). Regarding the last source, individuals will be shown to experience shame as the result of evaluating their actions according to understandings they attribute to members of a status category. Shame will result even when these understandings are known by the shamed to be antithetical to those shared among members of other status categories. Shame resulting from understandings that are, and are known to be, widely shared does not work in precisely the same ways as does that resulting from understandings that are viewed as being only shared within particular categories and relationships.

One of the differences is in identifying the shaming agents. For the very broadly shared understandings, those whose disapprobation is feared are the same for everyone. These "shamers" are the same group of prestigious men regardless of the status of the individual experiencing shame. With respect to aibu based in understandings taken by those affected as shared by some, but not most, community members, the shamers, obviously, are different according to what behavior is being assessed. The crucial and feared evaluations may be those of anyone occupying a status or statuses qualifying him or her as a likely judge as this is seen by the one concerned about a particular transgression. Those viewed as judges in one sort of transgression may well not be thought of as judges in another.

Double Status Relativity
and, Also, Uniform Judgment

The variation in the composition of the set of judges varies depending on the category the actor sees himself in (e.g., soccer player) and also on the categories of those he takes as concerned with what he is doing (e.g., soccer fans and kin but not those without interest in either the sport or the actor's general prestige). The double status relativity with its dependence on the actor's category as well as the categories of those whom he views as possible sources of shame does not apply to all judgments but is limited in its effects by three different considerations. Each of these limits leads to uniform, rather than dually relative, judgments.

First, there are a few broad value violations that are seen as shameful by nearly everyone without regard to whom the violator may be. Second, there is some general agreement on what is shameful resulting from the understood presence in the group of a status whose very high prestige members are taken to make judgments about shamefulness or its absence that are more difficult to ignore than others' are. Finally, an additional status exists whose members are characterized by their willingness publicly to disclose otherwise generally unknown shameful acts, thereby contributing to the operation of the first two considerations.

It will be shown that shame's operation is importantly affected by the fact that much of what anyone does is seen as judged by standards that differ according to the statuses of the shamers, while some of what is done is taken as judged by universally accepted standards. The differential importance of the judgments of occupants of different statuses in producing shame concerning much of what everyone does puts this powerful emotion behind the distribution of culture that occurs through the community's social structure, that is, set of interrelated statuses. At the same time, the uniform importance of the judgments of a single category of high prestige individuals as concerns a relative few of the things people do brings the same emotion to bear as a support for the existence of a single community embracing all its different statuses.

The interest here is mainly cultural and concerned with the functioning of the group rather than primarily psychological and concerned with the minds of individuals. Still, it will be suggested that although the internalization of values may be present, it is neither a necessary nor a sufficient condition for the effectiveness of shame as an influence on behavior.

"Shame"

The locus classicus for the differences between "shame" and "guilt" is the Piers and Singer volume (1971 [1953]). In brief, that source shows that the early idea division was between "shame societies" whose members do not internalize the values of the society and "guilt societies" where the values are internalized. Shame-motivated conformity is based in avoiding disapproval from fellow group members, while guilt motivates conformity through the effectiveness of the internalized values alone. Spiro, together with Piers in the latter's separate but contemporaneous formulation, rejects the notion that shame does not involve internalization of values. He holds that shame is distinguished by the fact that although values are internalized, the socializing agents for those values are not (Spiro 1958:406–422, Piers and Singer 1971 [1953]:25–33).

The position here is closer to Obeyesekere's, which sees "shame" and "guilt" as both referring to actors' reactions or contemplations of wrong-doing. In his view, the experience of shame is directly and necessarily related to social life, whereas guilt is not. While shame may involve internalization of the values whose violation is the process of interest, it does not depend on it. Obeyesekere (1981:131) puts this as follows:

> If . . . guilt were never given language formulation [because it is a primary mental process rooted in infantile experience] this was not true of shame. The [Sinhala] language has a complicated, incredibly large, subtly graded vocabulary of shame and its associated ideas pertaining to honor, status, loss of self-esteem, ridicule, vulnerability to slights, deference behavior, prestige and so forth. . . . Shame is a social emotion, though when it is internalized in a conscience it can act as a powerful mechanism of social control. Fundamentally, shame orients the individual to the reaction of others: he wants their approval and fears disapproval and ridicule.

I will follow Obeyesekere in the use of "shame" as referring to the actor's experienced or anticipated emotional discomfort arising from his understanding of the evaluation of his acts, omissions, or qualities made by others. Definition aside, it is an empirical fact that Swahili informants say that aibu sometimes results from the understanding that others do or will know about an act or quality and will evaluate it negatively. The informants also make it unmistakably clear that aibu can and does result from the actor believing that others view him as acting badly even if he himself considers his acts and qualities entirely proper and acceptable.

Finally, as we will see, informants also say that actors viewing their own behavior as unacceptable experience unpleasant emotions whether or not they understand that others share their views of what they did. These latter emotions are understood within the group as different from aibu, what I am calling "shame."

There is no reason to legislate here about the meaning of "shame" and the similarity between shame in this community and in all others. It is, however, my empirically based opinion that in the segment of American society in which I live, an emotion indistinguishable from Swahili shame exists, and the same is true of the two other societies in which I have done extensive fieldwork, Truk and Bena. Given the universal importance of evaluation in all societies, I find it difficult to believe that there are societies in which people do not experience bad feelings related to actual or anticipated unfavorable evaluations by others, but the concern with and intensity of such feelings probably differs measurably. I am sure that the Swahili experience such feelings, as well as talk about them, and that they influence their behavior. That is what is crucial for this discussion, which, however, may well have some hypotheses that apply generally.

The Power of "Aibu"

In the Swahili language "aibu" most nearly approximates what I have just defined as "shame." "Aibu" refers to dishonor, disgrace, loss of standing, and shame according to the three main Swahili dictionaries (Akida et al. 1981; Johnson 1959 [1939]; Krapf 1882). "Aibu" can be used in the broad and abstract sense in which English speakers use "shame," as in "Everyone tries to avoid shame" as well as in the somewhat narrower and more specific adjectival form, "It is shameful to cheat." The distinction between an act or quality that produces shame and the emotion that is shame is empirically and lexically difficult to make.

"Aibu," more than "shame," is used as a trope in which the act that produces the emotion of shame is mentioned but where the reference is actually to the emotion. A person is said to reveal his aibu when he tells of acts that produce shame, but since those who are insensitive to shame can mention acts that for others would be the source of aibu and, their detractors say, do so without aibu, it is clearly the emotion that is the central reference of the word "aibu." I will follow highly literate, English-speaking Swahili and use both "aibu" and "shame," with the latter being mainly reserved for the broad and abstract sense of the term.

So far as I know, there is no word in English that refers solely and specifically to what I have called "the emotional discomfort" that is the core of my definition of "shame," and the same is true of the Swahili language. "Anxiety" in English and *wasiwasi* or *mashaka* in Swahili refer to the emotional state, but the words by themselves can refer to bad feelings resulting from many different sources. In the Swahili language, more than in English, the word used for what I have defined as "shame" is used in direct reference to acts. Thus, one can say in Swahili, "His clothes fell open revealing his nakedness. What a shame!" without meaning "Isn't that too bad" or "What a pity." The Swahili usage just alluded to refers to the production of emotional discomfort in the one involved and not sympathy or any other reaction by observers. I will follow Swahili usage here with the understanding that the named acts are a trope for the discomfort they are taken to entail.

Wikans (1984) argues that honor may not be the direct opposite of shame, and this is mainly true for the Mombasa Swahili. As has been seen, fakhri, which can be glossed as "honor," is accorded individuals on the basis of their active, recognized adherence to shared values and cannot be won by the absence of aibu-producing behavior alone. Conversely, being without notable fakhri does not necessarily mean that the individual is filled with aibu. Informants all agree that virtuous but undistinguished people can be low in both shame and honor. People with fakhri are deeply concerned about aibu, and such concern is an essential part of having honor, but they are not free of shame because of their honor.

Those with honor are viewed as only relatively free from aibu. "Relatively" free because, informants all agree, no one is without aibu, and since the people with fakhri are very sensitive to aibu, the fact that they avoid most aibu-producing activities does not guarantee, indeed will not prevent, their having some aibu. The somewhat complex relationship between shame and honor will be seen as a source of power for prestigious men as recognized agents of cultural conformity, but for now it needs only to be clear that "aibu" cannot be taken to refer to the complete absence of fakhri.

Swahili individuals do not readily discuss aibu, their own or anyone else's. Men say that women discuss the aibu of their fellows quite readily, and at least some of my women informants agree. Men and women who consider themselves nobles also say that slaves and their contemporary descendants gossiped about everyone and, specifically, that this gossip was mainly concerned with people's aibu. Regardless of status, actors do not mention their own aibu at all readily, if ever, and all agree it is better not to mention the aibu of others either.

In fact, aibu are treated so circumspectly that their social manifestation is difficult or impossible to see under most circumstances. As among the Omani Arabs described by Wikans (1984:646 et seq.), overt expression of disapproval is not normally manifested. Even adulterers, drunks, and others whose aibu are serious and renowned, are generally treated just as everyone else is.

There are, however, circumstances, especially quarrels, when actors' aibu are openly mentioned. There is also a particular sort of person, a *fidhuli,* who is believed to have extensive knowledge of the aibu of his associates and who, if even slightly provoked, speaks of them publicly. We will return later to fidhuli and quarrels and their vital role in the operation of shame. For now, it is important to note the general reluctance to discuss aibu since that reluctance plays a part in the way shame operates in this group. The reluctance to mention aibu is part of a general Swahili emphasis on privacy, concealment, and secrecy. This emphasis is itself an important indicator of the importance attached to aibu in this society.

Secrecy and Shame

One of the most cherished ideals for a substantial proportion of the community is privacy or secrecy. "Siri," a noun used where English speakers might use verbs such as "protect," "keep private," "shelter," or "conceal" is a word often used in connection with this ideal. Bushes growing in front of a house's windows are said to provide "siri" for the house and its occupants. When a man dies, his widow sometimes laments that her siri is gone and wonders where it will come from now that the source of her prestige, personal protection, and material support is gone.

The opposite of siri is *aziri,* which refers to exposure in the widest sense. Aziri is what happens when clothes fall open to reveal the naked body, and it is also the word used to refer to having one's private deeds revealed publicly. Aziri is something to be avoided. Community members speak of it with enough feeling so that to say it is dreaded is not to put the matter too strongly.

Swahili go to considerable lengths to achieve siri and avoid aziri. People whom I know well are reluctant to tell me the names of their children or, even, how many they have. The remarkable reticence to provide information on who lives in which house and how the residents were related is, discussions show, explicitly aimed at maintaining siri and avoiding aziri.

How far this can go is shown by an attempt to get data about the ordinary course of family life and how it was seen to be changing. As part of this, in summer 1984, I paid youthful informants to tell me about their views regarding the differences between Swahili community life as it was in the past and as it is at present. I asked them to focus their attention on family matters and did not press them to talk about quarrels, improprieties, or anything that might cause them discomfort. I had some success with my limited objectives, but experience with two brothers shows something of the extent of secretiveness about family affairs.

The oldest brother came to one session and told me the names of the members of his immediate family but said he thought it would be better to keep the names of his grandparents "private." He did not keep his next appointment with me, and his brother told me that he—the elder—thought he should "protect family honor" by not talking to me. The younger brother (only a year separates this young man from his 18-year-old elder) came to several sessions but eventually failed to keep appointments. We had talked about the various places the family had lived in the course of his father's career as a school headmaster who was transferred around the country and about the ways he and his older brother helped his parents in household duties and in disciplining two younger siblings, ages ten and seven. No other matters were broached, but even these were enough to bring the brothers to discontinue participation.

The fact that one of the most dangerous and undesirable sorts of people in this society is a *mdaku,* a curious and inquisitive person, indicates the seriousness attached to keeping things private and out of general knowledge. Even the members of the socially disapproved category of boys and young men called "mahuni," whose behavior is generally understood as consistently contrary to accepted standards and whose indifference to the opinions of others is a central defining trait, show the pervasiveness of concern about aibu in the slogans written on the walls of their hideaways (gahden):

Tazama lako: lit. Watch yours, meaning Mind your own business.

Mtana wanatazama, usiku watalala: lit. In the daytime they watch [us], [but] at night they will sleep.

Informants agreed that these slogans show a concern about aibu despite the fact that the young men in the gahden take pride in being outside their natal community and flouting its standards. Informants say that although people differ in their sensitivity to aibu and in their concern about it, no one is without some concern. The founder of the branch of Sunni Islam followed by the Swahili, Imam Shafi, advises the faithful in a poem given me:

> Watch your tongue and
> don't mention the aibu of other people.
> Everyone of you, from the top of
> your head to your toes, is all aibu.
> The other people don't have a tongue,
>   they have tongues.
>
> If your eye spies out someone else's
>   aibu, say to your eye:
> "Oh my eye, look, the other people have eyes."

Whatever else aibu may be, it is ubiquitous and public knowledge of the acts that produce it is what actors see as providing the full emotional force that it has. It may well be, as Spiro says, that undiscovered shameful acts (whether committed or contemplated) continue to torment their perpetrators because the punishment that would end them has not been delivered (1958: 409). Still, the Swahili are uniform in indicating that a central defense against the undesirable consequences of aibu is keeping it secret or, at least, shielding it from public view.

That this may be, as Spiro's argument would suggest, a trading of psychic pain for social gain by concealing the aibu from public view is indicated by several further types of evidence.

One indication of this is the bitterness I have heard in Swahili complaints about false friends who induce you to tell them your aibu but never mention their own. Another and more explicit type of indication of the importance of concealment in preventing aibu is found in proverbs. The proverbs concerning shame that I collected are of two types: one emphasizes the importance of keeping personal matters private, and the other focuses on the readiness of people to gossip and the danger of that gossip. This danger, informants make clear, stems from the aibu the object of the gossip may suffer.

Concerning the importance of concealment, a widely quoted proverb says, *Nyumba yasitara mambo*: The house conceals [unfavorable] matters.

This proverb is used both to advise people to keep important matters within the family and, more often, to say that because you do not know about a family's aibu it should not be concluded that they have none. The latter point is also made by the proverb, *Kila nyumba inaondoa geneza*: Every house has a bier come out of it.

The idea that one should be careful about telling personal matters to people is contained in the proverb, *Penye kuku wengi, usimwage mtame*: Where there are many chickens, don't spill millet.

This last proverb also makes clear that people are understood to relish the aibu of others. A number of proverbs dramatize the danger in other people's talk, and although aibu is not mentioned specifically, informants are unanimous in saying that this danger is in revealing, or inventing, it.

Ulimi arobaini, fimbo arobaini: Forty tongues [are] forty spears.

Ulimi unanuma kuliko meno: The tongue wounds [worse] than the teeth.

Ulimi hauna dawa: [For what the] tongue [does] there is no medicine.

Shimo la ulimi mkono haufutiki: A hole [dug by] the tongue cannot be filled by the hand.

This emphasis on secrecy is evidence of what informants say directly and explicitly: aibu can only do its full harm to a person or family if it is generally known. The fact that even the disaffected young men who are known for their indifference to general standards are concerned about concealing their activities is taken as some indication that concern about aibu is very general in the group, not just to members of a few status categories.

Recognizing Aibu: Different Ideals and Different Agents

In Mombasa Swahili society, what is shameful depends in many instances on both the statuses of the actor whose behavior is being judged and on the statuses of those understood by that actor to be the judges. This implies that there need not be a single list of universally shared values or rules whose violation is aibu to all group members, that culture need not be uniform.

Further, the status-centered view of shame also implies that its cultural foundations include more than the understandings whose violation is shameful. Since the statuses of the judges and the judged are vital, the cultural bases for these status categories must also be included as part of shame's apparatus. Chief among these status constituents are the expectations that are the bases for judgment. Since it is through the expectations in the judging and judged categories and the salience understandings that brings these to bear on a particular judgment, the cultural distribution that constitutes the categories is central to the operation of shame. The nature of social structure, in other words, is a vital part of shame.

The understandings shared in the community provide the broad foundation for shame, but only a small minority of these understandings produce the possibility of shame for everyone, automatically. The rest bring shame only to occupants of some statuses when their actions are judged by occupants of some, but not all, of the statuses in relationships with them. Thus, what is possibly shameful is in part a result of the community's social structure and the places of the judges and judged within it.

Some Universal Bases for Aibu

I will begin the description of aibu's operation by identifying a few of the ideal understandings that are taken to be sources of aibu for members of this group regardless of who is being judged or who is doing the judging. When I asked informants to tell me specifically some aibu-evoking acts or qualities that they knew about and that were undoubtedly aibu producing for anyone, the following were mentioned: stealing; impregnating an unmarried woman and being impregnated if unmarried; using foul language in the company of "decent people"; being seen naked in public; dressing outrageously; using, selling, or supplying alcohol; making it clear to others that you would like them to give you goods or money; going to people's houses and making a nuisance of yourself by shouting or pounding on the doors, especially at night; and failure of a man to protect a woman of the community from assault by outsiders.

This is almost surely not a complete list of actions or failures constituting obvious and undoubted aibu for everyone, but it is important to note that most of the things mentioned here are of the gross, rarely occurring sort that figure little in everyday life for most people. Even these egregious activities may include some that are undoubted aibu only when taken out of their actual social settings and presented as isolated examples of evil.

So, for example, impregnating someone outside of marriage is aibu, but there are men—probably not a few—who have lovers outside their community-approved marriages and who sometimes impregnate these non-Swahili women. Is this impregnation an aibu for the man? It certainly is so far as the wife of the impregnator is concerned and probably also in the eyes of her parents and siblings. It most often is not for the man's male friends, many of whom would view his liaison as more admirable than shameful.

A Swahili woman being impregnated outside marriage is a great and undoubted aibu for her as judged by everyone including her peers. The impregnator is also shamed, and this event, rare as it is, is admired by no one. However, the same is not true if a Swahili man impregnates his non-Swahili lover. Here the existence of a basis for shame depends on who is doing the evaluation.

Aibu without Personal Belief in Having Erred

Actors surely do not need an abstract understanding of culture's operation for social life to continue any more than they need a knowledge of physiology to digest food. The fact that they are, willy-nilly, guided by culture makes shame a socially, as opposed to only personally, effective force. The importance of the cultural, as opposed to purely personal, element is emphasized by informants telling me that a person need not believe he has done anything wrong in order for him to have been involved in an aibu. An example will make this clear.

When a marriage takes place, it is usual for a drum to be put in front of the new wife's parent's house. This drum is beaten on the nuptial night to signal that the wife was a virgin and that the husband was successful in deflowering her. Many men view this practice as shameful, an aibu, because, they say, it concerns very intimate affairs about which the community need know nothing. Still, they say, they have no choice other than to allow the drum to be put out because the women—the wives, mothers, and sisters—think it is aibu not to have the drum.

It might be argued that the drum's presence is due to the women's concern about aibu and that the men accept it because of their concern for the sensibilities of their female kin rather than about their own aibu. Taking this view might seem to obviate the need to view aibu as occurring regardless of the actor's own evaluation of his behavior. This would seem to preserve the position that shame is invariably a consequence of the actor's understanding that he or she has violated one or more values, but it does not.

If we accept or reject what Swahili informants say, that aibu result from others' evaluations of your behavior regardless of your own understandings of it, or, as just suggested, we say that aibu influences behavior through intermediates whose aibu is of concern, the result for analysis is the same. This is that we need to know a good deal about understandings concerning who applies what standards to whom, in addition to the content of the values involved, when considering the shamefulness of particular behaviors.

In fact, it is through actors' knowledge of which people apply what standards to whom that a good part of the shame system works. It is not only feeling bad that lets actors know what standards apply but also knowing what is expected of others and what the others expect of the actor. The shame system has the same basis as the social system as a whole: the actors' sharing with one another at least some understandings about what people in different categories should do and actually will do in various circumstances.

These shared understandings enable actors to know not only what consequences their own behavior will have for their prestige and honor but also how they will be affected by the misbehavior of others. A young man, for example, was sitting with a group of friends when his father's brother, a ne'er-do-well, walked by. The uncle was very shabbily dressed, itself a shameful thing in this community, and, worst of all, was barefoot. After the uncle had passed, the young man said to his friends, "My father was the only one of those children who amounted to anything."

The significance of the young man's statement, of course, was that he knew what standards his friends would apply to his father's brother and what evaluation that would produce for the man. He also knew how that evaluation might affect his own honor and prestige with his peers.

There is nothing surprising about the young man knowing these things. They are the sorts of knowledge that make social life possible. Still, it is worth underlining their existence so that it can be seen clearly that shame involves a more complex cultural foundation than would be the case if it were necessary to consider nothing but what values are shared and what constitutes their violation. The young man's uncle violated a value concerning proper dress, and that is a part of the aibu the young man sought to avoid with his remark. To understand the incident, it is also necessary to examine the cultural elements that establish the nature of the relationship between the boy and his uncle and, given that relationship, the standards for judging the boy because of the uncle's behavior.

To take a more common but still similar problem, informants of both sexes and all social standings agree that the elderly mothers and aunts who often spend their last years living with a child and his or her spouse are a source of concern because of the aibu they might bring. The possibility that these women may go to neighbors' houses and accept tea or food and talk about the poor or scanty food in the houses of their sons or daughters is understood as real and frightening by their children. The feared "begging" does not shame the old women in their children's view; they are seen as being beyond shame. It is the shame that would come to the children from the implication that they do not or cannot care for their aged parent that is frightening.

It might seem that the old women show by their behavior that the children are violating accepted ideals of care and that once that is known, the shame in the situation is accounted for. This, however, misses a vital aspect of how shame works. This is that those who care for an aged parent need to have a full understanding of how others will judge the behavior of the old mother and of how this judgment will reflect on them. The children's concern about their aged kinswoman is based, in other words, in a more complex set of understandings than simply the ideal understanding (value) that may concern neighbors.

Both regarding the shabby father's brother and the resident old mothers, individuals suffer aibu, or fear they might, because of the behavior of other people rather than directly because of their own behavior alone. These instances were adduced to show that simply saying shame comes from the violation of values fails to take account of the fullness of social life and of the complex tasks culture must accomplish if it is to provide a basis for it. Taking a final example from the other side of my contention that feeling you have done something wrong is not a necessary condition for aibu, let us consider a man who felt he did something terribly wrong but who, nevertheless, was not judged to have committed an aibu.

A boy of about eight years very much wanted a bicycle. Many of his friends had them, and he asked his father for one repeatedly, but the father delayed getting it. One day the little boy went swimming in the ocean and drowned. The father was disconsolate. Long after the child's death he mourned the failure to give his son the bicycle he wanted. He obviously understood his failure to provide the bicycle as a grave omission, but it was not, informants agree, an aibu. It was, rather, a clear instance of guilt.

The last case shows that internalized values, in this case manifested in treatment of a son, are not always a sufficient condition for experiencing what is considered shame in this society. With regard to the marriage drum, the converse was seen: that internalized values are not a necessary condition for shame to be felt. This does not imply that internalized values are irrelevant to shame but only that they are but one element sometimes involved in a complex situation. Given the contingent nature of the role of internalized values, it is important to note that they cannot be assumed to be any more crucial or central to understanding shame's operation than such wider considerations as the statuses of those involved as judges and judged.

Aibu and Significant Others: Arbiters and Sanctioners

So far, emphasis has been put on the importance of who people think is judging the behavior at issue. It will be clear that if shame is to have social— as opposed to only individual—influence, establishing who one's judges are in various contexts must have a foundation in shared understandings.

My most general hypothesis about this foundation is that actors view themselves as being judged by two different sorts of fellow group members whom I will refer to as "arbiters" and "sanctioners." The arbiters are quite a small collection of individuals in this society. They are individuals of great prestige and of whom impeccable behavior is expected. Their judgments (rarely, if ever, openly made but often imputed to them by others) are given great weight across a wide scope of behavior, and when their judgments and those of nonarbiters are taken to disagree, the arbiters' evaluations are understood as more significant.

The men, and they are all men, I refer to by the term "arbiters" are not recognized as a class or group by community members, but each of them would be identified as being highly respected and as having a great deal of honor (fakhri). I will return to the arbiters after examining the numerically much larger collection of evaluators, the sanctioners.

Everyone in the society is a potential sanctioner. The term, like "arbiter," is coined here for analytical purposes and is not used by the Swahili. It applies to those who are understood as judging an act by those who perform or contemplate the act. The sanctioners for any particular act may well not include all the members of the society, but everyone is understood as a sanctioner by at least some others for some of the things those others do or think of doing.

Different sets of sanctioners may have, and/or be understood to have by the judged, different views of the same behavior depending, in considerable part, on the statuses of the sanctioners and of the judged. Those who are judged often believe they know more or less clearly what views of their behavior different sanctioners are likely to hold. When these views are believed to differ, the judged are usually well aware of the disparity in consequences for themselves deriving from the different judgments.

To take a clear example, consider the practice of taking a "secret wife" (*mke msiri*). Adultery (*uzinzi*) is a grave sin as the Swahili understand it, but Islam allows polygyny, and some men have wives who their "main wife" knows nothing about. These auxiliary wives are never Swahili, so far as I could determine, but sometimes are from families that were once Swahili slaves. A husband knows quite clearly both that the judgment of his wife and of her kin will be quite different from the judgments of some, at least, of his cronies and that the consequences of these judgments will be quite different. By controlling information, the judged can attempt to have his activity evaluated only by those whose judgments are likely to be favorable to him, and the favorable sanctioners will often not be swayed by the knowledge that other sanctioners take a different view.[2]

The existence of different sets of sanctioners obviously involves the presence within the community of differences in the values, rules, and beliefs held by different group members. Such differences undeniably exist in the Mombasa Swahili community (as we have seen with respect to sexual adventures and as the study of sharing in chap. 5 indicates more broadly), and these are not only differences between individuals. There are also differences between groups or collections of people such as those between men of certain ages, on the one hand, and wives of men of those ages, on the other. These sorts of differences in shared understandings among various categories of community members are important elements in what I am referring to as "the distribution of culture."

The Distribution of Culture

Despite the fact that sharing within status categories is a great deal less than uniform, group life is best understood as being based on a distribution of the total corpus of the group's shared understandings rather than uniformly shared among them. This distribution includes some understandings that are shared by all group members, others that are shared by many group members, and a substantial number that are shared among a relative few.

The predictability that is essential to social life (see chap. 1) requires that social relationships be based on a certain minimum sharing among participants of understandings concerning behavior in those relationships. This being so, whatever else is characteristic of the distribution of culture among different categories of actors, it always includes some sharing among the people involved of understandings concerning what is acceptable in the interactions involving them. This sharing may be mainly produced situationally by double contingency, which may sometimes be effective because of the exchange of tokens that are not also guides. Alternatively, it may proceed mainly on the basis of understandings commonly acquired through earlier socialization. Whatever its sources, it is essential to social life that there be some kind of sharing to serve as the basis for mutual predictability.

The understandings basic to many relationships, especially if they are multiplex, are rarely situational inventions. More often, they are relatively uniform for occupants of the same statuses through some combination of common socialization and the use of cultural models of the sort examined in the last chapter. To the extent that there is some uniformity, judges who sometimes have the same status as those occupied by the ones they judge will make their judgments on the basis of understandings similar to those guiding the participants. This is what would be expected given a uniform sharing of culture.

But there is no necessity that all others will make their judgments on the basis of the understandings that guide the participants; the relationships could operate quite effectively even if nonparticipants have different understandings about some or, even, all its aspects. In fact, such differences do exist among the Swahili (and, surely, elsewhere), so that some who evaluate relationships, and behavior in general, use different standards from those others do. These differences are a fundamental part of the "distribution of culture."

The basic element in cultural distribution is "status." As noted previously, the term refers to a mental category of individuals grouped together on the basis of understandings that identify what are taken to be significant characteristics that distinguish the category members from nonmembers. Associated with these understandings are additional understandings about what can be expected of category members and others concerned with what sorts of settings and circumstances membership in the status should and will take precedence over other category memberships.

Statuses as the Basis for Judgment

The understandings in statuses of what can be expected of members are the bases for determining aibu both by the members and by those who judge them. That is, each status has as one of its sets of associated understandings a series concerned with how its members should and should not behave and another set concerned with how people in relations with status members should and should not behave. These sets provide the foundation for differential assessments of aibu by different sanctioners, with these assessments equally affected by the statuses of those judged. The acts and their circumstances indisputably are, obviously, what is judged, but the statuses of both the sanctioners and those being judged determine what the judgment will be.

Most commonly, people in interaction with one another agree on the standards that apply to their relationship, and, in that relationship, each is in a position, in the view of the other, to serve as sanctioner for behavior in that relationship. Every now and again, however, relationships come about in which there is little or no agreement about applicable standards. These are instructive in showing how important such agreement, the result of cultural distribution, is. An example of a relationship lacking the results of the usual cultural distribution will make this clear.

Two Swahili brothers married and brought their wives to a house the brothers had inherited. One brother had married the daughter of one of the community's most prestigious men; the other had married a woman from the section of town that is renowned for its toughness, willingness to do manual labor (as fishermen, at least), and contempt for the "refinement" that marks the behavior of Swahili from the other sections of town. The sisters-in-law lived together for a time in an atmosphere that became progressively charged.

The wife from the "tough" section of town responded to any of the disagreements that joint living arrangements produced by saying such things to the more aristocratic wife as "Look at you! What man could love a woman with a behind like yours!" When more seriously provoked by her husband's brother's wife, the lower-class woman would bind up her clothing in a way that is understood as a sign of readiness to fight. The other wife was appalled by this behavior, which was quite foreign to her previous experience and contrary to what she understood to be acceptable. Eventually, the wife with the more delicate sensibilities got her husband to move out of the house and to take her to a place of her own where she was removed from her sister-in-law and the latter's shocking behavior.

As an insightful and perceptive informant told me in discussing this story, what the "tough" wife thought of as prestigious, the high-born wife viewed as aibu. The high-born wife could not bring herself to answer her sister-in-law in kind and was reduced to tears and shame by the latter's behavior. The women of the highest stratum of Swahili society are rarely seen, and for them meekness and gentle manners are a considerable virtue, both in their own eyes and in the eyes of their social peers. The women of the stratum from which the combative and insulting wife came are quite different: they admire bold and aggressive behavior in themselves and in their associates.

Both of the brother's wives shared Swahili values about personal dignity, autonomy, and rights of possession (the women quarreled mainly over who cooked what and when and with whose utensils and food). Their understandings about what procedures to follow in defending their rights and dignity and about how to evaluate the behavior shown by the other in that defense were, however, quite different. The differences between them in approach and evaluation were not only personal; each shared her view with many or most of the women of her stratum of the community.

The women of the "refined" status would—and did—judge their peer as having behaved admirably and the behavior of the woman of the "tough" group as having been shameful, while the women of the "tough" group would—and did—make opposite judgments. The question of where shame lies resolves itself into asking who the sanctioners of the behavior are. Their decisions, we see, depend on both their own statuses and the status of the one being judged. In the usual course of events in this society, actors as different in relevant statuses as the sisters-in-law in the above case do not engage in prolonged and close interaction.

Brothers do not often share a house after marriage, nor do they usually marry women of such different backgrounds. Having been brought together, however, the differences between the women's understandings were so great that interaction finally became impossible and they had to separate.[3] Their ability to deal with one another, including their ability to judge one another's behavior along the lines of what was aibu and what was not, was too limited to make continued interaction supportable.

The case of the sisters-in-law, like the example of the judgment of men with secret wives, shows the importance of cultural distribution in the shame process. These two sets of data make clear how there can be a variety of different sanctioners whose views of what is aibu and what is not can be quite different depending on both the statuses of the sanctioners and the statuses of those judged.

Status Differences and Privacy

The fact that sanctioners differ at least sometimes in their judgments helps explain the emphasis on privacy and secrecy found here. If no one knows about an actor's behavior, he has no realistic cause to be concerned about aibu (although he may be concerned anyway), but such secrecy is difficult or impossible in a small, mainly endogamous community of around 2,000 whose members live together in closely packed neighborhoods in a single section, Old Town, of the island of Mombasa whose whole area is only three miles by five miles (DeBlij 1968).

Moreover, some potential aibu, like the shoeless father's brother referred to earlier, are based in things that occur in public and cannot by their very nature be kept secret. Here actors cannot confidently use secrecy as the sole basis for attempting to avoid aibu once an act known to be taken by some as shameful has been committed or, in some cases, contemplated. What the actor can do is to lessen the likelihood that news of the act will circulate. Frequently, particular attention is given to keeping this news from those likeliest to judge the act unfavorably.

The distribution of culture in this group includes quite sharp differences among statuses in the expectations used in judgments. As we saw in the case of the sisters-in-law and also for those with secret wives, what is aibu for one group of sanctioners can be a source of honor and prestige for another. Complete secrecy, then, would prevent the actor from gaining prestige at the same time it protected him from aibu. This would seem to call for a strategy of careful information control, and that is, in fact, what we see.

It appears that Swahili women commonly are freer and more open in their relations with others, including being willing to discuss more of their own and others' personal affairs. This may be in some part related to the view, held by both men and women, that men are more preoccupied with avoiding aibu than women are. Given men's greater concern with aibu, it could be that men are more willing to forgo honor from a limited group of sanctioners than to risk aibu as seen by a much wider section of the community, while women more often take the opposite strategy.

Whatever differences there may be between men and women in their approaches to aibu and to honor, there can be no doubt that there are differences among sanctioners in their evaluations of others' behavior. These differences are often known to actors and, at least sometimes, used in calculating how to act and what information to allow to pass to whom.

Such calculations must take into account that judgments depend not only on the statuses of the sanctioners but also on the statuses of the judged and the act at issue. Thus, to consider only one of these dimensions, nuclear family members are less likely than outsiders to judge one another harshly as concerns such potentially aibu sorts of activity as eating low-prestige food or employing generally disapproved means to gain advancement in employment or school. The same family members, however, can be very severe judges as concerns use of family property, meeting of family obligations, and public displays of unseemly behavior.

Similarly, regardless of the activity being judged, rivals for something are likely to make consistently less favorable judgments of one another than those working together to get it. Generally, it is the specific role, the part of a status's collection of understandings concerned with relations with another in his status, that affects judgment. A son judging a mother proceeds on quite different grounds from another mother judging that mother, so that evaluations of performance in the mother status coming from the mother-son role

View of Old Town, Mombasa.

Two of the Mosques in the Old Town.

Young men praying outside the Basheikh Mosque in Old Town, Mombasa. Older men are inside where no photographs were allowed.

Girls in religious school (*chuo*).

Boys in separate religious school.

Ten important members of the Swahili community, mainly of the contested ethnicity that forms the basis for chapter 3; these are called "Swahili Arabs."

Men leaving meeting of the Muslim Association; many are not Swahili since the association includes all Mombasa Muslims. The man in the suit (*foreground*) is the provincial commissioner.

are based in expectations different from judgments in the mother-mother role. Statuses provide the understandings used in judgment. More particularly, evaluations are based in the expectations within the status that governs the relationship with the judged in the status relevant for the purposes of the judgment.

The roles occupied by sanctioners vis-à-vis those they judge affect not only the nature of the judgments they make but also which particular acts they will know about. So, for example, men are far likelier to judge the actions of their male peers in a variety of kinds of activities than they are to judge women of the same age and social standing for comparable activities and vice versa. Members of each of these status groups do judge members of the other as concerns some things such as propriety in sexual seclusion and marital fidelity, but they do not judge members of the other group on some behaviors that are quite important within that group.

Thus, men judge women's clothing and jewelry very little—they have little opportunity to know what unrelated women are wearing since women appear in public only when completely covered by the all-enveloping black buibui— although women use this as a major basis for judging one another. Women judge men very little on how the men follow etiquette, in considerable part because they see little of the relevant behavior since most public expressions of etiquette occur mainly in contexts where the sexes are separate. Men, especially those of the well-to-do sections of the community, judge each other quite closely in this domain. The judgments individuals make vary according to the characters of the individuals and of the relationship with the judged, but this variation is within limits imposed by statuses both as concerns what is judged and the basic criteria for judgment.

Sanctioners, then, differ in a number of ways, including the standards they use for judgment, how they apply these to different sorts of others, and the likelihood that they will make judgments on various kinds of behavior as carried out by people of different types. All of the differences among sanctioners, even the bases for individual variation, stem from the differential distribution of culture, which, as shown earlier, is a feature of the social structure with its differentiated and connected statuses.

In Swahili society, differences between men's and women's understandings about what is aibu and what produces honor, despite some important areas of agreement, are still great enough that men say that women care little about aibu. Wikans (1984:635–652) notes that in many studies of societies where honor is stressed, it appears that women have no honor of their own— or shame either—but only affect the honor of their husbands and male kin.

Such a view would result, of course, from the distribution of culture, leading researchers who work mainly with members of one sex to fail to know about the standards held by members of the other sex if, as is true for Swahili society and for the ones Wikans refers to, gender is used as the basis for differentiation involving importantly different understandings in the resultant statuses.

Differences between statuses are not limited to the type seen between men and women where members of one category are, or profess to be, ignorant of understandings important to members of the other category. There are also important differences in understandings about to whom and in what circumstances particular standards should be applied. Thus, the members of a particular family were fully aware of the understandings to be used in judging a person who engaged in a business dependent on the sale of alcohol (abhorrent in this pious Muslim group), and they would surely use these standards in judging an outsider, but the family members definitely did not use them in judging their husband-father who had grown prosperous through the sale of fermented palm toddy.

There is still another source of difference in assessing aibu which arises from the distribution of culture. This one results from the fact that everyone occupies a number of different statuses, each of which includes understandings, often different from status to status, about what constitutes proper and acceptable behavior by others depending on the statuses occupied by those others. Because of this, even actors who share many of the same statuses may, on the basis of their relationship to the judged person, use understandings from different ones of those statuses as the foundation of the judgment they make. This choice is not an entirely individual one but depends in part upon culture, specifically, on the type of status-associated understandings that I have called "salience understandings."

For example, some may judge what a fellow group member does according to understandings associated with the status "community member" while others may judge the same person according to the slightly—or grossly— different understandings associated with the statuses "neighbor," "friend," or "enemy." Which will be used depends upon the status the judge assigns himself and this is guided by salience understandings. A number of considerations affect these last including to whom judgment is expressed, but the nature of the relationship between the judge and the judged is often also important. Since the judgments made depend upon the status whose understandings are their base, saliency understandings play quite an important part in the operation of judgment just as they do in the operation of statuses generally.

Although everyone is a sanctioner as regards some acts, it is by no means true that everyone is, or ever will be, an arbiter. This is a status assigned to only a few members of the group who meet very demanding standards. As seen above, the judgments of different sanctioners of the same activity and individual often differ. Also different sanctioners, as such, are concerned with different categories of people, so that even when knowledge of some activity is widespread some kinds of sanctioners may not pass judgment concerning it.

None of this is so for arbiters. Within the rather narrow scope of public acts arbiters are understood to notice, judgment is taken as independent of any of the statuses of the person who commits the act. If an arbiter were to judge an act by someone differently from their judgment of another, his standing as an arbiter would thereby be put in question.

The arbiters are accorded great prestige mainly deriving from the understanding that members of this status set very high standards for themselves and live up to those standards. They are all men of middle age or older who can easily be recognized by the spotless traditional clothing they wear whenever their occupations make that costume possible. They are also distinguished by their erect posture, measured gait, modulated voices, and judicious manner. They follow the elaborate etiquette derived mainly from Persian Gulf Arabs, almost every one of them has visited Mecca during the pilgrimage season at least once, and they all have standard places at the front of the mosques where they customarily pray.

These men have a special presence that is obvious even to outsiders. It is, I am told, the men I call arbiters whom people have especially in mind when they say in praise of a young man or boy that he "fears the faces of the 'nobles.'" When young men lower their voices, improve their postures, and look at the ground, the man passing is surely an arbiter.

As the praise for youths suggests and as informants agree, the men I am referring to as "arbiters" are taken by group members as representing what is most honorable and worthy of respect in the community. These arbiters have no special designation. "Arbiter" is a name being used for analysis. Nor do they have a title; they are addressed as "sheikh," as are all mature males in the group.

Despite their importance in evaluation, they do not intercede in the affairs of other people to make explicit judgment. If anything, they are less likely to comment on the behavior of other group members than lesser people are. This is a consequence, informants agree, of their following the ideal that "nobles" do not gossip or discuss the actions of others. What is distinctive of them, and this is something that informants say about them and that they say about themselves, is that they "frighten" (tisha) their fellow group members.

What "frighten" means in this context is that people are sharply constrained in their behavior when they view that behavior as being considered by the arbiters. Even those given to making cynical and belittling remarks about the arbiters in private, and these are mainly disaffected youths and people whose group membership is marginal, are nevertheless distinctly restrained in their presence—even if they are across the street—and seem concerned about their opinions even as they declare their indifference to them.

There is an illness called mata ya wazima, the eyes of the grown people,[4] that afflicts youths and is believed to be caused by the young people behaving improperly in their presence. The "wazima" are all the mature men of the community, but informants agree that it is the high-prestige men of the kind I am calling arbiters who are particularly dangerous to youths who misbehave. The danger does not come from the men doing anything active when the youths misbehave. Disease is the direct result, I am told, of the impropriety being committed in front of the mature men, who do not actively participate to bring it about.[5]

The standing of mature men and, especially, the arbiters who embody the essence of their qualities is clearly an important aspect of cultural conformity here. Two anecdotes will illustrate how the members of this status group are viewed in the community and help explain that view.

A Swahili man living in a small city to the north of Mombasa noticed that corn was disappearing from a field he owned, and he resolved to spend the night in his field in the hope of catching the thief. After it became quite dark, he saw a figure enter his field and begin to pick his corn. The owner crept near where the thief was at work and on seeing the man's face recognized him as one of the town's leading citizens. On discovering this, he silently turned and fled. He told no one of his discovery until years after the event.

The second anecdote concerns a highly respected member of the Mombasa Swahili community and me. I had been hurt in an accident while traveling to Mombasa, and I could not leave my room at the Mombasa Club because my injury made it nearly impossible for me to walk. The respected man, a friend and patron of some years standing, lived only about a hundred yards away from the club and had heard, I was told by visitors less prestigious than he, that I could not walk. At first, he sent one of his sons to ask how long it would be before I could go to his house. I sent back the message that it might be several weeks before I could navigate beyond my room. That night he came to the club to visit me and told me that it was the first time he had ever set foot in the place despite its proximity to his house and his friendship with a number of club members.

I thanked him for visiting me and asked him why he had not been in the club before. He said that he knew the club had a bar (it does) and believed that members of the Swahili community sometimes drank beer or spirits there (I have never seen any). He said that if he had seen community members there drinking in contravention of Islam's prohibition, his "respect would be broken." By that, he explained, he meant that the drinkers would never again "fear" him and would "do whatever they wanted to" in front of him. This, he said, would ruin his reputation.

It was clear to me that only his concern for my welfare had brought him to risk this. Both coming to my room and leaving, he used a staircase that did not take him by the club's bar. This route may have been scouted for him by his son when the latter came to visit me the day before.

Self-Reinforcing "Fear"

The heart of both these anecdotes and, I hypothesize, a central element in the effectiveness of the arbiters in the shame process among the Swahili is the "fear" in which these senior members of the community are held. Because of this fear, informants report, people do not do aibu things that the arbiters are likely to find out about, and they certainly do not do aibu things in the presence of these men. I infer from this that anything done in the presence of the arbiters can be taken to be almost certainly free of aibu, and anything that would not be done in their presence has at least some taint of aibu about it. Informants agree with this inference (but seem to find it too obvious to mention).

Since the arbiters' views are taken so seriously in establishing whether behavior is shameful or not, actors have a considerable stake in knowing what these views are. On the one hand, this is made somewhat difficult because instances or examples of their judgments on particular individuals and their behavior are not available, since, as noted, they rarely or never explicitly make such judgments. On the other hand, everyone has a fairly good idea of what the arbiters are likely to think about a wide range of behavior from two related sources.

First, the arbiters are more or less explicitly seen as the representatives of traditional beliefs and values that are, of course, widely understood in the community. Second, the arbiters are all particularly pious Muslims in a community that is generally quite pious, and the views of arbiters are understood to be closely related to the precepts, and there are many, in the Koran. In addition, over the years, various individual arbiters have published their views about desirable and undesirable activities in pamphlets and Mombasa newspapers and presented them on radio and television. But probably more important than the publicly presented general views of the arbiters is the actual behavior of the arbiters themselves.

Arbiters attain their prestige because of the high standards they set for themselves and, importantly, because of their being viewed as living up to these standards. Their standards are understood to be more exacting than those of other group members, and if, given these standards, they can do it, it is not aibu.

The presence of the arbiters when particular behaviors are manifested also serves as an indication of what is acceptable. If they are present and something is done in their presence, the thing is unlikely to be aibu. In part, this is because most group members are strongly constrained by the presence of the arbiters. The fact that young men can actually get a disease from behaving badly in front of the arbiters and their lesser, mature brethren is an indication of how constraining their presence is. This constraint, it should be added, contributes to the prestige of the arbiters because it shows that people fear them, and that fear is a measure of their prestige. In addition, however, the arbiters try to avoid settings and contexts where aibu are likely to occur.

We saw this in the case of my friend's reluctance to visit me at the club. The high-prestige men in general make a point of avoiding places where men are likely to fight or where men and women are to be seen together as well as places, like the club, where drinking goes on. Aibu rarely occurs in the presence of arbiters, then, both because the arbiters avoid being where it might occur and because the real fear they inspire makes it unlikely actors will be bold enough to misbehave in their presence.

The process is an interactive and self-reinforcing one. The fact that aibu does not occur in their presence, even though partly due to their avoiding settings where it might occur, contributes to the arbiters' prestige, and that prestige is the basis for the fear that makes it unlikely that they will be confronted with others' aibu.

It would seem that in the case of the missing corn, the thief would have lost his prestige and would no longer inspire fear. There is almost surely, however, a generalization of the respect that derives from high standards and their maintenance. This generalization makes it difficult to disassociate from a person all the fear originally vested in him because of his reputation for righteous behavior even when he abandons that behavior. Just this process led the field owner to be silent and creep away when he found out who was stealing from him. The same respect, perhaps mixed with a concern that he would not be believed, led him to remain silent for years after the event. The theft was an aibu without doubt, but the "fear" of the thief made unmasking him impossible.

This story is an extreme one, of course. It is told among the Swahili as an illustration of how powerful the fear of the respected men is and how this fear can inhibit the behavior of the other group members. Even when an arbiter is obviously at a moral, psychological, and social disadvantage, an upstanding member of the community still cannot bring himself to risk his displeasure and disapproval by revealing the respected man's crime.

If this is true, when the ordinary group member has done nothing that could by any stretch of group standards be considered wrong, while the arbiter is personally involved in a serious aibu, how much truer it must be when the ordinary group member sees himself as having aibu and sees the respected man as evaluating the aibu from a position of unmatched moral and social standing.

Group members do not follow the views of the arbiters, as they understand these views, in all instances. The fact that these men receive a good deal of attention in conversation and a good deal of deference in interaction, however, strongly suggests that their understood views are a frequent source of influence on behavior. The arbiters can be looked at from the outside as representatives of the group's most respected standards, and the "fear" of the arbiters can be seen as a force encouraging adherence to those standards. This despite the fact that members of different status groupings may have their own standards that differ from one another and, even, from those attributed to the arbiters.

The arbiters' judgments override the differing judgments of different sanctioners in the sense, at least, that they leave in the minds of some of the judged and some of the sanctioners the clear notion—and this can be seen in informants' statements—that the behavior seen as disapproved by arbiters really may be aibu despite others accepting or, even, honoring it. In this respect, and it is a passive one, the arbiters' influence transcends the diversity of standards and judgments based in status differences and acts as a source of moral unity for the community as a whole.

Aibu as a Social and Psychological Process

When the concern individuals feel about the arbiters' judgments actually affects what they do, the influence of the arbiters is manifested socially, although this may or may not be known by the actors involved. Both for sanctioners and arbiters, even if their understood or anticipated judgments in particular instances do not affect overt behavior, they may result in anxiety for the actor and affect other instances or different behaviors.

The difference, however, between the influence of understood or anticipated judgments that results in the modification of behavior and the influence that results only in anxiety is considerable. Actors may be willing to suffer anxiety in return for the benefits they derive from the behavior in question. In fact, I know that members of this group do things—and refuse to do things—even though they understand their behavior to be unambiguously disapproved by arbiters and/or by one or more groups of sanctioners. A few group members, for example, do drink alcohol, engage in generally disapproved sex with other group members, and fail to meet obligations to kin or benefactors.

This happens, I hypothesize, more often when whatever psychological costs in the form of anxiety there may be are not augmented by direct social costs in the form of undeniable disapproval from either sanctioners or arbiters. A main way for actors to avoid these social costs once the disapproved act or failure is begun is to limit the availability of information about the act through taking advantage of the general emphasis on secrecy. However, there are two culturally based processes that militate against and limit this means of avoiding the social costs of aibu.

The first of these is that when people quarrel, they are understood to be fairly likely to use the proclamation of their adversary's aibu as a weapon. Family members may be reluctant to do this, but even they may become sufficiently enraged to forget their duties to their close kin and their own reputations and proclaim aibu that would otherwise never be known beyond the family home. Sanctioners who do not themselves disapprove of an action or failure know that other sanctioners and/or the arbiters do disapprove, and the former may use their knowledge as a weapon in a quarrel.

A second culturally constituted process that limits the assurance that information can be controlled as a means of avoiding or limiting the social consequences of aibu centers on a status whose members are called "fidhuli." A fidhuli is a person understood to be unusually interested in, and well informed about, the aibu of others and to be quite willing to broadcast his information. I know of no gloss for this status in English, so I will retain the Swahili word "fidhuli" to refer to them.

One such man is reported to have become annoyed at another for a fairly minor slight and to have said to the man publicly that the man should not forget that his grandmother always came to the fidhuli's house when she was sick. This allegation means that the man's grandmother was once a slave in the house of the fidhuli since slaves, and no one else, go to others' (i.e., their forebears' masters) houses for medicine and care when they are ill. For a person who claims to be a "noble" (mwungwana) or full member of the group, having a slave ancestor is a serious aibu that throws his whole social standing into doubt.

The fact that aibu can be revealed by fidhuli whenever they find it convenient to do so and that others may reveal it in quarrels limits the ability of actors to avoid the social consequences of their acts through limiting knowledge of them. Neither quarreling nor being a fidhuli is approved, and, as noted, the same is true even for discussing the behavior of others. However, these disapproved activities, somewhat paradoxically, have as one of their consequences the diminution of the judgmental relativity that results from the existence of different sets of sanctioners whose judgments depend, in part, on their own statuses and those of the judged. The disapproved revelation contributes to moral uniformity by making uncertain the actor's control of who will judge his actions.

Cultural Change, Shame, and Cultural Distribution

An aspect of the cultural dynamics involving the arbiters which has not yet been considered is who judges the members of this status. In fact, the arbiters, like everyone else, have more than one status, and in some of their statuses (father, government official, community member, Muslim, etc.) they are liable to judgment more or less as anyone else is. Having seen the case of the corn thief, however, it will be clear that separating an arbiter from his status is difficult. Arbiter seems to be one of the statuses, like priest, prostitute, and president in the United States, that "spills over" into other statuses occupied by the same individuals and affects the understandings that apply in those other statuses.

There is little question in the minds of the community members that arbiters have aibu. Community members agree that everyone, even Prophet Mohammed, has aibu, and only God is without it. Informants agree that the men I am calling arbiters are more concerned about aibu—their own as well as others—than anyone else in the society, which, they say, accounts in large part for their scrupulous maintenance of high standards. So long as group members show them deference and inhibit their behavior when they are present, the arbiters retain their prestige. Since no one is free of aibu, it is the arbiters' constant effort to avoid it, as people see it, that is the foundation of their prestige and of their ability to instill "fear" in others (*kuwatisha*).

Arbiters and Cultural Change

Earlier, it was suggested that if arbiters countenance behavior, that behavior is almost certainly not aibu. A fortiori, if arbiters actually engage in behavior, it is likely to be viewed as free of aibu. This suggests that the cultural complex centering around the arbiters provides, inter alia, the basis for a culturally constituted means for the acceptance of new understandings about what can and should be done and how to do it; a culturally constituted means, that is, for the acceptance of cultural change.

There is little reason to believe that arbiters can adopt new behaviors entailing new standards without any limits on how radically those standards depart from the status quo, since if an arbiter behaves in ways that make people stop fearing him, he loses respect (i.e., he is no longer "feared"). I would predict with great confidence that in the extraordinarily unlikely event that an arbiter were to convert to Christianity, that would not establish the understanding that such conversion is acceptable. It would only lead to the arbiter's immediate loss of prestige and raise questions about his mental health.

There are actual changes, however, that arbiters are involved in, and a brief look at one of them may be instructive. A senior man of substantial prestige who is undoubtedly an arbiter played an important role in making movie attendance relatively aibu-free some years ago.

As Muslims, the Swahili have, at best, an ambivalent attitude toward pictures of any kind, and activities that are purely for amusement, *upuzi,* are by no means completely admired. The fact that women in films are sometimes shown in revealing costumes, that scenes of sexual activities are shown, and that men and women attend the theaters together adds further possibilities for movie attendance being viewed as likely to entail aibu.

The arbiter, however, began to attend selected films in the late 1960s and went several times a year beginning in the 1970s. Sometimes other men of roughly equal prestige accompanied him. Their presence at the films together with the fact that none of them lost respect and all continued to be feared may have contributed to what both informants and I see as an increase in movie attendance during the 1970s by Swahili.

There are still men who report that they do not attend films and never did so. These men are all well into middle age, highly conservative, and generally suspicious of activities associated with the West. Many of them are themselves of the sort I would call arbiters, and it may be that the aura of acceptability of behavior stemming from other high-prestige individuals participating in it is more influential for lower-prestige individuals than for others with prestige comparable to those who participate.

For a considerable proportion of the community, however, film going is now accepted, and even those who do not go themselves seem to indicate no active disapproval of those who do. It is difficult to establish without doubt that attendance by the arbiter and his peers is the only factor involved in this change, but the time of their beginning to go to movies corresponds with the beginning of open and general attendance by increasingly large numbers of male community members.[6] A number of informants have told me that now any group member, even the "strictest," might go to the films without shame, if there is some attention to what films are seen and what theaters are attended.

The general hypothesis being advanced here is that the Swahili distribution of culture with its particular set of understandings included in the status "arbiter" results in the members of that status being in a special position compared to other group members in different statuses. They can engage in behaviors that might lead others to be judged as committing aibu, without being so judged, at least initially. If following their engaging in these behaviors, they retain their ability to "frighten" others and to be generally respected, the behaviors appear free from aibu and thereby become more acceptable to other group members than they might otherwise be.

Shame, Behavior, and the Distribution of Culture

Earlier, it was shown that individuals are exposed to a variety of judgments of similar acts with those of some sanctioners approving and those of others disapproving what was done or contemplated. Clearly, the different assessments cannot affect behavior equally in a given situation, so guidance is needed in choosing which to accord most weight. One of the factors in this is what has been internalized and another is who the holders of the different views are.

The weightiest assessment and the actor's own views may not coincide, but the variety of standards available through the multiplicity of sanctioners with different views offers the possibility of flexibility as well as uncertainty. With the guidance of both internalized beliefs and values and with knowledge, not necessarily explicit and formulated, of the status system, a person can satisfy his or her personal needs without either refraining from desired behavior or being negatively evaluated by any of a diversity of sanctioners.

The ability of the individual to respond to the diversity of standards associated with different types of sanctioners by controlling information about his activity and by inhibiting his behavior in some, but not necessarily all, social settings suggests strongly that he or she has not internalized all of the different—and perhaps conflicting—values concerning that activity with equal strength. This would be so, at least, if internalization usually results either in behavior in accord with what is internalized or in discernible anxiety when engaging in behavior contrary to the standards.

My data concerning how different individuals experience aibu and how it is involved in motivation are regrettably sparse as, so far as I can establish, are the comparable data from studies of shame in other societies reported in the literature. Swahili informants tell me that aibu is an unpleasant feeling that no one wishes to experience. People suffering from serious aibu are said to be unable to look others in the face, and anyone who customarily looks at the ground instead of at those around him is generally understood to be experiencing chronic shame. I am unable to determine, however, how effective aibu is as a force in motivation.

Informants agree that people, probably everyone including the worst, try to avoid aibu and that "good" people, like those I call arbiters, try harder than others. I do not have information that allows me to make statements about how far people are willing to go in avoiding aibu, and I cannot even approximate how experiencing it is weighed against the benefits and social costs of doing desired, but aibu, things. Nor can I comment on the emotional cost of not doing desired things because they are aibu.

Balancing Shame and Contrary Forces: A Little Case

A brief case suggests that at least sometimes group members will endure such psychic pain as they may experience from behavior that they agree is somewhat shameful, if the behavior has social benefits and acceptable social costs.

A young Swahili man told me that although he enjoyed the company of his male companions, they often caused him concern because of their drinking, smoking marijuana, and talk of sexual activities. He said that a "true Muslim" must lead others away from sin and he, although he saw himself as a true Muslim, did nothing to influence his companions to behave in more acceptable ways.

I take this to suggest that he felt some shame at his failure to do what he thought he ought to do. His views about what he should have done to influence his friends are in accord with what the Swahili say is true Muslim doctrine, and, although he never said so to me, I am sure he knew that. Still, he did nothing to correct his friends and continued to see them despite his misgivings. He never mentioned to them his disapproval of their actions but only, he told me, remained silent when they spoke of their activities and when they drank and smoked in his presence. However, he steadfastly refused to drink or do other things contrary to Islam despite the urging of his friends.

Insofar as my informant's account can be taken at face value (and the possibility that he sees me as a sanctioner vaguely aligned with men who are arbiters cannot be dismissed out of hand), his behavior appears to be more directed to gaining the benefits of associating with people who amuse him than with avoiding the feelings of aibu deriving from that association. It is to be noted that his associations had little or no social cost. The arbiters neither knew nor were likely to find out that he associated with the particular youths who were his friends, since their gatherings are in "cold houses" (cafés where cold soda and snacks are sold) where arbiters rarely or never went, and anyway, most or all of these youths were from good families and had done nothing sufficiently public and notorious to gain bad reputations. My informants knew of their aibu, but arbiters and others from sanctioner groupings likely to disapprove did not. From a personal perspective, he could—and did—console himself with his refusal to participate actively in his friends' sinful ways.

The youths themselves are, of course, sanctioners, and there can be no doubt they would have disapproved of any action by my informant aimed at "correcting" their behavior. Whether or not my informant and other group members would consider a negative judgment of this sort as a source of aibu (and I suspect they would not call it that), it would seem likely to be the functional equivalent in being a stimulant of feelings of being disapproved and losing prestige among the judges. At the same time, my informants did gain the social benefit of having usually amusing companions. The informant's aibu was, perhaps, not very great by his own standards, although he did feel he was behaving wrongly by not attempting to stop his friends from sinning or, at least, by continuing to associate with them when they did not stop.

Such emotional pain as this may have caused him, however, seems to have been outweighed by the social and personal gains of continued association and, perhaps, his personally virtuous behavior.

I do not mean to suggest that all cases result in feelings of aibu being overpowered by other considerations. My informant believed it was aibu-producing to drink alcohol, and he never did it despite teasing from his friends. I only mean to suggest that the existence of the feelings associated with aibu do not necessarily prevent the behavior that is identified as causing that aibu. Social considerations seem very weighty in determining aibu's effect on behavior, and many of these considerations involve an understanding by the actor that different "significant others" have different views of what is right and proper. Epstein (1984:40) says of the views of both experimental psychologists and psychoanalysts,

> common to these diverse approaches is the way shame is held to be intimately linked to threat to the image or negative evaluation of the self. [On the negative side are] . . . feelings of inadequacy, worthlessness, and the like . . . elicited by the exposure of some act or quality . . . one perceives as reflecting discredit on the self. . . . More positively, shame may also be seen as providing, at the level of the individual, a major thrust towards the development of a sense of identity, serving at the same time, at the cultural level, to protect and maintain basic social values.

I agree with Epstein. I would add, however, that shame is not a monolithic process in Swahili society but that it "protects and maintains" not only "basic social values" (those represented by the arbiters for the most part) but also the cultural distribution that is as basic to the existence of the society as are the fundamental values. The individual is motivated to behave in accord with widely held values because of the shame he would experience and the social costs he would incur if he ignored the judgments of the arbiters and such sanctioners as might support these values as they applied to him. The individual, however, is also motivated to act in accord with values different from, even opposed to, the fundamental ones because of the shame he would experience and the social costs he would incur if he did not.

Shame as a Support for Cultural Diversity

It is shame's operation as a support for diversity based in differences among statuses that is of particular interest in dealing with the questions raised by the fact that not all of culture's elements are shared by all of a community's members. The broadly shared values applying more or less equally to everyone, such as not going naked in public, serve more importantly as tokens than as guides. By following them, and it is effortless for almost everyone,

one affirms group unity, and members show each other that they behave as decent people do. However, the varying values and beliefs of the sanctioners, applying selectively but predictably, support a conformity to a culture that is differentially distributed among the statuses that make up the social structure and is not even fully shared within the status categories.

Like the models based in terms considered in the last chapter, shame not only promotes conformity to understandings shared by group members, it does so in a differentiated way. This differentiation is based on status differences with both the status of the judged and that of the judge greatly affecting the kinds of conformity expected of the judged. The sort of universally applicable pressure for conformity to universally shared understandings is limited to understandings whose importance for most sorts of behavior is rather slight. It is the status-dependent, differentiated pressures that promote much of the behavior that is vital for individual adaptation and community life. This sort of pressure for conformity allows substantial flexibility in the sorts of behavior found within the group and does not depend on broad sharing of large numbers of specific understandings.

The interest in statuses and their role in cultural processes in this chapter and those preceding it has focused more on how statuses function and their general properties as seen in Swahili culture and social life than on their operation as systems of interconnected elements. In the next two chapters, some of the effects of interconnected sets of statuses, that is, of social structure, will be examined.

9

Leaning on the Cow's Fat Hump

Medical Choices, Unshared Culture,
and General Expectations

Mtegemea nundu hawati kunona: *He [who] leans on
the cow's [fat] hump does not stop fattening. (The
proverb is used when someone is seen to use his connections with others to gain desired ends.)*

Shame provides one foundation for the differentiated cultural conformity
essential to the effectiveness of statuses. The part played by statuses in evaluation and shame among the Swahili has now received some attention, but their
involvement in cultural dynamics has not been specifically addressed. This
chapter turns to that by examining one of the ways statuses make it possible
for cultural elements to affect group members, including those who do not
share them.

This transmission of culture's effects results from a type of relation among
cultural elements that has received only limited attention as compared to what
can be called the "intrinsic relations" among them. The latter sort of relations
include the subset/superset relationship cognitive anthropologists have studied as it occurs in taxonomies (D'Andrade n.d.). Such relations among cultural elements depend on common internal qualities including their being
concerned with the same thing. There are, however, many possible sorts of
relations that link shared understandings together, and not all of them are
directly based in the contents of the understandings themselves.

Cultural Organization

All the relations among cultural elements can be referred to as "cultural
organization." There seems to be no limit to the number or kinds of relationships that can exist between understandings, and the same understandings—
singly or in complexes—can be present in any number of relationships.

Whatever sorts of relationships there may be among understandings, no understanding exists in complete isolation from all others in anyone's mind. This is true even as concerns remembering understandings as well as in considering or using them to guide action. For this, they must be related to one another at least with respect to priority, sequence, and whether they always entail one another, can never occur together, or can either occur together or not. In fact, the actual relations among understandings are far more complex than this last suggests, and much of this results, as will appear, from the social mediation of relations among cultural elements.

The shared or cultural organization of understandings, of course, is not necessarily the same as an individual's organization of understandings. Still, for people to behave with the predictability required for social life, they must have some common organization of the understandings that guide their behavior just as they must have some understandings in common. Thus, for example, if senior Swahili men are to greet people in a way acceptable to other senior men using the somewhat elaborate set of greetings they understand as appropriate, they must share not only a fair number of understandings concerning whom to greet and what to say but they must also be guided by them in similar sequences and settings.

The general importance of cultural organizations is not, of course, limited to such simple matters as greetings but extends across all of culture's scope. Below there is an examination of the elaborate understandings about body functioning, illness, and treatment shared by the practitioners of Swahili traditional medicine and the finely dove-tailed relationships among them. This organization unites a complex of intrinsically related cultural elements into an effective guide to behavior for the medical experts who share many or most of the understandings that comprise the complex.[1]

Limited Sharing of Vital Understandings and Organization

Although a substantial majority of the community share few or none of them, the practitioners of traditional medicine and serious amateurs share a much-elaborated set of understandings concerned with body functioning. The general ignorance of these understandings is perhaps to be expected given the limited nature of cultural sharing in all domains and, especially, laymen's ignorance in technical matters. It is striking, nevertheless, that people submit themselves to treatment, often for conditions they understand to be serious and painful, according to understandings they do not share or, even, for the most part, know about.

In fact, two quite different sources for the influence of these esoteric understandings will be hypothesized. Both are dependent on cultural organizations, albeit of dissimilar kinds, for their effectiveness. One of these is of the sort students of culture have long pointed out. It stems from the organizational fact that the understandings about the body and illness involve a fundamental cultural element that is also basic to social morality. The two sets of understandings are, or are part of, a "cultural pattern."

A Cultural Pattern:
An Intrinsic Organization

For the experts who share both the medical and moral understandings to be discussed, the presence of a common, basic understanding in both gives the medical understandings a force they would not otherwise have. For most members of the community, however, this appeal can hardly be present since, as shown below, more than 85 percent of them do not share the experts' understandings about how the body works. Nevertheless, it will be shown that the "balance pattern" does have a positive, if indirect, effect on the acceptance of medical care from practitioners who follow the balance theory of disease.

Another and more pervasive source of the ability of medical understandings to guide behavior will be shown to involve other cultural elements that often have no necessary reference to medical issues. These other understandings are the general expectations that are characteristic of relationships of the sort referred to in chapter 7 as "multiplex." These provide the basis for an organization of understandings that directly guides many patients' behavior. These general expectations lead the patient to accept advice on medical care, and this advice links the patient's understanding that treatment is needed with understandings about what sorts of treatment are available and desirable. This organization is not based on intrinsic relations among understandings with interlocked contents as some organizations are but is mediated through understandings about actors and the statuses of those actors.

This organization of medical understandings through the agency of cultural elements guiding social relations is broadly important in organizing Swahili culture generally. The organizational contribution of social relations in a different domain, kinship and marriage, will be seen in the next chapter. Organizations based on intrinsic relations among understandings are, of course, also vital. These are the organizations that most readily call themselves to attention and that have traditionally received close anthropological scrutiny. One of them, mentioned above, serves to strengthen the medical understandings held by practitioners and serious amateurs.

To examine the two types of organization closely, it is necessary to consider the understandings about the body and medicine held by experts and, separately, those held by interested laymen.

Expert Understanding of
Body Functioning and Illness

The traditional therapists (*matabibu*, sing. *tabibu*) understand the basic cause of most illness to be an imbalance among the four characters or elements (*matabia*, sing. *tabia*) that they take as fundamental to the body's functioning. This disruption is always due to improper diet, although other factors can exacerbate or lessen the disruption. The only effective treatment of the illness that inevitably results from disruption is understood to be dietary change supplemented by medicines, most of them compounded from herbs. The new diet and the medicines are aimed at reinstating the body's essential elementary balance and thereby restoring health.

The fact that the beliefs and values described in this section are shared among experts and not at all among the overwhelming majority of the community is crucial to an understanding of the cultural dynamics in this domain. Most community members have consulted "herbal doctors" (as I will henceforth call matabibu) several times or more, but this cannot be attributed to even sketchy knowledge of the basis for this medical view. Traditional medical care may be slightly less expensive than care from a university-trained physician, but many Swahili can well afford Western-type care. Although the basic understandings in Western medicine are shared no more than are those of traditional medicine, most people utilize Western medicine rather often.[2] In fact, as an estimate, I would say that a majority of the community uses Western medical services more than traditional ones, even though most people use both.

Fundamentally, the "balance theory," as it can be called, followed by herbal doctors holds that the proper balance of the body's four elements, hot and cold and wet and dry, is indispensable to health. Illness results should any of the elements fail to make its appropriate contribution to the body's operation.

A number of the herbal doctors and expert laymen commented on the fact that the understandings concerning illness they follow come from outside their own society. Many attribute them (correctly) to the early Greeks and, more specifically, to the well-known second-century physician, Galen, who is called "Galeni" in Swahili. The Mombasa Swahili, like their fellow ethnics up and down the East African coast, see themselves as part of the great, worldwide Muslim civilization, and a number of them, including many herbal doctors, know that the cultural heritage of this civilization includes the view of illness held in their own group. The view that balance theory is shared by other Muslim peoples in other areas of the world is, of course, correct (Temkin 1973). There are differences between the Swahili view of balance theory and the same basic theory as held in other Muslim groups (see, e.g.,

Good 1977), but the existence of similarities and a recognized relationship is worth noting.

All the Swahili herbal doctors save one learned their profession in apprenticeships, most commonly with their fathers. The one who has formal schooling went to a Muslim Institute in Lamu where he received a certificate for "general studies." He has far more elaborate offices than other herbal doctors, charges higher fees than they do, and told me that a group of visiting American physicians gave him $500 for a one-hour lecture on his approach to medicine.[3]

Body Functioning and the Bodily Elements

According to the herbal doctors, the body's functioning is to be understood according to what I have called balance theory. Their main attention to discussing body functioning is focused on the four elements (also referred to by English-speaking informants as "complexions" and "characters"): "cold" (baridi), "hot" (hari), "dry" (yabisi), and "wet" (rughtba). In Swahili belief, the same four elements are present in everyone, but there are important differences among people in their relative amounts and in the balance among them.

Each of the elements is centered in a particular part of the body and is associated with a bodily fluid. Hari (hot) is centered in the liver and is associated with blood. People with a predominance of hari tend to be hopeful and courageous in disposition. Hari is more powerful in men than in women and more powerful during youth than in old age. Women rarely get diseases caused by an excess of hot because their menstrual flow protects them from this excess by lessening the blood supply when they are young. When they are old enough for their menstrual flow to stop, they are protected by their advanced age, with its diminution of hot. Men, however, are quite susceptible to hot diseases until aging brings about a lessening in their natural tendency to hotness and makes them more susceptible to diseases of excessive cold as women are all their lives.

Baridi (cold) is in the lungs and is associated with phlegm. People with a predominance of phlegm are inclined to be sluggish, dull, and impassive. Cold is more powerful in women than in men and in old age more than in youth.

Unlike the case for cold and hot, there is no association between gender and the rughtba (wet) and yabisi (dry) elements, but wet is associated with youth and dry with old age. Wet is associated with yellow bile and is located in the bile sac. A person with a preponderance of wet is likey to be proud, quick tempered, and generally given to anger.

Dry is in the spleen and is associated with what the Swahili call maji, which is the word also used to refer to water. However, informants specifically deny that this "water" is the lymph that fills blisters, and it is a near certainty that it is the "black bile" Galen associated with the spleen as opposed to the yellow bile he associated with the liver and bile sac (Siegel 1968:258). Those in whom dryness predominates are commonly moody, depressive, and suspicious.

The fact that the Swahili refer to the elements by the same names used for physical qualities of temperature and moisture might lead to the incorrect inference that they are, in fact, directly connected with these qualities. This mistaken idea might be strengthened by the fact that the hot element affects the body, for good or ill, most readily in the summertime, while the cold element is most effective in the winter. In fact, season is understood to affect body functioning indirectly by the influence of ambient temperature on how food is digested. Thus, the cold element tends to dominate the body in the winter and hot in the summer because the foods promoting hot are more effectively assimilated in the summer, while those promoting cold are more effectively assimilated in the winter.

In addition to variations due to sex and age, each individual has his or her own particular balance, which is significantly different from all others. A fanciful balance rendered, strictly for purposes of illustration, in numerical values for the elements might be 3:1/2:2 for one person, while another might be 1:3/3:1. One consequence of these differences is that individuals not only differ in character as a result of the different weightings of the elements in their balances but they are also more or less healthy depending on how stable their balances are. Differences in predisposition to particular diseases and kinds of diseases result from the same individual variations in balance.

When the influence of one or more of the elements becomes excessive, an imbalance occurs and is manifested as an illness. Only reestablishing the individual's customary elemental balance will end the illness. Although the season of the year has an indirect effect on the balance of elements, only aging, sex, food, and drink affect it directly.

The Classification of Food and Drink in the Balance System

All food and drink is classified according to the four elements, or a combination of them, according to the way they affect the body rather than to the nature of the foods themselves. Thus, ice is not cold; it is dry since it contributes to the operation of the element that is given that name. Honey, even if it is taken directly from the refrigerator, is hot because of the nature of its contribution to body functioning.

Edible substances, in the Swahili view, can have another property in addition to the four components of the body's elemental balance, and this is being either "heavy" or "light." This dimension appears to be similar to another aspect of Galen's system. Galen, like his Swahili successors, believed that in addition to the four primary "qualities," there were "secondary qualities" that modified the primary qualities. As Siegel, an authority on Galen, puts it, "Galen regarded all parts of the body as a combination of primary qualities, but modified by the addition of secondary qualities. Thus, the blood is red; bile is bitter and yellow, and because of some other secondary quality each exhibits a varying viscosity" (ibid., 147).

In Swahili understandings, "heavy" foods facilitate the effect of, say, cold less than "light" foods do. For some foods, being heavy or light is an inherent property. Others, including most meats, are neither heavy nor light in themselves but can become either depending on how they are prepared and on how long they have been stored.

The classification of foods and drinks in this system is exhaustive, with previously unknown foods or drinks being classified by their observed effects on those who ingest them. Most foods are classified according to being either cold or hot and also according to being either wet or dry. Some foods, however, are so strong along one of the dimensions (hot or cold or dry or wet) that their standing on the other is negligible. Cold and hot are more powerful in their effects on the body than dry and wet, with hotness being a definite cause of dryness (i.e., if there is enough hotness, wet foods will be converted to dry), and excess cold can cause otherwise dry foods to produce the reaction of wet ones. Neither dry nor wet, however, can produce either hot or cold. Despite this, wet and dry must be in balance quite as much as hot and cold must be, if illness is to be avoided.

A few common foods and their classifications can serve as illustrations of the system:

Corn: cold and dry, light in the stomach
Wheat: cold and dry, heavy in the stomach
Millet: hot and wet, heavy in the stomach
White beans: dry and cold, heavy in the stomach
Red beans: hot and dry, heavy in the stomach
Beef: hot
Goat meat: hot and dry
Chicken: hot
Fruit: all fruits having juice are hot and wet, heavy in the stomach

Since foods are classified according to how they affect the body, it is not surprising that their classification changes as the food substances do. Thus, many foods are understood to change their effects with time, so that fresh cow's milk is hot and wet, but if it stands for some time, it becomes cold and wet, and if allowed to sour it is only wet without cold. Rice is hot, but if it is stored for a year or so it becomes dry. In the winter, bananas are hot and wet but in the summer cold and wet.

Similarly, the state, including size, or age of the source of a food is understood as affecting the food's influence on the body and therefore the food's classification. So, for example, the meat from immature chickens, that is, from hens that have not yet laid eggs and roosters that have not yet crowed, is hot, moderately wet, and fairly light in the stomach, but when the birds are older, their meat is hot, dry, and heavy in the stomach. In the same way, the flesh of large fish is understood to contribute to the hot element in the body but that of small fish to the cold. Even within the same food, the constituents can have different elemental standings, if these are taken to have different effects on the body. Thus, the whites of eggs are cold and wet, while the yolks are hot and wet.

Expert Understandings
of the Causes of Illness

The herbal doctors and dedicated amateurs say that most community members have a substantial knowledge of "balance" and the effects on it of various foods. As the evidence shows (see below), they are wrong in this, but, for the experts, physical well-being is understood as depending on diet, with all other determinants distinctly secondary.

Chief among these secondary sources are trauma and supernatural agencies, but even these involve the bodily imbalance based on diet. Injury and spirit attack can cause illness, but they can also lead to imbalance, which may bring on further, often more serious, consequences.

For illnesses resulting from either of these nondietary causes, becoming well again requires, as one step, that the effects of the external causes be terminated by overpowering the spiritual agency or overcoming the traumatic injury. This is done, for example, by exorcising the dangerous spirit, *pepo,* if it is a spirit-caused illness; by manipulating the broken bones if there be such; or by stopping the bleeding if that is present. This termination by itself, however, may not end the patient's distress. What seems to be shock, following broken bones, or various continuing symptoms, following attacks by supernatural beings, are taken as a sure indication that, in addition to the directly observable results, the body's fundamental balance has been upset by the trauma or spirits.

Infection is understood to operate in a manner quite different from that posited by Western medicine. In balance medicine, although it is diet that is the original cause, the person who has been "infected" is ill not because of *his* diet but because of that of someone else who has become ill in the ordinary way. This latter person's diet-based disease is transmitted to the one infected by it. The transmission occurs through small particles that leave the original patient's body and enter the second's through the openings in the skin where hair grows.

Diagnosis and Treatment

Regardless of complaint, the Galenic doctor's first step is to take the patient's pulse. This is done by putting the thumb, normally the right thumb but the left can be used, on the patient's left wrist. It is essential that it be the left wrist because it is understood that the major blood vessels that pass through the entire body are found near the surface only on the left side. By feeling the vessel in the left wrist, three vital diagnostic facts can be established: whether the force of the blood is strong or weak; whether blood flow is normal, fast, or slow; and whether the blood vessel itself is normal, thick, or thin.

A fast pulse and a thick-feeling vein are taken to indicate excess hot, since this condition is understood to involve there being too much blood. A slow pulse and a thin vessel result from insufficient blood and indicate an excess of cold, while too much dry is shown by a weak pulse and a thick vessel. Excessive wet, which is present when there is too much additional fluid (i.e., "maji") in the blood, produces a fast pulse and a thin vessel.

Patients are not asked to remove any clothing, nor is there any physical examination other than the taking of the pulse, but general appearance is noted with attention to paleness, flushes, obvious physical signs such as drooping eye lids, and signs of fatigue. After the patient reports his symptoms and is questioned about the location and nature of any reported pain, he or she is asked about appetite and diet, sleep, bowel and bladder performance, and changes in energy. The data collected in this way are used to establish the type of excess that is the basis of the patient's illness.

Once the type of excess is identified, the next step is to establish where in the body the excess is located so that treatment can be directed to that location. In all cases, therapy consists in overcoming the excess through contributing to the opposite element. Thus, excess hot is treated by increasing cold, excess wet by increasing dry, and so on. The medicines used vary according to the location of the excess, but the basic steps in the treatment of all diseases are similar and follow from understandings concerning the importance of the balance of the four elements.

When excess is located in the head, it is never necessary to cleanse the system since treatment does not involve digestion. The treatment of all other sorts of illnesses, however, often begins with the cleansing of the patient's system in order to ready the body for the changes that are to be made by the medications and dietary regimen that will be prescribed.

One of the herbal doctor informants said that the treatment of all illnesses not based in the head begins with a thorough cleansing in the way to be described in a moment. The other two agreed that cleansing is carried out in the way described, but they understand it to be necessary only sometimes and to be positively harmful when the patient is weak and/or old.

This cleansing is done by a single administration of a laxative in the summertime, when laxatives are understood to affect the body more fully, and of an emetic in the winter, when laxatives are understood to be only partially effective. The two methods of cleansing are seen as alternatives, and patients receive one or the other, rather than both, at the beginning of treatment.

There is only a single emetic in common use. A drink is prepared of one and a half "bottles" (roughly, liters) of water that has been boiled but whose volume has not been reduced and the juice of three limes. The water and lime mixture is allowed to cool and the patient is made to eat something (for obvious reasons it matters little what it is), and the mixture is drunk. The patient then waits for fifteen minutes when a twig 18 or 20 centimeters long and 1 to 2 centimeters in diameter with one end split and frayed into a brush, an *mswaki* (pl. *miswaki*),[4] more commonly used as a toothbrush, is put down his or her throat. This causes vomiting of a sort that is understood to include the entire content of the system, not just recently eaten food.

When the season calls for a laxative, there is a choice among a variety, with selection depending on the patient's condition. The components of the various laxatives interact and produce qualities in the compounds not present in the components by themselves. Although all laxatives are by their nature hot, there is substantial variation in the particular properties of specific compounds and choice among them is important to therapeutic effect. Like emetics, the basic purpose of the laxatives is to ready the system for medication and a new dietary regimen, but different laxatives have different effects and care must be taken to choose one that will not exacerbate the patient's illness. In some disorders due to excess cold, a properly chosen laxative can have therapeutic as well as preparatory functions.

It might be useful to consider a common illness and its treatment. The illustrative illness is one of a whole class particularly to be found in women and the elderly. It is understood to result from excess cold centered in the lungs. This type of disease results in weakness, loss of appetite, and coughing. Runny nose and difficulty in breathing are associated with some of the specific diseases of this type. Some of these diseases, including the one we will consider, can be fatal, especially in the elderly whose aged systems are understood to respond less well to attempts to reestablish balance.

A useful laxative for beginning treatment for this type of disease is compounded of cinnamon (*sanamaki*), tamarind (*ukwajuu*), and asafetida (*halilaji*). To compound this laxative, the cinnamon, tamarind, and asafetida (using only the small white kernels) are soaked for twelve hours in water and then boiled for five or ten minutes. The solids, after being taken out of the water, which is thrown away, are squeezed in a cloth producing a liquid that the patient drinks. A few spoonfuls to a quarter of a teacup is sufficient to attain this compound's desired effects.

The cinnamon contributes dryness, the asafetida hotness, and the tamarind wetness and coldness, with the result being a hot and wet laxative. This particular combination is both more effective and safer than others in cleansing the systems of all sufferers from excess cold. At the same time, it has some therapeutic effect in lung disorders, through its influence on balance in the lung area.

After the patient has had his system cleansed with the laxative, the full treatment regimen begins. Medications are given and dietary restrictions (*miko*) are imposed. Every disease has its own dietary restrictions, which are viewed as being as important in treatment as the medications are. The restrictions and medications are intended to work together in restoring the body's balance through what might be thought of as "an oppositional strategy." At least part of the treatment of a cold disease, for example, involves giving the patient hot medicines, keeping him or her from eating cold foods, and, perhaps, encouraging the eating of hot foods. Treatment is not as simple as this sketch suggests, since the patient's age and unique personal balance, the season of the year, and the effects of wet and dry also have to be considered, as does whether the foods and medicines are heavy or light in the stomach.[5]

The common lung disorder to be considered is called *balghamu* and is understood as resulting from an excess of wet abetted by an excess of cold. A patient suffering from balgamu has a fast and weak pulse in a blood vessel that feels thin. He or she will complain of a headache on the right side of the head only and will have a cough that produces phlegm (*makohozi*, sing. *kohozi*). When the patient awakens in the morning, there will be white matter in the corners of the eyes which is wet rather than hard. If the condition indicated by these symptoms is left untreated, it can result in paralysis.

It is generally characteristic of patients with balgamu to talk about the past and to tell stories of things that happened years ago. This behavioral pattern, like the illness it is associated with, is caused by excess wet. The wet-produced behavior varies across a wide range, from being so mild and similar to the patient's usual behavior that it is not noticed by relatives to being so extreme that it must be treated before or concurrently with the treatment of the physical manifestations of the disease.

The three herbal doctors agree that for these symptoms an emetic is given if the illness occurs in the winter and a laxative is given if it occurs in the summer, but two of them say that the cleansing must be delayed until recovery has begun if the patient has been weakened by the disease's progress before treatment. All agree that following the emetic or laxative, the patient is put on a restricted diet that excludes beef, apples, grapes, and all spices save vinegar (*siki*). In the early stages of the disease, the laxative and the regimen alone sometimes lead to a rapid cure without further treatment, but in more advanced cases, medication is needed.

The medication for balgamu is compounded of three components: three pennies' weight[6] of fennel seed (*shimari*), an equal weight of ginger (*sanamaki*), and six pennies' weight of rock sugar all ground to a powder. The three ingredients are mixed together, and the patient is given one soup spoonful three times a day. This treatment is viewed by informants as usually effective save in very advanced or difficult cases that have progressed to paralysis. For these last, different treatments focusing on dry herbs that also have cold properties are called for, with their exact formulations differing from case to case and established on a trial-and-error basis.

The intrinsic relationships among the understandings concerning balgamu and its treatment are now easily seen. The fundamental understandings involved concern the supreme role of the balance among the four elements in body functioning. These understandings are connected to understandings about what to do when the body is malfunctioning by simple extensions or implications: basically, the nature of imbalance must be discovered and the balance reestablished by adding elements opposite to the excessive one.

Morality, Illness, and Organization

The intrinsic organization of understandings focused around balance is not limited to those concerned with the body and its functioning. It is also found for understandings concerning social morality. A key requirement of proper social relationships is that they be balanced. This balance, like the one in the body, results from different but complementary contributions from the elements in the processes of interest.

The idea that there are important connections between understandings concerning misfortune, including illness, and the values held in the sufferers' group is well established (e.g., Douglas 1975:22–24). In the classical formulation, misfortune is experienced by those who suffer it in terms of the value system of their group (Weber 1922). The classical study of this in anthropology is, of course, Evans-Pritchard's (1937) study of the Azande. His central point is that an explanation of misfortune based on the physical facts alone is considered incomplete by the Azande, despite their being fully alive to natural causation. For them, the moral system embodied in the understandings about witches and their doings is essential to any such explanation.

The type of connection between the Swahili views about illness and their views about an area of considerable moral concern, that is, social relationships, is quite different from the Azande. For the Swahili, the occurrence of a type of misfortune, illness, is not caused by evildoers[7] as it is for the

Azande. Instead, understandings from one domain of morality are related to understandings about an unrelated type of misfortune, illness, by a shared emphasis on a common desideratum: balance.

My objective here is to show how this cultural organization actually works and to examine the part it plays in the continuing ability of the various understandings involved to guide behavior. Only the herbal doctors and a relatively few serious amateurs share the understandings about body functioning. Nevertheless, it will be shown that, like the unshared medical understandings themselves, the connection between understandings about what is proper in social life and about the body's functioning affect most or all of the group's members.

Balance as a Desideratum in Social Relations

The importance of balance in Swahili social relationships is most evident in the emphasis on reciprocity. In relations between individuals who are not equal, as between a parent and a child or a senior and a junior, the senior must give advice, guidance, and, in some relationships, material assistance. In return, the junior must give respect, deference, and obedience. When each of the participants does the different but complementary things he or she is called on to do, the relationship is understood by Swahili as being a "good" one that is likely to continue and to benefit its participants and those involved with them.

When the junior participant fails to respond to the advice and assistance of the senior or fails to show respect, however, the relationship is seen as "bad," and the junior is thought to harm him or herself as well as the senior and anyone else affected by the relationship. Specifically, the senior is in danger of having the respect in which he is generally held harmed by the junior's behavior, while the youth can lose standing as an upright member of the community and come to be looked on as a sort of hoodlum. No one will respect a senior, informants told me, if he accepts being treated badly by a junior instead of ending the relationship.

The same undesirable situation can arise from the senior failing to behave with proper balance toward the junior. A senior who shows excessive respect to a junior or who treats the junior as though he or she were a senior harms both himself or herself and the junior. The failure to assume the behavior appropriate to a senior puts the senior's own overall status in doubt and endangers the junior by undermining (*kumtimba*, lit. "to dig [under] him/her") his or her standing and, even, physical welfare. By treating a younger person as though he were older, the senior implies the junior may die first and, through the same sort of supernatural means involved in the evil eye (see chap. 7), may actually bring about the junior's premature death. To preserve his prestige and physical welfare, a junior in such a relationship must withdraw from it.

Nor are balancing but different contributions expected only between juniors and seniors. Among equals strict reciprocity is called for, with giving by one participant to be followed immediately by grateful taking and, later, by return giving. Whatever one gives the other, whether it is material, social, or emotional, the other should accept it gratefully and return its equivalent in the future. To fail to do so is aibu, shameful, as judged by most of the peers of those involved, just as is failure to conform to prescribed, complementary behavior in relations between juniors and seniors.

In Swahili values, then, the only lasting kind of relationship, the only one beneficial to its participants, is one where each makes distinctive contributions that are complementary to those of the other. This can be seen rather explicitly in several Swahili proverbs that recognize the inevitability of reciprocity, demand it, or bemoan its absence.

Mpaji na mpokezi, mtahamali, nani? A giver and a receiver, who is burdened [more]?

Unajua lete, jifunza twaa: You understand "give," [now] learn "take."

Ulichokula ndicho ununuacho: What you ate is that which you bought, that is, you are bound to return anything given you.

Bure ghali: Free things are costly.

Changumi chakove. Chakove sumu changu mimi: [What is] mine [is] yours. [What is] yours [is] poison for me.

This emphasis on reciprocity, on the importance and (sometimes tiresome) inevitability of participants making equivalent contributions in social relations, is clearly akin to what I have been calling "balance" in body functioning. The understanding that reciprocity is essential to rewarding social relations derives part of its force from understandings learned in early life. This learning concerns such primary issues as controlling the body and winning the approval of the parents and others on whom the infant and child depends.

The child finds that performing his bodily functions as his mother wants him to is more often followed by his mother doing something he wants her to do than is not following her wishes. More generally, the child finds that if he does what he should, those who care for him are likelier to do what they should. This learning has early manifestations, as in quite young children insisting that their playmates "be fair," give them their turn, and return favors. Children are also to be seen pointing out their own good behavior to parents as a reason for their being given what they want.

Swahili have a special term, *ngoa*, referring to the justified feeling of deprivation a person, particularly a child, has on failing to get what the expectations in his status indicate are rightly his or hers. If parents give one child a gift and do not give a similar one to the others, the others will experience ngoa, which, unlike the hated emotion, husudi, jealousy or envy, is viewed as right and proper. Envy stems from wanting what others have to which you have no right, while ngoa is based in your right to get as much of what is due you as others in your category do. The emphasis on reciprocity and balance has an important part of its foundation in the opposed values that each person should have what is rightly his but should not have what is properly another's.

Balance in Understandings about the Body and about Social Relations

A comparison of the moral values and beliefs that underlie social relationships with those concerning the body and illness shows interesting similarities. The body's elements each make a distinctive contribution to the functioning of the whole, and these different contributions must complement each other, must be in balance, or illness results. When that occurs, the condition is rectified by restoring the proper balance. If that is not possible, the body will eventually cease operating, that is, the patient will die.

The "elements" in social relations are people, not hot, cold, wet, and dry, and their contributions are, of course, different in nature. But the similarities between the understandings concerning the proper course of social relationships and those concerning the body and illness are striking. So similar, in fact, that it is hardly bold to hypothesize that a view of body functioning and illness that stresses the same sorts of relationships and the same kinds of values as those at the heart of social life is likely to be appealing to the holders of the social values. Holding these latter values is neither necessary nor sufficient for accepting the understandings that make up the Galenic theory of body functioning, but sharing the values is conducive to that acceptance.

It is possible that the correspondence of relationship values and body functioning theory is an illusion resulting from imposing on the two cultural complexes a similarity that is alien to the people themselves. That this is not likely can be seen by considering a serious sort of breach of propriety in social relations. This breach involves the same kind of activity harmful to healthy body functioning, and the same term is used to describe it: *mizani*. This term refers to a scale, either a balance beam or, sometimes, a spring scale, but it is also used to mean "measure," "appropriateness," and "good sense" in social relationships. The social reference of the term is always, so far as I know, to note the absence of the qualities referred to.

A person who says things that are inappropriate to a relationship or social setting is said to be without mizani. Thus, a man who mentioned sexual activity in the presence of senior men is without mizani, as is a person who discusses family matters outside the family circle. Like the welfare of the body being threatened when an element makes an excessive, that is, inappropriate contribution, the course of social relations are imperiled by a participant who ignores "measure."

This interpretation is strengthened by the fact that when herbal doctors refer to the body's balance, they use either the Arabic word *muutadil* or, more commonly, that same term, "mizani." When I mentioned the common role for balance in the two domains, experts in Galenic medicine found the idea slightly surprising but quite plausible.

Patterns, Nonsharing, and Cultural Organization

The common presence of the understanding that balance is vital for proper functioning unites the social and bodily domains in what can be thought of as a single cultural organization. Benedict's "patterns" (1934) as well as Opler's "themes" (1945) are based mainly or entirely on just this source of relationships between different cultural domains. A well-known example of this is Benedict's finding of common elements in the understandings that guide ritual and in those concerned with personal gratification. The same sort of organization of cultural elements has been identified by more recent researchers, as, for example, Geertz's tracing of the understanding *tjotjog* (to fit) in quite different complexes concerned with medicine, arithmetic, and a number of other domains of Javanese culture (Geertz 1973a:129–130).

This "common element" organization seems likely to increase the probability that the understandings in the different sets will actually guide behavior. The fact that an understanding is taken as important in one area of life does not necessarily affect its standing in another area, but it probably gives it an inevitability it would not otherwise have. When the understanding has sacred or value-laden connections in one of the areas in which it occurs, as with the Swahili understanding that balance is essential to proper social relationships, its obviousness and importance in another area is probably increased. This seems to be what Benedict, Opler, and others imply when they identify patterns and suggest that cultural conformity—whose presence is implied by a ubiquitous "style" of behavior in different domains—is enhanced by their presence. It is surely true that for those who share the Galenic views about the body as well as the commonly held values concerning social relations, the importance of the balance understanding in both gives the Galenic complex an appeal it might otherwise not have.[8]

Laymen's Understandings about
Illness and Body Functioning

As table 13B shows, more than 85 percent of those interviewed had not heard of any substantial part of the Galenic scheme. Eighty percent were without most of the understandings that are basic to the Western scheme. This being so, an organization of the understandings connecting those concerned with the body to those concerned with social morality through the common presence of a belief in the positive effects of balance is not possible for most of those interviewed.

The forty people in the survey provided information through conversational interviews. That is, they were not asked questions with multiple choice responses but were encouraged to discuss freely the issues brought to their attention. After saying that what was wanted was their views on how the body worked and what was mainly responsible for illness, they were encouraged to say whatever they wished.

If they had not mentioned the four bodily characters or elements fundamental to the Galenic view, they were told the names of the elements and asked to comment on them and what, if anything, they had to do with body functioning and illness. Those who did not mention the elements and how they worked in their "free" responses and did not identify two or more of the elements when their names were mentioned were taken not to have "heard of the elements in the Galenic scheme." If, however, their discussion of illness showed that they had a clear idea that particular sorts of foods had particular kinds of effects on the body, in the general way Galenic understandings indicate, they were taken as having heard of the elements of the Galenic scheme even if they did not mention or recognize the names of the elements.

In discussing the Western view, a basically similar approach was taken following from the same question about body functioning and illness. Informants who did not mention them in their spontaneous remarks about the sources of illness (even if they did mention the Galenic elements) were asked to identify *presha* (high blood pressure), tell what organs were involved in it; identify *ambuzika* or *wito* (infection) and comment on its working or origin; discuss *afia nzuri* (good health) with attention to what promotes it and what interferes with it; and discuss food with attention to its role in health and body weight. Those who spontaneously mentioned any two of the following six terms or otherwise indicated some knowledge of them were taken to have some understandings from the Western scheme. These six were "vitamins," "calories," "cholesterol," "virus," "bacteria," and "germs."

Whether they mentioned two or more of the six terms or not, understandings from the Western scheme were taken as present in those who were able to discuss blood vessels (*mishipa ya damu*) in a way that suggested a dis-

Table 13.   Sharing of Galenic and Western Medical Understandings by Recently Ill Swahili (n = 40)

A. Description of Sample

Sex		Age	
Male	*Female*	*Under 35*	*36 and over*
11	29	21	19

B. Heard of Elements

	Galenic scheme	Western scheme
Yes	5	8
No	35	32
Total	40	40
	(12.5% have heard)	(20% have heard)

C. Visiting Therapist and Sharing His Understandings

	Herbal doctor			Hospital doctor	
	One visit or more	*Never*		*One visit or more*	*Never*
Galenic elements			Western views		
Share some	5	0	Share some	7	1
Share none	27	8	Share none	30	2
Total	32	8	Total	37	3

tinction between arteries and veins or, in discussing the heart, indicated they were aware of the heart's pumping action or muscular composition. All those who participated in the study were given as much time as they wished to take to discuss illness, health, and the body's mechanics, and all were encouraged to comment on both Western and Galenic views.

Despite this encouragement, less than 15 percent of the sample indicated familiarity with the understandings basic to Galenic medicine and only 20 percent with the Western scheme. Given this lack of familiarity, a reasonable inference is that they could not choose among types of medical care on the basis of selecting therapists who shared their views of the body and its work-ings.[9] Not only were most informants immune to influence by the common importance of balance in social morality and the Galenic scheme of body functioning but they also could not be affected by whatever understandings in the Western approach might make it attractive since they did not share the elements of that scheme either.

In fact, patients usually consulted therapists without regard to whether or not the patients' own understandings were taken to have any correspondence to those they might attribute to those therapists. Table 13C shows that of the thirty-two patients and former patients who have consulted an herbal doctor at least once, twenty-seven (84%) share few or no understandings about the Galenic scheme followed by those therapists. Of the thirty-seven interviewed who have consulted a hospital doctor, thirty (81%) shared few or none of the understandings involved in Western medicine.

The situation regarding knowledge of medical understandings is similar in an important way to what Willis (1972) found among the Fipa in southwestern Tanzania. There the medical practitioners have an elaborate set of understand-ings about illness resulting from injury to social relationships as a result of the activity of spirits or sorcerers. Laymen understand illness differently as being the result of sorcerers poisoning food and drink because they are jealous of their victims. As with the Swahili, Fipa laymen and experts do not share understandings about illness. There is, however, an important difference be-tween the Fipa and the Swahili laymen: Willis reports the former as having a fairly elaborate set of understandings about the causes of illness,[10] while the Swahili laymen have no such set.

In some ways, the situation is closer to that Keesing (1987b) found among the Kwaio, where experts have a rich set of understandings about dying and going to the land of the dead, but those not especially concerned with such matters do not share these. The differences he found between experts and laymen led him to say, "Such diversity of knowledge in religious matters is perhaps not surprising, but it seems to me to render deeply problematic premises about culture as system [sic] of shared understandings" (ibid., 163).

This is not to suggest that the Swahili patients interviewed had no under-standings at all about illness and the working of the body. They did have what Roy D'Andrade suggested was "default knowledge" in that they rejected some suggestions as to how disease occurred and accepted others as possible (pers. commun.). For example, I mentioned to several young and early middle-aged informants that during my first year of visiting Old Town, twelve years prior to talking to them, I had been told by elderly Swahili that many people be-lieved that paving Mombasa's streets with asphalt caused illness by reflecting the sun's heat up and into people's bodies. None of those whom I told about this thought it was likely, and several of them thought the idea was laugh-able. At the same time, my account of having been told by the same elderly informants that oven-baked white bread (*bofulo*) and other Western foods caused illness was heard with interest. All agreed that such food might be harmful, although none save the few who shared Galenic understandings offered explanations of how it might produce disease.

Cultural Organization and Guidance: Choice without Understandings

For more than three-quarters of those interviewed, the decision about what help to get must be made on a basis other than a personal set of understandings about what sort of treatment would be most likely to produce desired results since they share few understandings about treatments and how they work. There is a good deal of sharing, however, of understandings about the signs of being ill. These include pain, sleeplessness, weakness, fevers, loss of appetite, changes in eliminatory activities, and, occasionally, aberrant behavior. There is, people say, some judgment involved in deciding one is ill because sometimes these signals can occur and persist without anything consequential following. Most people say that they come to the understanding that they are ill from the severity of the initial symptoms, from their persisting for an extended period, from the similarity of the symptoms to those leading to familiar illnesses, or because someone—usually a member of their household—convinces them that they are ill.

There is also fairly uniform sharing of the understandings that indicate a variety of types of medical help is available. Even though all believe that expert medical care for the sick is often needed and that many kinds are available, most lack a schema that directs them in what choices to make once they decide they are ill. Many have no understandings of their own which make it obvious that one sort of care is to be preferred above another.

In situations where there are no perceived alternatives, where all medical help is viewed as "the same" or different but in unclear ways, the individual need only understand that competent help is needed and where it can be got. When, however, there are sources of help that are taken to differ in important ways, the individual must be able to choose among them to avoid suffering the fate of the fabled donkey between equidistant and equally attractive bales of hay. As table 14A shows, there is a strong basis for believing this problem is present since the Swahili are aware of the availability of quite different types of medical care but understand little of their nature or specific differences.

Not much help in choosing among available therapists is provided by language. Many of the most commonly used names for illnesses are quite inclusive. *Homa* can be glossed as "fever" and applies to all conditions in which the patient has an elevated body temperature as evidenced by sweating, being warm to the touch, and, sometimes, having chills. *Kohoa* refers to a cough and is used for all illnesses involving that symptom. *Kitwa,* a word meaning "head," is used for any disorder involving head pain; *pua,* nose, is used for the symptoms often described as a cold in the United States; and all chest pain or difficulties in breathing can be called *kifua,* chest, or *pumzi,* lungs.

It is notable that none of these disease terms carries with it any intrinsic suggestions for action other than to seek medicine identified by the name of the illness. Thus, if one has a headache, one may buy *dawa ya kitwa* from a Western drugstore or one of the two herbal medicine shops. Even this, however, depends on deciding between the two kinds of medicine, and some basis for this decision is necessary. The decision could be—and sometimes is—made on the basis of the distance to the shops selling the different types or on their relative price. This is likely to be effective, however, only if the medicine chosen performs as the patient hopes it will. If it does not, the patient must decide what to do, and this may lead him or her to seek guidance. Lacking understandings about how the illness comes about, this guidance must be derived from sets of understandings of other kinds including, especially, the advice of those whom the patient trusts.[11]

There are names for specific conditions, such as *baridi kuu* (lit. great "cold" with the last word referring to the Galenic element) for stroke, *wito* for infections, *presha* for high blood pressure, *kipindupindu* for seizures and cholera, and *moyo* (lit. heart) for all heart diseases. These last, however, are experts' names and become known to many only after they or those close to them have undertaken treatment for them with herbal or hospital doctors.

Illness and Treatment

Once an individual has decided he or she is ill and that the illness is not going away by itself, the obvious issue is what to do about it. This second decision is almost always a choice among the following: do nothing and continue to wait, buy medicine from a shop, see a medical practitioner of some kind, or seek advice from someone. If the decision calls for anything other than waiting, further decisions are called for: what type of medicine, advice, or consultation to seek; which particular dispensers of these to use; when to make these visits; how much to expect from them; how much money will be called for; and, probably, others.

The decision about seeking help is partly based in the fact that a wide variety of kinds of medical care are available in Mombasa, and almost everyone knows about most or all of them. As table 14A shows, every one of those interviewed knew that there were at least two sorts of medical care available: that from herbal doctors and that from hospital doctors (*daktari ya hospatali,*

Table 14. *Choice of Medical Treatment*
(n = 40, see table 13 for sample description)

A. *Knowledge of Medical Care Available*

| | Mention | | Recognize | | Mention or |
	Yes	No	Yes	No	recognize
Herbal doctors	40	0	–	–	40
Hospital doctors	40	0	–	–	40
Spirit doctors	26	14	12	2	38
"Doctors" from other groups	19	21	15	6	36

B. *Basis of Decision to Visit:*

	Herbal doctor	Hospital doctor
Sent by "someone"	26	29
Know myself	2	6
Don't remember	4	2
	32*	37

C. *Sent by Whom to:*

	Herbal doctor	Hospital doctor
Parents	14	18
Spouse	7	6
Kin, friend, or person with similar illness	5	5
	26**	29

*These sums are less than 40 each and more than 40 together because some informants visited both herbal and hospital doctors and were advised about both sorts.

**These sums do not include those who chose on their own and those who do not remember who advised them.

as they are called). Most also knew about "spirit doctors" (usually referred to as *waganga,* sing. *mganga*) who, most informants agree, are also part of the Swahili "tradition." These practitioners control their own *majini* (sing. *jini*), that is, spirits mentioned in the Koran, who help them stop the bad spirits that are causing the illnesses. As of 1988, there were at least three such spirit doctors practicing in Old Town.

Another generally recognized type of medical practitioner is from other African ethnic groups and is also called *mganga,* as spirit doctors are, as well as *mchawi* (pl. *wachawi*). Such practitioners seem generally, but not exclusively, to be consulted by those who suspect sorcery and, thus, seem to be chosen according to intrinsically organized schemata.

A final category of curers can be formed of the more specialized practitioners, including midwives (*mku'nga,* pl. *waku'nga*), bone setters (*mkandaji,* pl. *wakandaji*), and teachers who treat illnesses with prayer (*Mwalimu,* pl. *Walimu*).[12] I did not systematically ask the forty informants about these specialists, but more than a quarter of them mentioned them and eight reported consulting one or more of them.

Medical Care and Advisers

Choosing among this variety of kinds of care is, unavoidably, on the basis of the organized understandings the individual has. Despite limited sharing of cultural elements, neither the understandings nor their organization is completely idiosyncratic. Table 14B shows that the original decision to visit either an herbal doctor or a hospital doctor was usually the result of advice rather than direct guidance by personally held understandings. Of the thirty-two who have visited herbal doctors, only two report that they did so on the basis of their own knowledge of what was wrong with them and what sort of practitioner was likeliest to be able to deal with the problem.

A substantially larger number of patients decided to visit a hospital doctor on the basis of their own understandings of what to do for their illness, but it is still only six out of the forty in the sample. Again, the largest part, around eighty percent, made the decision to seek this type of care on the basis of advice received.

Advice in Multiplex
Relations with General Expectations

As shown in table 14C, the adviser was a parent for a substantial majority of those who lived with or close to one or more parents. Next most common as a source of advice was a spouse with neighbors, kinsmen, and persons with similar illnesses (three of these were co-workers) taken together as the final, and smallest, category of advisers. The important common feature these advisers all have is that their relations with the patients were of the sort I have been calling multiplex. The responses to my questions about why the advisers were chosen and/or listened to all indicated that the patients accepted the advice because they viewed those who gave it as being truly interested in their welfare.

In almost all cases, the advisers had relationships with the patient that went far beyond medical matters and involved mutual expectations of a broad sort in many domains. This is unquestionably true of the parents and spouses, of course, and is hardly less true of the assorted kin and neighbors informants mentioned as advisers. Even the co-workers, in the few cases where they were the advisers, seemed to be understood by the patients as having a general concern about the patients' welfare, and it is probably more accurate to refer to them as friends. In the terms used in chapter 4, the expectations in all these relationships were general rather than specific and the relationships were multiplex rather than simplex.

In addition to being subjects of general expectations, the advisers were often characterized as "knowing about illness." This special knowledge was often seen as deriving from the adviser having had a similar illness or being familiar with it through a third person who did. In some cases, the adviser was characterized as having a good deal of knowledge about medical matters generally, and a few of the advisers actually gave medicine or other treatment to the patient as an early step in treating the illness.

The belief in special knowledge or experience does not obviate the importance of the generalized expectations in the relationship between the patient and her adviser; it supplements or focuses them. That is, patients usually have generalized expectations of help and concern of a number of people and they choose among these according to which of them presents herself (the majority of advisers are women, as were the majority of my informants about this) as willing to help and as particularly able to do so.[13] As would be anticipated given the importance of generalized expectations, in none of the cases was specialized knowledge or experience the sole basis for seeking and/or accepting medical advice. Thus, several of the patients reported that in addition to their advisers, there were people (almost always women) in their neighborhoods with whom they had no close ties but who had the reputation of knowing about medical matters. None of the informants reported going initially to these knowledgeable, relative strangers for advice, although several seem to have indirectly been influenced by them through their direct advisers talking with them.

It might seem likely that advisers had at least some medical understandings that many patients did not since the patients viewed them as qualified to give advice in this area. As seen in table 15B, however, only about half of those

Table 15. "Advisers" of the Ill (n = 12), Their Understandings about the Body
and Illness, and Their Recommendations

A. Description of Sample

Sex		Age	
Male	Female	Under 35	36 and over
2	10	4	8

B. Heard of Elements

	Galenic scheme	Western scheme
Yes	5	3
No	7	9

C. Advised Treatment by Practitioners following:

	Galenic scheme	Western scheme
Yes	9	11
No	3	1

D. Adviser Originally Found Type of Practitioner Recommended through:

	Kind of practitioner	
	Herbal	Hospital
Being told	5	5
Own understandings	4	5
Don't remember	0	1

who had advised someone to consult an herbalist had substantial understandings about the Galenic view of the body's elements and in what ways illness
was helped by the sort of treatment the herbalists gave.[14] Only a third of
those who recommended Western medical care had substantial understandings
about that view of the body and treating illness. The special knowledge the

advisers had, in many instances, was the result of their experience in consulting practitioners rather than their having understandings of their own about how the body works and how illness comes about.

The interviews with advisers included discussion of all the advice they recalled giving rather than only the advice they had given the patient I interviewed. Thus, the twelve advisers told me about twenty instances of recommending therapists rather than only twelve.

Table 15C shows that the advisers recommended hospital doctors slightly more often than they did herbal doctors. Those who reported more than one recommendation—four told of two each and two of three—divided them almost equally between herbal and hospital doctors, with only two of the six multiple recommenders referring people to only one kind of therapist. A major appeal of hospital doctors, the interviews make clear, is that such care is free and provides treatment quickly. Herbal doctors have to prepare the medicines they give, which sometimes takes hours or days while the herbs are found (generally in the same shops where laymen buy them) and compounded. In contrast, as informants say, the hospital doctor simply fills his syringe and uses it.

When the advisers recommend herbal doctors, they report, it is either because hospital doctors have already been tried and have not produced the desired results or, for some of the advisers, because they view the Galenic approach as superior in some or all kinds of illnesses. One adviser told me that hospital doctors get faster results but that their cures do not last. "Real" cures, in her view, came from herbal doctors, and she recommended hospital doctors only for quick relief.

Advisers' Understandings and Experience

What is particularly notable is that more than half of the advisers (see table 15B) shared few or none of the Galenic understandings and three-fourths shared few or none of the Western ones. Despite this, most of the advisers had recommended both sorts of treatment at one time or another, with hospital doctors being recommended slightly more than herbal doctors despite the slightly greater sharing of understandings about herbal doctors.

In fact, as table 15D shows, about half of the practitioners recommended were originally discovered through someone telling the adviser about the type of care in question. Advisers report that they discovered the usefulness of hospital doctors on their own as often as they discovered herbal doctors in that way. This finding, seemingly at odds with the fact that more advisers shared some understandings about the Galenic scheme than had comparable understandings about the Western scheme, suggests that advisers credit their own experience even if they have little basis for understanding why that experience was positive.

There can be little question that getting desired results is a central element in recommending that therapist to someone else. The question remains, however, how patients choose therapists in the first place, before they have experience with them. The existence of hospitals and doctors' offices with signs plays a role quite apart from elaborate understandings about the body and illness. People can decide to visit a hospital doctor because they have seen the hospitals they work in and, perhaps, because they are impressed by the number of people going in and out, the seriousness of the enterprise as indicated by erecting a building, or simply because they know that something concerning the treatment of illness is available. Similarly, they can visit an herbal doctor because they have heard it said that the care given is traditional, because the visit is less intimidating than going to someone in a white coat speaking English or standard Swahili,[15] or some other such consideration not necessarily based on the understandings involved in the Galenic scheme followed by the herbal doctors.

Social Relationships and Plans of Action: Cultural But Extrinsically Organized

For there to be a plan of action, or schema, enabling sick people to get medical care, they must be able to connect the understanding that they are ill with their understandings about the existence of a variety of types of medical care. We have seen that people share understandings about being ill and also about the existence of a variety of kinds of medical care. For the plan of action in dealing with illness to be cultural rather than idiosyncratic, however, the connections between the understandings about being ill and those concerning the existence of medical care must also be based on shared understandings.

Were the connection based on intrinsic relationships among the shared understandings, as are those, for example, that govern the playing of chess, the schemata would be culturally constituted in all its respects. In chess, the movement of the rook and the protection of the king are connected through understandings of how pieces move and how the game proceeds. For most people, such an intrinsic relationship between understanding one is ill and seeking help for the illness is not possible, since, as seen, they lack the medical and physical understandings such connections require. But this does not prevent them from having culturally constituted schemata, nevertheless.

These schemata are produced by connections between the understandings of the presence of illness and the availability of care which are shared but not mainly concerned with medical care. For most community members, the advice of others is the basis for forming a schema that takes them from understanding they are ill to choosing among therapies and therapists. It is also true that roughly half of the advisers interviewed were themselves advised about the kind of care they recommended. The advisers got their advice, as the patients did, from people with whom they had multiplex relations. Thus, for many who give advice, as for those who receive it, the decision about what kind of medical care to choose involves a social relationship as a crucial link in the organization of understandings that guide their behavior in giving advice.

Some of the patients and advisers formed intrinsically based action plans after they had had experience with various medical experts. Their understanding about what was currently wrong with them contained within it an indication of what sort of therapist to consult on the basis of similar symptoms having led in the past to successful therapy from particular practitioners or kinds of practitioners. This, however, does not change the fact that in many cases, the original plan of action was founded on advice sought and/or accepted on the basis of general expectations in the relationship with the adviser, with these expectations not being limited to medical matters.

The use of advice to form plans of action led to what might be thought of as social relationship-based schemata. Nor were these social relationships always limited to those between the patient and her adviser. I did not investigate where the advisers' advisers got their introduction to the type of care they recommended, but it is very likely many of them got it in the same way the advisers and the patients did: from consulting people with whom they had multiplex relations.

General Expectations and Cultural Organizations: It Isn't What You Know

The cultural elements concerned with medicine have just been seen to affect people who did not share them. A substantial proportion of the patients sought treatment from therapists whose understandings about the body and illness were utterly unknown to them. Even those who advised patients as to what care to seek did not, in a majority of cases, share the medical understandings of those whom they recommended. The direct effect of the medical understandings, of course, comes through the behavior of the therapist who is guided by them in giving treatment, so the key issue concerning how culture provides means for dealing with the effects of illness is how these therapists are chosen.

The choice of therapists was on the basis of the patients' expectations of others (mainly parents, spouses, and neighbors) rather than according to understandings of how the therapists understood illness and treated it. These others, in turn, at least sometimes gave their advice on the basis of *their* expectations of yet others with whom, almost always, they participated in multiplex relationships.

The transmission of culture's effects in the medical domain, then, is a social structural phenomenon. Patients submit to treatment as a result of the understandings that connect them in their statuses to others in theirs. Getting medical care is dependent most directly on the effectiveness of the understandings that connect patients and advisers, and also advisers and their advisers, rather than directly on the understandings that direct treatment itself. What gives these connecting understandings the ability to operate as they do is an obvious and important question.

Why Advice Is Followed

The advisers are older than the patients in almost every case. On this basis alone, the formers' advice is to be taken more seriously than that of younger people because of the understandings concerning the wisdom of those who are older. Two proverbs state this quite clearly:

Aliyeona jua kabla yako hata kwa siku moja ana akili kuliko wewe: He who sees [the] sun before your [seeing it] even for one day has sense more than you.

Asesikiza la mkuu kuvundika 'guu: He [who] does not listen [to the words] of [an] elder [is] breaking [his] foot.

There is evidence from other societies that older people may generally share more medical knowledge with one another and with medical specialists than younger ones do (Garro 1986), but it is not just knowledge that makes them important in the Swahili community. The influence of the understanding that those who are older are wiser is enhanced by the fact that the advisers are not just older than the patients, in many cases they are also their parents.

The parent status includes the widely shared general expectation that its occupants are genuinely concerned about their children, and this is surely closely related to the fact that patients say they "trust," "believe in," or (in a few cases) "obey" their adviser. In the numerous cases where the patient follows advice in getting medical care, the connection between his or her understandings about being ill with understandings about what sort of help to get and from whom derives from the general expectations just mentioned and derives its strength from the strength of the relationship.

A few patients and a slightly larger proportion of advisers do share either Western or Galenic medical understandings with each other and with the doctors. For these people, the organization of understandings that leads to getting medical care, and to advising about it, is intrinsically organized and not dependent on general expectations in relations with others for its effectiveness in guiding behavior. These fairly unusual individuals have multiplex relations with others who do not share the medical understandings, so they are in a position to meet the expectation that they show concern and provide help by providing a link between their partners' view of themselves as ill and the understandings concerning what to do about it.

The interview data suggest that sometimes there are chains of individuals linked together by the general expectations in particular roles and that one or a few participants in the chain have elaborate sets of understandings about medicine and use them to provide advice to a less-versed partner in a multiplex relationship. The latter, then, in time, passes on the same advice to others who may, in their turn, pass it on to yet others. In most cases, the advice will be effective even though none of those currently associated with it has a developed set of medical understandings. This is because effectiveness derives directly from general expectations of concern and help rather than from specific understandings about particular things.

Another group of advisers do not share the experts' medical understandings in any substantial number, but in the past, they have had personal experience with the therapist or kind of therapy (usually both) they recommend. These advisers form chains as well as the more knowledgeable ones do, except that these advisers often originally went to the therapist they recommend on someone else's advice. There seems always to be some kind of link between the therapists and the patients which does not depend solely on general expectations of help from people whose cultural competence in the area is not very different from the one needing help. This link, however, can be mediated through a substantial number of relationships, none of whose participants need have either much experience or much knowledge of the medical understandings at issue. A little knowledge may or may not be a dangerous thing, but through social transmission, it can go a long way.

Looking at this from the perspective of the social structure of the Swahili community, it is that structure, rather than the cultural elements concerning illness and treatment acting directly as a guide to behavior, that accounts for the choice of therapy and therapists in many cases. This social structure, the connections among statuses based in the mutual references in the understandings that constitute the expectations and salience understandings in those statuses, is a product of culture. Through statuses having different expectations, culture is distributed among actors so that some have understandings about Galenic or Western views of medicine, while others do not. Some have generalized expectations in their relations with particular others, and others do not have them in those relations.

But the social structure does more than distribute culture. It provides, as we have just seen, a basis for organizing elements of culture and providing schemata for individuals who have no means of forming them on intrinsic grounds. Through the mediation of social relationships—most specifically, the general expectations that are part of the statuses of those involved in the relationships—understandings are linked together so that people have a basis for action even though they do not share the understandings essential to that action.

Nor is this social structurally based cultural organization limited to medical understandings or to the Swahili community. It seems likely that the same sort of organization operates for Fernandez's West African participants in ritual who share few understandings about that ritual with ritual specialists in their group and Keesing's Solomon Islanders who know little of what their community's specialists know about what lies behind the ways they act toward the dead.

Illness, Nonsharing and "Patterns"

Earlier, it was shown that there is a "pattern" in Swahili culture of the sort Benedict made widely known. This pattern is the result of a common element, the understanding that balance is essential to proper functioning, that is present both in the complex of understandings concerned with proper social relationships and in the Galenic view of body functioning. The relations between the two are similar to those Evans-Pritchard demonstrated as present regarding the Azande's views of morality and their views of affliction. As for the Azande, the understandings concerning affliction are more acceptable and forceful because they are linked to broader moral understandings commonly shared throughout the community.

The effectiveness of this link as an influence on the behavior of community members, however, is put in serious doubt by the fact that many, even most, of them do not share the Galenic understandings. The understandings about social relationships are widely shared, in part because of the constant exposure group members have to the cultural models contained in relationship terms (this is a central topic in chap. 7), but the desired state of these relationships, balance, can hardly be connected to the Galenic understandings about health for those who do not share those understandings.

This does not mean that the pattern is without influence even on the behavior of those who do not share Galenic understandings. As seen earlier, for many people, advice from someone of whom they have generalized expectations is the link between the understandings indicating that they are ill and the understandings about what action to take to alleviate the effects of the illness. Many of the advisers, however, were themselves originally led to the kind of therapist they ultimately recommended by advice they had themselves received earlier.

Still, some of the advisers did share at least some understandings about Galenic medicine. For these individuals, the fact that both the body's healthy functioning and proper social relationships depend on balance would, it is worth hypothesizing, tend to make balance seem an obvious and attractive force in keeping things "right." If this is so, and I have only the limited evidence concerning the acceptance of explanations to be examined in a moment, the "common element pattern" involving balance would encourage using doctors whose approach to illness was based on reestablishing the body's balance.

More than this, those who share the Galenic understandings may well be readier to recommend Galenic doctors than those who do not, because, in part at least, they take the approach to illness these doctors use as self-evidently correct. In fact, all those who shared Galenic understandings recommended herbal doctors, while all those who shared Western understandings were almost as likely to recommend herbal doctors as they were hospital doctors.

Granting that sharing Galenic understandings increases the likelihood that herbal doctors will be recommended, the pattern would affect even those who do not themselves share the Galenic understandings through making it likelier that advisers would recommend herbal doctors. That is, even if those who give advice in particular instances do not themselves share the Galenic understandings, their advisers—those at a second remove from the patient whose illness is being considered—might. This would lead the pattern to affect those who do not share it in just the same way that understandings about the body affect those who do not share them: by being transmitted through social relationships in which the patients (or the advisers of the patients) have generalized expectations of benefit from those they consult.

And that is not quite all. The existence of the balance pattern may well give balance explanations of illness a certain validity even when those hearing the explanation had not previously known about the four elements in the body and the significance of their being in balance. Only a few patients told me that the herbal doctor they consulted explained to them why they were ill and why he was giving them the medication he did. But those few uniformly reported that they found these explanations satisfying and easy to accept. One of the reasons I was given for the popularity of the leading herbal doctor in Old Town was that he explained things so clearly and well. The similarity between the widely shared belief in the importance of balance in social relations may well be involved in making such explanations of illness easy to accept.

This "pattern-based" process was not seen for those who consulted hospital doctors, although they shared few or no understandings of the Western view of the body and illness. These few reported that the accounts they got were difficult to follow and not couched in terms they found familiar. This is surprising since the Galenic scheme also involves terms and understandings that are not encountered in ordinary affairs. There is no reason to believe hot, cold, wet, and dry as body processes are more obvious or initially convincing than infection, immunity, and vascular blockage. But it may be that the former scheme receives a friendlier reception than does talk of microbes, immunities, and cholesterol because health, like proper social relationships, results from the balanced participation of the different involved "elements."

Conclusion and Summary

General expectations in social relationships of the multiplex sort provide a connection between the elaborate sets of understandings shared among experts and the health needs of the majority of the community among whom the experts' understandings are not shared. There are a variety of types of medical care available to the Swahili. Galenic medicine, viewed by some as "traditional" Swahili medicine, and Western medicine are the most common and popular.

The experts' understandings in the Galenic approach hold that a balance among the body's four elements is essential to health, and this is strikingly similar to the balance in social relationships called for by Swahili ideals. This common element organization, or pattern, involving two different domains may serve to promote the acceptability of the balance understanding as a guide to behavior for those who share the balance understandings in both domains. Most community members do share the understandings about social behavior, but they do not share those concerning the body and illness. Nevertheless, the pattern may affect them through making it more likely that Galenic medicine will be recommended to them and through its having an intrinsically appealing structure.

When community members understand themselves to be ill, and these understandings are made on very similar grounds by almost everyone, they consult—or are given advice by—people they trust and of whom they generally expect help. These advisers as often as not direct the patients to practitioners on the basis of earlier advice they have themselves received. The schemata that lead patients to take advantage of the understandings shared by the medical practitioners are organized around the advice that has been given rather than around intrinsic relationships among the understandings concerning illness and medical care. Since the advice is accepted on the basis of the general expectations of help and concern that are part of the statuses of the advisers (most of whom are parents, spouses, kin, and neighbors), statuses are seen as playing a key part in the relations among understandings as well as among people.

In chapter 10, the part of social structure in culture's operation will be examined further. It will be shown that statuses affect the relations among understandings in ways quite different from constructing schemata through being vehicles for "importing" them.

10

A Wife Is Clothes

Family Politics, Cultural
Organization, and Social Structure

Mke ni nguo, mgomba kupalilia: *[A] wife is clothes,
[a] banana plant [is] weeding.*

We have seen that the relations between people, as guided by the general expectations in their statuses, provide a basis for those who consider themselves ill to choose a practitioner to treat them. In a similar vein, I will show that women's ability to get their husbands to spend money in ways the wives, but not the husbands, consider useful is mainly the result of a complex of role relationships including, but not limited to, that between spouses. The expectations involved in a number of those roles will be shown to play a central part in family politics generally and the power of wives in particular.

In fact, the central hypothesis here is that the power of Swahili wives in their relations with their husbands is mainly due to the distribution of culture by statuses and to the cultural organization that results from this.[1] The key element in this distribution is the unique set of expectations for men in the husband-wife role. According to the hypothesis advanced here, it is this distribution that explains the substantial power wives have with respect to their husbands, despite widespread sharing of explicit understandings, viewed as divine in origin, that specifically bar such power.

As seen earlier, the larger-scale structures of social relations as they existed in the various taifa ("tribes") and in the Nine Tribes-Three Tribes dual organization (see chap. 3) have declined in importance. Even neighborhoods have mainly stopped providing a framework for joint or cooperative activity despite their continued salience in personal identification and as a base for multiplex relationships outside the nuclear family.

The household and, more specifically, the nuclear family retains its position as the main center of social participation, division of labor, and the sharing of resources. It has taken on added significance with the decline of larger-scale groupings in a way characteristic of "modernizing" societies (Bott 1971:124 passim). The distribution of power within this vital family grouping is of substantial interest in itself and takes on additional significance in providing an important demonstration of how Swahili culture works in guiding the behavior of the community's members.

In the last chapter, we saw that social structure operated to shape people's plans regarding medical care through a series of linkages dependent on the general expectations the patients had of advisers in statuses such as mother, father, spouse, and neighbor. These "linkages" were in the form of acceptable ("attractive" would not be too strong a term) advice that made it possible for individuals to formulate plans of action aimed at dealing with their understanding that they are ill. Important as the giving and taking of advice is in transmitting the effects of culture to those who do not share the elements in question, I show here that there are other ways social structure affects culture's operation.

Power in Marriage

Mombasa Swahili informants of both sexes agree that with the exception of such strictly domestic activities as cooking, cleaning, and caring for young children, husbands have, as shared understandings hold they ought to, complete control of all affairs involving their wives and households. Observations and reports of specific incidents across a considerable spectrum of life's activities bear out these reports. Despite this, however, in an area of life the Swahili consider highly important to the household, it is the wives who get what they want even though the husbands say they do not share their spouses' goals in this area.

What is of central concern here is wives' power, with "power" being understood in the Weberian way as "the probability that one actor within a social relationship will be in a position to carry out his will despite resistance" (Weber 1947). The examination of wives' power will include an examination of the forces that lead them to seek ends they know their husbands find unattractive. Following this, the sources of wives' success in getting what they want will be considered, with particular attention to the fact that a substantial body of shared understandings holds that wives can never bring husbands to do what they do not want to do. Finally, attention will be directed to how wives and husbands explain and justify the wives' control in important contexts despite the broad and strong cultural foundation for husbands' monopoly on power.

In all of this, the partly autonomous social lives of men and women (see chap. 4) is a central fact. Based on the Swahili understanding of the separation of the sexes (*gawa* in Swahili) called for by Islam, men are mainly occupied in the neighborhood in its widest sense and, beyond that, in the city of Mombasa where they work, while women's main activities focus on the household and intensive interaction with other women, most of whom are either closely related and/or live in houses immediately adjacent to the woman's own.

Women's Social Relations and Prestige

The Koran requires every man to provide his wife with adequate clothing as well as food and shelter, but save for the small group of very poor families among the Mombasa Swahili, "adequacy" is not what women seek.[2] Western dresses or traditional women's garments, *leso,* are worn under the all-encompassing traditional veils, so that they are seen only by other women and by men of the wearer's immediate family. Nevertheless, this clothing plays a crucial part in the women's lives. "Allahu akbar!" (God is great!) women sometimes exclaim when they see a particularly desirable new fashion in a shop window. For many women, the intensity of their joy when they get such a garment is matched only by the intensity of their despondency should they fail to get it.

Women say that normally they buy one new dress or leso a month and that they try to get particularly fine ones for major social events such as weddings. When a woman arrives at the area set aside for females at a wedding celebration, she is closely examined by the others there after she removes her veil. What she wears under the veil will be fully discussed by her fellows over the next few days or weeks. Everyday clothing is important to the standing a person occupies in the sense that it provides a basis for demonstrating good taste and, especially, the ability to pay for attractive clothing. It is the special dresses and leso worn at festive events, however, that lend real distinction in relations with other women. Similarly, women who have an armful of the 22-carat gold bracelets (*bangili,* pl. *mabangili*) Swahili women often wear are the object of favorable comment, while those who have few or none of the expensive bangles are dismissed as paupers or as women who have failed to win and keep their husbands' love.

Having many bangles to wear at the weddings and parties when "best clothes" are called for will not by itself make a woman prestigious, nor will the absence of a respectable number of them totally destroy a woman's standing among other women. Character, piety, skill as a mother and household manager, reputation, and similar considerations are also sources of prestige. As with desirable clothing, however, the wearing of a substantial amount of gold jewelry is important, and failure to do so is a serious detriment to getting or keeping prestige.

Prestige is also connected to staging the rituals at which the elegant clothing and jewelry are worn. The marriage of a child, either a son or a daughter, can be the occasion for a celebration on a genuinely large scale. If a woman decides to hold such an event, and it is extremely rare for a man to make this decision, she will be occupied cooking great quantities of the most elaborate foods for many days and all night the final night before the ceremony. She will be aided in her efforts by most of the Swahili women in her neighborhood who will dance and sing as they work. The celebration traditionally lasts for a full week, and even now it sometimes continues for two or three days. The food, clothing, decorations, and orchestra involved can cost so much that few families giving them fail to exhaust their surplus funds. Sometimes debts are incurred to the extent that homes have to be mortgaged and, occasionally, ultimately lost. Funerals are not, of course, occasions for festivities, but women do stage very expensive ones providing the best sorts of food for virtually the whole community for an entire week.

Both men and women come to the weddings and funerals, but women phrase their interest in staging them with respect to other women. Women say, "I have gone to their weddings (funerals) for many years and now I must pay them back." A woman who gives an outstanding ritual will be remembered as someone with a real accomplishment to her credit, and a woman who fails to give any is likely to be consigned to the category of the impoverished or incompetent.

Both finery and rituals depend on money, which women do not normally control. Occasionally, an heiress will have sufficient funds of her own to outfit herself as she wishes and to stage rituals as she sees fit, but the vast majority of women get the funds they need for these things from their husbands. The crucial fact for present purposes is that although men do not share women's enthusiasm for spending money on clothing and rituals, it is only through them that most women can get the money necessary for the things that will protect or enhance their prestige among other women.

Men do not usually talk together about women, but when they do so, a good part of the time is spent railing against their extravagances, especially as concerns the women's interest in finery and rituals. No one who has heard Swahili men discussing expenditures for their wives' clothing and ceremonies can doubt that men are, at best, unenthusiastic about using money for those purposes, at least in the quantities the wives seek. The wives themselves are perfectly well aware that their husbands are not at all inclined to spend money on clothing, marriages, and funerals and that they must be brought to do so. This in the face of the fact that the women agree with the men that husbands are ideally and actually quite powerful and have every right to do just as they wish in their households without regard to what their wives may want.

The importance of admirable clothing and expensive jewelry rests in other women's response to it, but at least part of this response derives from what women understand about men's expressions of love. When women are very angry at one another and want to hurl the most telling insult, they say, "No man could love you." A woman who is unloved by her husband is taken to be a pitiful creature without the physical or character traits that are most prized by both sexes. Men's love for their wives, several different informants report, is shown in a number of ways, of which the most publicly visible is giving expensive jewelry and clothing.

It is perfectly well understood that men of modest means cannot give as much as wealthier men can, but, as other women understand it, women who are loved will manage to get at least an acceptable minimum of visible signs of their husbands' love. Thus, at least part of the reason that a woman's standing among other women is influenced by the clothing and jewelry she wears is that they are taken to indicate her standing with her own husband. The fact that the women themselves view the men as well within their rights in refusing the needed money is part of the reason women seek the money, since its availability to them shows they are loved, with all that entails.

Gender Statuses
and Salience Understandings

Before going further, it is useful to examine the statuses that are involved in the relationship between the husband and the wife. While the wife status is unique among all his relationships in the expectations it provides the man in the husband status, wives' power cannot be traced to this alone.

A key element in that power derives from the status of woman. The usefulness of positing the presence of a status is closely related to the observable effects of the understandings that make up that status. On this basis, gender statuses have undoubted usefulness in understanding Swahili behavior. Women are expected to behave differently from men when they are categorized in a variety of statuses, and the differences have a consistency that indicates clearly formulated expectations for each of the gender statuses even when they are occupied simultaneously with other statuses.

These gender statuses only rarely guide behavior by themselves, but their salience understandings lead to their expectations being joined with those from a considerable range of other statuses to guide behavior in a variety of circumstances. The only other statuses that appear to be even roughly equivalent in the extent to which their expectations occur together with others are the age statuses and the status, community member.

The joint influence of several statuses can be inferred when an individual's behavior meets the different expectations of several statuses in a single situation and relationship. A woman customer, for example, is expected to behave differently from a man customer, and the same is true of such broader statuses as neighbor, friend, or rival. The gender statuses bring similar expectations of their own to the other statuses with which they jointly occur and show their influence in cross-cutting similarities in otherwise quite different nongender statuses. Clerks and neighbors are different, but men and women clerks differ in some ways similarly to the differences between men and women neighbors.

This is not to suggest that the salience understandings in the gender statuses give them equal importance when they combine with all other statuses. Taking only statuses I know to be actually occupied by community members, women bank tellers are not expected to behave in a markedly different way from men bank tellers, and the differences between both religious and secular teachers on the basis of their gender statuses are real but limited. However, women neighbors are expected to act quite differently from men neighbors, despite similarities inherent in the expectations of anyone classed as a neighbor, and, in a simplex relationship, women customers are expected to act differently from men customers.

The expectations associated with the woman status involve openness, affectivity, and engagement. I had no opportunity, of course, to spend time with groups of women in "natural" settings, but in talking with women, it was striking how outgoing, responsive, and emotionally active they were as compared to men in a similar situation. The same differences I observed are noted explicitly by members of both gender groups who report themselves and the differences between themselves and the other gender group to be much as I observed. The gender statuses in this community are not only influential across a quite wide range of other statuses but they are explicitly recognized as being so. Further, informants are uniform in asserting that the differences between the genders in their various statuses are aesthetically and morally important. Women behaving in accord with a variety of different statuses are not only recognized to be different from men in many of the same statuses but the differences are explicitly valued.[3]

Gender Statuses and Differences between Them

Virtually all adult women maintain close social relationships with their neighbors, especially those, who may or may not be kin, from houses only a few meters from theirs. For some purposes—weddings and funerals are the most frequent and notable—relations with all the women in the mtaa (see chap. 3 for a discussion of the neighborhoods of Old Town) become quite active and, often, intense, and this sometimes extends to all the women of the community in an attenuated way.[4] The expectations in the women's neighbor-neighbor role are notable for their supportive and expressive character, but they also contain a great deal of open competition for prestige and power.

There are a variety of means whereby women attain precedence among their fellows, but the wearing of new and fashionable clothing and the display of an impressive collection of gold jewelry at weddings are very high among

these. I will show that the competition among women and the importance of
finery in that competition are crucial in leading women to made demands on
their husbands which both spouses see as burdensome and unwelcome to the
husband.

The man status and the expectations in that status are sharply different from
those in the woman status. Men's relations with one another are ideally and
often characterized by reserve and careful following of rules for proper behavior. Men of the higher classes have adopted what other community men
see as quite Arabized manners involving elaborate etiquette and reserve. In
relations among men of the other social classes, there is also concern for propriety and restraint, even if the expression of that concern shows less Arab
influence. Regardless of class, men avoid talking about "delicate" issues that
might bring shame to anyone present and there is a pervasive concern with
honor (fakhri). As the expectations in the woman status involve affectivity,
openness, and engagement, the man status's expectations emphasize calm,
reserve, and detachment.

The reserve and avoidance of things of personal and possibly emotional
significance (for that is what makes things "delicate") is characteristic of
men's behavior across a wide range of situations. When men are together at
their barazas, the talk is quiet, the topics are impersonal, and the tone is af-
fectively neutral. Male neighbors spend a good deal of time with one another,
but the laughing is muted if present at all and the conversations are far more
likely to concern politics, soccer teams, or religion than family affairs, scan-
dal, or experience of a personal sort.

Brothers greet one another much as they greet any other man, and even
close friends spend most of their time talking about neutral topics of general
interest. A man who is displeased with a shopkeeper most often states his
objections quietly and in a matter-of-fact tone, and the stinging insults mothers hurl at their daughters and, less, other women (see Swartz 1990a) are
more rarely heard from fathers directed at their children and almost never at
other men.

The competition between men, when present, is implicit. Men do not try to
outdo one another in any observable way and, unlike women, make no comparisons based on any traits, whether physical, characterological, or in possessions. Men may feel competitive, and there are hints that having more
honor than another—or at least not having less—is important, but there is
none of the open rivalry said to be characteristic of women.

The Swahili saying, "Women are not freeborn nobles" (*Wanawake si
wangwane*) is taken by men, the only ones who use it, as meaning that women
do not have proper regard for honor and the avoidance of shame. There are
women who agree that the members of their sex are less obsessed with shame
and honor than men, and they agree with the men that the difference is due
to God having created men and women differently. The difference in concern

about shame is based in broader differences with women being understood as more emotional, less logical, and less able to plan effectively than men are. These differences manifest themselves in a variety of ways, including greater freedom and emotional lability in relationships between women as compared to those involving men.

The God-given differences, as community members see them, between men and women find expression in gender status expectations. These operate jointly with the expectations in a wide range of other statuses to guide behavior across a broad spectrum of social life. Both men and women are expected to be helpful as neighbors, for example, but men's help is mainly limited to that of a practical and unemotional sort, while women's includes hugs, tears, and laughter.

Comparing Men's and Women's Social Relations

From what has been said about the man status, it will be clear that the kind of emotional expression and freedom broadly expected of women is quite improper for men. But the differences between social relationships involving men and those involving women are not limited to differences in affective display, as can be seen in considering their development in individuals' lives.

The social lives of males and females begin to diverge sharply as soon as the boys are considered old enough to go outside the house to spend the daylight hours playing with other boys or attending school. Most girls nowadays go to secular schools as their brothers do, but they still spend their out-of-school hours in their homes studying, doing housework, and cooking under the supervision of their mothers.

Unmarried girls were traditionally kept from the company of married women not closely related to them, explicitly to shield them from talk of sex. Thus, when their mothers' friends came to visit, the girls stayed in another part of the house. This is not strictly enforced in most homes now, but it is still true that only after marriage do women begin the rich social life to be described below. One of the main reasons commonly given by adolescent girls for saying that the most important thing in their lives is marriage is that it is essential for full acceptance into the company of adult women.

The situation for boys is quite different. From the time they begin to spend the daylight hours outside the home, they are encouraged to be friendly with other neighborhood boys from different households. They are urged to invite their friends home for lunch (the main meal), and boys who do this too little were traditionally, but only rarely currently, punished. Unlike females, it was desirable that males be known through the community and even beyond it. A man whose name is not known by every other Swahili in the city is thought a poor specimen. A traditional phrase in praise of a man was, "He who is not his brother is his slave." The phrase has not been wholly appropriate for most of this century, but the wide scope of approved social relations it refers to is understood as being as desirable in men now as it ever was.

Wedding Ceremonies and the Gender Statuses

Men's social relationships cross a wider range of the city's population and are more public, but they are also more restrained than women's are. Many of the differences associated with the differences between the two statuses are exemplified by the behavior that can be seen in participation in wedding ceremonies.

These ceremonies are generally held outside, near the house of the parents (either the groom's or the bride's) who are undertaking the responsibility for staging them. A large curtain, generally hung between houses, separates the women's festivities from the men's. From the women's side of the curtain comes the sounds of a band, laughter, shouting, and ululation. The women dance in a rather abandoned way with, one is told, their faces beaming and loud pleasantries freely exchanged.

On the men's side, the atmosphere is totally different. In the contemporary wedding celebration, rented wooden chairs are arranged into precise rows and the men on them quietly chat with those nearby. Boys and young men of the sponsoring family distribute soft drinks and snacks (often elaborate ones prepared by the women in a boisterous all-night session). When the groom, dressed in a turban and robes with an Arab-style dagger at his belt, is led to a seat of honor among the men, everyone turns to look at him during the brief period before he is led away to join his bride in the family house. During this period, there is a slight rise in the volume of the men's conversation, which can, nevertheless, hardly be heard above the din coming from the other side of the curtain. The commentary on the groom's fine costume, however, is short-lived and the men return to polite conversations about ordinary matters. After an hour or two, the men begin to drift away toward their homes, but the women's dancing and noise-making goes on far into the night despite the fact that many of them have been up celebrating and cooking all the night before.

The differences between relations among men and those among women seen at weddings are of the same sort found in everyday life. During their leisure time, the men come together at each other's houses, often not going inside but staying on the benches built into the front of houses that give their name, baraza, to the regular men's gatherings. At some of these gatherings, they sip coffee, although others view this as too Arabized. At all of them they discuss the affairs of the day. The groups form on the basis of a variety of common interests. Thus, one group is composed of men who are concerned with world affairs and politics; another of men with a greater than usual interest in sports; several of men who are fond of discussing religion; and so on.[5] All of the gatherings have one thing in common: they share an avoidance of personal topics. Deaths and hospitalizations are freely discussed, but nothing else personal is mentioned.

Talking about someone's wife, daughter, or sister—whether the man is present or not—is entirely unacceptable, and any man who did so, unless the context is illness or death, would be characterized as *Hana mizani* (without a sense of balance or propriety, see chap. 9). The general reluctance to discuss any specific member of the community is redoubled when the person is female and related by blood or marriage to someone present. The most valued topics for baraza discussion are all impersonal ones, and in a number of barazas "elevated" issues such as religion and philosophy are the most prestigious. Talking about specific people is considered unworthy of freeborn nobles and, especially, of men. For men, such talk is always bad, but they believe it often occurs among women and the low born.

The avoidance of gossip is not the only propriety in barazas. Each man is greeted on arrival by everyone already there with a handshake and a greeting consisting minimally of "Salaam Aleikhum" and generally of a considerably more elaborate sort. This is true even when the gathering is very large. Thirty or forty men were the most I ever observed at a baraza, with five to eight being more usual, but whatever its size, greetings occupy a good deal of the group's time. The tone of barazas I attended, whatever their particular content might be, was decorous, dignified, and restrained. The participants were invariably good humored and agreeable in their relations with one another, but reserve is the most notable trait.

Women's gatherings are less formal and structured than men's are. Unlike men's gatherings, which almost always involve the same men meeting at the same place, at the same hour, and lasting the same period of time, women come together whenever and wherever it is convenient and desirable. A woman may pop over to a neighbor's house to borrow a cup of sugar, and while there the two may chat for a long or a short period depending on how busy the two of them are and how interesting their conversation becomes.[6] Other women, if they are free and so inclined, may join the conversation and a casual group of four or five women might thus assemble. The same group of women could come together again within a short period of time, or no more than two of them might talk together again for weeks. Like the men, the women's groupings each draws on a limited roster of participants, but unlike the men's, the women's gatherings are spontaneous, casual, and irregular.

Another difference between men's and women's gatherings is that in the latter, I am told, there is little or no reluctance to discuss particular people and events concerning them. Tales of who is doing what and with or to whom are as common among the women's groups as they are rare among the men's. Also unlike the men's groups, among the women interaction rather often includes heated statements, arguments, and personal remarks including compliments and insults. Women share their joys, sorrows, and angers with one another rather freely; men hardly do so at all.

Relations with Close Kin: Warmth for Women, Restrictions for Men

The general differences between relations involving men and those involving women are as characteristic of relations among close kin as they are elsewhere. Relations among brothers are generally polite but in most cases distant. Informants explain that this is due to the fact that each may be reluctant to discuss the details of his private life with the other lest there be some shame involved. Also brothers may and often do see one another as potential rivals for their father's estate or, should one die with minor children, as the steward of the other's estate who may use it to benefit his own children rather than his nephews and nieces.

Women are less concerned with honor, shame, and matters of inheritance, and it is not unusual for women, especially sisters, to be mutually supportive confidantes. Women compete with one another for prestige, but sisters are generally allies rather than rivals. The concern for honor and the avoidance of shame that restricts relations even between brothers is mainly absent between women in general and especially between sisters. It is fairly common, women report, for women neighbors to be like sisters, including having the closeness and mutual support characteristic of that relationship.

As with siblings, men's relationships with their children do not involve the warmth and mutual support women often have in theirs. A father can express love and warmth for his very young children, but it is difficult for him to do this when the children are older. Daughters are said to occupy a special place in their fathers' affections, but after the girl begins to show physical signs of puberty, it is difficult for the father and daughter to be alone together. In conservative families, the girl does not even stay in the same room with her father, going so far as to speak to him from a hallway or adjoining room rather than face to face.

Although sons are not expected to avoid being in the same room as their mothers, the segregation of the sexes does divide them. The mother and daughter are both assigned to the home by the segregation of the sexes, and they spend most of every day cooking and doing household tasks together. The mother's relations with her unmarried daughters are close and emotionally labile (see Swartz 1990b), and the tie between them is a strong one in many families.

The mother's relations with her sons are quite different. She sees them only at mealtimes and in the evenings when the men return to the home, and the freedom of emotional expression in relations with daughters is mostly absent with sons. Although there can be little doubt that the survey data are accurate in reporting the tie between mothers and sons as closer than that between fathers and sons, the mother-son relationship is nevertheless far more restricted than that between mothers and daughters. It is important to note that widows live with their daughters rather more often than with their sons, despite the fact that this puts them in the houses of their sons-in-law who will be mainly responsible for their support even though they have sons with houses of their own.

The restrictions in the mother-son relationship that stem from the segregation of the sexes obviously do not apply to fathers and sons, but the father-son relationship is said to be the most tense and full of conflict in the family. Although some boys and young men obviously admire and even like their fathers and some fathers show considerable love for their sons, the majority of the boys and young men willing to discuss such things freely reported strained relations with their fathers.[7] In a group of eight young men not yet married but living away from their parents, four were living elsewhere because of quarrels with their fathers and three reported trouble living with their stepfathers. In the more usual situation where the son remains in the family home until marriage, the respect in which a father is to be held dampens emotional expression even when the relationship between father and son is relatively free of conflict.

Further data on the emotional character of relations involving fathers, mothers, and their children can be seen in table 16. It is notable that more than a third of both sons and daughters say that children should love their mothers more than their fathers, while none of the sons and less than 10 percent of the daughters say that the father should be loved more. Twenty percent of the mothers say that mothers should be loved more than fathers, but none of the fathers say that fathers should be loved more. All of the fathers say that children should love both parents the same.

One interpretation of this surprisingly unanimous response by fathers is that they really believe that children should love both parents equally. Another, and equally plausible one, is that the real alternatives fathers see for themselves are limited to two: being loved the same as mothers or being loved less. In either interpretation, there is no basis for believing that fathers see themselves as being the rightful or likely favored parent as contrasted with a fifth of the mothers who seem to. That both parents are realistic in this is indicated by interviews with young people about their actual family showing that fathers are, in fact, loved less than mothers in a majority of families.

Given fathers' common and expected conflict with their sons and their distant relations with their daughters as contrasted with the loving and close relations between mothers and children, it is clear that fathers' relations with

Table 16. *"Should children love their parents the same, their mothers a little more, or their fathers a little more?" (n = 51*)*

Informants' status	The same (%)	Mothers more (%)	Fathers more (%)
Father	100.0	0.0	0.0
Mother	80.0	20.0	0.0
Son	64.3	35.7	0.0
Daughter	54.5	36.4	9.1

* The sample for these tables is the same one used in chap. 5. See table 3 for a description of the sample.

the children are cooler and more isolated than the mothers'. Add to this the fact that a third of the offspring interviewed believe that mothers *should* be loved more than fathers and the effects of father's emotional limitations in relations with his children become quite clear.

The Spouse Relationship: Feelings and Funds

Marriage provides the one relationship in which men can express themselves freely and in which they can hope for warmth and emotional support. Women can also properly have close and unrestrained relations with spouses, but, unlike the situation for men, the marital relationship is by no means the only one where this is commonly true. Swahili unanimously report that love (upendo) is the most important single consideration in marriage. Even though first marriages were and mostly still are arranged by the parents of the couple, if love and the valued intimate mutually satisfying relationship does not develop, it is thought best for the couple to be divorced. Since one rather often hears Swahili men and women saying that "of the things God allows, He hates none more than divorce," this is a strong indication of love's importance.

Subsequent remarriages—being single is rare for men and only somewhat more common for women—are according to the wishes of the partners themselves, and if the love that ideally and usually led to the marriage should wane, again it is thought best to divorce. Love among the Swahili is very similar to Western love, with a romantic variety common among younger men and women and a calmer but more lasting type generally valued—and seemingly rather often present—for older couples.

The important fact for the present discussion is that the marital relationship is culturally constituted as one in which both partners are expected to be emotionally engaged and in which the male, as well as the female, is allowed to give and receive support and intimacy. The husband is ideally expected to make his wife happy by giving her his attention when he is not occupied in other ways and by showing her kindness and regard. The wife ideally devotes herself to her husband and indulges him with well-prepared meals, lavish attention, and such luxuries as massages with sandalwood. Informants report that these ideals are generally met most fully in the first year or two of marriage but that they set desirable goals for both spouses throughout life. It is surely true that not all Swahili share all the understandings about love and marriage, but it is equally true that there is no other relationship that so many community members view in this way.

The emphasis on the values and beliefs concerning love and the fact that men are uniquely able to give and receive emotional support in the spouse relationship should not obscure the contribution that economic and social considerations make in determining the nature of that relationship. Husbands and wives retain their own property on marriage, and what one earns or inherits during the marriage remains under his or her direct control. However, the legalities of the marital relationship—and they are given here according to Islamic law as the Swahili view it—fail to account for the social unity of the married couple.

The wife's standing in the women's groups is importantly dependent on her husband's social and economic position. We have already seen the importance of the husband's material support for his wife in the form of finery and ceremonies, but it is also worth noting that any blemish on his reputation, any shame attached to him, will redound to his wife's discredit and will be used against her by her rivals. This is what was meant by women's "indirect concern" with honor.

The wife's standing among women does not directly affect her husband's standing in the community, but if she exposes herself to shame by improper behavior—especially by being suspected of association with other men—his reputation and standing will suffer. More than the parties to any other relationship in this society, spouses are a social unit rather than quite separate individuals. This commonality of interest does not *make* their relations close and emotionally warm; it imposes obvious stresses resulting from the close interdependence. However, since divorce is easy, marriages that work have partners who are brought together by these social and economic pressures and couples that cannot accept them usually part.

Divorce, Death, and Gender Differences in the Significance of Marriage

Divorce itself can contribute to the prevalence of warm and supportive marital relationships among those that endure. Men are empowered to end their marriages simply by saying, "You are not my wife" (*Si mke wangu*) three times.[8] The most common reason for their doing so is the absence of love. Women have no formal right to end a marriage, but, in fact, they are usually able to do so by insisting that their husbands divorce them. A husband who refuses to listen to his wife's demand for a divorce finds himself living with a woman who will not speak to him, contribute to the functioning of the household, or participate in sex.

There are pressures other than personal satisfaction that affect marriages and their termination, of course, but one of the pieces of advice sometimes given the groom at the marriage ritual in the mosque is, "You have married peacefully; if it is necessary, then divorce peacefully as well." Divorce terminates about one in three Swahili marriages,[9] with more than sixty percent occurring in the first five years. There is sometimes an active effort by kin to try to convince married couples, especially young ones, not to divorce, but when it becomes clear that either partner's dissatisfaction is not temporary or trivial, the effort usually stops.

The marital relationship is crucial to both partners but on different grounds. For the wife, it generally provides the sole means of material support and of assurance she will have her children with her. Without a husband, or such rarely present alternative source of funds as an outside job or an inheritance, a divorced woman is forced to appeal to her male consanguines. Grown sons or brothers willing to contribute to her support and having means beyond what is needed for their own wives and children can provide a reasonably comfortable life, but this is rare. If, as is most common for divorced women, she lacks these alternatives and is unable to remarry, she is destined to a life of poverty.

A divorced woman has the right to support from her ex-husband for four months and ten days (the period deemed necessary to establish whether or not she left the union pregnant), and support for the children is due her until they are seven years old. After that, she has no clear right to assistance from her divorced spouse. He has the right to take the children to raise, and if he does, he supports them. If he allows his ex-wife to keep the children, he may provide funds for their care, but he has no legal obligation either in civil or Koranic law to do so. His support for the children is a matter open to negotiation and depends, among other things, on whether the woman has remarried. Whatever is done about the children, a divorced woman often finds herself in difficult financial circumstances. If she does remarry, her situation is rather often as good or better than it was before divorce even if, as will be seen, she has children in need of support.

Women are less able to initiate a new marriage than men are, partly because women have less freedom to seek a new spouse, and older divorced women often do not find a new husband since many men prefer younger women. It is very rare for a divorced person to marry someone who has never married before, but a few cases of men doing so were recorded.

Men encounter few if any material difficulties when they are divorced. In most cases, men remarry without delay and their lives go on as before with, perhaps, whatever caused the breakup of their marriage behind them. Even if they do not remarry, they can get servants or female kin to provide most domestic services. Materially, their condition is little changed since, almost always, they provided the income for the first marriage and, when they remarry, provide it in the second as well.

There can be little question that men are generally not adversely affected by divorce in any lasting way. It is important to remember, however, that they most often bring about the divorce themselves, or, less frequently, finally allow a wife who is making them miserable to leave them. For men, it is rarely rewarding marriages that end in divorce, and given their ability to find a new and perhaps more satisfactory wife, men generally benefit from divorce. Divorced women do not fare as well as men unless they remarry. When death rather than divorce is the cause of a marriage's end, however, women usually suffer decidedly less than men.

The traditional practice, *aida,* of women dressing in special mourning clothes and spending four months and ten days on their curtained beds is still followed. This long period of isolation is very hard on the women, their children, and any others who depend on their participation in household affairs. When women finally emerge from aida, they often suffer from the practical consequences of losing their husbands' income, but they do not usually show signs of serious and lasting emotional damage. Young widows often remarry, and older ones commonly find what some of them say is a reasonably satisfying life caring for their grandchildren in one of their children's houses.

Men are frequently more adversely affected by the death of a spouse than women are. A number of men seen shuffling feebly down the streets were pointed out to me by other men as widowers whose wives' deaths were said to have precipitated their current sorry state. At the baraza I usually attended, one of the regular attendee's wives died following a long illness. The man was in his middle fifties and had been married to the dead woman for decades, but almost a year after her death, this otherwise dignified and reserved man— or so he had been before his wife's death—would burst into tears without obvious reason.

Other men told me after we had witnessed an instance of the man's seemingly uncaused weeping that it is not uncommon for men to react that way on the loss of their wives. In the same discussion, I was told of several men who had been utterly ruined by the loss of their wives, and my informants said that mental breakdown or, even, drunkenness were familiar, if not common, reactions to this loss. Evidence is rather strong, in short, that despite the fact that women have to endure a prolonged postmortem isolation, it is husbands who most frequently suffer a lastingly adverse reaction to the loss of their spouses. At least part of the reason for this is that the spouse relationship has a significance for men that it does not have for women.

Husbands, Wives, Love, and Marriage

As their reaction to their death shows, men are very closely attached to their wives. There is, in fact, a sharp contrast between the spouse relationship and all the others the men participate in. It is only in marriage that men can express and expect intimacy and emotional support. For women, the spouse relationship is distinctive in its economic significance, but from the standpoint of intimacy and emotional support, the relationship is similar to a number of others including the women's relations with their children. Table 17 shows the quite substantial differences between wife/mothers and husband/fathers in the emotional experience they have in marriage and other nuclear family relationships.

A majority of informants say that there is more love between parents and children than between spouses, but it is notable that fathers and sons lead female family members in choosing the alternative statement that there is more love between spouses. The tense relations between fathers and sons may well play a part in the occupants of these statuses indicating that there is more love between spouses, since they both experience something different from love in their relations with each other. Since, however, it is true that sons (and fathers, after all, were and are sons as well) generally experience a relatively warm, if restricted, relationship with their mothers and that daughters (including those who are also mothers) have distant relations with their fathers, it seems warranted to look at the spouse relationship itself as the basis for the greater frequency with which males choose it as having more love.

We have seen that men's relations with everyone but their wives are restricted by various values and beliefs. There is tension between fathers and sons and competition between brothers. Considerations of honor (fakhri) and the avoidance of shame (aibu) prevent most men from having close relationships with peers. Relationships with daughters are circumscribed by respect and, like relations with the mother, attenuated by the separation of the sexes.

For men, the spouse relationship is unique. This is the one relationship in which men can expect emotional warmth and support and in which they can express themselves. Table 17 shows that the spouse relationship is chosen as the one with the most love by a larger group of sons and fathers than by mothers and daughters, with the women more often choosing the parent-child relationship. Although the same expectations in the spouse relationship apply

Table 17. *"In families around here (i.e., in Old Town), is there more love between*
wives and husbands or between parents and children?"

Informants' status	Between spouses (%)	Between parents (%)
Father	36.6	63.6
Mother	28.6	71.4
Son	38.5	61.5
Daughter	20.0	80.0

to women, for them the relationship is one of a number in which affectivity, a prominent expectation in the woman status, is freely expressed and in which warmth and support are common.

The Real Power of the Husband/Father

The fact that the expectations in the spouse relationship are unique for men in allowing affective expression but that this is common for women's relationships will be shown to be a central element in women's ability to get their husbands to do things they, but often not their husbands, want. It still remains to be shown, however, that wives getting things they want despite their husband's negative views is due to men being reluctant to use power they have rather than lacking the needed power and further, that this reluctance is connected to the unique character of the marital relationship for men and the potent, if unavowed and at least sometimes unrecognized, resource this provides for their wives.

It could be, of course, that women get the expensive things they want because the husbands simply do not have the power to prevent them from doing so. However, if "power" refers to the *ability* to control, there can be little question of men having insufficient power to prevent their wives from spending money if they wish to. The fact that husbands do have the power needed to deny their wives' demands is indicated by several types of evidence, including the unanimous views of all the Swahili who were asked about the distribution of family power or were heard to volunteer comments about it.

All of them indicate that the husband and father is the final authority in the family and that although it is desirable that he consult with other affected family members, all family decisions—save those concerning cooking, cleaning, and child care—are properly made by him alone. This applies quite unambiguously to decisions concerning money, since the husband not only controls it as the head of the family but also, in most cases, as the person who earned it. The latter fact is itself a powerful basis for the power to control the use of the money according to most community members' understandings. Adding this to the generally powerful position of divinely selected family head proclaimed in the holy Koran gives the father's authority a broad base.

Further evidence for the husband and father's power to make family decisions is seen in table 18, which shows that 90 percent of all fathers, mothers, and sons say that fathers are the ones with most influence on important family decisions. Only 63 percent of those in the daughter status make the same response, but inquiry reveals that that relatively low figure is due to several of the young, unmarried women in the sample whose fathers are dead having brothers (in the table, the latter are counted as in the son status) who act toward the women as fathers do when they are alive. The table is unambiguous in indicating that Swahili of both sexes *say* that fathers are powerful, and anyone who has discussed family relations with members of this community would agree that this view is nearly universally held. Still, attributing power to fathers may be a token that is not also a guide, to use the concept developed in chapter 6. It could be that saying fathers are powerful is the accepted and proper statement but that fathers have no real ability to get anyone to do anything the person does not personally want to do.

In fact, this is not so. The statements about fathers' and husbands' power do reflect social reality in the sense that husbands and fathers rarely fail when they actually exercise their power. This is particularly true as concerns their wives and, slightly less, their daughters, but least often so as concerns their sons. Even in dealings with the son, however, when the father/husband makes a decision and insists on it, that decision quite often determines what happens. Decisions concerning wives are even more uniformly successfully implemented, in large part because, unlike sons, wives do not usually eventually attain financial independence.

One man, for example, told his wife on their marriage that she was to associate with no one: not her relatives, not her neighbors, no one. Limiting women's associations with men to their husbands and close kin is, of course, universally supported by members of the Swahili group, but this husband was forbidding his wife to associate with anyone regardless of sex and without respect to relationship. The wife was said to be very miserable about her husband's decision, but she dutifully followed it throughout their long marriage. Only after his death did she begin to involve herself in the usual round of visiting central to the lives of all other wives. No one who told me this story, and several people did, thought the husband's restricting of his wife's activity was commendable, but it was equally clear that everyone understood that it was within his rights.

As a further approach to the issue of men's power, I showed the table, presented here as table 18, to informants of both sexes including some who had told me in general about, or who had cited instances of, women spending

Table 18.   "Who in the family has the most influence on important family decisions?"

Informants' status	Mother (%)	Father (%)	Daughter (%)	Son (%)
Father	9.1	90.9	0.0	0.0
Mother	6.7	93.3	0.0	0.0
Son	0.0	92.9	0.0	7.1
Daughter	9.1	63.6	0.0	27.3

money in ways that were at the limit of their husbands' ability to spend—or beyond it. After discussing the table's meaning with the informants, I asked them to explain how it was that men often gave in to their wives' demands for costly things when he was chosen by most informants as being the one with "most influence on decisions." Both men and women said there was no inconsistency between the husband/fathers having the most influence on decisions and important sums of money nevertheless being spent on things they did not support. If the husbands had insisted on smaller weddings, less expensive clothing, or less jewelry, then, the informants said, that is what would have been. In other words, men have power, but they choose to allow their wives to do things they want to do even if the men do not themselves agree with the wives about the desirability of those things.

This leaves little doubt that consistent with cultural understandings of their general power, husbands do actually have the ability to block their wives' access to the funds the wives seek for the things needed for full participation in the women's groups. The husbands, however, do not always or, even, frequently use that ability. In fact, although men have the cultural resources needed to control their wives' behavior, actually doing so requires an additional resource, emotional independence from the wife.

The Husband/Father's Real Need for Warmth and Emotional Support

Because of the nature of Swahili social relations, few Swahili men have the additional resource just mentioned and are consequently reluctant to employ their well-grounded power to block their wives' demands. Looking at the wives' cultural bases for power, it is difficult to see that they have many in the marital relationship other than the emotional dependence of their husbands. This, however, is often sufficient.

Despite their importance in family power use as well as their personal importance for those involved, men do not mention their emotional needs if they are aware of them, and the same is true of their wives and community members generally. According to very widely held ideal understandings, men should be self-sufficient and strong. Depending on their wives, or anyone else, for emotional support would be a direct contradiction of the ideal.

The reluctance to consider men's emotional needs and the part these needs may play in the spouse relationship leaves people with a difficult situation to explain: why do the powerful men give their wives costly things the men say they do not want to pay for? The most common explanation given by men concerns their wives' mental states. They say they could stop their wives from spending money in ways or amounts they do not agree with but that they sometimes withhold the use of that power because, and various forms of this phrase occur a number of times in my notes, they do not want to make the wives unhappy.

Women's views are quite similar to mens'. They agree that the husbands have the right to forbid them spending money on clothing, jewelry, and ceremonies, but they say that the husbands often allow them to do this because the husbands are "good." Their husbands, they report, buy them things even if they are not really in favor of spending the money, or spending so much money, because they "understand what it means to women" to have what the wife wants or because of the husbands' "love" for them.

Women's Happiness and Wives' Power

We have already seen that women are understood as having been created by God with greater emotionality and less planning ability than men. As part of this, people of both sexes generally imply or directly state that women cannot be happy if they are denied what they want no matter what the difficulties may be in giving it to them. It is not, of course, the view of anyone I talked to that women must or can be happy all the time. Nevertheless, given that it is only in his relations with his wife that a man can hope to express his own emotions more or less freely and only in relations with her that he can expect to get emotional support, this relationship takes on a very special standing for him. It becomes clear, then, why a husband would be willing to take considerable effort to see that his wife is not "unhappy" and why it is to his benefit to have his wife believe that he is "good," "understands what it (i.e., what she wants) means to women," and to show her that he "loves" her.

Men are not equal in their desire to have the opportunity to express themselves with some emotional freedom and/or in their wish to be given emotional support. Similarly, men's assessments of what they have to do to get the support and expression they want surely varies from person to person. Nevertheless, for most husbands, withholding the use of their power to deny their wives' deeply rooted demands and allowing the wives to have what they want is a readily available and widely effective approach for them to promote their getting whatever emotional satisfaction they may seek.

Understandings about Women, Social Structure, and Wives' Power

Men's emotional dependence on their wives is a key element in explaining wives' ability to get what they want from their husbands. Another element, and it is the one that makes the first effective, is to be found in the social structure. Out of the whole array of relationships involving adult men, all have expectations precluding emotional expression and support with the sole exception of the spouse relationship. That relationship takes on unique importance for the man because of its unique expectations, and this is the major factor in men's acquiescence to their wives' requests for money.

This explanation is not, however, the same as the one offered by the participants in the marital relationship. Their explanation of the ability of wives to get what they want has a dual foundation: the already discussed value on love as a basis for the marital relationship and the understandings concerning the nature of women, especially women's mental and emotional qualities. These latter understandings are important in that they not only play a key role in explaining why wives are able to get what they want but in that they also provide what Malinowski called a "charter" (1944:52, 111, 141 passim) for women's demands on their husbands.

It is basic to these understandings that women are seen as fundamentally different from men. Women are understood as being quite as intelligent as men and at least as likely to show such highly admired traits as compassion and consideration of others. However, the Swahili believe—and they buttress their views with references to the Koran—that women are less able to plan for the future than men are.

Women, however intelligent they may be, are believed to be less logical than men and to be unable to control their emotions as men can. Women's emotional lability, as seen at weddings, funerals, and everyday life, is taken by Swahili of both sexes as undeniable evidence of their deeply emotional natures. The widely shared understandings is that women cannot, as a result of their God-given natures, curb their desires on the basis of a logical assessment of what is possible and practical. There is some implicit belief that in areas where the women's own interests and emotions are not directly engaged (in matters of science, scholarship, or business, for example), women can be as logical as men, but there is general agreement that in their personal lives, it is not realistic to expect women to behave with control and on the basis of logic.

Women, including educated ones, accept—even embrace—this view. I was interviewing eight Swahili high school girls when I mentioned, with what was clearly a disclaimer in my voice, that a number of men had told me that women were highly emotional, poor at planning, and illogical. The girls were quite forceful in their response. "Do you think that is not true?" one of them asked. "Women are not at all like men," another said, "the Koran itself tells us that." I replied that perhaps women were different but asked whether it was not possible nevertheless that they be able to plan well and to control their emotions. All those present denied this vigorously and several of them picked up the theme—not uncommonly heard in a range of discussions with Swahili—that the Koran supported their views. They held that God had made women the way they were, and it was worse than ignorant to deny that this was so.

In discussing the allocation of power in marital relations with several male informants, I asked why husbands give in to their wives if, as they had been telling me, sometimes it is financially harmful for them to do so. One of them answered me with an analogy: "In some ways women are like children. It may be bad for them to have candy, but they want it and you can't explain to them that it is bad. They just become unhappy if they do not get the candy, so, because you love them, you give it to them even if it is not the best thing."

This was heartily agreed to by the other men present and is as close as I ever came to a direct, emic explanation of the ability of wives to get what they want. The men had told me, in sum, that there is no more point in trying to reason with women than with children and that if the women want something it is often best to give it to them since they cannot be brought to understand that it may not be really desirable. There may be some point in withholding desired things from (male) children since they may learn from the experience, but no such result is likely with women because of their God-given nature. The husband's love leads him to avoid causing his wife unhappiness, as the participants see it, and because of her nature, this involves giving in to her demands.

The shared understanding that women are unable to think logically or to control their emotions is not only used as a key element in community members' explanations of women's ability to get what they want but it is also important as a self-justification. So, women are at least as interested in the family budget as are men, yet some of them sometimes use substantial parts of their husbands' income—generally the family's only source of funds—on things they want but that contribute nothing to meet the family expenses for housing, food, clothing, and education. Some women explained that the use of even substantial sums of family funds in ways they particularly desire is not really frivolous. The gold jewelry, especially, is explained as a way to store wealth to be used in times of crises, which is particularly attractive given the Islamic prohibition on interest from bank savings.

Even here, however, when they are asked why it is that many women spend very considerable sums having goldsmiths rework their old jewelry into new and more fashionable designs—as is fairly common—the basic answer is that this is the way women are. Women, female informants told me, like to have things that are beautiful and they do everything they can to get them, especially if other women have them, even if doing so presents their families with financial difficulties.

In addition to comments and observations gleaned from talks with a variety of informants of both sexes, I discussed women's desires for finery and ceremonies intensively with four female informants. They all agreed that women were "not good at planning" and that they often spent money on things that did not really provide for their families', or their own, welfare. The informants reported that to some extent, at least, the many women who they believed used money this way could not help themselves. It was the way women were, and for many, there was nothing they could do about it. Three of the women said they knew of cases in which houses had been mortgaged to pay for elaborate weddings, with the wives and mothers being the principal ones responsible for the mortgaging. Although all of them condemned this as "dangerous" since the family home could be lost in this way, they also agreed that, as one of them said, "women don't think about the future very much . . . they just know what they want and they follow that."

Malinowski reserved the concept "charter" for the explicit justification of such organized sets of activity as those carried out by families, age groups, and religious congregations. These charters, often in myths, provided a statement of the "value, purpose, and importance" (1944:111 et seq.) of the groups' distinctive activities and contributions. The demands women make on their husbands are not institutions in the sense that families or religious congregations are, of course, but they are patterned and recurrent activities and the idea that women cannot avoid making them provides them with a culturally constituted explanation and justification. It gives the wives' demands a stature they would not otherwise have, because they are rooted in the belief in women's unique mental processes, which are understood to be as God wishes them to be.

Social Structure's Strictures:
More on Unshared Culture

As with medical treatment, wives' power needs to be looked at as the result of the operation of cultural elements, some of which are not shared—at least not in any active sense—by those involved in the phenomena they produce. Here, wives' power derives, in important part, from a social structure all of whose other statuses include expectations preventing their roles with men from including emotional support. Wives' power, in other words, is partly due to the restrictions in other statuses.

Understandings shared by many group members maintain that men need no emotional support, so the affectivity of the husband-wife role cannot be culturally based in the sense that people understand that role to be the proper venue for men's emotional expression. Women expressly deny the emotional importance of the spouse role to their husbands, since, as they say, their husbands are "too strong" to need such support. Similarly, the absence of affectivity in other relationships involving men—with their friends, parents, siblings, and children—is not a marked characteristic of those relationships. For those who share the understanding that adult men are without emotional needs, the absence of attention to such needs in specific relationships, if noted, cannot be difficult to countenance.

It is the nature of the other statuses in the social structure as much as the wife status that makes the latter unique for men. This uniqueness, that is, having expectations allowing affectivity in the role relationship with the husband, is mainly a *product* of Swahili culture rather than a part of that culture. The uniqueness is not the result of shared understandings overtly assigning emotionality to the spouse role or barring it in the other roles in which men are involved. Since men's emotionality is denied, its expression is not subject to explicit regulation. In fact, it is the generally close and private nature of the spouse relationship and the importance of love (upendo) in it that encourages such expression between spouses rather than explicit understandings calling for it. What is most unusual about the expression of affect in this relationship is less that it is prescribed than that, unlike the other relationships involving adult men, nothing interferes with it.

The spouse relationship thus makes a unique contribution to husbands. Its significance varies from man to man, but it seems rarely to be nugatory and provides a powerful, if unrecognized, base for wives' power in dealing with their husbands.

The expectations in the woman status are also important to the wives' power in the spouse role. Since women are expected to be emotional and alogical by their God-given natures, there is no advantage in denying them what they want in the hope that they will learn from the denial. Such educational prohibition is worth trying with sons but not with wives who, as women, will only become unhappy. Their unhappiness, through the strictures on all the other relationships the husband has, is easily transmitted to their husbands who need not have an understanding of why it affects them in order for it to do so.

As noted elsewhere (Swartz 1983), changes in the Swahili community offer the prospect that women may become more emotionally dependent on their husbands than they are now, but thus far this has not happened. It is, however, true that weddings are less important than they were just a few years ago (see chap. 3), so that wives' opportunities to turn their husbands' expenditures into prestige among women are somewhat reduced. So long, however, as the women in a neighborhood spend much of their time with one another, it will take substantial changes in a number of the statuses occupied by women (including "woman," "Muslim," "wife," and "neighbor") and in other parts of the social structure to diminish their wish to gain prestige with their peers and the importance of their husbands in their ability to get the means for doing so.

11

The Dynamics of Swahili Culture

A Status-Centered View

As it has for centuries, the culture of the Swahili community continues to provide a basis for its members' social lives and acceptably effective procedures for pursuing their individual interests and personal needs. The sets of understandings that make this possible are changing, as they always have, with new elements, new organizations, and new distributions emerging at a rate that may be faster than in previous eras. But there can be no reasonable doubt that this culture works to serve those who variously share its elements. The aim of this book has been to illuminate the processes that make this possible, and a number of hypotheses have been proposed which attempt to do that.

For much of anthropology's history, the main approach to explaining culture's operation has been to invoke "shared beliefs and values." Once beliefs and values were identified as part of culture, the means whereby they actually affect those who share them received only slight attention. Since all group members share the same beliefs and values, the existence of the ones concerned with the behavior or institution at issue was often taken as a sufficient explanation.

There can be no serious question but that culture's effectiveness stems from its contents being shared. Even if all of its elements were shared by everyone, however, the processes involved in their operation deserve the sort of attention cognitive anthropologists have been giving their psychological aspects. And although the social processes also require attention, they have received only a limited amount.

The fact that sharing is less than universal for many or most cultural elements makes this an even more pressing matter. The ways in which understandings shared by only a small proportion of the community's members influence the behavior and lives of the whole community, including those who do not share them, has received little attention. The same is true of how understandings shared by everyone are effective, but the problem is more dramatic and obvious when our concern is with those cultural elements that may be unfamiliar to the majority.

There are a few understandings that seem to be shared by all, or almost all, group members. Those that are specific enough to guide behavior are usually of a broad and inflexible character of little use in dealing with the intricacies of life everyone faces every day. These sweeping and general understandings are of undoubted importance to both the individual and social life, but their usefulness in action depends on their being supplemented by a host of understandings whose sharing is often unevenly distributed among community members.

This type of distributed sharing is characteristic of most understandings. Some of the cultural elements most vital to the continuation of the community and to the adaptation of each of its members are shared only among a minority. This limited sharing is obviously characteristic of the procedural understandings that are the basis for such skills as compounding herbal medicines, the teaching of Arabic, and elaborate lovemaking, but it is also true of understandings concerning the specifics of performance and evaluation as a mother, a Muslim, or a debtor. Much remains to be learned about how this distributed sharing and its involvement in cultural organization operates, but there can be little doubt that just what is shared, by whom, and the social relations among the sharers and nonsharers are among the most vital aspects of cultural dynamics.

Clearly, much of the distribution of sharing is according to statuses of the sort just mentioned (see Schwartz 1978 and 1989:119–121, for a somewhat different view of the same phenomenon), but even within status-based categories, the sharing of understandings concerning the status itself can be distinctly limited. This has been shown not only for the Swahili (see chap. 4) and the four European groups to which they have been compared (Swartz 1982a) but also for American college students (Holland 1985, 1987a). Holland reports such sharing as concerns both the romantic and academic activities of the students she studied. For the Swahili, incomplete sharing was found in all three of the domains studied: nuclear family life and relations (chap. 5), intergenerational relations (chap. 6), and body functioning and illness (chap. 9).

It might be thought that the limited cultural sharing found in the Swahili community is an indication of the group's decline as a consequence of its cultural disintegration. Modern urban societies are famous for their fragmentary nature and the isolation of their nuclear families from one another and from other groupings (e.g., Bott 1971), and the Swahili are unquestionably urban and in many respects "modern." Moreover, the community has experienced some notable changes in recent decades.

Despite these, and they include changes in community structure and the nature and frequency of collective action, the community remains the focus of its members' lives. Even without the broad-scale economic, political, and ritual activity that once characterized it, the community continues to serve as the matrix for its members' social relationships as well as the source of most of the means they use to satisfy their needs and, more broadly, pursue their personal goals.

Walking through Old Town in the evening, one encounters groups of Swahili young men standing in front of the houses and on the corners chatting among themselves. When their neighbors from other ethnic groups pass by, they greet them politely and even, sometimes, exchange a few pleasantries. But the "outsiders" do not stay to pass the evening. These groups of Swahili youth are just that; members of other ethnic groups do not belong even if they live next door. In fact, for community members of all ages, despite the constant association with people from other groups at work and in school, close relationships of any kind with outsiders are very rare.

In addition to almost all voluntary association being with other Swahili, the views and actions of fellow community members are taken most seriously in social, personal, and family matters. Those of outsiders have far less social and moral weight, however important they sometimes are economically and politically. The community, in sum, endures as the prepotent source of moral assessment, as well as of social life, for its members.

Invoking "Shared Beliefs and Values"—and Why Not

Perhaps the enduring value of the community is not surprising. The Swahili are a "traditional" community with a long, unbroken history, and one expects the culture of such a community to be effective. The temptation to explain this effectiveness by reference to "shared beliefs and values" is a powerful one. It can, after all, hardly be doubted that shared beliefs and values are the bedrock of life in this, as in every, community.

The fact that these beliefs and values, these understandings, are shared by some and not others complicates the explanation. But even if the issues focusing around sharing are set aside, major difficulties in understanding culture's effectiveness on the basis of calling attention to its contents remain. Thus, if all the understandings shared by community members were identified, the accomplishment would be only a very limited contribution to an explanation of the nature of the community and its members' behavior. In part, this is because, as Spiro has shown (most recently, in Spiro 1984), the sharing of culture does not always or necessarily entail behaving in accord with that culture.

In addition, then, to identifying the beliefs and values that people share, it is also necessary to address the vital issue of cultural conformity. If a large enough portion of the population is not influenced by the understandings shared among community members, it is hard to imagine how the group can be said to have an effective culture—or how it could exist.

Simply determining whether or not group members are guided by cultural elements is insufficient in assessing the contribution of the elements to the culture's effectiveness. This is because cultural elements that are not associated with the behavior they call for can nevertheless contribute to the effectiveness of the culture as a whole.

This last consideration has been discussed here (see chap. 6) as the part "tokens" play in social life. In short, people sometimes give indications of sharing beliefs or values with others even though those cultural elements do not actually guide their behavior. The indications themselves, however, encourage and smooth the course of interaction and the continuation of relationships, thereby contributing to culture's effectiveness despite the fact that they do not affect behavior in the way their contents seem to indicate.

"Tokens," as these not necessarily guiding understandings are called, are one aspect of processes that proceed on the basis of limited sharing. Another important issue, and one that has received virtually no attention, is how understandings affect group members who do not share them. Several processes by which this occurs have been described here. A brief review of them may be useful.

How Cultural Elements Affect Those Who Do Not Share Them: Statuses, Cultural Distribution, and Prediction

The importance of the processes whereby cultural elements affect those who do not share them is rooted in the fact that some, possibly many, of the understandings that serve to provide means for dealing with crucial problems are shared among only a relative few group members. Since it is true that despite this the culture serves the needs and interests of all group members a considerable proportion of the time, an examination of these processes is clearly vital to any adequate understanding of culture's functioning.

As Schwartz (1978) was first to point out, cultural elements are unevenly distributed even among those who are directly affected by them. Less than universal sharing of elements within a group is not necessarily a hindrance to the effectiveness of those elements or of the culture as a whole. In fact,

Wallace (1970) has argued persuasively that the simple—and undeniable—fact of incomplete sharing of culture's elements does not hinder the ability of culture to serve as the basis for social life and personal adaptation. Incomplete sharing, in fact, has quite positive functions.

> Many a social subsystem simply would not "work" if all participants share common knowledge of the system. . . . [C]ognitive nonuniformity subserves two important functions: 1) it permits a more complex system to arise than most or any of its participants comprehend; 2) it liberates the participants—from the heavy burden of learning and knowing each other's motivations and cognitions (ibid., 35).

Wallace's well-known solution to the explanatory problems presented by the recognition of the incomplete sharing of culture's elements is what he calls "the organization of diversity." This guarantees orderly relationships "not by the sharing of uniformity, but by [the participants in the relationships] . . . capacity for mutual prediction" (ibid., 24). There are difficulties with Wallace's view of culture as "policy" as developed in his classic *Culture and Personality,* but there is a substantial basis for agreeing that mutual prediction plays a key role in culture's functioning.

Part of this mutual ability to predict the other's behavior is based in beliefs and values actually shared by those in interaction. However, even setting aside the fact that the universal sharing of cultural elements is not a necessary condition for their effective functioning, it is also true that when such sharing is present, it may not be sufficient for that functioning. Cultural sharing only affects what people do directly when the shared understandings are used as active guides for behavior. Sharing without sometimes conforming to some of what is shared makes some contributions to social life, but this only sets the stage, as tokens do, for the influence of understandings that are both shared and serve as effective guides. What is needed for many results is quite clear guidance, allowing people to accomplish their ends and to provide the limited predictability essential to social relations.

But the specific understandings that might provide such guidance are often inadequate. On the one hand, the understandings that are shared by all, or nearly all, community members are usually so coarse in their behavioral guidance as to preclude their effectiveness as a basis for predicting behavior or, even, accomplishing ends save in the most familiar circumstances. More directly to the point, these widely shared understandings are usually very broad and following them does not necessarily instill the needed confidence that behavior can be predicted, especially in the multiplex relationships that are crucial to individual and community life.

In chapter 8, it was noted that all interviewed community members mentioned a few of the same activities as shameful, and this suggested that they all agreed that avoiding these behaviors was desirable or essential. Included among these prohibitions—and they all were that—was not being seen naked in public, not stealing, not using or selling alcohol, and not begging for food. These are undoubtedly important prohibitions and may add a significant, though sharply limited, element of predictability to relations among community members. However, they hardly qualify as a basis for making the predictions on which social life depends, especially not in the relations among kin, neighbors, and friends on which many aspects of community life depend.

The necessary predictability, however, can be based on the sharing, limited even in multiplex relationships, that seems to be characteristic of humans provided either that the relations are strictly limited in their scope or that they are mainly based on general expectations. In the first case, one needs few expectations to deal with bus conductors, and, in the second, those fundamental to relations with parents, spouses, and neighbors may be effective even though they are vague and general.

What is important about this is that culture's functioning as the basis for social relationships can depend on mainly specific understandings when only a few are involved, but in wider scope relations, the functioning can proceed on the basis of only a few, broad cultural elements. In either simplex or multiplex relations, then, limited sharing is quite sufficient for the relationships to proceed. Group members' belief in broad sharing may be useful, and may be provided by tokens, but in reality such unanimity of understanding is not called for.

Statuses: Bringing Culture to Bear on Everyday Concerns for Sharers and Nonsharers Alike

It has been a central tenet throughout this book that understandings, whether shared by many or few and whether specific or general in their reference, are useful as guides for behavior only as part of a cultural complex, "status," having three distinguishable sets of understandings. These three sets indicate who belongs in the category that is the basis of the status, under what conditions and what combinations with other statuses the one in question operates, and how those in the category can be expected to act and react in various situations and relationships. Through these three sets of understandings working together, culture's elements are brought to bear on individual's interests and problems as well as on social relations. Through their three sets of elements, statuses are a culturally constituted means whereby culture's elements are distributed among group members according to the situations that arise. Through this distribution statuses bring culture's components to bear as guides for behavior in actual circumstances and relationships, thereby making culture not a heap of assorted understandings but a useful means of dealing with life.

Without the same emphasis on status as given here, Roberts (1964:438–452) made the general point concerning culture's ability to serve all of a group's members, although most of its elements are shared by only some of them. His view of culture is as an information economy involving storage, retrieval, and decision making. Roberts's approach has been materially elaborated as "distributed cognition" (Hutchins 1985), and recently there has been further development of the concept and an important empirical demonstration of its functioning (Cicourel 1988).

Evaluation as the Foundation of Social Life, Status as the Foundation of Evaluation

The distribution of understandings by statuses is both central to their effectiveness and unavoidable. It is only by understanding what people (and what sorts of people) do what under what circumstances that social life is possible and at least a minimum of one's needs and interests are attended to. Nor are statuses limited to their vital function as guides for social relationships and interactions. In fact, it is the evaluative functioning of statuses, more than any other single factor, that lies at the heart of culture's effectiveness. Hamlet's "There is nothing either good or bad, but thinking makes it so" would be a fuller, if less lyrical, characterization if it were clear that "thinking" is closely tied to the understandings in the statuses to whose categories we assign ourselves and to the understandings in the statuses whose occupants we evaluate and understand to be evaluating us.

The evaluations embedded in statuses are the bedrock of social life. As concerns actual behavior, interaction cannot proceed without those involved understanding each others' behavior as being within the limits set by the expectations of the statuses they assign to each other and themselves. It is in interaction that the basis for evaluation[1] is manifested, and it is the statuses of both the evaluator and the evaluated (with all parties being both) which provide the standards for evaluation. Multiplex relationships depend more on inclusive evaluations of overall performance and less directly on particular behavior in specific contexts than simplex relationships do, but the evaluation process is central to both types of relations.

In the discussions of cultural models (chap. 7) and of shame (chap. 8), there was substantial evidence to show that the Swahili, like everyone else, are nonstop evaluators of everything they encounter, especially of the people (including themselves) they deal with. At the same time, everyone is very much alive to the fact that he or she is being evaluated by those same people.

Given the importance of the evaluations of those with whom one has on-going relationships, there is a powerful impetus to act in ways understood as likely to win approval (or, at least, avoid disapproval) from partners in those relations. Putting this in terms of the status complex of understandings, those in interaction come to some agreement as to which statuses are salient and to meet, to some degree at least, what they take to be the expectations in those statuses.

In order for this to happen, the agreement must include what statuses each party occupies. This agreement emerges from and is confirmed by signs (actually symbols) of acceptable evaluations of the behavior that each participant gives the others. Such evaluation usually derives from at least partially shared understandings about what is acceptable and what is not. In other words, it is in social life that shared understandings (culture's elements) become "visible" as such through the behavior they guide and its acceptance. The acceptance of behavior as demonstrated by positive symbols from partners seems to be taken as acceptance of at least some of the understandings that guide that behavior.

The direct and immediate importance of social relationships to group members and the central part played by mutual evaluation in those relationships puts the understandings actors take as the base for evaluation at the center of culture's ability to operate. This is a point long emphasized by social theorists (e.g., Hallowell 1955:105–110, Durkheim 1961:52–55). Because of the central contribution of morality to cultural dynamics, I first proposed a definition of "culture" as "the sum of the morally forceful understandings acquired through learning and shared by the members of . . . [a] group" (Swartz and Jordan 1976:46). It is now clear, however, that this definition is seriously flawed in that it requires shared understandings to be "morally forceful" if they are to be included as part of a culture.[2] This directs attention away (technically, it precludes it) from the empirical study of the presence or absence of moral force in shared understandings when such study is clearly worthwhile.

How Unshared Evaluative
Understandings Serve to Affect Behavior

Moral or aesthetic judgments affect behavior, when they do, on the basis of two different sorts of understandings. One of these is "values," the evaluative understandings concerning what is good and bad, beautiful and ugly. Unlike these, the other sort is made up of descriptive understandings concerned with how people actually evaluate what one does and what the social consequences of behavior are likely to be.

These two sorts of understandings can, and sometimes do, affect the individual in similar or identical ways. This happens when the individual holds evaluative understandings that would lead him to act in ways that he understands others to view as he does.

The two sorts of understandings, however, sometimes do not work together. This happens as the result of the actor believing that the evaluator holds evaluative understandings concerning the behavior at issue different from his. One way, and a common one, this occurs arises from the role relationship of the judged and the judge. Thus, understandings that hold that men having secret wives (see chap. 8) is a bad thing coexist in the culture with understandings saying it is satisfying and rather delightfully manly.[3] Men who make such marriages understand many others to condemn them, but their own view is that such marriages (at least *their* marriage) are acceptable and, since they are permitted by Islam, quite free of sin or blame.

What seems important about the partial independence of the two sorts of understandings is that either can function independently of the other. It is obvious that people are affected by ideal understandings that they hold even if others do not share them. It may be less obvious that ideal understandings people do not share can also affect their behavior through the effect of descriptive understandings concerned with how others evaluate. So long as actors care about the evaluations of the likely evaluators, the evaluations the latter are understood as likely to make will affect what the actors do regardless of how accurate the understandings may be. Even should no one in the group personally understand secret wives and disregard of others' rights as intrinsically bad, the belief that they do may well affect what those who care about their views do.[4]

Statuses as a Source of
Morality When Understandings Differ

The present point is that for morals to affect behavior, it is not necessary that the understandings concerning the virtues of that behavior be shared by those affected. Some or all may share them, but the behavior could be the same for the sharers and the nonsharers provided that the latter are concerned about the evaluations of the former and respond to understandings that they *believe* some or all of the others hold.[5] Much or all of this belief is the result of status-guided interaction where status assignment includes the attribution of expectations including what category members are believed to value.[6]

Broader Consequences
of Social Relationships

As important as social relationships are in themselves, their significance is by no means limited to participants' concern with the specific relationships occurring at the moment. Many Swahili care little about the simplex relationships with grocery clerks, bus conductors, and tailors, but most of them do care about the results of those relationships, about what they get from participating in them. They care about the food they buy, the trips across town that they take, and the clothing that they wear.

To get these things, they must sustain relationships with the clerks, conductors, and tailors long enough to accomplish their ends, and this depends on meeting some of the expectations in the appropriate roles. One may care little for clerks' good opinions, but one turns over to them the money called for and refrains from too much quarrelsomeness to avoid trouble while getting the desired things they control. More than this, to some extent, one's interest in the food, trips, and clothing usually derives in some part from one's relationships with those who share meals, live in the places traveled to, and whose opinions about clothing matter. Finding a basis for getting along with occupants of statuses that matter little in themselves is, in fact, essential to getting along with occupants of statuses that matter a great deal.

"Delivery Systems" and
Cultural Guidance for Life's Problems

The vital function performed by statuses in distributing culture's elements among actors and situations warrants a brief concluding examination. This distribution depends on the basic fact that in all interaction people are always categorized, by themselves and by others, according to identifying and salience understandings. These latter understandings provide what might be called "the delivery system" for bringing the expectations with which they are associated into the relationships where they guide behavior. Since situations result from an interaction between events and the statuses assigned and assumed by those involved, this process not only assigns particular cultural elements to specific individuals but does it with regard to the problems of the immediate situation.

The statuses people assign one another have expectations that work as the common standards in double contingency and determine to a considerable extent how they treat each other. Thus, a situation involving two men is one of patient care if the assigned and accepted role pair is practitioner-patient and is one of informal chatting if it is baraza member-baraza member. In this way, by agreeing on the complex of understandings that make up statuses—identifiers, expectations, and salience understandings—those in interaction jointly provide a culturally constituted means for the distribution of culture by mainly establishing the situation[7] and by providing guidance for one another based on such sharing of understandings as may be present and effective and on each being willing to adapt to the other's apparent evaluations.

Nor is cultural distribution the only function statuses serve in addition to guiding social relationships. In order for culture's elements to have any utility, those who share them must be able to choose among them, rank them according to precedence, decide which call for or preclude which others, and group them according to similarity and difference. Such organization of culture's elements is a sine qua non of culture's effectiveness in guiding behavior. Cultural organization, like cultural distribution, cannot be understood without close attention to statuses and their operation, especially in guiding social relationships.

Limited Sharing within Statuses and the Sources of Statuses' Effectiveness: The Issues

The fact that culture is only very partially shared and that this is true within status categories as well as between them raises the question of how they can work effectively. A closely related question concerns the foundations for the differentiated cultural conformity without which such sharing as may exist has little significance either for individual survival or group continuation.

These two sorts of questions, concerning sharing and concerning conformity, are closely, in some instances inextricably, connected. The sharing issues are concerned with the processes involved in having at least the minimum interpersonal agreement necessary for statuses to operate. The conformity issues are concerned with the processes involved in expectations actually serving as guides to interaction. Together, the processes concerned with the issues involved in sharing and in conformity provide both the necessary and the sufficient conditions for interaction.

Both the reaching of agreement and the following of the expectations agreed on depend on social relations actually proceeding, since statuses function mainly in interaction rather than in the mind alone. Since this is so and since interaction only occurs when the participants believe they can predict each other's behavior, predictability is essential not only to guiding social relations but also to culture's general effectiveness as the basis for individual and group adaptation.

Conformity and Status Effectiveness: Universal Sharing and the Role of Tokens

A necessary step in statuses being generally effective is specific statuses being effective, with some of these contributing materially to the effectiveness of others. In Old Town, and probably everywhere, among the statuses that contribute most broadly to the effectiveness of other statuses, there are inclusive categories that are rarely given names but might be referred to as "community member" or "decent person." These statuses, and their identifiers are historical and associational, involve a quite limited range of expectations, including those based on the few universally shared understandings about what must and must not be done (see above). Nevertheless, they play an important part in promoting the general effectiveness of many of the community's statuses.

A substantial part of the effectiveness of these statuses derives from the expectations of others understood as characteristic of those categorized in them. Importantly, these include highly visible behaviors, mostly of the sort that are carried out (or, more often, avoided) in public. To be well thought of by "decent people/community members" is understood to entail a broad range of behaviors. If one fails to meet expectations for obvious, publicly performed activities, one is likely to be negatively evaluated for the whole range. Conversely, and importantly, if one meets the expectations for public behavior, one is at least eligible for positive evaluation in far more significant domains.

The consequences of the community member status extend beyond the restricted, direct guidance they provide for group members' overt behavior. These derive from the fact that behavior guided by them serves to reassure community members that those around them are like them, that the base for the predictability that is indispensable to social life is present. Even between community members who have substantial differences in their understandings of emotionally charged issues, there are exchanges of tokens that give them reassuring indications that they share beliefs and values allowing continuation of their relationships with one another.

In chapter 6, the tokens involved in generational relations were seen to contribute to their continuation despite serious differences in understandings concerned with the foundations for such relations. The tokens in the form of statements in a particular context gave each of the age groups a basis for believing that those in the other group were willing to take their sensibilities into account by suggesting sharing in areas where, at least as concerns the guidance of much behavior, it does not exist. The assertions members of each age group make about the sources of intergenerational strife provide tokens for the members of the other grouping.

"Tokens" are functionally defined. Any symbolic exchange in which the participants directly or indirectly indicate to one another that there is substantial sharing of understandings between them involves an exchange of tokens. These tokens may also be guides for behavior beyond the exchange in which they occur, but they need not be. The symbols that serve as tokens are not all expressed in speech. By never appearing naked and, probably more important in daily life, by appearing in the kind of clothes community members regularly wear,[8] Swahili proclaim their membership in the group.

By dressing as other group members do and by wearing clothing slightly different from that of the members of any other group, group members give one another tokens suggesting that there are important similarities uniting them and differentiating them from people outside the community. They show that they accept the identifying symbols of being a "community member" and thereby can be taken as predictable and safe for interpersonal relations. Indicating interest in and agreement about important issues reinforces and continues this.

If it can be accepted that interaction is vital for social relationships, that the functioning of social relationships is vital for statuses, and that statuses are at the heart of culture's general effectiveness, then tokens can be seen to play a significant part in cultural dynamics through their contribution to the interaction. Tokens can be based in understandings that are also guides, but even when that is not so, they contribute to social life through promoting what might be called a social and psychological "medium" that is conducive to interaction.

When Tokens Are Not
Guides But Have Manifest Results

Working from the hypothesis that tokens play an important part in cultural dynamics by helping to provide the medium for the social interaction essential to culture's functioning, a further hypothesis emerges. This is that tokens differ among themselves in their contribution to cultural dynamics, with some having distinct dangers to those dynamics built into them.

It seems likely that tokens that are not guides serve best in encouraging a productive social climate if they leave no "footprints," that is, if they do not interfere with the effectiveness of the complex of understandings in the relationships they promote. When tokens are of the sort found in the study of generational differences, the fact that they are not guides has limited consequences.

The younger Swahili can continue to act as they wish regarding clothing, demeanor, and such, despite saying, in what appears to be their "community member" status, that their own actions are both "bad" and a result of their personal shortcomings. In their statuses as young people, however, they are not bound by their public assertions of self-blame. Similarly, the older people are speaking as community members when they blame themselves for the misbehavior they report, but when they act as parents or as fellow mature men or women, they are not hampered in denouncing the youth and their behavior. The relative isolation of members of different generations from each other outside the home renders token use less likely to cause difficulties than it would if there were more open and frequent association.

Such insulation from the consequences of asserting views in one status which are less than consistent with those taken in another, however, may not be present or effective in all situations and roles. Tuzin (1976:177) reports that among the Ilahita Arapesh, there is a widespread avowal of the virtue and commonality of fraternal co-residence but that, in fact, brothers often do not live with one another. He notes that normative statements are of a different order from descriptions of experience and that "while they [i.e., the statements of norms] appear to refer directly to experience they are actually of a different logical order, one which, up to a point, cannot be contradicted . . . by the statistics of 'real' behavior" (ibid., 197).

However, he goes on to note that continual and frequent violation of the norm, expressed as a "token" in my sense, leads to an undermining of the effectiveness of the understandings as useful guides.

> These many exceptions [to the "rule" and asserted practice of fraternal co-residence], taken collectively and over the long term, pose a serious and increasing threat not only to the particular norm but to the wider set of values to which it contributes. [If group members come to perceive the invalidity of the statement that brothers live together, this] . . . would expose the prescription as starkly, *massively* [emphasis in original] unworkable and, by pernicious implication, invalid. Here, then, is the psychological raw material of revolutionary and counter-revolutionary ardor, of the unutterable bleakness of cultural collapse (ibid., 198).

What Tuzin's discussion of the Ilahita suggests is that tokens that are not also guides work best when they have least direct bearing on aspects of social reality manifestly at odds with the tokens' content and unavoidably perceptible by the tokens' users. If the tokens can indicate deeply important sharing between users and still offer little possibility that their referred to understandings will be seen as false, they would seem likely to be both highly effective and free from the sort of danger to shared understandings generally that Tuzin notes.[9]

The exchange of tokens serves to increase the likelihood that partners in interaction anticipate acceptable behavior from one another and, therefore, that they are willing to interact. As Tuzin's work suggests, however, tokens can produce a "crisis of faith" in the ability of those in contact with one another to predict each others' behavior. This happens if the tokens' references are to observable conditions that are manifestly contradictory to what the tokens assert.

Even when they work most effectively, tokens that are not also guides have distinct limitations on their contribution to individual satisfaction and group continuation. They can serve to make social life smoother and to encourage participation in it, but unless they are also guides, they contribute nothing to the "business" of life. Cooking meals, treating the sick, earning a living, and the like depend on social relationships, to be sure, but these relationships need to be more than just social links. The statuses of those involved must contain substantial expectations concerning cooking and who shares the meals they prepare, how to treat illness, and the rest of the concerns addressed in the relationships. More than this, the expectations must at least sometimes be met.

Some understandings must be guides some of the time or there can be no continuing social life or any basis for individual adaptation. Despite the importance of tokens, the Swahili community has not endured for centuries on the basis of a culture limited to sources of mutual reassurance that are no more than that. The necessities of individual and social life depend on statuses whose expectations contain understandings that, if followed, lead to some sort of satisfaction. Such statuses are effective only if there is at least minimal sharing of some of their constituent understandings and at least some conformity to these.

Divergent Understandings and Double Contingency

The minimal sharing just mentioned is all that is required for social relationships. Some time ago, Wallace (1970:32–34) argued on the basis of a gedanken experiment that group members need not share even one cognitive map. He argued that useful and productive relationships can be and are carried out on the basis of what he called "equivalence structure." As noted earlier, Wallace views predictability rather than sharing as the basis for social life, with the needed predictability arising from "equivalent mutual expectations . . . [that] may be termed an *implicit contract* [emphasis in original], in the general sense of the word contract" (ibid., 35).

Although Wallace does not say so specifically, it would appear that any actor's behavior can be affected by what fellow participants in an interaction do and that their behavior, in turn, is affected by what the first actor does in response to their act (ibid., 27–29). This is similar to Talcott Parsons's (1964:36–43) "double contingency" (see also chap. 7, above), which involves the mutual adjustment of actors to one another's behavior. That is, in any interaction, what the second actor does is contingent on what the first actor did and the first's response to the second's response takes account of what the latter response was.

There can be little doubt that double contingency is a fundamental element in social life. Through smoothing the course of particular interactions, it contributes to the continuation of relationships. The process is one characterized by continual self-correction, with each participant reassessing his own and his companions' statuses according to clues received in interaction.

The primary task of double contingency, as far as interaction beginning and continuing is concerned, is to achieve agreement on mutual status assignment. People may not begin an interaction with shared understandings about their own and their partner's category memberships, but they will respond to each other's cues until they do or they will cease trying to interact. Even if they share—or come to share—identifying understandings about their own and the other's category and its salience relative to other categories, they must also come to agree on the expectations the other will manifest in response to what the first does. They will respond to each other's cues and reach agreement, or the interaction will stop when it is hardly begun.

The Necessity for "Common Standards" and the Question of Sharing

Double contingency is much influenced by the immediate responses of those in direct relations with one another, but their responses are not completely ad hoc. Parsons (1964:37) is quite explicit in maintaining that an element of shared "orientation" ("understandings" is close to this in this context) is essential to the operation of this basic process: "The orientation of one actor to the contingent action of another inherently involves evaluative orientation, because the element of contingency implies the relevance of a [shared] system of alternatives . . . the particular acts of evaluation on both sides should be oriented to common standards."

In order for people to be concerned about how others respond to them and about how they should act themselves, they have to have some commitment to the relationship. It is also essential that they have some ability to predict the partner's response, and it is hard to see how this can be based in anything other than some sort of understanding of how the partner will choose among alternatives. This last is an understanding of the evaluations of different courses of action the partner is likely to make. Insofar as the understandings of alternative evaluations held by the different participants are similar, their interactions are probably likelier to lead to results they will find acceptable or desirable. Since, however, evidence supports much of Wallace's skepticism about the existence of sharing of understandings, it seems worthwhile to examine processes whereby what Parsons calls "common standards" are brought into action.

As has been made abundantly clear here, an "all by all" model of cultural sharing is quite unjustified by the facts. If acceptable, it would account for Parsons's "common standards," but the fact of generally incomplete sharing precludes its invocation. At the same time, a "none by none" view is clearly

untenable. Some sharing among at least some group members is always present. Every study devoted to the topic has shown that sharing is limited, even
sharply limited, but all of them, from Roberts's study of the Navaho at the
beginning of the 1950s to Holland's study of university students at the end
of the 1980s, show the presence of some sharing. The question is not whether
there is sharing, then, but what is shared and by whom?

Universal Sharing and the
Importance of Relationships: "I Know You!"

Among the Swahili, universally shared procedural understandings are
mainly limited to such behaviors as not appearing naked in public. There is,
however, universal, or nearly universal, sharing of another order of understanding. As seen in chapter 4, members of the Swahili community are quite
uniform in their attachment to and concern about certain relationships. Individuals differ to some extent about which particular relationships are more
important to them than others. They also differ in the intensity of their commitment to the relationships they find most important. Despite these differences, everyone has some relationships in which his or her behavior points
to their being understood as having deep emotional and/or social significance.

In every case I know about, all such relationships are based on kinship,
marriage, and neighborhood. These are the relationships to which people de-
vote most of their energy and attention and the evaluations of partners in them
are generally the most weighty and lasting in effect. The broad importance
for culture's dynamics of the expectations that are the bases for evaluation in
these relationships can hardly be overemphasized. It is a central hypothesis
of this study that these expectations in multiplex relationships are fundamental
not only to those relationships but to the processes that make culture an effective base for individual and community life.

Relationship Terms and Cultural Models

One of these processes depends on the cultural models expressed in the
standard terms used to characterize social behavior, including, especially, behavior in the multiplex relationships themselves. These evaluative terms serve
to promote the common standards essential not only to those relationships but,
more generally, to interaction within the community as a whole. The terms
do this by bringing these standards to bear on individual behavior in a direct
and explicit way, with particular relevance to what the individual himself
views as the most important relations.

Lakoff and Johnson's influential work (1980) has shown a similar role for metaphor, but here the process focuses on the direct use of words in ordinary speech to characterize in a value-laden way how people behave, especially how they behave in social relationships. Through their relatively uniform use when applied to different individuals, these characterizations provide an impetus to uniform standards in similar social relationships.

None of the terms used for these characterizations is neutral. Some are approving, though most Swahili terms concerned with behavior in relations indicate disapproval. But in either case, their applicability to acts and types of behavior is quite unambiguous. The terms as used thus openly and explicitly display for all those exposed to them understandings of what is desirable, acceptable, good, and beautiful, or, more often, the opposite. They apply particularly and directly to relationships with others, including those from the social groups (family, neighborhood, and community) that matter most to most people. They thereby serve as models of the parts of the culture applicable in various key relationships for occupants of particular statuses and, by extension, to other relationships.

The approval—more commonly, disapproval—involved in the terms harnesses, so to speak, the concern people have for the evaluations of those who matter to them and makes them amenable to the pressures for conformity to the common standards they imply. These terms, in other words, serve as cultural models that not only display shared understandings but do so in a way that is conducive to their actually affecting behavior.

Keesing (1987:374), views a "cultural model" as constructed from elements of the same general sort as the relationship terms of interest here:

> What . . . makes them models? Presumably, it is their paradigmatic, world-proposing nature. These cultural constructions of the everyday world do not consist of disconnected bits of cultural wisdom, expressed in precepts, parables, proverbs, or pragmatic, probabilistic operating strategies, but of world-proposing . . . models embodied or expressed in these bits.

As chapter 7 makes clear, the relationship terms used in Swahili evaluations concerned with characterizing how people act in social relationships are not "disconnected bits" but unite particular characterizations into overall, integrated models. These models find their most direct and behaviorally effective expression when they are applied to individuals by their partners in multiplex relationships through characterizing them, their general behavior, or their behavior in some limited context according to emotion- and value-rich terms.

These terms differ in their scope, but they always involve evaluation of the performance of their subjects in some of their statuses. Sometimes the statuses to which the terms apply are only situational (e.g., apply only to hosts or guests), and sometimes they are broad, such as "Muslim," "man," "woman," or "community member." There are terms that are appropriate only for occupants of particular statuses, but there are others that can be used for everyone. The meanings of some terms are the same regardless of the statuses of those to whom they apply or who uses them, but others vary according to the statuses of the referent and/or the user. Some are uniform in their implied judgments, but many relationship terms entail different judgments according to the statuses of the user and the person referred to.

The existence and, especially, the use of quite standard terms that evoke the understandings of what is and what is not proper behavior in particular statuses direct the universal concern for evaluations into active interpersonal and psychological forces promoting the "common standards" Parsons rightly places at the base of social life. The judgments involved in applying the relationship terms to any community member supplies all those who are aware of the judgments, not just those to whom they are applied, with a compelling opportunity to become aware of common standards for behavior or, more often, to be reminded of the costs or benefits flouting or following them bring. The fact that the standards evoked by the terms are applied to or about a specific person carrying out particular behavior gives the standards a clarity otherwise hard to attain. That the terms clearly entail approval or disapproval is often obvious by the manner of their use and application, and this approval or disapproval is often unambiguously associated with strong positive or negative emotions.

In the same way, the judgments made by those about whom one cares are obviously more compelling than those made by others about whom one cares little, but there is often a transitivity involved. If A cares for B and his judgments and C also cares for B, the possibility that A and C will have common standards is much increased, despite their indifference to or ignorance about one another, by their common concern about B. This calls for A and C each understanding B's judgments of him as being based on the same set of understandings. The likelihood of this is increased when B's judgments of both are expressed in the same relationship terms. The use of the terms in characterizing particular actions of specific individuals, not just their existence, much reduces their ambiguity and is a key base for their part in encouraging common standards.

Similarly, if A's relations with B are very important to A, B's views about A's behavior in the relationship A has with C are likelier to be effective than otherwise. This insertion of a third person's standards in a relationship not involving that third person offers the prospect of a standardization of understandings in such relationships when their participants have important relationships with similar "third persons." If the views of the "middle man" (B) are those often expressed in the ordinary relationship terms, with the common specificity these involve, the likelihood that this standardization will be broader and more generally effective is increased.

The terms that Swahili use to characterize participation in social relationships provide exposure to a constant source of clearly implied—sometimes explicitly stated—understandings about how people should and, more often in actual use, should not behave. They are less often of the "X is a bad person" sort than of the stated or implied "X's having done what he did in his dealings with Y is an *mshenzi* [uncivilized person]," with the connection to X's behavior, his relationship to Y, and the condemnation as an "mshenzi" being quite clear.

Because of this clarity, the terms often make clear the standards that are used in positive and in negative judgments of easily identified behavior in particular relations.[10] The fact that the terms apply to and are not infrequently made by partners in multiplex relationships enhances their ability to affect behavior.

The Importance of Positive Assessments: A Universal Lesson and Ubiquitous Source of Cultural Conformity

It may well be that the particular "shalts" and "shalt nots" taught in childhood socialization are not the most important lessons of this crucial period as concerns culture's effectiveness. They are unquestionably important, but what is learned varies from family to family and person to person. This variability is far less characteristic of the teaching of two quite unspecific things.

The first is that the judgments passed on one depend on others' assessments of one's behavior. The second is that positive assessments are far more desirable than negative and that this is truer as the judges matter more. If group members learn these two things, and they do in every society as an essential part of becoming human, a solid basis is laid for participation in social life that is independent of extensive and uniform sharing of the specific understandings that guide behavior, including behavior in social relationships.

Learning that evaluation is constant and that positive evaluation is profoundly desirable has a number of important consequences for culture's effectiveness. One of these is making the cultural models displayed through the use of common terms characterizing behavior an effective force for cultural conformity. These models are not the only source of the common standards essential to interaction, but they use the universal concern with evaluation to encourage the operation of a reasonably uniform foundation for interaction. They do this regardless of differences among individuals concerning the virtues or vices of specific behaviors by depending less on particular beliefs and values for their strength than on everyone's awareness of being constantly judged by people whose judgments matter.

The judgments may or may not involve understandings that the judge, the judged, and those aware of the particular judgment all share in the sense that they had similar knowledge of them beforehand or in the sense of all equally accepting them as just, true, or desirable. What they do is provide schemata concerning what is and is not desirable in social behavior as that is understood by some group members. These are presented in a concise but value- and emotion-laden way through relationship terms whose use in evaluation is unmistakable.

Cultural Conformity:
Bases for Shame and Guilt

The effectiveness of this process, of course, depends in part on people's concern with others' evaluations. Such concern is not equally present in every- one or equally common in different communities. An oversimplified but use- ful division is according to the nature of the goals sought. One sort of schema aims primarily at supplying the individual with the positive evaluations of his fellows. A related, but different, schema puts its focus mainly on attaining intrinsically rewarding goals, with others' approval of them or of the means for attaining them secondary.

The difference between the exact behavioral guidance provided by each of the schema would not be obvious. One might seek goal A because one un- derstood that others admired the quest, or, alternatively, one might seek A because one wanted it for itself. In either case, the directly observable be- havior is A being sought. Differences would appear in how the individual felt about gaining or not gaining what the schemata called for and the nature of the pleasure or pain experienced.

If painful feelings associated with others' negative judgments are the re- sult, it would appear that what was in operation is what Obeyesekere calls "shame" (1981:131). This is the meaning of the Swahili term *aibu*, a word often heard in Old Town.

A concern with the correspondence between one's actions and one's own evaluative understandings independent of others' judgments is a different sort of process, one that is nearer to what is sometimes called "guilt" (e.g., Piers and Singer 1971 [1953]:26–27). Although it occurs among the Swahili, it is less commonly heard about there and, possibly, less common in occurrence (see Swartz 1988).

Aibu does not depend on the actor evaluating himself or his behavior in a negative way but on his belief that others do. The Swahili are by no means unusual in experiencing feelings of disgrace, dishonor, and dysphoria as a consequence of believing others do or would disapprove of what they do.

They may, however, be different from the members of some other groups in the extent to which a very substantial proportion of them dwell on the possibility.

Conformity to Communitywide and Status-Specific Understandings

Two different sources of shame can be distinguished among the Mombasa Swahili (see chap. 8). One sort comes from the judgments of what I called "sanctioners," with every community member being a sanctioner as concerns the behavior of some others under some circumstances. The sanctioners' judgments are, and are taken by community members to be, dependent on the category in which the person judged is classified for purposes of judgment and, also, the category that is salient for the sanctioner when the judgment is made. In the status of brother-in-law, for example, a man's judgment of another's adultery is strongly negative, but in the status of crony, the judgment is quite different even though it could be of the same acts by the same man were he not married to the sanctioner's sister.

The importance of status-specific cultural conformity will be obvious, and the emotional consequences of the sort of judgment sanctioners make is an important support for just such differentiated conformity. It is worth noting that such judgments are not limited to communities like the Swahili where shame is a frequent and active focus of attention. Although a pervasive concern with shame may make others' judgments more poignant for more of the population, it is not at all a necessary part of their influencing behavior. If this is so, it implies that even without the extra emotional impetus of shame, the judgments that people attribute to others are universally important in encouraging differentiated conformity even if substantial cultural heterogeneity is present.

People are not, of course, equally concerned about all judgments of themselves. One of the aspects of the social world being divided into culturally significant categories is that assignment to one or another establishes the judgment of a potential judge as being more and less important as concerns the assessment of what an individual does as a member of one or more of his categories. This "choice" of sanctioners is central to the shame process, but it is not limited to shame. Even in instances when the judgments carry little emotional charge, their prospective social consequences can make them a force for conformity to the judge's expectations when the judged understands them as significant. The one judged, then, plays a main part in the potency of a judgment by the status he assigns the judge. Moreover, since the judge's expectations are what determine his judgment, the status he assigns himself and is accorded by the judged vis-à-vis the behavior at issue is crucial. There is, thus, a dual dependence on status assignment at the heart of the socially, culturally, and psychologically vital assessment process.

It should be made explicit that those involved in this process are not necessarily limited to the actual participants in the role in which the judged behavior occurred. Judgments on behavior are often made on one's performance in a status by people having no direct connection to that status. Thus, one's mother may judge one's performance as an employee, and her judgment may be important to one's behavior because of the character of the multiplex relationship with her.[11] A neighbor's judgment of the same behavior, however, might be far less influential despite there being a multiplex relationship with him as well. It might be, however, that the neighbor's assessment is nevertheless more influential than that of a customer who is nothing more than that since the simplex relationship, customer-employee, is likely to be influential in only a limited way.

By definition, multiplex relationships cross a number of life's domains, and their participants are the same individuals over long periods of time. The statuses that are the basis for participation in these relationships provide expectations that may serve as bases for evaluations of performances by fellow participants in situations and interactions where the judge may not be directly involved or, even, present. Simplex relations, by contrast, may be highly important to role performance, but their importance is limited to the role in which they exist.

Since people are aware of the "outside" judgments involving multiplex relationships and wish to be positively evaluated by their partners in these relationships, various strategies based on shared understandings are used to increase the likelihood of such evaluation. In the Swahili community, none of these is more striking than control of information.

Even the rather extreme secrecy of the Swahili, however, does not prevent almost every act from being subject to the judgments of sanctioners. More than that, in the Swahili community (and possibly elsewhere), there is an additional and much more limited set of judges, the "arbiters."

These are men of substantial prestige who are distinctive in that they are said to *tisha,* frighten, their fellow community members. Their judgments are not, as the sanctioners are, relative to the status of the judged. Every community is judged in a similar way, with little attention to differences in gender and age and none to differences in wealth, learning, or anything else. The standards they employ are universal: what is unacceptable for one is unacceptable for all.

Interestingly, however, they make no explicit judgments, nor do they act differently toward those who are supposed to have won their displeasure. Young men—young women may be spoken of similarly, but I never encountered it—are praised for "fearing the faces of the mature people" (*kucha uso wa wazima*),[12] and this means that the young men behave in accord with universally applicable standards *as though* they feared the judgments of high-prestige men, the arbiters. The arbiters make no public—or, as far as I know, private—statements about who is naughty and who is nice. Nor are they explicit about which behaviors are judged as one or the other.

The arbiters are, in fact, a sort of evaluative Rorschach. The understanding that they would disapprove of something is what is important since they do not actually disapprove, or approve either, of anything in ways that can be perceived. Not only do they refrain from making explicit judgments but they also continue to behave toward the judged with the same dignified and restrained politeness they show everyone else.

They function in at least one respect as an internalized set of standards does: the judgments are no less real for having no external signs. From the perspective of an observer, doing something to avoid displeasing the arbiters is indistinguishable from doing something because conscience dictates it be done. As with internal prompting, the person involved "just knows" what the arbiters approve and disapprove. In neither case is there a social process others can see.

The only thing that can be seen and that connects the arbiters to approval or disapproval of specific behavior is what can be inferred from their own behavior. What they openly do is almost always viewed as acceptable for everyone since they are the avatars of good behavior.

The arbiters have no Swahili name, but this unmarked category is as much a status as are those occupied by the sanctioners. The arbiters, unlike the sanctioners, have but a single status, and their imagined judgments are virtually uniform regardless of who is judged. Still, both sorts of judges are effective only if their statuses are. Only when men tisha (inspire fear in) others are their judgments taken with the seriousness arbiters' judgments are, and inspiring fear is a main expectation of those in the arbiter status. Similarly, a brother-in-law's disapproval of one having a "secret wife" is in accord with the expectations of his status vis-à-vis one's own as sister's husband and, therefore, is likely to be taken seriously so long as the brother-in-law demonstrates the general interest in his sister's welfare called for by his status's expectations. In effect, then, the ability of judgments to affect behavior depends on the judgments of the judges, whether arbiters or sanctioners.

Statuses and Cultural Conformity

According to the argument to this point, a number of important inducements to cultural conformity operate differentially based on the status of the individual and that of those judging his behavior. "Sanctioners," and everyone is one, may make quite different judgments of the same act depending on the statuses of the judged and the status salient for them when they make the judgments.

Even the recondite "judgments" of the arbiters can be understood only in the light of the complex of understandings that form the arbiter status and the mainly undifferentiated status, "community member," assumed by those who take themselves as judged. Here the judgments of the same act are understood as uniform provided only that the judged is a community member.

This judgmental process with its two different sorts of judges provides support for the differentiated conformity called for by the differences among the expectations in different statuses and their roles. It also supports a broad general conformity to a relatively few universal expectations applying to all community members. "Sanctioners" are surely present in every society, and every human is one, but "arbiters" may not be ubiquitous. It is likely that universally applicable standards work in a similar way even if they are not seen as embodied in the judgments of high-prestige individuals.

Judging and Sharing:
Conformity Independent of Consensus

From the point of view of cultural dynamics, it is important to note that one need not share the understanding that is the basis for judgment to be judged by it or agree with it to be affected by it. Since evaluations are relative to the statuses of both the actor and the assessor, the shared understandings brought to bear are not from a widely shared and generally applicable inventory of evaluational rules. Instead, the expectations in the roles that unite the statuses of the judge and the judged provide the basis for the assessment.

Since every status has as many roles as its occupants have relations with different categories of others, the expectations of a given status may be quite different according to the status of the individual with whom there is a relationship. The husband has expectations in the husband-wife's brother role that are quite different from those in the husband-crony role, and the judgments will differ accordingly.

The diversity of standards presents a potential difficulty for the evaluated and, since everyone is constantly evaluated, for all the members of the group. To put it melodramatically, the differentiated conformity called for by the fact that everyone has many statuses and an even larger number of roles offers the potential for painful individual conflict about the existence of potentially contradictory evaluations. Social difficulties also threaten in that individuals may be reluctant to participate in some kinds of relationships due to uncertainty about which standards will be applied to them.

If the numerous pressures for conformity to different, sometimes contradictory, expectations all work simultaneously, the individual's situation could
become impossible. The fact that people not participating in a relationship,
as well as those directly involved, assess behavior in it makes this even more
difficult. Virtually everything a person does could be approved by some with
whom there are important relationships and, simultaneously, disapproved by
others with whom relations are equally vital.

To complete the melodrama, the social and individual dangers inherent in
there being a variety of standards by which conflicting judgments may be
made for the same behavior are not greater than the threat posed by a single
standard being uniformly followed by all. If none of the differing pressures
for conformity to different, sometimes contradictory expectations are effective in producing a differentiated conformity, there is the prospect of status
distinctions failing and, with them, the performance based in different expectations that is indispensable to social life and individual satisfaction.[13]

Since Swahili individuals continue to function and the community perdures,
there are unquestionably ameliorating factors at work which allow differential
conformity and, at the same time, reduce the incidence of contradictory pressures on people. One of these is the limitation on the array of statuses likely
to be occupied by those who know about a given behavior.

This reduction in contradictory expectations and judgments, no doubt,
comes about in a number of ways in different societies, but in the Swahili
community, it is in some part the result of the quite sharp separations in the
personnel and the location of activities involved in different domains. This
serves to limit the range of statuses occupied by both judges and the judged
in each domain and, thereby, limits the variety of expectations bearing on
particular behaviors.

The business of earning money is mainly separated from family relations,
juniors are separated from seniors, and, for most of the day and the great majority of activities, men are separated from women. This, of course, reduces
the likelihood that the same behavior will be subject to judgment according
to different standards by reducing the range of statuses whose occupants are
aware of the activities.

An even more pervasive source of reduction in the difficulties arising from
conflicting judgments derives not from social structure but directly from culture, namely, the widely shared understandings that the restriction of information about one's activities and those of people with whom one is closely
connected is, pari pasu, always to be preferred to the broad dissemination of
information. Insofar as this understanding guides behavior, it promotes uniformity in judgments by reducing the number of judges and reduces conflicting judgments by allowing the judged to choose who will have the information
needed.

Limiting Cultural
Diversity with Cultural Models

A closely related problem to that of multiple evaluators is that of multiple standards. Anything that encourages those involved in a relationship or interaction to apply similar understandings to participation and evaluation will lessen diversity of judgment, if only "locally," that is, to the individuals or situation at hand. The processes that promote "local" homogenization include double contingency and, a key source of its effectiveness, the use of emotionally loaded mnemonics such as those found in the use of relationship terms. These two processes are more focused and current than socialization and enculturation on which they depend, to some extent, for their effectiveness. More immediately and directly important to the effectiveness of double contingency and the display of cultural models is that those judged care about the relationship in which these processes occur.

Judgments are likelier to be effective when they are made by partners in multiplex relationships. Since these relationships are broad in scope (but by no means all-inclusive) by definition, their effectiveness in strengthening evaluations applies rather broadly and, since membership in them overlaps, making broad networks of relations, is conducive to some uniformity within the community.

The uniformity promoted in this way is not a uniform commitment to a single set of understandings. Mothers do not expect sons to perform in the mother-son role as they expect them to perform in the sister-brother role, much less the student-teacher role, but the mother's assessment of all of these roles is often influential. The woman who is mother, that is, may introduce or maintain some uniformity in effective understandings by her assessments of those who are in family roles with her and also in other roles that concern her. The "uniformity" they promote is, of course, differentiated according to the statuses and roles in which she judges her family members.

Note that since the son who is evaluated by his mother in the employer-employee relationship is reacting in some part to his mother's evaluation and by his actions is affecting the employer, the employer's behavior is affected by his worker's mother's standards whether the employer shares them or not. This sort of process does not guarantee uniformity throughout the group, but it is surely a force in that direction.

The pressures for uniformity based in evaluations are always through roles, not statuses as wholes. A mother's behavior is evaluated differently by sons, by daughters, by teachers, and by other mothers, with uniformity promoted less as regards the mother status as a whole than as regards its component roles. This is probably a considerable part of the basis for the finding here and, possibly, in Holland's study (1987a) that status occupants do not share more of the understandings concerned with their statuses with fellow status members than they do with nonmembers.

Mothers evaluate one another mainly in the mother-mother role and have only a limited basis for assessing, or directly influencing, one another in the other roles of the mother status since they are rarely present when these roles are played. Nuclear family members, however, not only interact with the mother in their particular roles but also influence her in her other roles involving fellow family members. Thus, the "local" homogenization in the family leading to more sharing among family members as concerns the mother status than among people who are all mothers but operate in different families is quite in accord with the processes hypothesized here.

The cultural conformity that is essential for social life and for individual adaptation is a highly differentiated one. Actors must follow at least some of the understandings that constitute the expectations in the various statuses they occupy in response to the requirements of their current situation and its relationships. Their conformity is not to a single set of expectations but, rather, must be attuned to the behavior of others in the particular situation and must shift as statuses and their roles change from situation to situation and relationship to relationship.

The sort of judgments sanctioners make provide impetus for just such conformity through the judgments' constant dual-status dependence—on that of the judged and on that of the judge. It is crucial to this process that people do not respond equally to all judgments by all judges. Because of the greater commitment to them, the judgments by those with whom the judged share multiplex relationships are usually more significant across a broader range of domains than judgments by those in simplex relationships. Participation in multiplex relationships, in other words, helps organize the various understandings available for guidance in a particular situation. Those likelier to guide behavior so that a positive evaluation in multiplex relationships results have an attraction in the Swahili community that understandings in simplex relationships do not have.[14]

Multiplex Relationships, Conformity, and General Expectations

Individuals differ as to which of their multiplex relationships are the source of more influential judgments and which less, but it is always from partners in *some* such relationships that people draw the judgments that affect their behavior most. In the Swahili community, there are shared understandings that encourage this focusing more on certain multiplex relationships than on others.

A Swahili cultural model, expressed in proverbs as well as relationship terms, emphasizes the importance of permanent relationships (mainly of kinship) as opposed to more transitory ones. To the extent that attachment is associated with sensitivity to judgment, this promotes the effectiveness of judgments made by those in such relationships.

The judgments in all relationships, whether simplex or multiplex, always involve the expectations in the statuses of those in the relationships. Expectations, however, are not always different in substance from the other types of understandings that make up statuses. It has been noted several times that the three types of understandings that make up statuses are analytically distinguishable but not necessarily different in fact.

Often, identifying understandings overlap with expectations so that what people do influences how they are categorized. Both kinds of understandings work together to indicate the salience of category membership in different situations and, when several are appropriate at once, to indicate its proper strength in combinations with other statuses. It is what people do that can be seen and assessed, however, and therefore it is expectations that are the understandings most directly tied to evaluation.

But expectations are never divorced from identifiers and salience understandings. Metaphorically, the expectations are the tool's edge, but the haft is composed of identifiers and salience understandings. The three distinguishable components of statuses, however, are subject to joint influence. By having direct influence on expectations, that is, by calling for some rather than others, the social pressures in judgments, double contingency, and cultural models also affect the other parts of statuses through their indications of which are appropriate.

Some expectations are quite specific. A bus passenger is understood to give the conductor money, and in return the conductor is understood to allow the passenger to ride. The ability of the parties to such a simplex relationship to determine whether or not their expectations have been met is to a considerable extent dependent on little more than direct observation and very limited interpretation.

This is not so as concerns many or most of the expectations in multiplex relationships which are of the sort called "general expectations" here. These are broad in scope and only loosely identified with specific behaviors. Although multiplex relationships include specific expectations, the sort that are most vital to them are not met through specific behaviors but rather by a general interpretation of a whole range of actions.

The broad behavioral scope of these general expectations gives them a kind of flexibility in influencing behavior that is particularly important to culture's effectiveness. Because of this, as will be seen in a moment, the importance of participants in multiplex relationships meeting their partners' expectations goes beyond the relationships themselves to affect how the community as a whole operates.

In an important sense, general expectations differ from specific expectations with respect to the amount of interpretation of behavior they call for. When Swahili say that in relations with those closest to you, your satisfaction or lack of it is due less to what your partners do than it is their nia (purpose or intentions), they are referring to just what is meant by "general expectations."

General Expectations, Cultural Sharing, and the Scope of Multiplex Relationships

Whether or not A's behavior meets B's general expectations is a matter involving A's *interpretation* of events quite as much as the events themselves. In the grocery clerk-customer relationship, the clerk does not usually need to make abstruse interpretations to decide whether or not the customer has handed over the payment asked for. In the Swahili husband-wife relationship, however, it is far more difficult to establish whether, for example, the husband has "shown love" to the wife even though doing so is frequently mentioned as an expectation in this relationship. Because of their dependence on general expectations, multiplex relationships have two notable qualities.

First, the relationships can function despite participants not sharing many specific understandings, including some of those concerned with the relationship itself. Some sort of balance of satisfied as opposed to violated expectations is probably essential to the maintenance of social relations. This balance, however, is more likely a psychological than a quantitative one. Many failures to keep the bathroom floor dry can be outweighed by a single manifestation of what is understood as concern and love. To the extent this is true, family relationships, and multiplex relationships generally, function in some part, at least, through their participants' general, empirically broad, expectations of one another which lead them to interpret quite a wide range of behavior as in accord with their most heavily weighted expectations.[15]

Second, the relationships have an indefinitely broad scope, since just what each participant can, should, and might do for the other is not, by their nature, specified in the general expectations. In the specific expectations most characteristic of simplex relationships, the limits of commitment and responsibility are usually rather clearly understood as part of sharing the understandings that constitute those expectations.

In multiplex relationships, there are no such sources of limitation. A person whose nia toward you is "good" is one who can be called on for a very broad range of things, and if your nia is similar, you can be similarly called on. Each of you may understand issues and circumstances that cannot or should not be dealt with within the relationship, and some of these limiting understandings may be shared, but the boundaries are very wide.[16]

Sharing Identifying Understandings

What seems most consistently and broadly shared by participants in multiplex relationships are the understandings that identify participants to one another. Such sharing of identifiers is characteristic of all relationships, especially multiplex relationships. The sharing of the identifying understandings may not be quite as complete as community members sometimes indicate it is, since people sometimes do identify as "friends" those who privately identify themselves as only acquaintances or who even understand themselves to be enemies. But the sharing is usually general, so that almost everyone is quite sure who their partners in multiplex relationships[17] are. Given the importance of general expectations in multiplex relationships, the sharing of identifiers (which sometimes include these expectations) for these relationships entails a sharing of such expectations as well.

As we will now see, these expectations play a key role in cultural dynamics beyond their direct service in multiplex relationships. Working together with the ability to identify those in multiplex relationships and the indefinite boundaries of expectations in those relationships, these inclusive expectations are an essential basis for transmitting, so to speak, the effects of understandings to those who do not share—or even know about—them.

It may well be that there are a considerable variety of processes by which this takes place. Two of them were recognized among the Swahili. In one, understandings are "imported" from one relationship to another. In the other, limitations in similar expectations in all but one in a set of connected multiplex relationships give a highly distinctive character to the one relationship, husband-wife, that does not have those limitations.

Importation in Swahili Medical
Treatment: It Isn't What You Know

An instance of the transmitting of understandings and their effects through what might be called importation was seen in the examination of Swahili understandings about the body and illness and how people choose among types of medical care (see chap. 9). This choice was not commonly made on the basis of intrinsically organized schemata involving selecting a medical practitioner on the basis of understandings about the practitioner's views of illness being in accord with the patient's. Most patients were found to have few understandings of any kind about either the treatment of illness or differences among types of practitioners.

Rather, the choices were made according to the advice of people, usually kin or neighbors, of whom the patients had general expectations to the effect that the adviser would help the patient and could be trusted. These expectations made the advice worthy of following. When it was followed, it led to the patient being affected, in the choice made and the treatment received, by understandings about medical care held by the adviser or often, at a further remove, only by the adviser's adviser or her adviser.

What is particularly striking about the advice is that it is usually accepted. The patient goes, or allows himself or herself to be taken, to the kind of medical practitioner the adviser recommends. When this happens, the nonsharers are affected by the medical understandings that are, according to the definition of "culture" used here, part of the community's culture despite the patient's ignorance of them. If two or more members of the community who maintain some sort of an active relationship with one another share an understanding, it is part of the culture of the group. The fact that there are individuals who do not share the element does not bar it from being part of the culture. Swahili culture would consist of nothing save understandings such as that one must not go naked in public if only universally shared items were included.

Nor is this only an arid definitional matter. If culture's ability to promote individual life and social relationships is to be explained, and if a substantial proportion of culture's contents is less than universally shared, it is obviously essential to examine closely whether understandings shared by only a few affect others who do not share them. When this does happen, and it is surely quite a common phenomenon, the processes whereby it happens call for description and analysis. The Swahili medical care study is an attempt to do just that for one domain.

The understandings that lie behind medical care affect those who receive that care just as the understandings behind the generation of electricity affect people who read by electric light even if they are innocent of understandings about coils and magnetic fields. Medical care, unlike electricity in modern cities, is not "just there," that is, so much a part of life that it requires effort to avoid.

Everyone I talked to knew that Mombasa has a variety of different medical practitioners, and everyone was quite clear about knowing that different people consulted various of them when ill. But understanding that there are practitioners who can be consulted about your illness does almost nothing to lessen the effects of that illness. Only choosing one and accepting the treatment offered may do that. Having no clear understandings about how illness arises and none about how different medical practitioners deal with illness, the basis for this choice is not obvious. It is constantly made, of course, but the basis for it cannot, for most, be understandings concerning the body and its treatment since they do not have these.

For most people, the choice is made on the basis of advice from partners in multiplex relationships. Their advice is taken seriously enough to be the immediate basis for action as a consequence of the general expectations in those relationships. These relationships "transmit medical understandings" in the sense that they expose patients to activity based on them (what practitioners do when the patients come to them) whether the patients themselves have any familiarity with those understandings or not.

Repeatedly, informants said that they sought the treatment of a practitioner recommended to them not because of what they directly knew about the practitioner or the theory of body functioning and illness he or she followed but because of their relationship with the adviser who recommended the practitioner. When asked why they followed the advice given them, the patients usually said that the adviser "cared about" them (and so would give "good advice") or that the patients "trusted" the adviser or, less often, that the adviser "knew about" the illness in question or medical matters generally. Thus, for the overwhelming majority of the community who are ignorant of medical understandings, these understandings affect their lives through the agency of quite different understandings; namely, the expectations in their relations with others when these others were kin, friends, or neighbors.

There is little new or enlightening in observing that medical knowledge is limited in its distribution and that medical practitioners share understandings (with other practitioners and, to a limited extent, with a relatively few "dedicated amateurs") that most group members do not share. What is worth noting is that the medical understandings affect people because those people have expectations of others, including others as free of medical understandings as they themselves are, which lead them to accept the treatment of the medical experts.

Those in the relationships who give advice are only sometimes more knowledgeable about body functioning and medical care than are the patients they advise. When they are not, they get information from a third person about what should be done. This third person may share a substantial body of medical understandings with practitioners, but it appears that the "chains" of social relationships between the medical practitioner who ultimately treats the patient and the patient can sometimes be rather long. In each link of this chain, the connection between adviser and advised is more often through shared general expectations than through shared understandings about the body and illness.

Cultural Organization and General Expectations

The schemata that commonly serve Swahili as bases for getting medical treatment have components that are extrinsically connected to one another. People use general expectations about advisers as a connection between the understandings that they are ill and need treatment and those that hold treatment is available and can be obtained from a specific source. Since "cultural organization" refers to the relations among shared understandings, in the extrinsically based schema, the general expectations take over the part played by the intrinsic relations (of the sort used by chess players in deciding on moves) in organizing the elements in that schema.

Nor is organization through statuses involved only in extrinsically based schemata. Some organization derives directly from understandings about understandings (Swahili proverbs sometimes express these) wherein doing or being one thing is said to be better or more important than being or doing something else. A substantial part of establishing relations among understandings, however, is due to the functioning of statuses and their constituent roles in determining what is appropriate, what is more and less important, and, as already seen, what is likelier to be approved by whom. This depends mainly on the significance of evaluation in the relationship, so understandings whose guidance leads to behavior that is positively evaluated by partners in multiplex relationships thereby have a quality affecting their desirability and choice other understandings do not have.

A rather extreme example of the choice among understandings immediately guiding behavior can be seen in an aspect of the relationship between Swahili mothers and daughters. A woman cooking in her kitchen, for example, can sometimes be heard to direct strong insults to her own daughters.[18] Women tell me that they would not use such insults on their peers or even the daughters of their peers but that with their own daughters such behavior is acceptable and they are not despised by anyone, including the daughter, for using them (Swartz 1990*b*). The mother-daughter role involves, inter alia, the understandings that the mother status occupant is dominant, that mother's abuse of a daughter "means nothing," and that daughters accept their mothers' behavior, even if it is harsh, as "instruction."

What goes together with what and what does not, that is, one of the relations among guiding understandings, is established according to statuses and the expectations they have in various roles. Without organization to indicate which understandings can and cannot be used together, what comes first or last, and what is more salient than what, the elements of culture are useless in guiding behavior. The main base for this organization is the expectations in the statuses, and this is as true for general expectations as for specific ones. However, general expectations have effects that specific expectations do not.

"Patterns" or Common Element Organizations

An example of the organizing effects of general expectations beyond what is involved in schemata can be seen as concerns the type of cultural organization often referred to as "patterns." This organization is one in which a common element is present in the complexes of understandings associated with a number of different domains. The common understanding provides an element of similarity in the different domains in the way exemplified by Benedict (1934) in her distinction between Apollonian and Dionysian cultures. This similarity may be one of style, substance, or both, but its presence presumably serves to promote cultural conformity through harnessing habituation and the sense of rightness that comes with familiarity.

As shown in chapter 9, at least one instance of just this sort of cultural organization is found in Swahili culture. Understandings concerned with the usefulness or desirability of "balance" are a common element in several different domains. Thus, in the domain of body functioning, Galenic medicine is based on understandings about the close relationship between elemental balance and health; in social relationships, the balance involved in maintaining status differences and meeting expectations is valued; and in character, the highly important "balance" calls for adherence to the differential proprieties in different situations.

A "Pattern" and How It Can
Be Effective Given Limited Sharing

The understanding that balance is desirable provides an organization based on the presence of a common element in the diverse sets of understandings that severally concern their different domains. In all of them, the desirability and benefit of including the "proper" proportions of different things is noted and also the cost of not doing so. The simple existence of the same sort of understanding in quite different areas of life may make it likelier that the understanding will be influential in each of them. To the extent that the understanding is a morally charged one, as balance in social relations and character is, it becomes even more effective and able to influence or guide behavior in a variety of areas.

The difficulty with these common element organizations, "patterns," having a substantial effect on general cultural conformity is that their influence depends on there being a good deal of sharing of the understandings involved. On the face of it, the balance notion in body functioning can only be made compelling for those who share it and also share the balance understandings concerning relationships and character. Since most people know nothing of Galenic medicine, including its emphasis on balance, the acceptance of this type of medicine would, it might seem, hardly be increased by the fact that those same people are committed to balance in social relations and in character.

There is a substantial basis, however, for the pattern being effective in promoting conformity despite the widespread lack of sharing of its component understandings. This basis is in the fact that somewhere in the chain of advisers who serve to supply the "missing link" between the understanding that one is ill and the understanding that there is help in dealing with illness, there is usually someone who knows about balance in medicine as well as in social relations and personal character. By inclining the experts or serious amateurs who know about Galenic balance to recommend Galenic practitioners rather than other kinds, the organization affects some of those who do not share the balance understandings in some domains.

It may be of some interest to suggest that not only do understandings affect those who do not share them but organizations can affect those who are innocent of their components. At least one process by which the latter occurs is the same as the one that brings about the former. This is, of course, that people accept advice from each other, with an important source of the acceptance being the general expectations in the multiplex relationships within which it is given.

Transmission by Simplex
Relationships and Its Limits

Clearly, advice is also given and accepted in simplex relationships. The practitioner-patient relationship is an example of this. Here acceptance, when it occurs, is usually on the basis of the specific expectation that the practitioner knows about illness and can make useful recommendations. In order for the patient to continue to accept the practitioner's advice, however, the patient must see acceptable results, that is, the specific expectations in the relationship call for particular things to happen within a relatively limited time span.

The general expectations vital to multiplex relationships do not call for highly specific returns, and the time spans involved in exchanging whatever is exchanged may be quite long. A mother who sends a son or daughter to a practitioner whose treatment does not help as soon as the patient thinks it should is, nevertheless, quite likely to be asked for advice again. The patient is likelier to abandon treatment from the practitioner than advice from the parent. The "pay-off" in multiplex relationships is quite different from that in simplex relationships, making the former far more resilient in most cases.

Moreover, the general expectations in multiplex relationships provide a far broader scope for the relationships than is found in simplex relationships. Parents or neighbors are consulted because they are expected to be committed to one's interests as much or more than because of the breadth of their command of understandings.

Simplex relationships do serve to transmit unshared understandings in the way seen for Swahili medical care, but their "reach" is limited and their "cost" is high. Simplex relationships, by definition, begin and end in a single domain, and their specific expectations are all within that domain. One does not have a relationship with a medical practitioner, if the only role is prac-titioner-patient, outside the domain of medicine. This relationship can be part of a broad transmission of the effects of understandings to those who do not share them by those who take themselves to have benefited but only if the links in the chain of transmission that follow it are the general expectations in multiplex relationships.

Generally, simplex relationships cannot serve to make cultural organiza-tions effective in the way multiplex relationships can and do. A practitioner may study and practice Galenic medicine because of understandings in other domains which make the balance understandings in that scheme attractive to him, but his ability to bring people to accept the kind of medicine he practices depends more on the actual results they believe he achieves than on *his* advo-cacy of the scheme.

In a multiplex relationship, the partner's enthusiasm, which may be based in her being struck by the inherent "rightness" of the balance, or some other, understanding does matter in that her advice is followed not so much because of the qualifications she has for giving the advice but more because of her understood commitment. If a mother wants a child to consult an herbal doctor, a central reason for following the advice is that she gave it. General expec-tations do not call for specific results, nor are they based in understood com-mand of specific understandings. Their broad and vital part in cultural dynamics is mainly a consequence of these two facts.

The effects of general expectations in the operation of patterns and in the transmission of the results of unshared cultural elements suggest that these broad expectations have effects beyond the relationships in which they occur. In fact, through their central part in multiplex relationships and the broad consequences of these relationships for the social life of the community, they play an important part in the operation of social structure as a whole. These broad expectations not only bind together spouses, parents and children, neigh-bors, and many others who "mean" a great deal to one another but also play a central part in making the whole culture effective. Their contribution to the community's whole social structure is particularly critical.

Social Structure as an Independent Influence on Behavior

"Social structure" here refers to the statuses in a community's culture and their connections, direct and indirect, by mutually involving references in their expectations and salience understandings. Since the statuses making up social structure are each composed of shared understandings and since these statuses are joined by the mutual references of one of these sorts of component understandings (i.e., expectations), it is a culturally constituted system. As will be seen, however, despite its being composed wholly, but not quite solely, of culture, social structure has effects that are independent of culture.

A social structural perspective focuses attention on how the statuses that guide relationships affect one another and, therefore, the nature of the guidance available within the community seen as a system, sensu stricto, of relationships. A social structural point of view directs attention to the connections among understandings rather than directly to the understandings themselves.

As an example of the results of a social structural perspective, consider recent changes in the statuses of Swahili women. These changes in the expectations in the statuses daughter, sister, and wife as well as woman lessen the difficulty women have in being in statuses, especially "employee," whose expectations call for spending a good deal of time outside the home. The expectations in these "outside" statuses affect the statuses women (or, perhaps, "respectable women"), daughters, sisters, wives, mothers, and neighbors and the wide variety of roles involving these statuses. These changes in women's statuses and roles, in turn, affect the statuses connected with them and *their* component roles, thus altering the sets of understandings that affect a wide range of the community's relationships.

The Social Structural Importance of Multiplex Relationships and Their General Expectations

Every status affects all the others directly or indirectly connected to it in role relationships through the presence of the mutual references in the roles' expectations. This is true whether the relationships are simplex or multiplex. The examination of how medical care is obtained illustrated how multiplex relationships such as mother-child affect simplex relationships such as practitioner-patient by leading people to participate in them, but it should not be thought that all influence flows from multiplex to simplex relationships. The influence goes the other way as well. So, for example, the expectations in the statuses in such simplex relations as employer-employee doubtless affect expectations in the statuses of a variety of multiplex relations within the family and neighborhood.

Given this caveat, it is nevertheless true that the statuses in multiplex relationships are particularly important to a community's social structure. Because their general expectations are flexible and inclusive and because, by definition, the relationships involve a number of different domains, it is multiplex relationships that most often bring the effects or products of a wide range of the group's culture to community members who may not share the understandings they rest on. No one in any group has even indirect access to all the cultural elements available in all of the statuses in the community's social structure, but such access is not necessary to be affected by them. Relations with others who do have access to these understandings, whether direct or indirect, may serve to transmit their effects provided the relations have expectations promoting such transmission.

The hypothesis that has been advanced here is that it is multiplex relations with their general, rather than specific, expectations which do this. The transmission may be through the sort of advising that was seen in Swahili medical care, or it may be through one participant in a multiplex relationship bringing the effects of his or her participation in a quite different relationship to bear on the fellow participant.

The latter can involve a sort of chain reaction effect. For purposes of illustration, imagine that A is in a multiplex relationship with B, B is in any relationship with C, and C in any with D. D imposes expectations on C deriving from relationships D has about which C need have no understanding. The effect of this on C leads him to impose expectations on B who, in turn, knows nothing of their provenance but is affected by them and imposes them on A. A knows nothing of what led B to impose the expectations he did, but A is affected by them nevertheless. Since the A-B relationship is multiplex, the limits to the kind and extent of the influence that B brings into the relationship as a consequence of his relations with C are quite wide. Thus, the imposition of expectations by D affects the relationship between A and B even though neither of them need be aware of the relationship between C and D for this to happen. (See Swartz and Jordan 1976:86–98, for a fuller discussion of this process and an example.)

The point is that through advising and through the sort of chain reaction of expectations, social relationships spread the effects of components of the group's culture so that they affect individuals even if they do not share those components. Simplex relationships can and do operate in these processes as well as multiplex relationships, but the former, unlike the latter, are probably limited to the domains in which they mainly operate, so that, for example, economic relations can only transmit the effects of mainly economic understandings.

This limitation is to be expected since it is the expectations in social relationships that serve to transmit cultural influence to those who may not share the particular understandings that affect them as concerns the matter at issue. Given the central part played by expectations, it must be remembered that it is the identifying and salience understandings that make the expectations effective. These latter status components are the culturally constituted means for promoting the culture's groupwide effectiveness regardless of less than complete cultural sharing.

Multiplex relationships and their general expectations are a particularly important part of this because of their scope and their relative immunity to the weakening of relations that can result from the failures to meet specific expectations that are inevitable and generally more harmful to simplex relationships. There are failures to meet specific expectations in multiplex relationships, of course, but the broader and more diffuse foundation of these relationships often diminishes the harm these do to the relationships and makes them a more enduring part of the community's social structure.

Social Structure as an Independent Influence on Behavior

The interconnected set of statuses that forms the group's social structure is crucial to the functioning of the community's culture through the operation of the components of the statuses, but that same social structure also serves to influence behavior independently of the culture that is its base and most of its substance. I say "most" of its substance because community members need not have understandings about the connections among statuses for those structural connections to affect behavior. A father can be affected in his status as employee by his boss's expectations, some of which stem, for example, from the boss's spouse relationship. The father may impose expectations on his children as a consequence of the expectations imposed on him as an employee even though neither the father nor the children know the boss is married, much less how his relations with his wife affect what he expects from his employees.

The connections among relationships derived from the mutual reference and interdependence of expectations have an influence on behavior that stems from, but is independent of, shared understandings themselves. Parsons is the locus classicus of the view that social structure has an influence on behavior that is independent from culture (1964 [1951]:6, 17–21 passim), and this view is important to the scheme developed here.

In an earlier work, I used data from Pitt-Rivers's (1961) study of an Andalusian village to illustrate one of the processes by which this operates. The Spanish villagers were shown to respond to expectations in one of their social relationships despite having no understandings about the usefulness or desirability of the expected behavior itself. Some of the expected behavior, in fact, was contrary to shared understandings about how people should behave (Swartz and Jordan 1976:93–98).

The expected behavior was forthcoming solely because of the importance those involved attached to maintaining the relationships in which the behavior was expected. This importance, in turn, was a consequence not of the value or utility of the relationship in itself but of its connections to other relationships (ibid., 89–92). In a sense, the influence of the one relationship can be, and frequently is, derived not from understandings about its intrinsic merit or worth but from its connection with other relationships that are understood as valuable in themselves.

Culture and "Cultural Products"

In the Spanish case, influence comes not from people's shared understandings about the behavior at issue but from their commitment to the social relations themselves. Thus, the social structure affects behavior independently from culture. Nor is this the only way in which that occurs. To appreciate this source of influence in its proper context, it is useful to look at social structure as a product of culture much as tools or buildings are products of culture.[19]

People are affected by the tools they use, the buildings they occupy, the food they eat, and the clothes they wear without respect to their sharing the understandings that produced the tools, buildings, and clothing. People are usually led to make use of cultural products such as tools they do not know how to make or repair through their participation in social relationships. Frequently, they actively seek ends they clearly recognize by means they are thoroughly unfamiliar with, as most Swahili patients do in striving to become well. This sort of intentional striving, however, is by no means an essential part of all the processes whereby cultural elements affect those who do not share them.

Wives' Power de nihilo: Social Structure's Effects Independent from Culture

Chapter 10 showed that almost every understanding concerning Swahili spouse relations holds that wives are subordinate to their husbands and must accept their decisions. Almost everyone I talked to regardless of sex said that women are subject to the authority of men because it is part of God's plan as revealed in the Koran. In fact, those men who do exercise this divinely commanded authority over their wives in ways that deny them the expensive ceremonies and finery most want appear to be entirely successful in doing so. These men are not negatively evaluated by men or women.

And yet many women actually do spend very considerable sums of money in ways their husbands say they disapprove. The women's expenditures, the men say, are the single most important factor in the Swahili being less prosperous than the Arabs and Indians among whom they live in Old Town.

Without repeating the argument and evidence, it is enough to say that the central issue is why men choose not to exercise their very real power when dealing with their wives' wishes to use money in ways the men do not approve and from which, in fact, the men derive little direct benefit. The answer to this, the evidence indicates, is to be found in social relations—not just those between husbands and wives but the various relationships involving men and involving women.

Examination of men's relationships shows that intimacy and emotional support are not readily available to them in any relationship other than that with the wife. Expectations in the broad "man" status make emotional warmth and support difficult to give and to receive in almost every relationship involving men save that between spouses. For women, however, many relationships have expectations that encourage warmth and support, so that for them the spouse relationship is only one source among many.

The men's emotional dependence on the spouse relationship together with the women's relative independence gives the wife a source of power she need not admit, or even recognize, in order to use. Her unhappiness resulting from not getting what she wants is transformed, more or less without her willing it, into her withdrawing emotional support from the husband who frustrated her wishes. For most husbands, this leads to serious efforts to avoid wifely unhappiness. The women need not admit, even to themselves, that their husbands are emotionally dependent on them. All they have to do is act as they feel—and doing this is an expectation of the status "woman"—to increase the likelihood that their husbands will give them what they want. For present purposes, what is important about this source of wives' power is that it demonstrates a means whereby a community's social structure affects community members in ways independent of, in fact, contrary to, the directly concerned elements of culture.

In considering Swahili medical care, it was seen that understandings can and do affect community members, including those who do not share them. Here we see behavior affected in ways that do not depend on *anyone* sharing understandings that produce the effect seen and without anyone needing to acknowledge, or know about, the basis for what is happening. There is no understanding, certainly not one people admit, holding women have the ability to use their husbands' money as the women wish regardless of their husbands' views. Yet they do.

Social Structure's Effect: Blocking and Channeling

Men say they believe and are aware that sanctioners act as though they believe that it is improper, impolitic, or shameful to be emotionally expressive and to accept emotional support. In their relations with all of those with whom the relationship is in any way open to observation, including those with mother, sister, and other female kin, such behavior is negatively evaluated by those involved, including the men themselves. This is not true of women's relationships, most of which include expectations of emotional expressiveness.

The unique presence, for men, of emotionality in the spouse relationship needs to be seen in light of the fact that this relationship is carried on entirely in the privacy of the home with no one but family members ever seeing spouses together. It is not so much that the expectations in the spouse relationship openly and explicitly admit male dependence as it is that the privacy in which much of this relationship takes place makes its expression possible. Further, the positive evaluation of "love" between spouses encourages giving and accepting support and warmth. This support for husbands is not specifically called for and need not be recognized by either husbands or wives, but it is available in the spouse relationship, in large part as a consequence of love and privacy. A good deal of evidence has been cited in support of the hypothesis that men do, in fact, derive emotional support from their relationship with their wives even if they never talk about it or admit its presence.

As seen, from a cultural point of view, the shared understandings concerning the spouse relationship accord men complete control, so that the wives' power to get their husbands to give them money is de nihilo, or so it seems. In fact, the social structure of the Swahili community—or, more exactly, the unique character of the spouse relationship within the structure—is a key resource for wives in dealing with their husbands.

This is the key fact here, and it is the consequence of the differences in the whole set of statuses and roles focusing on husbands as contrasted with the set focusing on wives. This difference is the main basis for wives' power, which is to say that their power is directly attributable to the social structure, not, as we saw, the elements of culture that, in fact, give all power to the husband.

The statuses that make up the social structure are all culture and nothing but culture. The structure itself, however, is not just the sum of its cultural parts. It also involves the relations among these parts, including the effects relations have on one another because of the connections between them. Some of these connections are not the result of understandings in any community member's mind but of the effects relationships have on one another through the influence of their expectations "spilling over" into one another. Some such mutual effect of relations on one another is understood by participants, who know, for example, some or all of the ways an employer-employee relationship can affect a parent-child relationship. But the effect of one relationship on another can come about without such understandings through the meeting of the expectations in one or more relationships affecting the expectations in some other relationship.

This is just what is seen in the spouse relationship. The expectations restricting emotionality in all of men's other multiplex relationships give the spouse relationship an importance for them it would not otherwise have and that, because of the different expectations in their multiplex relationships, it does not have for wives. Since social structure is a cultural product, culture's part is hardly a distant one. But its effects come from the way it channels behavior through expectations that encourage it here and block it there. There is no understanding to the effect that wives should spend substantial sums on weddings and bracelets even if husbands object. Quite the opposite. What there is, is a complex series of statuses and their roles that give wives alternatives for emotional gratification but give none to husbands.

Culture contains statuses that guide relationships and indicate what these relationships contain and do not contain. These have consequences for other relationships and the occupants of the statuses in those relationships. Wives' power is one of these consequences.

Hakuna refu lisilo ncha:
Nothing is so long that it has no end

There can be no question that the culture of the ancient Swahili community works, even though it has been seen that most of its elements are shared only among various sized parts of the population rather than by all. In asking how this culture works, then, a basic question has been how cultural elements affect those who do not share them.

The main answer to this has been through statuses, with particular importance attributed to the statuses in multiplex relationships and the general expectations that are vital to them. These bundles of understandings are taken to bring culture's guidance to specific issues and situations and, at the same time, to serve as a central part of a variety of processes that make culture's components, or the result of their use, available to community members, including some who do not share them.

If the perspective derived from this study can be summarized in a single statement, it is that culture is a sort of ouroborus, the Greek snake with its tail in its mouth. Social relationships cannot operate without the culturally constituted statuses that guide them, but culture cannot operate without the social relationships that distribute its components and are the main force in organizing them.

Culture is not ineffable; it is a natural phenomenon, though a very complex one, that can be increasingly well understood as more useful concepts and theories are developed. This book has been an attempt to contribute to such concepts and theories and to test them on a body of ethnographic data collected from some of the world's most gracious people.

Notes

1: Ethnographic and Theoretical Introduction

1. The term "Swahili" as used here applies only to the members of this group who are part of the Mombasa community. My findings are based solely on work in Mombasa, and it is my clear impression that there are substantial differences among the Swahili community in that city and those elsewhere on the coast and on offshore islands. This is so, I believe, despite important similarities among the different communities and the presence among Mombasans of a generally shared understanding of being similar to those of other communities. There is no doubt that there is a Swahili ethnic group, but there is a good deal of disagreement about its boundaries (Eastman 1971; Salim 1973:46–52; Arens 1975; Swartz 1978).

2. There are indications that Keesing has abandoned his "building blocks" model (see Keesing 1982, 1985). The comments here are directed to the position stated in Keesing 1970.

3. See Swartz and Jordan (1976:88–112) for my initial statement of the position that is substantially elaborated and modified here. With a few modifications, I use the same basic approach here to "status" and "role" as culturally constituted means for the distribution of culture. My first formulation of social structure and how it functions as an influence on behavior that is independent of culture's direct effect (ibid., 89–95) has been greatly expanded (see chaps. 9 and 10), but the original position presented in Swartz and Jordan is part of the overall view here.

4. This is a point that has occupied students of social structure for a long time. In a 1953 paper, Fortes notes, "The concept of the 'person' as an assemblage of statuses has been the starting point for some interesting enquiries. A generalization of long standing is that a married person always has two mutually antagonistic kinship statuses, that of spouse and parent in one family context and that of child and sibling

in another" (1953:37–38). The concern with what I call "salience understandings" is also seen in Fortes's statement.

5. It is, of course, not relationship terms alone that serve to promote such conformity. For example, in Turner's (1968:214–216) analysis of the Ndembu girls' initiation ritual, *nkang'a,* he shows that certain objects, such as the white beads called *kasenzi,* are symbolically powerful. They evoke understandings about the proper nature of social life ("status expectations," as they would be called here) in compelling ways that promote conformity. Thus, the beads stand for the desirability of fertility, motherhood, and good relations with affines.

6. The use of "role" is quite different from Goodenough's use of the same term to apply to an inclusive set of understandings (in my sense) applying to a broad status category (1965:16) or Keesing's use of "role" in a way that is closer to my use of "status" (1970:424). It is, however, closer to its basic source, Linton's original use of role as "when [the status occupant] puts the rights and duties [of his status] into effect, he is performing a role" (1936:114), and to those who follow Linton's usage (e.g., Parsons 1964 [1951]:25).

7. Roles are necessarily identified by the names of the statuses of the participants in a relationship, so we speak, for example, of the "fisherman-fisherman" role and of the "fisherman-customer" role.

8. Social structure is always a product of culture in that its elements are the shared understandings that compose statuses. It may sometimes be, of course, that these shared understandings are themselves the product of other forces such as those of production, consumption, or reproduction. Even in these cases, culture is the proximal source of social structure.

2: Akher Zamani: Mombasa Swahili History and Contemporary Society

1. It seems that Mombasa and the other Swahili cities of the east coast have not made much of an impression as indigenous African cities, even on specialists. Thus, in a paper on African urban studies, Mitchell (1966:37) says "towns of considerable size, outside the Arab north, existed in the Sudan and West Africa long before European industrial expansion into Africa."

2. It is likely that the preceding Swahili group, the one ruled by a Shirazi dynasty, was absorbed by the Twelve Tribes successors.

3. There is substantial disagreement about the actual role of a Persian or Shirazi element in Mombasa and more generally in Swahili history. Allen (1982:24–25) argues strongly that it is entirely unfounded to believe "that East African Shirazis must be ultimately descended from immigrants from the Persian Gulf. It is clear that, even if there were such immigrants and some of them played an important role in the early days, the Shirazi phenomenon is a purely African one which could have arisen without them." (Cf. Spear 1984, Nurse and Spear 1985:74–79).

Further, the exact reference of the term is difficult to pin down. Although "Shirazi" applied to specific families and even villages along the coast, it was used more by the colonial officials than in common speech (Prins 1967:14).

4. In addition to the Portuguese attacks and intermittent rule, the Somali-related Galla, a nomadic people from the northeast, were raiding and, sometimes, destroying

the north coastal mainland Islamic settlements, including those immediately adjacent to, if not actually on, Mombasa island (Oliver and Mathew 1963:114).

5. The term "tribe" may summon up notions of a separate ethnic group, but this is definitely an inappropriate reference for the word as it applies to the Mvita and other constituents of the Twelve Tribes. *Taifa* in Swahili usually refers to nation, and this gloss—with its reference to common origin and political unity—seems closer to the meaning properly assigned to the "tribes" of the Mombasa Swahili than does the usual significance of "tribe."

6. The fear of Galla attacks, which were continuing at the time, may have had a role in the Three Tribes finally moving onto the island where they were relatively more secure behind the arms of the Indian Ocean which form barriers around Mombasa (Berg 1968:47).

7. Although the Kilindini came to the Mombasa area from the south, their place of origin, as they themselves report it, is the famous Shungwaya on the mainland coast north of Mombasa from which they claim to be the advance guard of the movement of peoples to the south which began no later than the middle of the sixteenth century (Berg 1968:47). There is considerable controversy among historians as to just where Shungwaya was and what its role was in the beginnings of coastal and Swahili society (see Allen 1983 for an important review and an inclusive bibliography; also, ibid., 456–457; Spear 1974, 1977; Pouwells 1987:11).

8. Cooper (1977:78) is probably right in noting that the immigrants may have married slave women, but since their descendants would lose their standing if such a marriage were admitted in their ancestry, it is to be expected that one is told that these immigrants married "noble" women.

9. Prins (1967:98–99) lists the relationships between Swahili taifa and neighboring peoples during the nineteenth century showing that like the Three Tribes, the Nine Tribes maintained patron-client relations (activated mainly for war but also involved with trade) with various of the other coastal peoples. Kindy (1972:47) lists the most important alliances as the Three Tribes with the Digo and the Duruma and the Nine Tribes with the Giriama, Rabai, Chonyi, Jibana, Ribe, Kauma, and Kambe.

10. The reason I say "if it has ended" is that although I have observed no activity involving the whole community as such since I began working in Mombasa in 1975, the framework for separate identity still exists in that most Swahili know what section they belong to. Several informants have mentioned the competitions between the two sections in the past, and, although the actual conflicts that sometimes have attended those competitions are decried, the wish to reinstate the competitions has been expressed by both younger and older men from both sections or confederations.

3: The Brotherhood of Coconuts: Unity, Conflict, and Narrowing Loyalties

1. I collected the proverb quoted here in Old Town, and when I needed exegetical advice (as I did with all those whose use was not repeatedly seen and heard), I discussed them with a number of informants. My friend and associate, Sh. Yahya Ali Omar, who helped me with most aspects of this study and is prominently mentioned in the preface, is a particularly subtle and thoughtful interpreter of proverbs. I am especially grateful for his assistance in their interpretation and also for his active assistance

in their collection. Some of the proverbs I collected are also listed in Scheven's (1981) inclusive compendium of proverbs from most of the Swahili communities along the East African coast, especially those south of Mombasa.

2. According to Swahili informants, *uzomba* refers to Muslim beliefs or practices, so that the root of the term is clearly based in the common Muslim religion of the two groups. Indian Muslims, however, are not referred to by this term.

3. This dish is sometimes called "mush" in the ethnographic, and other, literature but is too dense to be eaten with a spoon. It is eaten by using the thumb and first two fingers to break off a quantity from a bowl and roll this into a ball with the tips of the first three digits. Rice is eaten in the same way, and, given the Swahili preference for cooking that results in the grains retaining their individuality, a good deal of dexterity is required to dip the rice "ball" into its sauce or gravy (*machuzi*) without dribbling on one's face, clothes, and the mat on which one is seated.

4. A number of Swahili strongly supported the Germans in World War II, and there was a baraza whose main topic of daily conversation was the latest news that indicated German strength and success. Such actions as the rationing of rice may have had a role in the anti-British, pro-German feeling, which, however, had strong and deep roots in, inter alia, the antislavery campaigns and their promotion of Christian missions over the decades since they assumed an active role on the coast.

5. Stroebel calls these societies *lelemama* after the dance that they most frequently performed (e.g., 1979:56–58). Informants, however, consistently called these groups "vyama" when they mentioned them to me.

6. According to Stroebel, the competitive dancing involving women's groups still continued in the 1970s among women in Mombasa who were not considered waungwana by Twelve Tribes members (1979:181), but I have never succeeded in witnessing it. I was told of the existence of vyama similar to those of Old Town in another section of town among women, including, I was told, the descendants of slaves of Swahili families, whom the Old Town Swahili consider not to be of their group.

7. The boys in the sectionally based soccer teams do not seem to be interested in, or even aware of, the sectional differences between teams. The teams are formed according to neighborhood, and these are based on sectional alignment. This lack of explicit intention or awareness, however, does not prevent the long-standing sectional opposition from being reinforced by the competition between the teams since they unite with their teammates and against the opposition regardless of their not using the names "Nine Tribes" or "Three Tribes."

8. Gluckman (1963:1–2) makes a concise statement of these dynamics in his BBC lectures:

> This is the central theme of my lectures—how men quarrel in terms of certain of their customary allegiances, but are restrained from [community-destroying] violence through other conflicting allegiances which are also enjoined on them by custom. The result is that conflicts in one set of relations, over a wider range of society or through a longer period of time, lead to the re-establishment of social cohesion.

9. The "secret wives" are seemingly rather rare now, but they still exist and are sometimes referred to as *suria,* "slave wife," as they were when they actually had that status. Informants say that men took some of these wives from among the descendants of their family's slaves, as their fathers and grandfathers had from the slaves

themselves, until just a decade or two ago, and according to some informants, this is still occurring. However, the rising cost of living is making it difficult for most men to support more than one household. In my long experience among the Swahili, I know of only one man who has two wives whom he openly treats as such and who are publicly known to be his wives. In this case, one wife is a Swahili and the other is a member of another ethnic group from which some Swahili slaves came.

10. The Swahili value *siri,* privacy (secrecy is not too strong a word), and are extremely reluctant to discuss even the most prosaic personal matters such as how many children they have or who shares their houses. *Faut de mieux* much of my information comes from individuals who do not share the value on siri as strongly as the majority do. My only census data come from asking such individuals to tell me who lives in specific houses and how they are related to one another. During the fifteen years I visited the Swahili, I never overcame the general reluctance of most individuals, including some men with whom I maintained friendships of years' duration, to discuss even routine family matters. The sources of this reluctance are examined in chapter 4, but there can be no doubt that it has limited my information, as it will, I am certain, the work of any others who study this community.

11. The word "baraza" refers to the benches built into the front of a common style of Swahili house and the gatherings of men that take place, ideally on these benches, on a fairly regular basis—usually between the *magharibi* (postsunset) and *isha* (final) prayers. The word *baraza* in standard Swahili (i.e., as taught in Kenyan schools) refers to the sitting room or reception room of a house and, by extension, to meetings held in such rooms. I wrote a good deal about the "baraza" among the Bena of Tanzania (e.g., Swartz 1966) where the term refers to dispute settlement sessions sometimes held in the reception room of a chief's or headman's house. This latter usage does not apply to the Swahili.

12. Until the late 1970s, weddings focused on the bride's virginity and, secondarily, on the groom's potency as demonstrated by bloody sheets brought out by the woman's sexual adviser (a grandmother or a woman descended from family slaves) and exhibited to the multitude with loud beating on a drum (see Swartz 1983). Informants say that this was extremely stressful for the groom and hardly less so for the bride, who had long been told that her wedding night would be the most painful experience of her life. The practice seems to have been abandoned as of the early 1980s. Now couples are married secretly, and the rather modest wedding celebration is held weeks after its consummation when the union is publicly announced.

4: He Who Eats with You:
Kinship, Family, and Neighborhood

1. In the Swahili language, gender is not noted, so the gloss "he/she" would be more nearly precise. Since it is cumbersome, I will follow general practice in the literature and use the masculine pronoun with the understanding that the original is without gender reference.

2. Up to and following World War II, the members of an mbari attended weddings as a subunit within their taifa (see chap. 2). Those giving the weddings distributed the materials for betel nut chewing by taifa (see chap. 2) with a subdistribution by mbari.

3. It is worth noting that a term, *wajoli* (sing. *mjoli*), is used among people who were, or whose families were, slaves belonging to the same family of waungwana (i.e., free-born community members). Wajoli is not a kin term, but I am told (I have never heard it actually used and would be surprised if it still were since the status of slave descendant has very few openly avowed members) that it is a way of calling attention to the fact that those who refer to one another by it are "like kin," as one informant put it.

4. Several young men who were in conflict with their fathers told me that they did not have to worry about their fathers withholding radhi because there was no proper basis for the fathers to do that. Only, they claimed, if they behaved contrary to Koranic prescriptions would God actually give weight to a father's, or presumably a mother's, withholding of radhi.

5. Fathers, like mothers, say of a child who has behaved in an intolerable way, "Matumbo yangu hakuzaa" (My womb has not borne), i.e., they disclaim the child as not being their issue.

6. Cousin marriage is viewed as "easier" in that the parents of the new couple know one another and are unlikely to raise any difficulties. A badly regarded young man (generally so because of rowdiness, poor prospects, or bad reputation) is likelier to marry a cousin than a nonrelative because, I was told, the bride's family "wants to help their relative." Similarly, a young woman with a bad reputation (much rarer than for males) will also marry a cousin more often than a nonrelative, and the same is true for women who simply have no outsiders asking to marry them. Cousin marriage is also easier because quarrels between the spouses are likelier to be adjudicated by their families rather than exacerbated.

7. Elderly women, but not men, are properly greeted with the expression, *Shika mo* (said to be a form of "shika mgoo," embrace [your] foot) as a sign of the respect in which they are held, and this is true not only of kin of the parental and grandparental generation but of all elderly members of the community.

8. Not giving money to sons may contribute to a man's positive evaluation in the father status when the evaluation is by other fathers, neighbors, and, sometimes, wives. The evaluation by the son, however, is at least sometimes highly negative and the father is evaluated as not having shown love. As chapter 8 shows in detail, the importance of the statuses of both the evaluated and of the evaluator are quite as important in determining judgments for general expectations as it is for specific.

9. There are Swahili in the restricted sense I am using the term who live outside Old Town in the area immediately to the west of the boundary formed by the Digo Road. Because of my focus on the Old Town group, I spent time in only one household in this area, called Majengo, whose residents are mainly members of Mijikenda and inland (*barani*) ethnic groups. Old Town Swahili say that the descendants of slaves once owned by Swahili families live here as well as some waungwana who through financial reverses, sometimes generations before, lost their Old Town homes. This last may be why the family I visited was here rather than in Old Town, but I never established that that was so.

10. A woman was weeping inconsolably at the funeral of her stepfather who had not married the woman's mother until the woman was fully mature. "Mazoeizi," she wept, "mbaya kuliko upenzi" (Accustomedness is worse [more painful] than love).

11. People do rent rooms in their houses to nonrelatives, but the few cases I have

both census data for and a personal knowledge of who lives in the house suggest that "roomers" are not included in answer to questions about who lives in the house.

12. The verb and noun should be in quotes because adoption involves the adoptive parents taking on the sole rights and duties of parents, whereas this is not the case, as will become clear, with *wazee walezi* ("adoptive" parents) who share these rights with the *wazee wazaazi* (birth parents). For the sake of brevity, however, I will henceforth use "adopted" without quotes.

13. *Hanithi* is a word that applies to passive homosexual males and also to men who are impotent. A community member with serious physical disabilities was said to have remarked several times that he would prefer to be referred to as "hawezi" (He is unable) rather than as "hanithi."

14. It is impossible to say precisely how many girls and young women I have talked to over the years. In 1976 and 1980, my friend, the late Gamal Khan, arranged group interviews for me with Swahili students at Coast Girls' High School. There were a total of 65 in those interviews, but less than half participated actively. In addition, I have interviewed 23 girls and young women in private sessions at their homes or the homes of their relatives. I have had no group interviews with boys or young men but have had private, lengthy interviews with 17 and briefer talks with many more.

15. In a third case, a young woman was to marry a Persian Gulf Arab who was going to take her with him when he returned to his homeland. She did not directly oppose her family's decision but expressed serious misgivings about leaving Mombasa, her friends, and relatives and living in a society where the restrictions on women are greater than they are in contemporary Old Town. She was subsequently possessed by a *pepo* (a *djin* or spirit) who, when asked by a spirit medium (*mganga*) what she, the possessing spirit, wanted, replied through the medium, "Sitaki kilembe. Nataka msuti" (I don't want a turban [man]. I want a suit-man [i.e., a "modern" man]). Her parents called off the wedding and she recovered.

16. A young man told me that there are young, unmarried women in the community who are willing to engage in anal or oral sex but not intercourse because they want to preserve their virginity. Although another young man agreed this was so when I asked, a number of others denied it and said that few if any community women will engage in sexual activity of any kind before marriage even if there is reason to think they would like to.

5: Understanding Is Like Hair: Limited Cultural Sharing and the Inappropriateness of "All by All" and "Some by Some" Models for Swahili Culture

1. Children under 12 years of age were excluded, as were married children.

2. A fuller description of Kahl and La Jolla can be found in Swartz 1982a:317–318. Comparisons involving various aspects of cultural sharing among the Swahili and all four of the other groups in that earlier study are found in the 1982 paper.

3. A rather different and less satisfactory explanation for this is offered in Swartz 1982a:323–324.

4. Since in Wallace's view, there is only very limited sharing, but social life goes on, its basis must be provided through what he called "the organization of diversity"

(1970:24). Wallace's own view about the relation between culture and social life is somewhat obscured by his taking what seems to be two different positions on the definition of "culture." First, he tells us, "culture . . . becomes not so much a superorganic entity, but policy tacitly and gradually concocted by groups of people for the furtherance of their interests, and contract, established by practice, between and among individuals to organize their strivings into mutually facilitating equivalence structures" (ibid.). Culture, as defined in this statement as a contract, obviously influences social processes. Later (ibid., 37), however, he approvingly quotes Radcliffe-Brown's remark, "To say of culture patterns that they act upon an individual . . . is as absurd as to hold a quadratic equation capable of committing a murder."

6: Close One of Your Eyes: Concealing Differences between the Generations and the Uses of "Tokens"

1. I am told that the Swahili shave off all body hair save that around the eyes. Beards are seen in Old Town, of course, but those having them are either unconnected to the Swahili community (often unassimilated Ibadhi Muslims from Oman) or young men of the sort to be discussed in this chapter.

2. "Adoption," discussed in chap. 4., presents a special case. The adopted children are treated as "own children" by the adoptive parents (often siblings of the birth parents), but the birth parents retain their interest and concern as well.

3. I am grateful to Michael Downs for doing this coding.

4. Some Swahili have a small callus in the middle of their foreheads. A young man told me that some young people, when no one is around, rub their foreheads against wood or other substances to induce and speed the formation of the callus. It is understood that a callus on the forehead comes from much prayer, involving, as the evolutions in the five-times-a-day prayer performed by all pious Muslims do, pressing the forehead on the ground. A callus is, therefore, a token of piety based on the understandings that guide prayer and given by its owners to all those who notice it.

5. The possibility that a certain proportion of what is found in the ethnographic literature must be viewed as tokens, rather than guides, deserves serious consideration.

7: Liking Only Those In Your Eye: Relationship Terms, Statuses, and Cultural Models

1. There is no necessity for statuses to have names, although many do. They are recognized, both by observers and community members, according to members meeting criteria set out in understandings that may, but need not, include their being labeled in speech. Those who follow the understandings that are called "etiquette" in English are labeled as "polite" in English, and this is a status label. So far as I know, there is no commonly used label of a comparable sort in the Swahili language as used in Old Town, although the term "mpole" is used this way by members of at least some other groups who speak Swahili as a second language. Nevertheless, those Swahili who are considered to follow the understandings concerning proper greetings, what to say on getting and giving gifts, and so on are categorized together. They have

expectations associated with them when that category is taken as a salient one for them, and these do not apply to those not in this category.

2. I am both called and referred to as "Professor" in Old Town by all but my closest friends, who still use that title in reference but call me "Marc." During the fieldwork period, there had been no anthropologist working in Old Town, but there had been several historians and linguists. The idea that I was a student of Swahili society was taken to mean that I wanted to know about history, folk tales, proverbs, and language.

3. "Multiplex" and "simplex" apply to relationships. Extending the concepts to statuses has the difficulty that, as noted, the statuses in multiplex relations can be involved in simplex relations. Even though the reverse is not true, it may be that con fusion is possible from speaking of "multiplex statuses" instead of "the statuses involved in multiplex relationships." The economy in the less strict usage, however, justifies the risk.

4. A fair number of late-middle-aged and elderly Swahili women have spent their lives in the rather strict separation of the sexes (*tawa*) followed in this community and have never ridden a bus. Some of them call buses "Kenya" because the bus company operating within Mombasa is the Kenya Bus Company and has been for many years. When referring to the country, I have heard an elderly woman say "Kenya, si gari, nti" (Kenya, not the vehicle, the country).

5. Multiplex relationships can, of course, supersede simplex relationships, and the statuses appropriate to the simplex relationship may not be employed. I got on a *matatu* (a jitney bus) with a Swahili friend and the conductor did not ask my friend for his fare as he did everyone else. When I asked what happened, my friend told me that the conductor had been his pupil in school and never asked him for a fare. Even in these situations, however, the mutual identification is unavoidable if more complex.

6. During British rule, there were members of the Swahili community who held positions in the colonial administration. In addition to teachers in the government schools, Old Town men were employed in the native administration where they served under Britons but had substantial authority of their own. Their ranks were *kadhi* (judge in Islamic courts), *mudiri* (administrator of the second rank either supervising minor areas or being assistant administrators in larger ones), and *liwali* (top administrators in major areas so that there was a liwali for Mombasa and a superior one for the Coast Province).

7. The similarity of "general expectations" to legitimacy as a basis for political power is intended. "Compliance," I wrote regarding legitimacy, "is motivated by the belief (which may be only vaguely formulated) that at some time in the future . . . [the locus of legitimacy] will satisfy the compliers' expectations" (Swartz, Turner, and Tuden 1966:14–15).

8. While interviewing a group of high school girls, I said that although men of their own community had told me that girls and women were less rational than boys and men, I did not necessarily share that view. Hands shot up all over the room, and several girls heatedly said that it was God's will that girls and women be less rational than men but that that did not mean they were less intelligent or good. Why, they asked, was I denying what was obviously true, part of God's plan, and a perfectly honorable state for females?

9. The dialect of the Swahili language spoken in Mombasa, Kimvita, is one of the several dialects spoken in different Swahili communities along the coast. The Swahili spoken throughout Kenya as well as in Tanzania, Uganda, the eastern Sudan, northern Mozambique, and elsewhere is not viewed by the Swahili people as the true and proper version of their language. It is true that most non-Swahili who speak the language learned it in later childhood or adolescence as a lingua franca. It is the first language of the Swahili themselves whose version has not been subject to the decisions of the colonial Interterritorial Swahili Committee, which regularized the grammar and ruled on proper usage beginning in the 1920s and continuing until independence.

10. Adult men, over 30 or so, fought with weapons in the few accounts I have of their fighting. The traditional walking stick, bakora, was used as a weapon (see chap. 3), and at least some men carried a knife. Younger men are reported to fight with their hands when they fight, but this is also rare.

8: Tongues Are Spears:
Shame and Differentiated Conformity

1. The Swahili word that I am rendering as "a-i-b-u" can also be spelled "a-y-b-u." The difference represents a slight difference in pronunciation, and following fairly close attention to the word while in Old Town in summer 1988, I am inclined to believe that the spelling used here is nearer the way most community members pronounce the word. Akida et al. (1981:4) is the only dictionary listing the term and the spelling there is a-i-b-u.

2. Acknowledged polygyny, as noted in chapter 4, is extremely rare, but polygyny involving secret marriages may be more common. As would be true anywhere, getting information about such practices is difficult. In this community it is, if anything, even more so.

3. Predictability is necessary to continuing social relations, but it is not sufficient. Most who are familiar with lions confidently predict that they will eat you. This does not usually lead to a social relationship.

4. It is not entirely clear where mature women and young women fit in this. My mainly male informants say that the youths who misbehave are always male and that the mature women are not around (being subject to tawa, the separation of the sexes) to see them doing it, so that it is always young men who become sick because of their misbehavior in the presence of mature men. It could be that young women who misbehave in the presence of mature women also become sick from mato ya wazima, but I have no information on this to indicate whether this is or is not so.

5. This seems to function in the way jito, the evil eye, does but is said to be entirely different in that husudu, jealousy, is absent.

6. Most informants say that women and girls should not go to the movies as a general part of their not going out in public save for school and, increasingly, work. Some families, however, allow their daughters to go to the special women's showing of Indian films that are mainly patronized by women from the large Indian Muslim community in Mombasa. In the mid-1980s, I have seen young Swahili women attending Western films with other women, their brothers, or, sometimes, their husbands.

9: Leaning on the Cow's Fat Hump: Medical Choices, Unshared Culture, and General Expectations

1. My research on understandings concerning the body and illness was in two distinct phases. I spent a good part of the time I was in Old Town during summer 1987 interviewing three practitioners of what they and others said was "traditional Swahili medicine." I also talked to a number of other informants who viewed themselves as "interested" in medical matters and who proved to be remarkably well informed. This last group included women who are known for their medical knowledge by their families and neighbors and who sometimes actually treat the latter, something men who were not "doctors" seem never to do. I returned in summer 1988 and spent most of my visit interviewing people, chosen because they were willing to be interviewed and had reported themselves as ill or having recently been ill. These informants were not screened for their knowledge of or interest in medical matters or their lack of it. I also interviewed some who advised the first group on how to deal with their illnesses.

2. The Republic of Kenya provides its citizens with free medical care at government facilities including a number in Mombasa and a large hospital in Old Town itself. Medications have to be bought, however, and a considerable number of the members of the Swahili community consult private physicians and use one of the several private hospitals in Mombasa. Private physicians were charging between $2 and $5 for a consultation in 1987. Medications are mainly imported but are not subject to import duty and seem slightly less expensive than in the United States. Given the incomes of Swahili families where more than $3,500 a year is considered prosperous and half of that is taken as an acceptable income for a small family, these fees and costs are by no means low, but many people manage to meet them anyway.

3. This herbal doctor rejected my offer of $12 for an hour or less of interviewing but, in the end, saw me and answered my questions willingly and without charge. The other two herbal doctors were obviously quite pleased with their honorarium, and I am quite sure I would not have been able to continue interviewing them had I not paid it.

4. These twigs are sold at small shops throughout the Swahili section of Mombasa. They are typically cut from either one of two trees, *Salvadorus persica* or *Dobera loranthifolia,* but vendors sometimes substitute others when these are not available.

5. All treatment involves the danger of side effects resulting from the excessive effectiveness of the treatment or from an unwanted interaction of the disease and its treatment. Excess success in removing an excess can result in the appearance of symptoms of a new excess that is opposite to the one originally being treated. For example, the attempt to lessen excess hot can produce symptoms, or even full-blown illnesses, of excess cold or the treatment can lead to excess hot, manifesting itself in abdominal difficulties and expressing itself in pain in the teeth, neck, and jaws. Some part of the tabibu's skill consists in his or her ability to compound medications that, together with the prescribed diet, will correct the existing imbalance without inducing a new one.

6. A "penny" is a Kenyan ten-penny piece that weighs approximately 28 grams.

7. The Swahili do have understandings that hold individuals can be harmed by the malice of others in rather the same way the Azande do. Some of these have been

mentioned in chap. 7 where envy was seen to be a destructive force through the operation of mato, the evil eye. In addition, Swahili understandings include those that see persons of bad will as able to use jins as agents or to employ sorcerers from other ethnic groups to harm their enemies. When people whisper of an illness, *kuna mkono wa mtu* (there is the hand of a person), they are referring to sorcery in most instances. However, most Swahili do not understand most illness to result from "the hand of a person," and a considerable number believe that illness is never caused in this way.

8. The hypothesis that the relationship goes the other way—that the views of social morality are strengthened by the importance of balance in body understandings—cannot be dismissed, of course. My evidence about this hypothesis is slender, but it may well be true or, as is even more likely, the understandings strengthen each other through an interaction.

9. It could be that the patients had no very well formulated view of how the body worked but, nevertheless, thought that herbal doctors—or, equally possibly, hospital doctors—had views they approved of. There is, however, no evidence to support this view. Patients seemed either surprised at or uninterested in the implied suggestion that they might have substantial views of the body's functioning and illness's sources or that they should be concerned about the correspondence between their own understandings of how illness comes about or is cured and those of the therapists who treat them. In most cases, informants seemed indifferent to differences in approaches to illness and were concerned only with success in treating it.

10. My work with the Bena who live several hundred miles south of the Fipa shows that Bena laymen have understandings about disease similar to those of the Fipa, but, unlike the Fipa, many of the same understandings were held by Bena experts as by Bena laymen (Swartz 1969b). It is notable that jealousy is understood by laymen, experts, or both as a major source of illness in such diverse African societies as Fipa, Bena, and Swahili as well as in societies on other continents such as the Gujerati of India (Pocock 1973). The relation of jealousy to illness suggests the presence of some cultural organizations of similar sorts in quite different societies despite differences in economics, religion, kinship, and politics.

11. Advertising provides a set of understandings that can be used in place of those allowing the patient to choose a course based on his or her view of what is causing the illness. These understandings conveyed by advertising are often very broad, suggesting the suitability of what is advertised to a variety of problems. One of the most commonly encountered ads in Kenya is for Aspro, a headache, fever, and cold medicine. Its motto is *Aspro ni dawa ya kweli* (lit. Aspro is medicine of truth/genuine[ness], i.e., Aspro is genuine or true medicine).

12. The Walimu pray in the ordinary way for a sick person's recovery or for the preservation of his or her health. A few of them also provide a sort of medicine by writing Koranic verses in henna on plates and then putting water on the plates. The patient drinks the water with the dissolved henna in it.

13. As noted in the preface, the difficulties in getting informants in this community makes all data-gathering difficult. It would have been preferable to have as many male informants as female, but there is no evidence to indicate that what is said here applies only to women and that men have a broad and general set of understandings about medical care or get advice from people with whom they have simplex relationships. Similarly, the advisers of the patients in the original sample I was able to talk with

were all parents (8) or spouses (4), and I was not able to interview any advisers who were neighbors, siblings, or co-workers. I do not believe this affected the findings.

14. Garro (1986) found that there was little difference between curers and non-curers in the specific cultural elements shared, but curers and older people shared more with one another than young people shared among themselves. This latter part of Garro's findings are similar to those here in that advisers, who are older than patients in the Swahili group, do share more medical understandings with curers than young people share among themselves. It is not true in the Swahili group, however, that curers and others differ little in what they share. This may well be true because of the technical nature of what the "curers" (i.e., herbal doctors and hospital doctors) share in Mombasa as compared to what is shared among the comparable group in Garro's study.

15. The Swahili, as noted in chaps. 1 and 2, speak the Kimvita dialect of the Swahili language. Older people sometimes complain about outsiders (i.e., those who are not Swahili from any of the recognized communities along the coast) misusing the language and, especially, its form as taught in the schools of Kenya and used in public life. Everyone understands standard Swahili, and all but the oldest people can speak it without difficulty, but some are not pleased by it and avoid situations where they must use it.

10: A Wife Is Clothes: Family Politics, Cultural Organization, and Social Structure

1. In fact, cultural organization is not exactly the "result" of cultural distribution since the latter is partly as it is because of cultural organization. The nature of the relations among cultural elements is affected by the expectations in statuses and their roles since, in part, the expectations in relationships preclude following some understandings in favor of following others and require that yet others never be allowed to guide behavior in the relationship. In this and related ways, cultural distribution affects cultural organization. At the same time, the cultural elements are distributed among statuses, in part according to what is understood as more, less, and not at all appropriate for the different categories of people. This last is clearly a case of organization influencing distribution. Some cultural organization is governed by understandings alone and has nothing to do with their distribution (e.g., it is always better to be healthy than sick), but that source of organization aside, it is probably true that cultural distribution and organization are always in interaction.

2. Stroebel (1979:57) seems to interpret the proverb that opens this chapter to mean that a woman's clothes are among the things she can expect from her husband according to Muslim law. My slightly different view is that the proverb is used to mean that just as you cannot have a banana plant if it is not weeded, you cannot have a wife if you fail to provide clothes for her, and, in both, the requirements are taxing.

3. Holland (1987:240–243) reports a general tendency for the American college women she studied to exhibit more intense emotion about both gender types and school types than the men she studied did. Even if this difference in affectivity is generalizable beyond Holland's study, there may still be differences between her American college students and the Swahili in that the latter not only expect women to be more

emotional than men but they also say they *should* be, whereas that may not be so for the American sample.

4. Active relationships among women from different neighborhoods and, even, from different parts of the same neighborhood have become less frequent and less important over the period from 1975 and 1988 during which I did fieldwork. With the decline of large weddings, the occasions for large groups of women to gather have become less common, and the greater unwillingness of people to venture into the streets of Old Town, especially at night, has added to this.

5. During World War II, I was told, there was a pro-German baraza that devoted much of its attention to news or speculation indicating that the Germans were winning the war. This baraza began to break up after D day and was no more before the Allies crossed the Rhine. Despite some considerable proportion of the community favoring the British and their allies, there seems not to have been a particular pro-British baraza. This may be because most of the news-oriented barazas were mainly pro-British anyway.

6. There is a proverb that is mainly used by women who would like to stay and chat with a neighbor but are forced by the necessity of their household tasks to leave: *Mwenye kibiongo halali kwa tani*: The hunchback does not lie on his back; i.e., unavoidable necessity prevents one from doing what one wants to do.

7. This is one of those findings that needs to be handled with care. Sons who are willing to talk about relations with their fathers thereby demonstrate their rejection of the understandings holding that family matters should be kept strictly within the family, so that, given the importance assigned these understandings, few of them are likely to be among those deeply committed to the family as a group. This does not mean their information is false or worthless but only that it must be recognized that it comes from a rather special sort of family member and must be looked at together with other data.

8. There is some disagreement in the community as to whether saying, "You are not my wife" three times constitutes a divorce regardless of whether it is said on the same occasion or whether each *talaka* (pl. *talaka*, as the divorcing statement is called) must be pronounced on a quite different occasion, normally a different day. In both cases, the reason there must be three, informants report, is that it would be wrong to divorce a wife in anger and the multiple talaka help ensure serious and enduring intent.

9. As noted in chap. 4, Stroebel's (1979:88) estimate of the divorce rate is one of every two marriages. Her estimate was arrived at in a way quite different from mine.

11: The Dynamics of Swahili Culture: A Status-Centered View

1. This "basis for evaluation" is usually the behavior *in* the interaction, but sometimes it also includes accounts or other indications of the behavior of others not now in interaction.

2. The initial definition is also faulty in its failure to note explicitly that "culture" includes all understandings shared by any two group members. This omission has been dealt with in the discussions of the culture concept in chap. 1, chap. 5, and earlier in this chapter.

3. The few men who would talk to me about sexual matters agreed that sex with

a wife may be more restrained than is desirable, with this being especially true if she is a kinswoman, as the "main" wife is in a large minority of marriages. A suria, a "slave" wife, which is what most secret wives are, is never a true member of the Swahili community. She is often the child of a family once owned by a Swahili family, sometimes that of her husband. She does not command the deference a kin wife does and may not share the understanding, mentioned by several men, that a woman should not show pleasure lest she be thought an mkware, a woman with a strong—and dangerous—interest in sex. Since men are actually married (it requires only a single other male believer to solemnize a marriage) to their "secret wives," there is no sin involved however enraged the "main" wife and her family would be should they find out about the marriage.

4. It may well be that no one needs to hold an understanding in order for it to be an effective influence on behavior so long as there is a belief that such an understanding is held by others. The Bena of Tanzania believe sorcery to be common, and many of their fellows practice it. Much of what many members of this group do is influenced by the understanding that sorcerers exist and have a body of understandings they follow in order to harm others (Swartz 1969).

It may well be, however, that, in fact, there are no developed understandings concerned with the details of ensorcelling people. That this may be so is suggested by the fact that all accused sorcerers denied that they knew anything about, much less practiced, sorcery. This denial would be expected since sorcery is severely punished, but the absence is also suggested by the fact that a number of Bena, having unable to find instruction in sorcery locally, had traveled hundreds of miles to the coast in the belief that sorcery techniques could be learned there. These travelers returned disappointed, complaining that they could find no one to instruct them there either. At the same time, people from the coast come to the Bena area to learn magic, and they too returned home having learned nothing except that sorcery.

5. Spiro's distinctions among levels of holding cultural elements is crucial here. "Sharing" understandings may entail holding understandings in such a way that they instigate behavior or, as here, involve nothing more than believing others hold the understandings. I am speaking of the latter as "not sharing," in the sense that sharing would involve at least some commitment to and influence by the understanding.

6. Gearing (1976a:184–187), 1976b) presents a strong case for the importance of interaction, "transaction" in "encounters" is how he phrases it, as a means whereby the cognitive mappings of different individuals come to change through association with one another, i.e., as they influence one another.

7. Statuses are always important to establishing situations and generally so outweigh other factors that they often seem to do it by themselves. The setting, the clothing of those involved, or even the kind of speech used can be important in establishing a situation, but these are almost always status identifiers and not independent determinants. If men always assumed the status "worshiper" when in a mosque, the setting would be a prior determinant of the situation. Since, however, other considerations affect the statuses assumed in the mosque (where men lounge and chat between prayers and where, sometimes, homeless men sleep at night), this setting is only a very partial status determinant as many other things are. Statuses are not, of course, assumed at whim. Sometimes they are produced by events external to the relationships of those present, and these events are the main determinant of the statuses and of the situation.

If the roof of the mosque were to fall in during prayer, the statuses of the worshipers would quickly become something else and the situation would cease to be one of prayer.

8. Group members never explicitly mention the understandings about how one should dress when asked what understandings are broadly shared. These understandings are almost surely part of that very large class that are similar to the rules of language in being broadly shared and followed but neither explicit nor consciously available without the prompting provided by the actual situation.

9. Ritual seems a likely source of tokens meeting the requirements just noted. In many rituals, those involved see others behaving in ways highly similar to their own, indicating a similarity of understanding fundamental to mutual prediction. More than this the similar behaviors—speech, singing, body movements—are concerned with the sacred, suggesting to at least some of those involved that the common actions imply that they are united in having similar views about nothing less than the nature of the supernatural and the meanings of existence. This believed-in similarity may well serve as an important foundation for confidence in the predictability of coparticipants in the rituals. Unlike Tuzin's residence "rules," behavior outside the exchange of tokens (i.e., in extraritual settings) is unlikely to contradict the tokens' import in any direct and unambiguous way. This is so because the ritual entails no directly observable behaviors beyond those involved in its own performance.

10. Holy and Stuchlik's (1981:26–30) discussion of the influence on social life of what they call "folk models" examines the ability of these models to influence and be influenced by other behaviors. I quite agree with the view about the dialectical relationship between models and action. Which relationship terms the Swahili use in which settings has to do with who is involved, what the goals of those involved are, and what their salient statuses are in the relationship in question. My interest, however, is to call attention to the ways cultural models presented through relationship terms operate to enhance awareness of and formity to common standards in interaction. I do not wish to suggest that their "political" significance (i.e., how they are used in individuals' pursuit of their own goals) be overlooked but only that their broadly cultural importance be noted.

11. The evaluation made by the mother is of "son as employee," which is a combination of the two statuses "son" and "employee" and uses expectations from both. The son, however, need not combine expectations from the two statuses in guiding his behavior as an employee, though it is common enough for actors to combine expectations in multiplex roles with the expectations they are guided by in the statuses they occupy in simplex roles.

12. The term "wazima," mature person, is not limited to those who are what I call "arbiters." Anyone who is 35 or so is an *mzima* (plural *wazima*), but only the most prestigious men among these are in the category I call arbiters.

13. This is the situation Gluckman with Mitchell and Barnes (1963) tellingly portrayed in showing that the village headman could not "win." If what he did pleased his colonial superiors, it displeased his village constituents and vice versa. Academic department heads sometimes portray themselves as in the same, impossible situation with respect to their colleagues, on the one hand, and the administration of the university, on the other.

14. It may be that in other societies evaluations in simplex relationships are as weighty, or even more so, than those in multiplex relationships. The values involving "independence" in "modern" cities suggest this, although the urban Swahili do not show it.

15. What leads people to make such interpretations is an extremely vital and, so far, unanswered question. Like legitimacy in politics, where "legitimacy" is used to refer to such beliefs as that a leader will "bring peace," "promote justice," or "establish general prosperity," the processes whereby general expectations are established and continued, as well as those by which they are deracinated, are little understood and deserve investigation.

16. The similarity between "general expectations" and "legitimacy," as well as between "specific expectations" and "coercion," as I have used the concepts in political analysis (e.g., Swartz 1967:30–37, 1975), is intended. I hope to explore their similarities further in subsequent studies.

17. It may be that people have different identifying understandings that lead to similar conclusions. That is, although it is true that all Swahili—and surely members of all other communities—identify those who are closest to them with unfailing reliability and are very frequently identified similarly by those others, it may be that different individuals use different means for doing this. If there were a substantial number of highly correlated "signs," such a finding would not be surprising. Thus, A recognizes B as a "friend" because B tells A things that would be shameful if told to others. B recognizes A as a "friend" because B can ask A for money or food whenever he wants to. The understandings that lead to these identifications are different, but they are highly correlated. Anyone you can ask for money or food is also someone who can be told things without shame and vice versa.

18. One of the most frequently used of these is the rather surprising, given who says it, "Your mother's cunt."

19. The established practice of calling cultural products "material culture" is not only a contradiction in terms but also blunts analysis by failing to direct attention to the consequences of the understandings that guide people in producing and using the products.

References

Adair, J., and E. Vogt
   1949   Navaho and Zuni veterans: A study of contrasting modes of cultural change. *AA* 51(4):547–560.
Adams, Richard N.
   1975   Energy and Structure. Austin: University of Texas Press.
Akida, Hamisis, et al.
   1981   Kamusi Ya Kiswahili Sanifu. Dar es Salaam: Oxford University Press.
Akong'a, Joshua J.
   1979   Social training: Perspectives on obedience and autonomy in boys among the Swahili of Old Town, Mombasa and the upper middle class of La Jolla, California. Ph.D. dissertation, Anthropology Department, University of California, San Diego.
Allen, J. DeV.
   1982   The "Shirazi" problem in East African coastal history. *Paideuma* 28: 9–27.
   1983   Shungwaya, the Mijikenda and the traditions. *Int. J. Afr. Hist. Stud.* 16(3):455–485.
Arens, William
   1975   The Waswahili: The social history of an ethnic group. *Africa* 45:428–438.
Beer, William
   1980   The concept of the person in the Hellenic intellectual tradition in Islam. M.A. thesis, Anthropology Department, University of Chicago.
Benedict, Ruth
   1934   Patterns of Culture. New York: Houghton Mifflin.
Berg, F. J.
   1968   The Swahili community of Mombasa, 1500–1900. *J. Afr. Hist.* 9(1): 35–56.

1971   Mombasa under the Busaidi Sultanate: The city and its hinterland in the 19th century. Ph.D. dissertation, University of Wisconsin.

Berg, F. J., and B. J. Walter
1968   Mosques, population and urban development in Mombasa. In B. A. Ogot (ed.), Hadith 1. Nairobi: East African Publishing House.

Berlin, B., and P. Kay
1969   Basic Color Terms: Their Universality and Evolution. Berkeley and Los Angeles: University of California Press.

Bern, John
1979   Politics in a secret male ceremony. *JAR* 35:47–60.

Bott, Elizabeth
1971   Family and Social Network: 2d ed. New York: The Free Press (1st ed. 1957).

Bourdieu, Pierre
1977   Outline of a Theory of Practice. Cambridge: Cambridge University Press.

Bujra, Janet
1968   An anthropological study of political action in a Bajuni village in Kenya. Ph.D. dissertation, Anthropology Department, University of London.

Caplan, A. P.
1969   Cognatic descent groups on Mafia Island. *Man* 4:46–54.
1975   Choice and Constraint in a Swahili Community: Property, Hierarchy, and Cognatic Descent on the East African Coast. London, New York, and Nairobi: International African Institute by Oxford Press.

Caws, Peter
1974   Operational, representational, and explanatory models. *AA* 76(1):1–10.

Cicourel, Aaron V.
1987   The interpretation of communicative contexts: Examples from medical encounters. *Soc. Psych. Quarterly* 50(2):217–226.
1988   Aspects of formal and tacit distributed knowledge in the collaborative organization of medical diagnostic reasoning. Unpublished manuscript.

Cooper, Fredrick
1977   Plantation Slavery on the East Coast of Africa. New Haven and London: Yale University Press.

Dahl, Robert A.
1968   Power. *In* David L. Sills (ed.), International Encyclopedia of the Social Sciences. Vol. 12. New York: Macmillan and the Free Press. Pp. 405–415.

D'Andrade, Roy
1984   Cultural meaning systems. *In* R. Schweder and R. LeVine (eds.), Cultural Theory. Cambridge: Cambridge University Press.
1985   Character terms and cultural models. *In* Janet Dougherty (ed.), Directions in Cognitive Anthropology. Urbana: University of Illinois Press.
1987   Modal responses and cultural expertise. *Am. Behav. Scientist* 31(2):194–202.
n.d.   Cultural cognition. *In* M. Posner (ed.), Foundations of Cognitive Science. Cambridge: MIT Press. In press.

DeBlij, Harm Jan
    1968   Mombasa: An African City. Evanston: Northwestern University Press.
Douglas, Mary
    1966   Purity and Danger. London and Henley: Routledge and Kegan Paul.
    1970   Natural Symbols. New York: Pantheon Books.
    1975   Implicit Meanings: Essays in Anthropology. London, Henley, and Boston: Routledge and Kegan Paul.
Durkheim, Emile
    1949   The Division of Labor in Society. Glencoe: Free Press. Pp. 128–129.
    1961   Elementary Forms of the Religious Life. New York: Collier Books.
Eastman, Carol
    1971   Who are the Waswahili? *Africa* 41:228–236.
    1979   "Culture-loaded" vocabularies and language resurrection. *CA* 20(2):401–402.
    1984   Language, ethnic identity, and change. *In* Carol Eastman (ed.), Linguistic Minorities. London: Academic Press.
    1985   Establishing social identity through language use. *J. Lang. Soc. Psych.* 4(1):1–20.
    1988   Women, slaves and foreigners: African cultural influence and group processes in the formation of northern Swahili coastal society. *Int. J. Afr. Hist. Stud.* 21(1):1–20.
Eastman, C. M., and M. T. Topan
    1967   The Siu: Notes on the people and their language, Swahili. *J. Inst. Swahili Res.* 36(1):24–48.
Epstein, A. L.
    1984   The experience of shame in Melanesia: An essay in the anthropology of affect. RAI Occasional Paper No. 40.
Erikson, Erik
    1950   Childhood and Society. New York: Norton and Co.
Evans-Pritchard, E. E.
    1937   Witchcraft, Oracles, and Magic among the Azande. Oxford: Oxford University Press.
Fernandez, J.
    1965   Symbolic consensus in a Fang reformative cult. *AA* 67:902–929.
    1974   The Mission of Metaphor in an Expressive Culture. *CA* 15:2,119–145.
    1982   Bwiti: An Ethnography of the Religious Imagination in Africa. Princeton: Princeton University Press.
Fortes, Meyer
    1953   The structure of unilineal descent groups. *AA* 55:25–39.
Frake, Charles
    1962   Cultural ecology and ethnography. *AA* 64:53–59.
Freeman-Grenville, G. S. P.
    1963   The Coast, 1498–1840. *In* R. Oliver and G. Mathew (eds.), History of East Africa. London: Oxford at the Clarendon Press.
Garro, Linda
    1986   Intracultural variation in folk medical knowledge: A comparison between curers and non-curers. *AA* 88:351–370.

Gearing, F. O.
    1976a   Steps toward a general theory of cultural transmission. *In* J. I. Roberts
             and S. K. Akinsanya (eds.), Educational Patterns and Cultural Configu-
             rations. New York: David McKay. Pp. 183–194.
    1976b   A cultural theory of education. *In* J. I. Roberts and S. K. Akinsanya
             (eds.), Educational Patterns and Cultural Configuration. New York:
             David McKay. Pp. 194–205.
Geertz, Clifford
    1973a   The Interpretation of Cultures. New York: Basic Books.
    1973b   After the revolution: The fate of nationalism in the new states. *In* Clifford
             Geertz, The Interpretation of Culture. New York: Basic Books. Pp. 234–
             254.
    1973c   Thick description: Toward an interpretive theory of culture. *In* Clif-
             ford Geertz, The Interpretation of Culture. New York: Basic Books.
             Pp. 3–30.
Gluckman, Max
    1955   The Judicial Process among the Barotse of Northern Rhodesia. Manches-
             ter: Manchester University Press.
Gluckman, Max, with J. C. Mitchell and J. A. Barnes
    1963   The village headman in British Central Africa. *In* M. Gluckman (ed.),
             Order and Rebellion in Tribal Africa. London: Cohen and West.
Good, Byron
    1977   The Heart and what's the matter: The semantics of illness in Iran. *Cult.,
             Med. and Psych.* 2:125–128.
Goodenough, Ward
    1951   Property, Kin, and Community on Truk. New Haven: Yale University
             Publications in Anthropology No. 46.
    1965   Rethinking status and role. *In* Michael Banton (ed.), The Relevance of
             Models for Social Anthropology. London: Tavistock.
    1970   Description and Comparison in Cultural Anthropology. Chicago: Aldine.
    1971   Culture, Language, and Society. McCaleb Module in Anthropology.
             Reading, Mass.: Addison-Wesley.
Gouldner, A.
    1970   The Coming Crises in Western Sociology. New York: Basic Books.
Hallowell, A. I.
    1955   Culture and Experience. Philadelphia: University of Pennsylvania Press.
Harries, Lyndon
    1962   Swahili Poetry. Oxford: Oxford University Press.
Heider, Karl
    1970   The Dugum Dani: A Papuan Culture in the Highlands of West New
             Guinea. New York: Wenner Gren Foundation. No. 49 in Viking Fund
             Publications in Anthropology.
Holy, L., and M. Stuchlik (eds.)
    1981   The Structure of Folk Models. London: Academic Press.
Holland, Dorothy
    1985   Feelings about jocks: An interactionist corrective to the status-centered
             model of intracultural variation. Presented at the annual meeting of the
             AAA.

1987a   Culture sharing across gender lines: An interactionist corrective to the status-centered model. *Am. Behav. Scientist* 31(2):234–249.

1987b   Romantic identification, cultural transmission, and social reproduction. Paper presented at a symposium organized by Sally Lubek, "Cultural Acquisition and Modification through the Life Course," annual meeting of AAA, Chicago, November 1987.

Holland, Dorothy, and Naomi Quinn (eds.)

1987   Cultural Models in Language and Thought. Cambridge: Cambridge University Press.

Holland, Dorothy, and Debra Skinner

1987   Prestige and intimacy: The cultural models behind Americans' talk about gender types. *In* Dorothy Holland and Naomi Quinn (eds.), Cultural Models in Language and Thought. Cambridge: Cambridge Univesity Press. Pp. 78–111.

Horton, Mark

1986   Asiatic colonization of the East African coast. *J. Roy. Asiatic Soc. Britain and Ireland* 2(1986):202–213.

1987   The Swahili Corridor. *Sci. Am.* 257(3):86–93.

Horney, Karen

1937   The Neurotic Personality of Our Times. New York: W. W. Norton and Co.

Hutchins, Edwin

1985   The social organization of distributed cognition. Unpublished manuscript.

Johnson, Frederick

1959   A Standard Swahili-English Dictionary. London: Oxford University Press. Orig. ed. 1939.

Jordan, David, and Marc J. Swartz (eds.)

1990   Personality and the Cultural Constitution of Society. Tuscaloosa: University of Alabama Press.

Kasim el Mazrui, Mohammed

1952   Mirasi katika Sheria ya Kiislamu. Approved by Sh. Al Amin bin Aly. Mombasa: East African Muslim Welfare Society 50(2):217–226.

Keesing, Roger

1970   Toward a model of role analysis. *In* R. Naroll and R. Cohen (eds.), A Handbook of Method in Cultural Anthropology. New York: Natural History Press. Pp. 423–453.

1972a   Paradigms lost: The new ethnography and the new linguistics. *SJA* 28(4):299–332.

1972b   Simple models of complexity: The lure of kinship. *In* P. Reining (ed.), Kinship Studies in the Morgan Centennial Year. Washington, D.C.: Anthropological Society of Washington. Pp. 17–31.

1974   Theories of culture. *Ann. Review Anthro.* 3:73–98.

1978   'Elota's Story: The Life and Times of a Solomon Islands Big Man. St. Lucia: University of Queensland Press.

1979   Linguistic knowledge and cultural knowledge: Some doubts and speculations. *AA* 81:14–37.

1982   "Cultural rules": Methodological doubts and epistemological paradoxes. *Canberra Anthropology* 5:37–46.
1985   Conventional metaphors and anthropological metaphysics: The problem of cultural translation. *JAR* 41:27–39.
1987*a*   Anthropology as interpretive quest. *CA* 28:161–176.
1987*b*   Models, "folk" and "cultural": Paradigms regained? *In* Dorothy Holland and Naomi Quinn (eds.), Cultural Models in Thought and Language. Cambridge: Cambridge University Press. Pp. 369–394.

Kindy, Hyder
1972   Life and Politics in Mombasa. Nairobi: East African Publishing House.

Knappert, Jan
1970   Social and moral concepts in Swahili Islamic literature. *Africa* 40:125–136.
1979   Four Centuries of Swahili Poetry. Nairobi: Heinemann.

Krapf, L.
1882   A Dictionary of the Swahili Language. London: Trubner & Co. Reprinted 1969. New York: Negro Universities Press.

Lakoff, G., and M. Johnson
1980   Metaphors We Live By. Chicago: University of Chicago Press.

Lambert, H. E.
1958   Chi-Jomvu and Ki-Ngare; Sub-dialects of the Mombasa Area. Studies in Swahili Dialect 3. Kampala: East African Swahili Committee.

Linton, Ralph
1936   The Study of Man. New York: Appleton-Century-Crofts.

Malinowski, Bronislaw
1944   A Scientific Theory of Culture. Chapel Hill: University of North Carolina Press.
1960   The problem of meaning in primitive languages. *In* C. K. Ogden and I. A. Richards, The Meaning of Meaning. London: Routledge and Kegan Paul. (Orig. published 1923).

Martin, Esmond B.
1978   Cargoes of the East: The Ports, Trade, and Culture of the Arabian Seas and Western Indian Ocean. London: Elm Tree Books.

Mathew, Gervase
1963   The East African coast until the coming of the Portuguese. *In* R. Oliver and G. Mathew (eds.), History of East Africa. London: Oxford at the Clarendon Press.

Mirza, Sarah, and Margaret Stroebel
1989   Three Swahili Women. Bloomington and Indianapolis: Indiana University Press.

Mitchell, J. Clyde
1966   Theoretical orientations in African urban studies. *In* Michael Banton (ed.), The Social Anthropology of Complex Societies. ASA Monograph 4. New York and Washington, D.C.: Praeger.

Murphy, Michael D.
1978   Between the Virgin and the Whore: Local Community and the Nuclear

Family in Seville, Spain. Ph.D. dissertation, Anthropology Department, University of California, San Diego.

Nurse, Derek, and Thomas Spear
1985   The Swahili: Reconstructing the History and Language of an African Society, 800–1500. Philadelphia: University of Pennsylvania Press.

Obeyesekere, Gananath
1981   Medusa's Hair. Chicago: University of Chicago Press.

Oliver, Roland, and G. Mathew
1963   History of East Africa. I. London: Oxford at the Clarendon Press.

Opler, Morris
1945   Themes as dynamic forces in culture. Am. J. Soc. 51:198–206.

Ortner, Sherry B.
1984   Theory in anthropology since the sixties. Comp. Stud. Soc. Hist. 26: 126–166.

Parker, Carolyn
1974   Aspects of a theory of proverbs. Ph.D. dissertation in Anthropology. University of Washington.

Parsons, Talcott
1964   The Social System. 2d ed. Glencoe, Ill.: The Free Press of Glencoe. Orig. ed. 1951.

Pelto, J. P., and G. H. Pelto
1975   Intra-cultural diversity: Some theoretical issues. Am. Ethnol. 2:1–18.

Piers, Gerhart, and Milton B. Singer
1971   Shame and Guilt: A Psychoanalytic and a Cultural Study. New York: W. W. Norton and Co. Orig. ed. 1953.

Pitt-Rivers, Julian
1961   People of the Sierra. Chicago: University of Chicago Press.

Pocock, D. F.
1973   Mind, Body, and Wealth: A Study of Belief and Practice in an Indian Village. Oxford: Blackwell.

Pollnac, R. B.
1975   Intra-cultural variability in the structure of the subjective color lexicon in Buganda. Am. Ethnol. 2:89–109.

Pouwells, R.
1987   Horn and Crescent: Cultural Change and Traditional Islam on the East African Coast, 800–1900. Cambridge: Cambridge University Press.

Prins, A. H. J.
1967   Swahili-Speaking Peoples of Zanzibar and the East African Coast. 2d ed. London: International African Institute. Orig. ed. 1961.
1971   Didemic Lamu. Groningen: Instituut voor Culturele Anthropologie der Rijksuniversiteit.

Radcliffe-Brown, A. R.
1940   On joking relationships. Africa 13:195–210. Reprinted in A. R. Radcliffe-Brown, Structure and Function in Primitive Society. Glencoe, Ill.: The Free Press, 1952.
1949   A further note on joking relationships. Africa 14:133–140. Reprinted in

A. R. Radcliffe-Brown, Structure and Function in Primitive Society. Glencoe, Ill.: The Free Press. Pp. 105–116.

Reisman, Paul
1977   Freedom in Fulani Social Life. Chicago: University of Chicago Press.

Roberts, John M.
1951   Three Navaho households: A comparative study of small group culture. Peabody Museum of America Archaeology and Ethnology Papers, vol. 40, no. 3.
1964   The self-management of cultures. *In* W. Goodenough (ed.), Explorations in Cultural Anthropology: Essays in Honor of George Peter Murdock. New York: McGraw-Hill.

Rosen, Lawrence
1984   Bargaining for Reality: The Construction of Social Relations in a Muslim Community. Chicago: University of Chicago Press.

Salim, A. I.
1973   The Swahili-speaking Peoples of Kenya's Coast. Nairobi: East African Publishing House.

Sanday, P.
1968   The psychological reality of American-English kinship terms: An information processing approach. *AA* 70:508–523.

Sankoff, G.
1971   Qualitative analysis of sharing and variability in a cognitive model. *Ethnology* 10:389–408.

Saunders, George
1976   The family bond: Individual and communal experience in a modernizing Italian village. Ph.D. dissertation, Anthropology Department, University of California, San Diego.

Scheven, Albert
1981   Swahili Proverbs: Nia zikiwa moja, kilicho mbali huja. Washington, D.C.: University Press of America.

Schneider, David M.
1976   Notes toward a theory of culture. *In* K. H. Basso and H. A. Selby (eds.), Meaning in Anthropology. Albuquerque: University of New Mexico Press. Pp. 197–220.

Schwartz, Theodore
1972   The size and shape of a culture. *In* F. Barth (ed.), Scale and Social Organization. Oslo: Universitetsford. Pp. 215–252.
1978   Where is the culture? Personality as the distributive locus of culture. *In* George D. Spindler (ed.), The Making of Psychological Anthropology. Berkeley, Los Angeles, London: University of California Press. Pp. 419–441.
1981   The acquisition of culture. *Ethos* 9(1):4–17.
1989   The structure of national cultures. *In* Peter Funke (ed.), Understanding the U.S.A.: A Cross-Cultural Perspective. Tübingen: Gunter Nagg Verlag.

Siegel, R. E.
1968   Galen's System of Physiology and Medicine. Basel and New York: S. Karger.

Spear, T.
1974   Traditional myths and historians' myths: Variations on the Singwaya themes of Mijikenda origins. *Hist. Afr.* 1:67–78.
1977   Traditional myths and linguistic analysis: Singwaya revisited. *Hist. Afr.* 4:230–245.
1984   The Shirazi in Swahili traditions, culture and history. *Hist. Afr.* 11:165–181.
Spiro, Melford E.
1958   Children of the Kibbutz. Cambridge: Harvard University Press.
1961   Social systems, personality, and functional analysis. *In* B. Kaplan (ed.), Studying Personality Cross-Culturally. Evanston: Row, Peterson, & Co. Pp. 93–128.
1984   Some reflections on cultural determinism and relativism with special reference to emotion and reason. *In* R. Shweder and R. LaVine (eds.), Cultural Theory: Essays on Mind, Self, and Emotion. Cambridge: Cambridge University Press.
Stroebel, Margaret
1979   Muslim Women in Mombasa: 1890–1975. New Haven: Yale University Press.
Swartz, Marc J.
1966   Bases for compliance in Bena villages. *In* M. Swartz, V. Turner, and A. Tudin (eds.), Political Anthropology. Chicago: Aldine.
1967   Introduction. *In* M. Swartz (ed.), Local Level Politics. Chicago: Aldine.
1969*a*   The cultural dynamics of blows and abuse among the Bena of Tanzania. *In* R. Spencer (ed.), Forms of Symbolic Action. Seattle: University of Washington Press.
1969*b*   Interpersonal tensions, modern conditions, and changes in the frequency of witchcraft/sorcery accusations. *Afr. Urban Notes* 4:25–33. Reprinted in Max Marwick (ed.), Witchcraft and Sorcery. 2d ed. Harmondsworth, Middlesex, England: Penguin Books, 1982.
1975   Legitimacy and coercion: Sources of participation in a Bena political activity. *In* L. Cliffe (ed.), Political Penetration in East Africa. Oxford: Oxford University Press.
1976   Hyperbole, politics, and potent specification: The political uses of a figure of speech. *In* W. O'Barr and J. F. O'Barr (eds.), Language and Politics. The Hague: Mouton.
1977   Legitimacy and coercion in Bena politics and development. *In* L. Cliffe and M. R. Doornboch (eds.), Government and Rural Development in East Africa. The Hague: Martinus Nijhoff.
1978   Religious courts, community and ethnicity among the Swahili Mombasa: An historical study of social boundaries. *Africa* 49:29–41.
1981   Sources of Swahili women's power in Kenya. *Africana* 8(4):27–28.
1982*a*   Cultural sharing and cultural theory: Some results of a study of the nuclear family in five societies. *AA* 84:314–338.
1982*b*   The isolation of men and the power of women: Sources of power among the Swahili of Mombasa. *JAR* 38:26–44.
1983   Culture and implicit power: Maneuvers and understandings in Swahili

nuclear family relations. *In* M. Aronoff (ed.), Yearbook of Political Anthropology. New Brunswick: Transaction Press.

1984   Culture as token and as guides: Swahili views and behavior concerning generational differences. *JAR* 40(2):78–89.

1985   Relationship terms and cultural conformity among the Swahili of Mombasa. *In* Joan Maw and David Parkin (eds.), Swahili Language and Culture. Vienna: Afro-Pub.

1988   Shame, culture, and status among the Swahili of Mombasa. *Ethos* 16(1): 21–51.

1990a   "God curse you and the curse is that you be what you already are": Swahili culture, power, and badtalk. *Maledicta* 10:21–47.

1990b   Aggressive speech, status and cultural distribution among the Swahili of Mombasa. *In* D. K. Jordan and M. J. Swartz (eds.), Personality and the Cultural Constitution of Society: Essays in Honor of M. E. Spiro. Tuscaloosa: University of Alabama Press.

1991   On the two bodies: Understandings of the body and society. *In* Joan Maw (ed.), Concepts of the Body and the Self in Africa. Vienna: Afro-Pub.

Swartz, M. J., and David K. Jordan
1976   Anthropology: Perspective on Humanity. New York: John Wiley & Sons.
1980   Culture: The Anthropological Perspective. New York: John Wiley & Sons.

Swartz, M., V. Turner, and A. Tudin (eds.)
1966   Political Anthropology. Chicago: Aldine.

Swartz, M. J., et al.
1980   A questionnaire used in a five-society study of nuclear family cultures and culture sharing. Unpublished manuscript in the Library of the University of California, San Diego.

Temkin, O.
1973   Galenism: Rise and Decline of a Medical Philosophy. Ithaca and London: Cornell University Press.

Trimmingham, J. S.
1964   Islam in East Africa. Oxford: Oxford University Press.

Turner, Victor
1968   The Drums of Affliction. Oxford: Clarendon Press.

Tuzin, Donald F.
1976   The Ilahita Arapesh: Dimensions of Unity. Berkeley, Los Angeles, London: University of California Press.

Wallace, A. F. C.
1952   Individual differences and cultural uniformities. *Am. Soc. Rev.* 17:747–750.
1970   Culture and Personality. 2d ed. New York: Random House. Orig. ed. 1961.

Weatherford, Jack McIver
1977   Family culture, behavior and emotion in a working-class German town. Ph.D. dissertation, Anthropology Department, University of California, San Diego.

Weber, Max
  1922   The social psychology of the world religions. Originally published as Die
          Wirtshaftsethik der Weltreligionen. I. Tübingen. Translated and re-
          printed in H. H. Gerth and C. W. Mills (eds. and trans.), From Max
          Weber: Essays in Sociology. New York: Oxford University Press, a
          Galaxy Book, 1958. Pp. 267–301.
  1947   The Theory of Social and Economic Organization, translated by A. M.
          Henderson and T. Parsons. New York: Oxford University Press. Orig.
          ed. 1922.
  1958   Religious rejections of the world and their directions. Reprinted in
          H. H. Gerth and C. W. Mills (eds.), From Max Weber: Essays in Sociol-
          ogy. New York: Oxford University Press. Pp. 323–359. Orig. ed. 1915.
Weller, S. C.
  1984   Consistency and consensus among informants: Disease concepts in a
          rural Mexican town. *AA* 86(4):966–975.
Whitely, W. H.
  1955   Kimvita. *J. E. Afr. Swahili Comm.* 25:10–39.
Wikans, Uni
  1984   Shame and honour: A contestable pair. *Man* 19(4):632–652.
Willis, Roy
  1972   Pollution and paradigms. *Man* 7:369–378. Reprinted in D. Landy (ed.),
          Culture, Disease, and Healing. New York: Macmillan.
Wolff, R. J.
  1969   Modern medicine and traditional culture: Confrontation on the Malay
          Peninsula. *In* R. O. Tilman (ed.), Man, State and Society in Contempo-
          rary Southeast Asia. New York: Praeger.
Young, Michael, and Peter Willmott
  1973   The Symmetrical Family. Harmondsworth, Middlesex, England: Pen-
          guin Books. Originally published by Routledge & Kegan Paul, 1971.
Zein, A. el
  1974   The Sacred Meadows. Evanston: Northwestern University Press.

Index

Designer: U.C. Press Staff
Compositor: Prestige Typography
Text: 10/12 Times Roman
Display: Helvetica
Printer: Bookcrafters, Inc.
Binder: Bookcrafters, Inc.